Shocking S

of

Antiquity

Racial Wars of Bronze Age,

Unusual Artifacts, Technolithic Engineering

& the Two Cataclysms that

Buried History

Jason M. Breshears

Archaix

2

cover design by author

Table of Contents

4

32. **The Greatest Secret of Them All**

1.

Dark Realities

Learn what others are afraid to know

The materials offered in *Shocking Secrets of Antiquity* are for those unafraid of the dark, who want the truth undiluted, direct. The ancient past, behind-the-scenes happenings throughout all time periods, censored histories, the academic cover-ups, *real* facts about race, religion, subversive societies and even psi-based *predictive* systems of analysis by which future events can be known beforehand are uncovered and explained.

The study of history is today so strictly disciplined as to render it almost meaningless. Its like studying a clown while ignoring the circus. Such rigid compartmentalization of knowledge by today's scientifica has abstracted the past in to a series of indefinites. The once-unified histories of earth are now so tangled that seemingly disparate realities are no longer recognized as orders within the same series of events.

The Big Bang...Creationism...natural selection...evolution, either phyletic gradualism or punctuated equilibrium, *two* versions supporting a bogus theory ...directed panspermia...quantum mechanics...superstring theory- so many nicely packaged theories with supporting "facts" that morph into mere suppositions under scrutiny...all of them *wrong,* victims of the Heisenberg Uncertainty Principle, Murphy's Law and the occasional maverick genius. We are condemned to exult in feigned intelligence, to construct beliefs from the wisps of phenomena, causes unknown. Scientist and religionist locked in combat with facts as amorphous as fictions, both victims of a programming designed to delude. The astronomer envisions galaxies beyond sight as the faithful hope in an even more distant heaven. Both are in error. The truth lies in none of these; prisoners of a nightmare in disguise. The truth is *astonishing.*

I present to you a disturbing idea, a new theory that does not practice exclusions in its effort to be persuasive, a sort of unified field theory of calendrics. Uncomfortable information but not overwhelming, not without its use. But theories require thinkers, those rare individuals with the acuity to assess an idea's viability to perceive its merit. The world is full of critics, those imaginatively-impaired deniers whose implacable distrust of the unconventional serves only to impede real investigation. The earnest searcher in reading these posts would do well to intellectually disengage from any preconceived notions. Paradigms are products of our programming, intricate veils designed to conceal more than they convey. Only by choosing to look more closely will we begin to see the cracks in the holosphere.

My expertise is *chronology.* Anyone who has gazed upon my 510-page *Chronicon* can easily see that I have spent two decades reading and data-mining 1157 nonfiction books. And 10,000+ hours studying the annals of antiquity guided me to a startling discovery. The records of the distant past were originally *three* separate chronologies of events but only two of these timelines were *human*. This site, www.nephilimarchives.com, serves to disentangle these histories, identify their participants and expose, remove and explain the misinformation manufactured to hide historical chronology from modern discovery.

Relative dating methods are all heavily dependent upon a number of assumptions whether they be radiocarbon dating, potassium-argon, thermoluminescence, thermal ionization mass spectrometry, dendrochronology or ice core drilling- such methods produce at best only approximates. But today we have a much more reliable way of dating ancient historical events, one that science has virtually ignored. There are *thousands* of old chronologies, annals, traditional datings, archeological texts, dated monuments and religious writings preserving dated events all today translated into English, German and French.

Today we are overwhelmed with new books offering new theories or new explanations for the failure of older models now threatened by the accruing of modern discoveries. Scores of variant historical models all supported by convincing *cherry-picked* data has done little but engender confusion and promote a vast knowledge gulf where the majority of even the learned know relatively nothing at all about the astonishing events of the ancient world. A novel idea is introduced and again the curious public is left with more questions than answers.

Every genre of science and history has been analyzed to support one model or another *except one...*chronology. The last published chronologist was 360 years ago and a staunch religionist which hurt his credibility with Establishment historians. He was Archbishop James Ussher and over three and a half centuries ago he did not have the benefit of the *hundreds of thousands* of modern discoveries and translated, *dated* monuments and texts of the 18th, 19th, 20 and 21st centuries.

Our prestigious universities would never deign to acknowledge the importance of so meticulous a study because it is the *opinion* of academics today to assume that our predecessors were simpletons unable to accurately record observed events, even when two different peoples from opposite hemispheres writing in different languages reported the same events and dated it at the same time.

Anti-Establishment historians tend to be an unpopular lot and my work will undoubtedly serve to reinforce this attitude by those who have published garbage adorned as history. It is my intent to make academic enemies, to topple their cherished pillars, to silence those charlatans who have sold their fictions off as facts. My mission is to educate those willing to know, having no doubt I will lock horns with many along the way.

I take a more Gnostic approach to the study of human antiquities, the Gnosis older than Christianity and maintaining fragments of records from even older belief systems and histories. As students of the Gnosis we agree that we do not agree on everything. Each walks his own path and deals with their own demons. We also all have our own gifts, and mine is my ability to see whole sequential pictures out of what others merely see as thousands of pieces. My gift is evident in the writings of www.nephilimarchives.com.

Principal tenets of this research serve to shatter several paradigms. The public majority are not ready for these revelations nor are the majority capable of processing the information unveiled in this work.

Fundamentals this work endeavors to show:

> Material reality maintains observable and measureable properties of a *hologram*; henceforth referred to as the *holosphere*

> This holosphere maintains programming protocols designed to deceive human sense-perceptions

> The holospheric matrix is *imperfect*; there are historic instances when programming errors have occurred, when humans witnessed these glitches and even when the actions of humans have induced a hurried *correction* in the holography

> The holosphere is an advanced psi-based medium programmed to reflect back as phenomena what is *projected into it*

> Projections altering, creating or continuing "reality" steadily feed the holospheric generation of personal and collective conditions

> The holosphere is *not* reality; it is a sentient biogram containment field quarantined away from the *real* Universe

> There exist intelligences that can and do enter and exit this holofield, even *removing* men and materials from the holosphere

> The historical record exhibits evidence that humans are not the only victims of past holospheric imprisonment

> Homo inferior breeds were created for slave labor by an Enemy that is still today trapped in this holography; their

activity against mankind continues today but is *governed (i.e. restricted)*

> The original holosphere was a DNA development preserve able to   generate complex biospheres to study the ancient and mysterious coding of DNA under controlled conditions; in the holosphere new life forms could not contaminate the *real* Universe

> The fossil record contains proof that *explosions* of life forms in the tens of thousands have appeared on earth *suddenly* with no traces of preexisting transitional forms

> Homo inferior was later modified by a *benefactor* who deliberately committed the ultimate trespass; the introduction of the benefactor's own genetic material was a *prohibited* act of cross contamination between the holospheric containment area (our reality) and the *real* Universe that resulted in the creation of homo sapiens

> The benefactor race, *Homo Anunna* {i.e.Anunnaki} were trapped in the holospheric medium because of the violation- the containment holography became *locked down.* With no escape out of the programming, the holosphere became home

> Humans were not a part of the Original Design, our existence and   potential is a threat. But this threat cannot be edited out due to a most unforseen development. Immortal spirits from *outside* the containment apparatus have found freedom in residing inside humans as they are conceived

> This new spiritual development of a prohibited sentient species has created a rift between opposing factions of

Homo Anunna both inside and outside the containment field

> The multidimensional spatial charactoristics of the holosphere are convincingly generated from multiple sources both *outside and inside* the holofield

> Only *after* genetic manufacturing of homo sapiens did *new* programming and subroutines infiltrate the biogram. Mechanisms were set in place to *depopulate* humanity, to impede development, to deter the influx of uncontainable immortal souls

> These cataclysm protocols occur at *fixed dates;* their timing is *governed* and therefore predictable. Despite earth's altered orbit, decelleration around the sun, the supposed loss of mass of intruder planets Phoenix, NIBIRU and the Dark Satillite, these objects have all been viewed in historical times on the very ancient *fixed date* timelines- ONLY AS PROGRAMMING could this precision be possible in linear time though the qualities of *spatial properties* have changed

> The core programming of the exact past and future dates of the holofield's Cataclysm Protocols are encoded and easily seen in numerous rectilinear dimensions in the scientifically-verified measurements inside the Great Pyramid of Giza in Egypt and in NO OTHER PYRAMIDS

> Some of the oldest records in the world were written from the perspective of *nonhuman* beings who conveyed their accounts to humans who later committed them to writing

> The holospheric containment apparatus is an interactive three-tiered mechanism of fantastically advanced

technological hardware and biogram software operating from outside *and* inside the holosphere:

a) observers *outside* the holofield manipulate the holography through nodal apertures disguised among the stellar canopy as *variable stars.* These apertures between dimensions bathe earth with energy to create terrestrial phenomena. Variable stars are rare, not even .01% of the visible luminaries are variable stars

b) *Governors* are spread throughout the solar system that perform different functions, all disguised as lunar bodies, planetoids and astroids. These immense vehicles are stations/ machines still performing according to fixed protocols though the advanced, ancient civilization that constructed them may no longer exist; our Moon...one moon of Mars...planetoid Ceres...one moon of Jupiter...one moon of Saturn...the Phoenix Orbiter...the NIBIRU waystation...the Dark Satillite

> The older Homo Anunna civilization trapped in this holography with homo sapiens currently reside in vast interconnected underground bases and Deep Earth Biospheres, complexes that antedate the existence of homo sapiens on the surface. The vast amount of energy expended throughout antiquity to convince humans that "gods" came from the heavens and modern UFO culture are *programs* that serve to misdirect all attention to the thriving Homo Anunna civilization in our *underworld.*

> The cosmological concept from distant antiquity of an inaccessible heavens above, a Middle Earth (Midgard) where humans dwelt on the surface, and an underworld that was home to *fallen* gods, the origin of today's Heaven, Earth and Hell model, ultimately derived from the historic understanding of the holospheric containment field's

function of *separating* the Sol system from the rest of the Universe, where humans dwelt unprotected on the surface as an older, more advanced race occupied Deep Earth Biospheres, a fallen species unable to escape the holosphere.

2. Petrified Jellyfish & Fossilized Humans: Evidence of a Flash-Frozen World

I was 12 years old in 1985. While other kids played in the park, I sat there in my own little world amidst piles of white rocks with my tackle box full of fossils. In Bedford, Texas I excavated various kinds of specimens from three different fossil-rich city parks. My research went far afield as my father took us on camping trips and as he acquired hanger space at two municipal airports where I found numerous fossils for my collection.

As I found among the bleached stones yet another rock reminder of an ancient life form my mind would race with scenarios of how it came to be there. In the park surrounded by people, I was lost in a Jurassic dream, the very essence of my entire being in rebellion against those explanations forced upon me by my teachers. My school career was a disaster. Ever dissatisfied with the conclusions offered me but unable to refute the textbook arguments due to my lack of knowledge, I receded into myself. Distrustful of teachers and textbooks, I began to search for other sources of information. My imagination became my instructor and this inner insurrection led me down paths of learning so few have had opportunity to tread. But this revolt extended into every aspect of my life and landed me in Texas prison where I spent 26 years and 48 days...reading. Little did I know that this was God's way of giving me what I wanted- a true education- giving me exactly what I wanted despite all I had to pay to get it.

Archeology is the science of reading the rocks and is probably what the priest-prophet Ezra meant when he wrote that in the Last Days the "stones will speak," (2 Esdras 5:5) imparting knowledge to the wise. Today the stones are speaking and what they are telling us is vastly different than what we are taught. Let us look at these discoveries without prejudice to exhume some truth out of a mire of falsehoods.

Fossils are anything but normal. For any once-living organism to petrify, the mineralization of organic tissue, is a baffling anomaly. Fossils are not created today. Animals and plants decay rapidly. Because fossils appear in all of the strata then by the Establishment standards we are looking at layers of anomalous events creating fossils that occurred over and over again. A ridiculous notion. The evidence recorded in the rocks is quite clear. Our planet is one immense fossil of a once-global ecosystem that met with a disaster so sudden that fauna and flora had no time to deteriorate before they were entombed in solid stone. The idea that sedimentary and fossiliferous strata formed layer by layer over vast epochs of time is directly contravened by many startling proofs. I have a new tackle box, one filled with astounding discoveries exhumed from reputable reference books.

That a fossil is a stone is an effect that is traced to a cause far more unbelievable and mysterious than we commonly believe. There is a vast amount of evidence that the ancient world was flash frozen or flash burned, that the atmosphere itself collapsed. Billions of life forms froze to death in the space of a second and this freezing even preserved deep sea life.

Among the more delicate organisms in our seas are jellyfish. They are boneless beings of fragile tissue yet they have been found numerous times petrified in solid rock. This is cogent evidence of being quick-frozen. (1) On land their soft-tissue counterpart would be the earthworm, animals also found in fossil form. (2) These creatures were not instantly petrified to be later found in stone, such a scenario makes no sense. No, these animals were thriving in an ecosystem and their WHOLE WORLD FROZE instantly, silt, dirt, mud, turning over time into solid rock. Only instantaneous freezing of land and sea, the entire biosphere, can explain how an ichthyosaurus could be petrified whole underwater where it lived at the instant it was giving birth to an infant whose head was still between the pelvic bones of its mother. (3) Also, this scenario accounts for the find of a fish fossilized in the act of swallowing another fish (4) and the fossil of a 14 foot long fish with a petrified 6 foot fish in its stomach still undigested. (5) Further, whole beds of fossil clams have been found with their shells closed. This is not normal, for when clams died their muscles relax and shells open wide. (6)

That anything beneath the ocean's surface could mineralize into solid rock and not become the meal of carrion creatures of the deep is profound. This freezing to death was accompanied by rapid compression and and rapid change in sea levels. Sharks have been found flattened to a fourth of an inch in thickness with their tail fins still upright, suggesting RAPID BURIAL. (7) Not only sea life, but fish and saurians have been found in immense log jams packed and petrified together.

Segmented deep sea mollusks called neopilina perished 500 million years ago in the Devonian Age, their fossilized remains not uncommon. But not a single specimen has been located in later strata. This would not be so mysterious had not it been discovered that neopilina were thriving alive and well today. (8)   In 500 million years why has this creature not evolved into a kraken?

New microbiological research is exhibiting hard evidence that the evolutionary chronology is untenable. Shells found locked in 180 million year old Jurassic strata have been found that still have amino acids within protein structures. (9) Also, corals are sensitive organisms that can only live within a couple hundred feet of sea level, however, remains of corals have been discovered deeper in the oceans demonstrating that ocean levels have risen considerable. Corals and fossils undersea... perhaps God is a girl, a leviathon medusa whose All-Seeing Eye had mineralized all that she had made.

Having adopted my own belief by following the evidence I now feel compelled to advance my position. This involves a measure of hypocrisy , for Creationists and avid Flood-adherents are equally guilty of allowing preconceptions to guide their efforts. On the other hand there is the sage advice of Charles Fort- "To have an opinion is to be ignorant of, or to disregard a contradiction...for if you don't take something for a standard of opinion, you can't have any opinion at all." (10) So in tracing effects to their causes I offering the following nigh unbelievable findings as further evidence that entire seas and oceans were quick-frozen before sections of ice fragmented off and were entombed, mineralized and preserved in solid rock or cavernous regions.

In 1460 CE miners tunneled to a depth of 100 feet in the mountains near Berne, Switzerland, searching for metals. To their astonishment they happened upon a preserved and entombed wooden ship carved with well-fashioned ornamentation. Its masts were broken and an iron anchor was found. To the horror of the miners they also discovered among the timbers in the rock the skeletons of 40 sailors who dies with the ship. (11) It was 43 years later that a windstorm dislodged a huge chunk of rock from a high mountain overlooking the Sea of Naples, Italy. The locals set out to investigate and found to their astonishment the large fossil of a primordial ship, a vessel unlike any of that time period. An Italian historian and statesman named Giovanni Pontano was one of the many to witness and study the find. (12) Thirty-seven years after this near Callao, Peru, Spanish miners searching for silver and gold removed earth in a deep mineshaft and were shocked to discover a buried wooden ship of extreme antiquity unlike any they had seen before. (13) Three ships documented in the modern historical records, found inside mountains. I visualize a calm sea suddenly flash-frozen, ships encased in ice, weighted down, sinking. Buried in silting, sediments, mud, layers of materials adding pressure- an irradiated world bereft of an atmosphere suddenly burned, volcanic resurfacing, sediments hardened into stone...and three ships later discovered beneath mountains.

With me, mere probabilities are not accepted as truth until they are tested against the weight of all else I've come to accept. Men spend their careers and lives chasing fictions, dressing their evidences to conform to their fantasy.

Though I'm no Christian, the Good Book has excellent points- "Ever learning and never able to come to the knowledge of the truth..." My own tackle box will never be full. But each relic protected within is scrutinized under the same lamplight that advises all men- "Keep that which is committed to they trust, avoiding profane and vain babblings and oppositions of science falsely so called..."

{1. Poleshift p. 74; 2. Darwin's Mistake p. 29; 3. ibid; 4. ibid; 5. Evolution Cruncher p. 470; 6. Evolution Cruncher p. 466; 7. Evolution Cruncher p. 469; 8. Evolution Cruncher p. 478; 9. Evolution Cruncher p. 484; 10. Book of the Damned p. 74, 83; 11. Secret Cities of Old South America p. 417; 12. ibid; 13. ibid}

Fossil Humans, Petrified Dinosaurs...Whole Land Surfaces Entombed

Deserts and mountain ranges have a common link little discussed...they are packed with fossils. The petrified remains of a world that once was. An ancient planet frozen solid with massive melt water seas carving vast tracts of its surface still clearly visible today. Mexico is known both for its deserts and mountains.

A great bane to conservative scientists now totally edited out of the modern books is the discovery of 33,000 mysterious artifacts discovered at Acambaro, Mexico, of figurines and statuettes showing humans performing all sorts of activities, even feeding and training anatomically correct dinosaurs! But this is impossible, of course, for the Age of the Dinosaurs ended 65 million years ago by the impact of a large rock from space. A beautiful theory, assuming this rock was more catastrophic than the meteorite that in 1954 fell from the sky to crash through the roof of a house in Sylacuaga, Alabama to strike a radio before hitting Anne Elizabeth Hodges on the hip leaving a dark bruise. Just maybe some of the prehistoric animals survived as did Mrs. Hodges, who was struck by a rock from space that took 65 million years to get here.

The concepts of evolution, natural selection and uniformitarianism popularized in the 19th century by Charles Lyell and Charles Darwin were hypotheses based upon a plethora of assumptions that required filtering out a tremendous amount of anomalous data in order to be presented to others as plausible. Knowledge filtration is censorship. These ideas were placed upon an arbitrary pedastool pretending itself to be scientific theory that morphed into a belief blindly accepted and now pushed onto us through institutions of learning as an incontrovertible fact. But there is an absurdity involved in accepting these concepts- to date the fossilized remains of organisms by the rock strata they are discovered in...strata that is solely dated by the index fossils found petrified within it. This circular reasoning is precisely why another Charles, the infamous Charles Fort, wrote, "We've been damned by giants sound asleep, or by great scientific principles and abstractions that cannot realize themselves." (1) It is axiomatic that we cannot take two unknowns, defining one another, and conclude that we have learned anything at all.

The scientific approach concerning the formation of fossils is one steeped in hypocrisy. Science requires direct observation and by multiple witnesses confirming conclusions. But petrification in nature has never been observed and recorded. The cause has never been studied, no living life form has in recorded history ever turned to stone. Only the catastrophist models can adequately explain them but the Establishment scientists continue to censor verifiable findings because they upset the prevailing theories and most often scientists rationalize this unscientific behavior, the filtering away of anomalies from professional study, believing that they can be explained away at a future date when more data is available. So archeological treasures get "lost" awaiting a validation that never comes. Charles Fort remarked concerning the scientists and their pet theories- "Who would not be a prize marksman, if only his hits be recorded?" (2)

Evolution, survival of the fittest and the uniformitarianism view of history with its slow geologic time table are not supported by the evidence of archeology, but they are made palatable by quietly disregarding the wealth of informations that oppose them. My own position is not the same as Creationists and other Bible-believing proponents for I am convinced that the findings of archeology they rely upon to support their position that the Great Flood accounts for all of the anomalies, actually supports the position that THREE major global extinction-level cataclysms occurred and all three occurred not millions of years ago but VERY recently...the third just prior to the advent of writing. A VERY OLD world of prehistoric reptillian and amphibian life forms existed on this planet BEFORE Earth was orbiting in its present position between Venus and Mars, when a second sun illuminated the skies. That luminary exploded tearing away Earth's atmosphere before collapsing into a Dark Star currently located at the Cygnus Rift.

Earth plummeted toward Sol. The Daystar explodes ejecting materials and an immense wave front of iridium shreds through earth's atmosphere. The entire tropical

Jurassic world is flash-frozen, gradually to mineralize into fossils. Today a dark clay stratum containing extraterrestrial iridium encapsulates the Earth called the K-T Boundary [Cretaceous-Tertiary]...the layer marking the sudden death of a planet. (3) Orbiting Sol the planet awakened, was reseeded by offworlders and a civilization emerged of great intellect and accomplishment, very different than the Neanderthal before them. These were the Cro-Magnon. They suffered a catastrophe that resulted in Earth's orbiting Sol for 270 years with its axis pointing at the Sun. Half the world frozen in darkness for 270 years while the other half was perpetually sunny and warm, facing Sol. Earth rolled around the sun in its orbit. More will be said of the Cro-Magnon, but for our purposes here it must be mentioned that these people were advanced, intelligent, had a lengthy history and were survivors bereft of a vast infrastructure they once enjoyed.

After 270 years of chaos, of men turning into monsters, little different than animals, Earth captured Luna into a dead orbit and this tilted Earth's axis allowing the planet to rotate and turn its darkened, frozen hemisphere toward the sun...day and night created the firmament above according to Genesis. A melting hemisphere, a warming world and intense volcanism created a Venus-type vapor canopy and almost overnight the Age of the Megafauna was started. The PreFlood World began, animals, plants and people grew to astonishing sizes by virtual of the ambient radiation and thick vapor canopy.

And then 1656 years after the pole shift of 3895 BCE at beginning of the Megafauna Age, the Great Deluge occurred in 2239 BCE just before the advent of writing, the Flood a direct result of the collapse of the vapor canopy.

Three global cataclysms and several lesser hemispheric disasters account for everything we have found in the archeological record and geologic column. The each-layer-of-rock-equals-millions-of-years teaching is total crap because those layers all contain fossils; the extreme rarity of petrification nullifies the chance that such long periods of time could even produce the immense amounts of specimens we have excavated.

I do take heed to remain open to other, unforeseen possibilities. John Keel's words are relevant here-"To subscribe to any one of these beliefs is to exclude all other possibilities. We should consider every possibility, avoid belief, and accept only the hard facts." (4) Despite the scientific ridicule by pompous bastards stuck up on their pretended learning, I cannot conceive of dinosaurs being 65 million years ago because this would mean that homo sapiens sapiens would also be 65 million years old. This I cannot accept. DNA is fantastically ancient and complex and interstellar, but mankind is a very recent addition to the Sol system. We have discovered human fossils...petrified just like the dinosaurs. It is not humans who are as old as the prehistoric saurians but the dinosaurs who were as young as mankind. That human fossils have been unearthed is the most damning evidence against the current paradigm. Read of these findings.

The oldest historical record of the finding of a human fossil to my knowledge is from the 6th century BCE Rome. King Tarquin began the Temple of Jupiter on the Capitoline Hill and the workmen excavating the site were astonished to find a human fossil head with facial features still intact. Of course, Etruscan diviners at the time interpreted this find as an omen that Rome would be the

24

head of all kingdoms. (5)   In 1812 on the coast of the French Caribbean island of Guadeloupe a human female fossil was discovered in limestone dated at 28 million years. She was 5'2" tall and completely preserved in a two-ton block that was cut out and transported by ship to the British Museum where she was placed on exhibit as evidence of Noah's Flood. Sixty-nine years later in 1881 the Royal Society, adopting the evolutionary model, quietly had the relic taken down and hidden in the basement. (6) In the London Museum is an artifact not on display today. It is a fossilized sandal print preserved in 600 million year old rock that clearly shows stitching impressions along the perimeter of the sole and a heel impression. Shockingly, this sandal print has crushed beneath it a petrified trilobite fossil! (7) Why is this hidden? First, humans wearing sandals in ancient times is just unbelievable. What did they need to protect their feet for? Especially 600 million years ago. Trilobites are Index Fossils used to date strata believed to antedate the dinosaurs by millions of years. 400 million years before the dinosaurs to be exact.

Human fossilized remains have been found in places evolutionary geologists refuse to accept, preferring the convenience of ignorance to the remodification of their position. In 1967 human bones were discovered in a vein of silver in a Colorado mine accompanied with copper arrowheads four inches long. (8) In California human skeletons have been found fossilized in gold-bearing strata underneath several layers of lava deposits. (9) According to the current models, silver and gold require immense time periods to form.

In Germany in 1842 a fossilized human skull was found in solid coal. A coal miner in West Virginia in the same year found a perfectly formed human leg that had changed into coal. (10) Dr. Johannes Heurezeler of Basel University, Switzerland found a complete human skeleton hundreds of feet deep in a coal mine in Italy, dating it to be 10 million years old. (11) The jawbone of a human child was found compressed in coal in Tuscany in 1958. It had been flattened like a piece of sheet iron. (12) The famous Calaveras Skull of California was discovered in 1866 by Professor J.D. Whitney from a depth of 130 feet under several lava deposits and beds of auriferous gravel. (13)

In the desert of Mesopotamia at a place called Xari Suste archeologists found an entire town buried beneath the sand. Skeletons were crouched as if praying- others in a sleeping position. Pottery was discovered in perfect condition and laid out ready for meals. The excavators claim that this civilization was terminated abruptly about 5000 years ago. (14) This is almost as good of evidence of a global freezing as the petrified jellyfish. Imagine, a desert full of sand preserving what a flood once wrought. And dated rather accurately too. A little further east at another desert, the Gobi, this hot and arid region also boasts evidence of an ancient quick-freeze. Archeologists in the Gobi desert excavated the fossil remains of a velociraptor and protoceratops, backs arched, still locked in mortal combat-frozen to death instantly, buried in sediments and fossilized. (15) At Glenrose, Texas along the Paluxy River I personally walked the valley and stepped into the huge dinosaur tracks as a teen in my fossil-hunt wanderings. It was only years later did people make significant finds at the park. Giant human footprints were found fossilized near the dinosaurs prints. Also, a few miles away at Chalk Mountain a human finger was found, all fossilized with fingernail clearly defined. Examination by xray showed that not only had the bone survived inside, but the marrow as well. (16)   George Adams of Glen Rose found two fossilized human skulls and a seven foot tall female skeleton. (17) In 1815, a mummified human female fossil with finely chiseled features showing her to be young was found in the labyrinthian recesses of Mammoth Cave, Kentucky. (18) That human prints are spread about with dinosaur tracks is not so remarkable. Fossilized hand and foot impressions of humans have been found alongside ammonite fossils which were supposed to have become extinct 65 million years ago. (19)   Some humans were never fossilized but remained frozen, like Ice Man, who was discovered in 1991 in the Italian Alps, believed to have died of hypothermia 5300 years ago. Found on a mountain in a desert of snow.

3. A Fossilized World vs. Scientific Fantasy

Over 2000 years ago the Roman statesman and master orator wrote, "For it is impossible to write anything about men of ancient epochs when they themselves have left us nothing, and no one else has left any records about them." (1) While this may have been true in his day it is definitely in error now for the innovations of science through many disciplines in archeology and anthropology provide us several modern windows into distant antiquity where textual evidences are lacking. It is by the testimony of rocks and soil that we comprehend so much history. Our present dilemma finds its origin not in any faulty conveyances from the strata or the petrified specimens within, but with the official interpretations of phenomena that can be explained in more ways than one. Omission is the new commission that secures serious scholarly peer review. Many are the scientists who violated this creed and found themselves without funding, denied publication and opportunities for advancement.

The fossil record is only confusing to the uniformitarians and evolutionists who strive to derive interpretations of it meaningful to their pet theories. Those studying from a different perspective clearly realize that the distribution of anomalies, the gaps and sudden reappearances of life forms, many having no ancestral counterparts, see the unfolding of events far different than what is scientifically acceptable today. The erudite and multidisciplinary approach of Immanuel Velikovsky secured for himself many avowed Establishment enemies and forced him to conclude that our teachers are "Purveyors of fossilized notions offered as ultimate truths." (2) My own favorite comment relative to this official prejudice was uttered by Clara Jessup Bloomfield-Moore in 1886, who said, "Science is not only very blind, but glories in her blindness. She gropes among the dead seeking the origin of life." (3) In their defense the sages of today take refuge when ridiculed for the position, an Aristolean approach, the philosopher writing in Metaphysics that "...it is altogether impossible for there to be proofs of everything." (4) Scientists can easily take refuge in other's inability to refute many of their arguments because Establishment agents have spent over a century editing out all evidence to the contrary. Many are the books written citing proof that the Smithsonian has been involved in a campaign of destroying artifacts and fossils in the tens of thousands. Even an outright lie has the appearance of being right when supported by a multitude of half-truths.

The foisting upon the public curriculum the idea of evolution was more like an experiment in mass psychology, which has as one of its basic tenets that any explanation is better than none. (5) Our ever-cynical philosopher friend Frederich Nietsche wrote, "That all the world believes so is already an objection to it." (6) But evolution is the prevailing belief by those who merely accept the explanation without studying for themselves. As Seth Payson put it in 1800- "The most egregious and absurd falsehoods, if told with confidence and confidently repeated, will at length gain credit and influence..." (7) Seventeen centuries before Payson, the Roman Tacitus wrote, "Some believe all manner of hearsay evidence; others twist truth into fiction, and both sorts of error are magnified by time." (8) This is what the scientific establishment has performed in just 150 years of knowledge filtration, in popularizing collaborative evidence while remaining silent or actively silencing actual archeological discoveries and archeologists that would collapse this house of cards. The truth is everywhere, but we are accused of ignorance if we believe it. As Fort summed it up, "Things are exhumed only to be buried in some other way." (9)

To discover the truth about the history of our world is not as simple as the uniformitarians or evolutionary biologists assert. The package as presented to us was tailor made with preconceptions tainting the design. The scientific world, noted by Schwaller de Lubicz, "...likes to believe in things stripped of all meaning, while other more meaningful and logical explanations are rejected as fantasies and hallucinations." (10)

LIVING FOSSILS & DORMANT PREHISTORIC MICROBES

In using 65 million year old paint to decorate their version of history the Establishment scientists must brush away the many findings that do not conform to their fantasy. The case of the coelacanth is famous. A prehistoric fish, hideous, that roamed the seas 70 million years ago that was used as an Index Fossil by scientists to date the surrounding strata it is located in. Apparently about five of them did not die, the first caught in a net by a South African fishing trawler in 1958, a living fossil five feet long. (11) Also well-known is the 1977 capture of a 30 foot long, 4000 lb. 100 million year old plesiosaur by Japanese fisherman off the coast of New Zealand. It was not a fossil, but a floating carcass. It is a creature resembling the Loch Ness Monster descriptions by the locals in Scotland. Though Asian countries minted coins in commemoration of the find and marketed t-shirts, posters and other memorabilia, little to nothing at all was broadcast in the west due to the scientific dogma and western academic censorship...they had to protect their paradigm. (12)

One of the strangest and most heavily censored discoveries concerns the amazing find of a fossil hunter named William Webster Jr. at Antelope Springs, Utah, who discovered a human footprint, petrified, stepping on a trilobite fossil. Trilobites are index fossils dated at 65 million years old. Intriguingly, the footprint that had smashed the trilobite was sandaled...all preserved in Cambrian strata. (13) Scientists refuse to study the find because it is obvious to them that humans did not exist 65 million years ago. It's that simple for them. They are blissfully unaware and ignorant that the fossil is probably less than 10,000 years ago which easily allows for the presence of a sandal-wearing human. Mere faith in their geologic model allows them to professionally ignore the fact of the finding.

Then there is the mystery of the cockroach. Here we have a little unarmored creature that has survived every extinction-level event including the two major ones of the Permian-Triassic and the Cretaceous-Tertiary...relatively unchanged. (14) No evolutionary development. It's almost as if these little animals drop from the sky from time to time, for their continued, unchanged existence defies every model we have conjured to explain the past. The official scientific belief in evolution mandates that these creatures should be RULING the world as sentient, logical beings, a vast sophisticated civilization of evolved people descended from the roach. But no, we are asked to accept that a hundred million years of evolutionary development is why the life forms on our world are the way they are while also accepting that the cockroach has not only remained unchanged during this magnificently protracted period without any development, but that this creature had survived so long. Again, its not that roaches are so old but that the global prehistoric destruction was not very long ago.

Here is an intriguing insectoid factoid- Prehistoric insect remains preserved in fossilized amber supposedly tens of millions of years old yielded forth dormant microbes that scientists REVIVED in California, a finding that made news everywhere. Either insects are imbued with godlike immortal DNA or those fossils are nowhere near the age they are passed off to be. The same can be said of another discovery- Paleontologist Mary Schweitzer discovered

proteins in the fossils of a Tyrannosaurus Rex.
Hmmm...old Rex sounds to be just as young as the roach.

 The blindness of science is a psychological phenomenon.
A maverick professor named Charles Hapgood once wrote
that men only find what they are looking for. (15)   The
mind constantly edits out unwanted information. As
Nietsche says, men discover in things only what they put
into them. (16) Long before our time, over 2000 years ago,
Lucretius wrote, "What wonder is it then, if the mind
misses everything, except what it is itself intent on? So
from small signs we draw great inferences and lead
ourselves into error and delusion. (17)   Higher learning
involves the process of editing out discrepancies, of
compartmentalizing data in order to make some kind of
sense out of the maelstrom of evidence. Proof is ever a
matter of opinion easily contradicted by the findings of
others also heralded as proofs. It seems as if knowledge
itself it knowledgeable enough to evade any concrete
affirmations. Russian-born scientist Itzhak Bentov sums
this up beautifully when he wrote- "I speak from my
present level of ignorance. The more you know the more
ignorant you become, because ignorance grows
exponentially- the more answers you get the more new
questions arise...one's level of ignorance increases
exponentially with accumulated knowledge." (18) David
Hatcher Childress wrote, "Geology is not a very exact
science, nor are there any real geological 'facts.' Geology is
a matter of opinion and theory, and many scientific theories
taught as 'fact' in schools may never really be proven." (19)

Through censorship of anomalous findings our scholars
have deluded us. But we are also at fault for blindly
accepting authority as the truth rather than truth as the

authority, as Gerald Massey warned over 120 years ago. (20) Avenues for personal research are open to us everywhere. When an idea forced upon us becomes so fossilized we can detect its falsity it is our duty to amend our thinking and search for the right of way. I must agree with our honorable publisher of curious facts, Benjamin Franklin, who in 1731 wrote- "When men differ in opinion, both sides ought equally to have advantage of being heard by the public, and when truth and error have fair play, the former is always an overmatch for the latter." (21) This fair play has been denied us. Our institutions foment a fictive model of the past and use our taxes to do it. Joan d'Arc in Phenomenal World wrote, "Humans have a tendency to perceive only what can be incorporated into an established frame of reference, and tend to perceptually block out anything that does not fit into preconceived notions of the physical world." (22) This is why censorship is so dangerous; opportunities are available to the open-minded but those who have been trained to believe in false histories guarantee they will not recognize the false trails they are led into in the future.

It was a saying of Paracelsus, and adhered to by Nostradamus, that true learning begins where schooling ends. Schools are centers of disinformation, collective brainwashing, where teachers pass off as fact the fictions they have themselves been trained to believe. We are taught to disdain the biblical record, to view history through the scope of science but the entire topography of our everyday world shows evidence of a massive flooding. We are brainwashed to accept concepts that are repulsed by our intuition, to mistrust the evidence of our eyes in favor of the erudition of the elite. Fort noted- "So there is a revolt against the science of today, because the formulated utterances that were regarded as final truths in a past generation, are now seen as insufficiencies." (23) In my own search for the real from the imagined I have come to discard the pessimism of Democrates who believed that either nothing is true, or at least, truth is hidden from us. I nod in recognition of Tacitus in that truth is surrounded by mystery. (24) And these mysteries are only impenetrable when viewed in light of misconceptions that serve to mold our thoughts to conform to popular ideas rather than obvious facts emerging from the evidence. For my own part I am unable to learn and withhold information from others meant to be known. As Theognis lamented over 27 centuries ago- "What good is knowledge if only one man knows?" (25) My own position is that of Henry Frederick Amiel, Swiss philosopher who died in 1883 who wrote that, "Truth is not only violated by falsehood; it may be equally outraged by silence."

FOSSIL TREES STILL GROWING TODAY

The past freezing of the whole world is evidenced by a a cursory glance at any modern globe. Where did the expansive glacial sheets of the Arctic and Antarctic come from? That the northern and southern extremities of our planet were once as tropical and the equatorial zone is proven by the abundant fossil impressions of leaves, stems, wood, ferns and giant ferns. (26) Coal beds have been found two miles above sea level and a mere 200 miles from the South Pole. Also found here were vertebrate fossils and petrified reptiles. (27) The Arctic is not dissimilar from the Antarctic findings. Large fossil reptiles have been found near the Arctic circle along the Dvina River in Russia. (28) In Canada whole fruit trees have been found

fossilized with palm trees with fruit still on their branches.
(29)

 As our teachers corrupt the tree of knowledge by
consigning its branches to abstract assertions supported
only by pet theories we who search deeper with better
clarity can easily see why the arcane symbol for life was
that of a tree. The world of old was a mighty forest that
covered continents. Immense jungle woods and forests
were instantly frozen and then petrified, some deteriorating
into vast coal seams. Coal is produced when enormous
amounts of plants and even animals are compressed and
heated by the weight of overlying sediments that creates
intense pressure. Around the edges of coal seams has often
been found identifiable traces of plants. (30)   In some
places there have been found 15 to 18 levels of buried trees.
(31) Of particular interest is the presence of polystrate tree
fossils, upright trees extending through multiple strata,
often right through coal seams.

If these levels of fossiliferous strata represent the remains
of millions of years of Cenozoic, Mesozoic and Paleozoic
skins enveloping our planet, how old these trees must be!
Which begs the question: were Earth conditions so tranquil
that 60 foot high petrified trees NEVER fell as the world
turned to stone, geologic layer after layer, millions of years
apart, burying these trees higher and higher? If so, how
were open-air trees petrified to begin with? Not only trees,
but gigantic ferns 65 to 100 feet high with proportionate
subsurface roots penetrating through several layers of rock.
(32) Because these findings are not supposed to exist we
shall call these anomalies Genus Fernus Ridiculus.

I think the geologic column so cherished to the
Establishment evolutionists should be called the Geologic

Tree and then dendrochronologists could count the rings of millions of years into the planet's history. But these tree scientists are not to be heeded too seriously. A while back they paraded the bristlecone pine as the oldest living tree on earth. (33) Then it was learned that a tree ring does not signify a year of time, therefore all of their prior calculations were off. Tree rings are created by wet seasons separated by dry seasons. A ring forms in spring when well-watered for this promotes growth. The dry summer stunts this growth as trees conserve their moisture. The fall rains bring about a second growth ring that is sometimes thicker than the spring ring. Dendrochronology is nothing but guesswork no better for accuracy than the myriads of relative dating methods like carbon-14 invented by Libby and all its descendants. A year could result in a single thick ring if waterfall was continual, the summer mild. Under ordinary conditions trees form two rings a year. (34)

With this realization, the Sequoia Gigantea, or Redwoods of California, are the oldest trees, living fossils that average at 4000 years old. Termites and parasites do not affect them; they do not die unless knocked down or cut down by men. Perhaps we got it wrong...the Tree of Life was a forest. In California. But then a dendro-miracle occurs. Imagine a Miocene Forest of great antiquity long ago filled with species of animals no longer alive reduced to pitiful sculptures of nature formed of stone. These are the Metasequoias known as the Dawn Redwoods, great trees that became extinct 60 million years ago but for some strange reason quite a few are still alive and well, unchanged, in China today. (35) Amazing unpetrified fossils.

My own theory of earth history is that in the very recent past, just prior to or in 5239 BCE, the Sol system was a part of a binary involving two luminaries, both having their own planetary systems as one star orbited the other. A nova occurred that catapulted our Moon, Earth, Phoenix, Nibiru, the Dark Satellite and other objects out of the dying system that orbits Sol and into the Sol system to orbit the sun. The orbital histories and evidence of the existence of Phoenix, Nibiru, the Dark Satellite and the sudden appearance of Luna [the Moon] are fully detailed in When the Sun Darkens, in Anunnaki Homeworld and my third book on these topics titled Nostradamus and the Planets of Apocalypse. The nova tore away Earth's atmosphere in seconds and the entire prehistoric world was FLASH-FROZEN [see previous post- Petrified Jellyfish & Fossilized Humans: Evidence of a Flash-Frozen World]. A very short time later Earth was renovated, a program of accelerated development initiated. Many reptilian, amphibian, marine and insectoid creatures are again manufactured and reintroduced to the post-cataclysmic biosphere, some with deliberately planned and designed modifications to permit them to flourish under the new conditions. Feathered birds are created using reptilian DNA. Marsupials, or proto-mammals and the placental mammals are introduced on land and sea with thousands of new types of flower-bearing flora all delivered to the surface from offworld repositories. The mammalian DNA was brought from somewhere else and deposited on Earth as a newer group of species able to thrive in the new post-Nemesis Sol system. The planets were no longer bathed by the light of two stars. Earth was originally an amphibian-reptilian world.

The nova and instant freezing following by gradual thawing and mineralization of the entire world into layers of fossils did not occur over millions of years...but in VERY recent times. The entire Ice Age scenario is that of a world thawing out after such a freezing, the warming up of the planet due to its NEW ORBITAL position between Venus and Mars.

It has been said that a theory is only as good as its best evidence. The absence of transitional forms in the fossil record, polystrate artifacts lying through several layers of strata, fossil reversals, dormant DNA specimens inside petrified remains and a host of other conveniently ignored facts will not change the present paradigm, ever propagated by the prestigious. People are sheep who bleat what they are told, few searching on their own. As Baltasar Gracian observed so many centuries ago- "We live for the most part by what is told to us; it is little that we see; thus we live in the faith of others...the truth is sometimes seen, but rarely heard." (36)   Evolution as a belief is a faith and all attempts to give it a true scientific foundation are no different than the theologian who asserts what is tangible from the textual. Both make conviction the criterion for truth. I for my part offer you the stone jellyfish as my best evidence of a variant theory. But I cannot provide you any proofs, only evidence that conforms to my own faith. The search for absolutes, to borrow the words of Charles Fort, is like looking for a needle no one ever lost in a haystack that never was. (37)

4. Mysterious Origin and Fate of the Cro-Magnon People

One of the greatest anthropological mysteries of prehistory is how the Neanderthal abruptly appeared all over the earth. (1) Evolution cannot explain the abrupt disappearance of Neanderthal, a whole well-entrenched species. (2) So baffling and damaging is this sudden appearance that the scientific acadummies have over and over been caught manufacturing fake fossil hominid predecessors to Neanderthal.

No anthropoids have long hair growing from the top of their heads. (3) So how did humans acquire it? The anthropoids have thick body hair, humans are basically hairless. Natural selection could never have phased out body hair while increasing hair atop the head. (4) Humans do have chimpanzee DNA, but the entire archeological record of any evolutionary development between chimp ancestors and descended humans exists NOWHERE on Earth.

Professor Eisley- "I voiced the suspicion that homo sapiens became separated from the ape tribe by a deliberately planned mutation." (5) David Icke- "The reason science has been unable to find the missing links in human genetic evolution is because there aren't any. The sudden changes in the human form were due to extraterrestrial intervention." (6) Max Flindt and Otto Binder wrote- "If something does not work solely by blind chance, who is tipping the scales?" (7) My answer is Homo Anunna, more popularly referred to as the Anunnaki.

Pre-5239 BCE: Homo Anunna return to Earth's surface to find that their robust , dark-skinned hominid upgrade manufactured at their previous visit, Neanderthal, were inadequate for their mining needs. Unsupervised, this primitive homo inferior has fallen into disorganized hunter-gatherer groups who domiciled in caves rather than worked them for ore.. While bred for strength they were intelligent and artistic. The disappointed Anunna visiting Earth let them be and redesigned homo inferior into a more capable worker- Cromagnon Man. Today scientists accept that Neanderthals were NOT human ancestors but were an entirely different race. (8) Mitachondrial DNA analysis concludes that Neanderthals did not contribute substantially to the modern human genome. (9)

Cro-Magnon Man is an anomaly, superior to Neanderthal and of an independent lineage. Cro-Magnon appeared suddenly, with mysteriously improved skeletal characteristics and with a cranial capacity that is amazingly in excess by 100 cubic centimeters of that of modern man. (10) M. Don Schorn in Elder Gods in Antiquity wrote that, "Cro-Magnon man simply appeared suddenly on Earth, within the midst of the Neanderthals. Science simply does not know how such an event occurred." (11) What? These brainiacs assert that the dinosaurs were wiped out 65 million years ago and that Cro-Magnon were supposed to be 64.5 million years CLOSER in time to us today and they can't solve this local mystery. So much for nicely package theories.

Cro-Magnon man is classified as homo sapiens sapiens. (12) It is a theory that Cro-Magnon wiped out the Neanderthal. (13) The Cro-Magnon are not descended from Neanderthal no more than homo sapiens are direct descendants from Cro-Magnon. In fact, the mystery of the Cro-Magnon is heightened when comparing his anatomy to ours. Though his average height was 6'1.5" but with relatively short arms (a sign of high development), his braincase was extraordinarily large in capacity. (14) Much larger than ours today. The larger Cro-Magnon are measured at 6'7" feet tall, and interestingly, Cro-Magnon women were petite. (15) This is evidence of a race with superior intellectual development and a LONG history of civilized living allowing for their females to cease growing to a proportionate stature with the males of their race. M. Don Schorn relates that the Cro-Magnon was a powerfully-built Caucasoid race, white, wearing sewn embroidered clothing of skins who also wore modern trousers, jackets and hats. (16) Cro-Magnon people looked like any midwestern farmer of the 1930s rural America. Cro-Magnon wore a cap, trousers, tunics and moccasin-like shoes. (17) The men sported beards and mustaches and the women had elaborately parted or braided hair. (18)

A global freezing ended the conditions and civilization of a prior world where Cro-Magnon thrived as the Neanderthal waned, a history for which they are no monuments, no artifacts, no memories and virtually no ancient records save a few fragments that mention the prehistoric catastrophe before the beginning of our own homo sapiens age of urbanization that began circa 3400 BCE. The Cro-Magnon we have excavated and studied, a post-cataclysmic culture after an Ice Age period, is clearly seen in that the Cro-Magnon lived and hunted in the world of the megafauna, enormous mammals like the mammoth depicted in Cro-Magnon art now known to have been a temperate to tropical animal. (19)

The high cultivation and potential of Cro-Magnon were the magnum opus of Homo Anunna's genetic engineering, and therefore, a threat. In unrecorded history prior to 4309 BCE when their civilization was destroyed, Homo Anunna visited Earth, created Cro-Magnon after using mammalian DNA after a period of development and failures. The product complete and performing as intended, Homo Anunna departed.

Upon their return to the planet, they found the thriving Cro-Magnon civilization was in full bloom. They had broken the chains of slavery, driven Neanderthal to the caves of the Earth, mastered nature, established societies, learned how to modify holospheric reality to conform to their will and Cro-Magnon genius had discovered the greatest revelation of all...their immortality. That physical life was merely a temporary path to a personal eternal existence. Homo Anunna found to their dismay that they had manufactured a sentient species having the potential to rival their own superiority, having the intellect and spiritual intuition to some day realize that they were actually confined in a holospheric prison and quite possibly...how to collapse it.

Furious, Homo Anunna modified Cro-Magnon coding in a dangerous series of alterations that created monsters bereft of souls, hybrids, insensate bodies, creatures more than creations. DNA is fantastically ancient and still a mystery to extraterrestrial civilizations. Homo Anunna learned that DNA is pro-life, self-aware, sentient and that the creations of new sentient beings can only be effected by merging preexisting coding with preexistent sentient DNA. Before seeking to destroy them, Homo Anunna manufactured Cro-Magnon to perfection by simply taking chimpanzee mammal DNA and grafting in whole sequences of their own, Anunna, DNA. Not enough Anunna DNA resulted in the earlier Neanderthal and too much resulted in Cro-Magnon. The genetic palindromes and latent genes "switched off," are mysterious but it is obvious that once created, DNA itself maintains fail-safe guardian protocols that prohibit the erasing of life form imbued with intelligence. The coding defense mechanism disallows conception, disallows propagation of a contaminated species. The Anunna, having made Cro-Magnon close to their own image, discovered to their dismay that they could by no manipulation, unmake him.

Their first trespass was now compounded by another. The Anunna made diluted DNA clones that could not reproduce. Production of clones resulted in a worthless workforce. With Cro-Magnon thriving on Earth the Anunna further added to their crimes in the design, manufacture and implementation of a devastating device- the Phoenix Weapon. My books When the Sun Darkens and Nostradamus and the Planets of Apocalypse as well as several posts go in to great detail on this Anunna technology [see Phoenix Calendar]. It has been shown extensively that deployment of this weapon causes terrestrial disasters of local, hemispheric and sometimes global dimensions and always bathes the earth in a red dust that falls to the surface like fine powder or as a rain like blood visited with terrible earthquakes. The first deployment of the Phoenix weapon was again Cro-Magnon civilization. Many millions died, survivors scattered during a cataclysm of quakes, volcanic resurfacing, flooding and red mud fallout from the sky. It is this history that solves a great anthropological mystery that has perplexed the acadummies...the use of red ochre in dressing the dead for burial. Red ochre use is evidence of a sentimental race wanting all of their dead to be rejoined in an Afterlife. The nightmarish end of their civilization was dressed in red blood rains, mud from the sky and choking reddish dust and from that point onward Cro-Magnon added to the dead host on The Other Side all those who passed afterward.

Cro-Magnon believed in an afterlife, burying their dead with possessions. The bones of the dead were specially treated with red ochre after the flesh was removed. (20) That Cro-Magnon man died out as the Neanderthal is not the case. As homo sapiens spread prolifically the Cro-Magnon elements were absorbed. Only a little Cro-Magnon blood entered the Basque and Iberian streams but by far the most is to be found in the early Native Americans. (21)   The Cro-Magnon we are familiar with were post-Cataclysm hunters of the megafauna and gatherers barely surviving in newer regions away from the destroyed lands of their nativity. Despite collapse of their civilization, Cro-Magnon, like the older Neanderthal, survived. The year the Phoenix Weapon was used to depopulate the Earth, induce volcanic resurfacing to push up more rare earth metals and ores to the surface, was 4309 BCE...twenty-one centuries before the very first pictographic writings emerged by the next wave of Anunna creations.

With Cro-Magnon we have a Caucasian race whose art remained unparalleled until the 1st millennium BCE; they were an advanced people who had lost everything. Even Establishment archeologists have been perplexed as to why mathematics, astronomy and calendar systems only appeared thousands of years after the last Ice Age. (22)
   The answer is a simple one: in 4309 BCE the Phoenix Weapon shattered every faith the people had in the heavens and its stability, inducing a global freezing and series of disasters critically depopulating the planet. With Earth's axis pointing at Sol it slowly rolled around the Sun for 270 years with one hemisphere frozen and dark while the other bathed in continual sunlight day and night. Calendars became obsolete and the Cro-Magnon civilization collapsed as Neanderthal again multiplied against them, hunting them for food. The existence of the Cro-Magnon culture is evidence of a totally UNKNOWN highly developed civilization on Earth that had collapsed in unrecorded antiquity, perhaps in the Anunnaki NER nodal dates of

5239 BCE or 4309 BCE in the very first historically recorded Phoenix Cataclysm.

In northern New England, Nova Scotia and Labrador, in eastern Canada, survived an archaic culture called the Red Ochre People, or Red Paint People. These people ceremoniously buried the dead and sprinkled mineral red ochre over the bodies of the deceased and their interred possessions. (23)   The Red Paint People built megalithic chambers, used metals and were a seafaring race, also called the Maritime Archaic. Some of their burials estimated to be 5000-7000 years old. (24)

The pole shift of 3895 BCE totally rearranged the planetary topography. Traces of human occupation are found the world over dating to this period, undeveloped paleolithic communities scattered about in hunter-gatherer bands. The extent of human development is quite clear...people were little more than tool-using animals. During the shift, which would have lasted for days, possibly a week, vast tracts of the Earth's surface slipped under the ocean, a 30 degree displacement moving the lithosphere by 2000 miles, whole seas scouring dry land of its topsoil to leave deserts in their wake. Whole human populations vanished, survivors relocating by following the fleeing herds. Neanderthal and Cro-Magnon, more suited to the conditions of cataclysm than the softer humans the Anunna deposited on the surface, teetered on the edge of extinction. Neanderthal were hardy and vicious and archeologists have discovered evidence that the last holdouts of the Neanderthal race hunted homo sapiens. Human bones with butcher marks have been found charred in excavated Neanderthal camp sites. (25)   Though the Cain and Able story was Jewish fiction, it conveys a real fear in this period. Cain feared that his banishment from the human family would result in his death by "the others." Neanderthal stalked the mountains and hills as the descendants of Cro-Magnon wandered the valleys and forests. In Croatia was discovered evidence that Neanderthal-Cro-Magnon interbreeding did occur. (26) The new homo sapiens had much to fear in this world before the Great Flood. The 1986 discoveries of the Fontbregoua Cave in France have yielded evidence that Cro-Magnon man had also engaged in cannibalism. Humans were butchered, processed, raw meat stripped off the bones which were then broken to extract marrow. (27)

Concerning our 3895 BCE Phoenix Cataclysm pole shift we have testimony from Plato in the Statesman- "In the fullness of time, when the change was to take place, and the earthborn race had all perished...the Pilot of the Universe let the helm go...reversed the motion of the world...and the world turning round with a sudden shock, being impelled in an opposite direction from beginning to end, was shaken by a mighty earthquake, which wrought a new destruction of all manner of animals." (28)   Much of the Greek concept of mankind's beginning was borrowed from Egypt and the Near East, necessarily so, as no Caucasian, Aryan, Semitic people yet existed. To Plato, who knew that gods in the heavens made all the races of mankind, the older races of non-homo sapiens pedigree were regarded as earthborn. In his time period the designations Neanderthal, Cro-Magnon, homo inferior, were unknown. This pole shift catastrophe is a fact of geology, paleobotany, geography and other disciplines though it is hardly remembered in human memory. Many of our historical account prior to the 20th century BCE were recorded retrospectively through transmission of oral testimony, or as will be shown, revealed to literate humans by nonhuman benefactors.

Cro-Magnon artifacts of France reveal a high culture of artistic sophistication. Lewis Spence wrote that, "...the race

which produced it cannot be classified as merely savage.
In fluency and originality, at least, Aurignacian [pre-
Magdalanian Cro-Magnon] art is, indeed, greatly superior
to that of either of Egypt or Babylonia, and to achieve a
standard of such surpassing excellence it must have
persisted elsewhere than in the area where it arrived at
fruition for many thousands of years." (29) It "...have
had a long history in some other region." (30) It was
"...greatly more advanced than those of any other
paleolithic civilization." (31) Spence wrote- "We have an
art fully developed and obviously having behind it many
centuries of evolution, suddenly appearing in a locality in
which there are no signs of its earlier phases." (32)

Concerning Aurignacian art, Spence wrote, "Its
beginnings cannot be traced anywhere in the known
world." (33) "The walls of the caverns they occupied are
in many cases covered with drawings of animals and men
which, for accuracy of design and modelling have never
been surpassed. (34) Cro-Magnon art sometimes used
natural protuberances to enhance artwork with three-
dimensional effects. (35) Macalister wrote that the origin
of the European Cro-Magnon was NOT Europe. Upon
their arrival they had already developed over a period of
time elsewhere. (36) Spence wrote that the Cro-Magnon
man was cut off from his home by some cataclysm,
marooned upon the shores of the Atlantic coasts of Europe
and Africa to spread into the Mediterranean BEFORE it
was a sea. (37) The Mediterranean Sea we know today
was back then a series of valleys and fresh water lakes.
The Aurignacian culture did not spread into central or
easter Europe (38) but they populated the lands and coasts
of north Africa, Sicily, Spain, France and Italy (39) as a
culture of fishermen (40) at a time when the Mediterranean
basin was not a sea, but a system of fertile valleys with
large lakes and vast forests teeming with game. The study
of Cro-Magnon civilization is impeded by our assumption

that the present geography and condition of our planet is the same now as when it was then.

Spence wrote that the Aurignacian race "...was physiologically far superior to any human type presenting existing. (41) If cranial capacity is a measure of intellect, then Cro-Magnon had greater intellectual potential than modern homo sapiens. As a highly developed race both physically and mentally we must conclude that our current discoveries of Cro-Magnon man are of his post-cataclysmic degenerative state. While later Aurignacian further blossomed into the Magdalenian Cro-Magnon culture this development was not a fundamental change but rather a difference in degree.

In 2239 BCE the land bridge at the Strait of Gibraltar [Pillars of Hercules] broke from quakes allowing the Atlantic ocean to flood the basin burying the majority of Cro-Magnon sites and artifacts. Cro-Magnon people migrated into the Mediterranean region prior to this catastrophe. There is no sign that Cro-Magnons ever migrated into central Africa. (42) They suddenly appeared along the Atlantic coast, of Spain and France, in the regions of Biscayan, Pyrenean and Dordogne, at the END of a glacial period, the end of the LAST true Ice Age. (43) This was not approximately 11,000 BCE as the acadummies purport, but some time between 5239 and 4039 BCE.

Cro-Magnon is not a type of homo inferior. In fact, today's homo sapien species is a slightly diluted, sabotaged, genetically-impeded form of Cro-Magnon. Cro-Magnon are considered homo sapiens and it was further genetic modification on Cro-Magnon man that resulted in modern homo sapiens sapiens. (44)

Humans today are DNA-designer products of Homo Anunna who used Cro-Magnon coding with newer modifications to develop homo sapiens sapiens and fashion distinct races of Negroid, Mongolid to High Oriental, Amerindic and Dark Caucasoid. The white Caucasians did not yet exist; in fact, the first appearance of white-skinned, blue-eyed infants among the antediluvians is one of the major themes from the traditions of the preFlood world. Even the preFlood Sumerians prided themselves as being "the black-headed people," and all their depictions in statuary and reliefs show them as a smooth-skinned, beardless people. The establishment of black, yellow, red and brown races on earth from the older Cro-Magnon stock was a deliberate act of divisiveness by Homo Anunna...induced arrested development, a managerial act to prevent humanity from succeeding at whatever feat of accomplishment Cro-Magnon had obviously attained in prehistory.

The history of the world is very racial. How the offended will howl! I search for the truth in all matters and strive to convey it. If you are among the vacuous, media-influenced sensitive puppets of the Establishment who take offense at my conclusions on the origin of human racial types then write your own book. Then compare your bibliography with mine. Or you can write a rebuttal so I can answer it.

5. The Anunnaki Homeworld Nibiru and the Once-Inhabited World...the Moon

Our Moon is many times larger in proportion to Earth than any other lunar body in the solar system compared to its host planet. This is highly unusual. In fact, compared to the combined moon-planet proportions of the four largest moons orbiting Jupiter (Ganymede), Saturn (Titan), Uranus (Titania) and Neptune (Triton), our Moon is still much larger in comparison. The Earth-Luna system is widely out of proportion in this solar system. (1) This is because it is not a true host-satellite pairing. The earth-Moon relationship is actually a double-planet system.

Jim Marrs in 2013 in Our Occulted History, wrote, "Mainstream science now accepts the theory that the moon originated elsewhere and entered the Earth's gravitational field at some point in ancient times. (2) Isaac Asimov notes that the Moon is too large to have been captured by Earth. (3) Luna was placed deliberately in its near-perfect circular orbit and its rotation synchronized with its period of revolution so one side always faces Earth. (4) Spence notes that a captured body should have a pronounced elliptical orbit- our Moon's orbit is too circular and scientists are at a loss to explain why. (5)

In the inner solar system, Earth is the only planet to have a moon. Mercury and Venus have no moons and Mars has two asteroids orbiting it, not moons, and these two asteroids did not appear until 1877 AD, first documented by Asaph Hall. Before that they had never been seen though Mars was the object of much scientific study prior to 1877.

Moon's distance is so perfect it totally occults the sun at eclipse. It is now known to be far older than previously believed. Odd lights have repeatedly been reported by those studying the lunar surface, yet, scientists have found no evidence of volcanic activity on the Moon. (6) Though this is not the focus of this post, we will soon review evidence that the Moon exhibits much evidence of former habitation. Scientific analysis of moon rocks indicate that it is without a core, or hollow. (7) There are many, even scientists, now holding to the position that our Moon contains hollowed deep-interior bases or installations and that it has for thousands of years been used to watch over our world. Whole crater basins have been seen from Earth to have opened like massive doors with light inside from time to time. On the lunar surface are gigantic artificial constructs called the Shard in the Ukert Region and the Tower in the Sinus Medii, both upright and totally unexplainable by known natural processes. (8)

That the Moon is a recent addition to the inner solar system and the Earth system was the opinion of naturalists over twenty-three centuries ago. Aristotle wrote that the PreAchaean Pelasgians occupied Arcadia before there was a Moon in the sky. (9) Anaxagoras and Democritus taught that there was a time in human memory when Earth was a without a moon. (10)

Hans Hoerbiger was a Viennese engineer who devoted his life to the study of cosmic origins. He held that Luna is a captured planet. (11) This is the subject matter of my book Descent of the Seven Kings to be released by Book Tree in the Summer of 2017. The capture of Luna was actually a steering of the Moon to its present position and this occurred on one of those anciently venerated Great Years of 600 years known to the Sumerians as the NER Chronology, the history of the cosmos and world in 600-year intervals. Many fragments of this time-keeping tradition have survived around the world. The Moon was attached to Earth's orbit in the year 4039 BCE, or 1800 years (600x3) before the Great Flood cataclysm of 2239 BCE.

In 4039 BCE the Moon is moored to the Earth and our world begins rolling more rapidly, the planet beginning to warm. As the frozen hemispheres thaw the earth and moon are locked in a geosynchronous rolling in orbit around the sun as the same hemisphere on earth faces the same hemisphere of the moon as if the two bodies were connected by an invisible axis. Like a barbell of unequal weights, they roll around the sun as the ice melting into seas evaporates on the continually-dayside of the planet. A thick vapor canopy spreads from the solar heated hemisphere that knows no night. This melting of frozen glacial sheets and oceans on one side of the planet continues 144 years. Still, small bands of Neanderthal and Cro-Magnon humans live, the solar-facing hemisphere supporting life. Our planet was a frozen fossil-world with minimal life surviving in the caves and subterranean biosphere. Our lunar body earlier had orbited the sun alone after being ripped away from Tiamat's explosion (Astroid Belt) till Earth came along and trapped it in its gravity. Our Moon was formerly called Kingu before it began orbiting Earth. It orbited the 4th world (present Astroid Belt), called Tiamat, which had 11 moons.

Albert T. Clay, Near East scholar and translator, in 1923, wrote that the Tiamat monster conflict at the Creation symbolically "represents an unfriendly power," and that "the belief existed that there had been a great conflict prior to the Creation of the heavens and the earth, between God and the primeval monster, with whom were associated other beings termed dragons. (12) As found abundantly in my prior works on Phoenix and NIBIRU, intruder planets and comets coming very close to Earth throughout history by many cultures were referred to as dragons. Tiamat's dead body provided water that fell to the earth- a glaciosphere turned vaporous and torn away from a dead world to rain on ours. In 1902 L.W. King wrote that the Moon was as a "Planet that was laid waste." Sitchin notes that the Moon, or Akkadian Sin, derived from SU.EN, or Lord of Wasteland. (13)

In Porphry's Letter to Anebo the Egyptian as related by Augustine in City of God X ch. 11, he wrote that demons were of the moon, and inside it. Occult tradition derived from Tibet reads- "Here we touch upon a hidden mystery, of which the solution lies revealed for those who seek, in the fact that human beings and certain groups of devas are no longer found on the moon. Man has not ceased to exist upon the Moon because it is dead, and cannot therefore support life, but the Moon is dead because man and these deva groups have been removed from off its surface.." (14) "The Moon, as you know, is a shell, an ancient form..." (15) There are several theorists offering convincing evidence today that many of the impact scars and craters on the Moon's surface were not from meteorites but are actually blast craters...the relics of major weapons impacts.

Earth's new orbit, rotation and axial tilt occurring in 4039 BCE is confirmed indirectly in research of Scott Creighton and Gary Osborn in The Giza Prophecy, showing convincing evidence of a geoastronomical timeline encoded in the architectural distribution of the Giza monuments identifying the approximate date of 3980 BC (59 years off from 4039) for an ancient poleshift cataclysm when Earth assumed its 23.5 axial tilt. They confirmed their Sphinx timeline by independent analysis of 39" Queens Chamber shaft that pointed directly at Al-Nitak of Orion's Belt in about 3980 BC. (16)   Also from Egypt comes evidence closer to the mark.   The temple of Dendera in Egypt built by the Ptolemys in accord with an ancient plan was designed to commemorate the Zodiac. Paul A. LaViolette, Ph.D, admitting that he did not know why, wrote that Dendera's zodiac encodes the date 4040 BCE. (17) An estimate only 1 year off from 4039. A stunning find- truly a band of constellations could have no meaning to a planet not rotating on its present axis. The Zodiac was literally born on 4039 BCE because prior to the Moon's presence the terrestrial poles would have been different, thus making the band of stars we see today as the Zodiac to have been a totally different strip of the starry heavens.

In this year of 4039 BC an unusual surface-scarred world appeared in a dead orbit around Earth. The Moon. It was once inhabited. It's installations have been reactivated in the last century. It was brought to the inner Sol system and deliberately placed in orbit around Earth. We are far from finished in our study of this remarkable object in our every night sky.

THE HOMEWORLD OF THE ANUNNAKI...NIBIRU

There is a vast object very much a part of this solar system that has returned with such regularity that its appearances have been documented and these records put together to paint a harrowing picture of Earth's past. This object is not to be confused with the Phoenix I write so much about. Both are intruder planets, the relics of a former binary system of two luminaries. The older luminary collapsed into a Dark Star, the younger luminary is our own sun, Sol.

The Phoenix object visits the inner system every 138 years and it now a barren world of red earth. Its glaciosphere was torn off and rained upon our planet in 2239 BCE, an event remembered globally as the Great Flood cataclysm. This second and more obscure object is known popularly as NIBIRU and was introduced to us by Zechariah Sitchin in his Earth Chronicles series.

This NIBIRU object spends exactly 732 years far outside the inner solar system on its journey orbiting Nemesis (the Dark Star is a compressed star). It spends precisely 60 years in the inner solar system orbiting Sol at its perihelion. This 60 year period, twice before the Deluge and once after it is well marked in history for it is these times when the Anunnaki are busy among mankind constructing technolithic monuments for which humans then spend millennia trying to replicate long after the Anunnaki depart. Sitchin introduced the Anunnaki but never predicted the date of NIBIRU's return for he did not have its orbital history. When Book Tree of San Diego decided to publish *Anunnaki Homeworld* by Jason M. Breshears in 2011, this is what they wrote on the back cover-

"The Anunnaki is a legendary race that appears in the oldest documents preserved by mankind. They are said to inhabit an outermost planet that orbits our sun in an extremely elliptical orbit. Each time this planet gets near to the earth it creates planetary cataclysms. Many researchers claim it will be returning soon. The work of Zecharia Sitchin, author of the Earth Chronicles series of books, focuses on the Anunnaki and their previous visits. Many have asked Sitchin, "When will this planet return?" He never gave an exact date, but said it was more than halfway back. Jason Breshears gives an exact year, and does so confidently, due to his extensive research. He delves not only into historical records, as Sitchin had done, but also uses scientific cycles and mathematical formulas that relate to our concepts of planetary time and orbits. The historical records, chronologically presented by Breshears, help in identifying cyclical patterns. He also employs advanced geometry, interprets complex crop circle patterns, and uses biblical prophecy in support of some of the astronomical events he has predicted. He does not cover much on the mythical aspects of the Anunnaki gods themselves, but focuses more on the actual sciences that can predict their return. Ancient stories and carefully documented proof are two different things. For these reasons, this book is highly recommended."

Breshears' introduction elaborated more about the actual book's contents and demonstrates that outside of his own research there are no publications that provide more information about NIBIRU than he does. No one has ever published an orbital chronology and then backed it up with so much data. His introduction to *Anunnaki Homeworld*-

This work restored what our scholars have lost. The truth about our planet's past and future. This author's prior work, *When the Sun Darkens*, concerned the history and 2040 AD return of planet Phoenix, a fragmenting and uninhabited world having little bearing on then present thesis. The fact is herein demonstrated that there is indeed a second wandering planet that occasionally visits our inner solar system, a gigantic broken and present populated world that is now fast approaching Earth and will arrive at 2046 AD. This planet is NIBIRU, and its orbital history completely forged the unfolding of human events.

This is the *Anunnaki Homeworld* and its return was a constant fear of the ancients. The most magnificent architectural wonders from the Old World, the Great Pyramid and Stonehenge, as well as the earth's most archaic dating systems all remain as mute witnesses of the presence and orbital chronology of this alien planet. Even the modern misinterpreted Mayan Long-Count system, when accurately interpreted, as will be shown herein, was a sophisticated countdown to the exact date of the return of NIBIRU and its Anunnaki occupants in 2046 AD. The popularized year of 2012 AD was never the end of the Mayan system, and this will be conclusively proven in this book.

The pyramid was not a tomb. Stonehenge was not a temple. It is not mathematically possible for 2012 AD to be the end of the Mayan Long-Count calendar (Editor-Breshears' book published 2011, written 2009, three years before 2012). These are the assumptions of men trained to think one-dimensionally, those blind to the silent atavistic patterns appearing mysteriously in our grain fields that beckon us to search deeper into the messages of universal geometry. We are being warned. These warnings concern 2046 AD.

Whatever preternatural forces are at work behind these amazing crop formations, it is abundantly clear that the exact same formula exployed in interpreting the three-dimensionasl calendrical geometry of Stonehenge I and II and also the method for understanding the calendrical messages of crop patterns. READER BEWARE...what the masses believe and what this thesis demonstrates cannnot both be true.

Sitchin was a brilliant researcher and scholar, but he made mistakes. One of his most glaring was assuming every reference in the Old World records to a celestial object and attendant disasters was a reference of NIBIRU. Breshears has separated the chronologies of Phoenix and NIBIRU, and has done so providing so much evidence that after Book Tree released his initial works, *When the Sun Darkens* on Phoenix and *Anunnaki Homeworld* on NIBIRU, he amassed so much new material on these two separate orbital chronologies that he had to write another book. This is what Breshears said-

After years of researching into chronological and calendrical systems from around the world I made a single profound discovery not found in ANY published books EVER. Over thirty ancient destructions and eyewitness accounts specifically dated and confirmed by multiple recorders from widely separated civilizations left us writings today that DATE the appearance of a vast red object approaching earth and passes leaving earthquakes, volcanic ruin, floods and a red mud, rain or reddish dust blanketing our atmosphere. These findings, coupled with what ancient writers mentioned of the very old legends of the Phoenix, led me to write *When the Sun Darkens*, published by Book Tree of San Diego in 2009. My discoveries did not end with the publication of this work, but so much new materials came into my possession that I had to write *Nostradamus and the Planets of Apocalypse*. I was shocked to find so much proof of my theory, especially my newer findings concerning NIBIRU.

Book Tree hurriedly released *Nostradamus and the Planets of Apocalypse* in 2013, publishing this description on its back cover-

This book maps out the entire historical chronology of planetary cataclysms starting in 4309 BC, covering the cyclical return of Nibiru, the planet Phoenix, and more. It also reveals the code for understanding the prophecies of Nostradamus, showing when they have occurred in the past, or when they will occur in the future. It takes the work of Mario Reading, who first broke the code, and shows how it perfectly applies to all of Breshears' previously made cataclysmic predictions for the years 2040 and 2046. Mr. Reading made mistakes in interpreting some quatrains for the years 2001-2012 that did not involve his code, so his work has been largely dismissed. Breshears brings Reading's work back to life with stunning clarity, and takes it one step further in our understanding of prophetic events. Also covers the predictions of Mother Shipton, who was not only a contemporary to Nostradamus, but made the exact predictions Breshears and Nostradamus made concerning two large scale global catastrophes that will occur six years apart. Despite the many predictions of others, the year 2012 passed with no worldwide cataclysmic events because, according to the author, they were never interpreted or explained correctly, until now. The author remains unmatched in his in-depth research regarding historical and geological cycles, which in turn allows him to accurately map major planetary events, past and future, many of which are outlined in this book.

We hope this post has been helpful to those wanting to bear out the truth of our ancient past and the relevance history has for us today and in the coming years. Breshears' findings should concern everyone. This is not some doomsday pulpit routine hollaring about a unspecified future with unspecified dates. This is data-packed research demonstrating mathematically what we can expect will happen to our planet and civilization on May 2040 and November 2046, two cataclysms back-to-back plummeting humanity right back to Year One where we found the Cro-Magnon people who were sophisticated but totally bereft of their infrastructure; how we found the earliest Sumerians in possession of advanced knowledges but not comprehending their value and preserving these things in ritual, ceremony and ridiculous religious traditions.

6. PreFlood Memories of a Prior Creation

Some of the most beautiful scenery in the world provides us the visual proof of vast destructions of our planet in antiquity by the agency of water.

The most misunderstood aspect of antiquated calendrical systems is that none actually span back to the very beginning, though many are believed to by those that adhere to them. By all accounts the oldest dating systems seem to universally span back to some distant apocalypse or widespread, civilization-destroying cataclysm. Those that do not start in like fashion begin with mankind, such as the Hebraic system and Annus Mundi, but still found wanting are any stretching back to an alleged creation. Our planet's past was ancient by the time humanity was created and planted on this garden planet.

The arrival of the first 200 Anunnaki is best understood by first being aware of the state of the earth at their arrival. It is commonly held that God created the heavens and the earth in six days, this concept of course being that of core fundamentalist Christians and those of the Judaic faith. This supposed creation event was by their reckoning less than 6000 years ago. But the scriptures do not convey this fiction. There was a vast time period between when in Genesis 1:1 the heavens and earth were originally created and later in verse 2 when the Anunnaki found the earth covered in darkness in a state of chaos [tehom]. Even Genesis 1 makes the distinction between created [bara] and made [asah], the latter carrying with it the connotation of renovation. The only new creation in Genesis 1 after the earth was restored from the chaos was mankind, the center of controversy between the Godhead and the Anunnaki, and man was commanded to "replenish" the earth. This command is void if the earth had not been filled with life priorly.

This mystery of a preAdamic world was known to the Sumerians and later Babylonians. The Euphratean cultures rewrote the original inscriptions of the Sumerians concerning the creation and changed object nouns and descriptions of phenomena into pronouns, the names of nonexistent deities. In the seven tablet series called Enuma Elish we find a retelling of the same cosmogony found in Genesis 1 in that the world was originally subject to the waters of chaos. The Jewish redactors of the old Babylonian records literally took the six phases of conflict between the Chaos Dragon and newly arisen gods and turned it into the Six Days of Creation in Genesis. The idea behind this manipulation was because the elder traditions concerned a teeming world of paradise prior to humanity that rose up in insurrection against the gods and was destroyed utterly by the Dragon. They merely merged concepts that seemingly belonged together, and while this has been a vex unto scholarship, to their credit, the Babylonians were right.

Before the sun and moon were present, in the Enuma Elish text we read, ". . . Anshar and Kishar were created; they surpassed them. Long were the days, years were added." (1) Though the scribes altered the texts considerably, attempting to place gods where none existed, we see in Anshar and Kishar not deities, but elements of time. These are Sumerian personifications of heaven [AN] and earth [KI] time. In fact, as probably already noticed, they are affixed to the Sumerian designation for time period [shar]. The phrase ". . . long were the days, years were added," reveals to the reader that earth during the epoch of chaotic ruin had virtually ceased rotating, making what should have been 24 hour rotational periods to extend to month-long or even years-long days and nights. And the fact that "years were added" probably infers that it took a lot longer for the planet to orbit the sun. The Genesis creation story in its original form was a preflood account narrated to humans by the Anunnaki they lived among, an account that was later written down by the Sumerians. Centuries later the Akkadians translated the Sumerian creation accounts and it was these Akkadian cuneiform texts that were used by the Babylonians to compose their Enuma Elish, which now positioned deities in the place of what was earlier only phenomena. About a thousand years later these badly altered tablets were studied in Babylon by Jewish scholars who saw more than one version in the eldest writings so they composed the book of Genesis using both creation accounts (Genesis 1 and 2).

In essence, the Anunnaki arrived 144 years prior to Year 1 Annus Mundi to a dead planet. There is no other reason for this Babylonian text to have preserved such an unusual statement unless it was the elements of time that brought earth back out of its stupor, the Anshar and Kishar that rescued the planet after a period of divine judgement. Having ceased rotating the earth was dead, probably just another Wanderer [arcane designation for planet] far away from the sun [universal symbol of Deity] and Genesis 1 did not occur until something with a powerful gravitational field passed closely to earth's surface generating sufficient friction to cause the earth to spin again while pushing it back into a trajectory that would then allow it to gravitate back to a stable orbital belt, the passing object [gigantic fragmented planet] forming the appearance of light before the sun naturally appeared as shown in Genesis 1 and initiating the first "evening and morning." The Babylonians are to be praised for preserving these elements, however, this restorative process did not begin with Anshar and Kishar but with the appearance of a broken planet that voyages from the vast Abyss that serves the Godhead as a sufficient prison for the [AN]unna[KI]. This broken planet Passover is the origin of the first 200 Anunnaki who descended 600 years [NER] before 200 more descended in Jared's day in 3439 BCE.

Scholars are at odds concerning the second verse in Genesis 1 but all accounts agree it is a textual anomaly. Though God very clearly commanded man to "replenish the earth," or to fill it again, theologians and academics are apprehensive in considering the possibility that this passage describes the result of a planetary cataclysm before humanity. But the evidence, scriptures, ancient textual and even mythological passages and traditions from around the globe are enough to convince the unbiased trier of fact that Genesis 1:2 describes a world lost in space, encased in dark ice and frozen solid until it returned toward the warmth of the sun, defrosted, and then its heating up evaporated the frozen moisture below back into the atmosphere to create a firmament above [vapor canopy like Venus] and below as Genesis 1 describes. The world was one vast ocean until the water canopy was again above the earth, an aquatic atmosphere that again collapsed in 2239 BCE [1656 AM] at the Flood.

The chaotic waters were called tehom, from which the Babylonians personified into the Dragon Tiamat. Translators claim that the word tehom is a ". . . veritable survival from prehistoric antiquity, an ancient word older than the text itself, which was written in Hebrew, derived from hum [to roar: rage]." (2) These translators and researchers have for over a century now held that Moses had access to old writings when compiling Genesis, and probably studied an ". . . ancient primeval record of the formation of the world." (3) It was because of this ancestral memory that Aristotle in Book I of his *Metaphysics* wrote, ". . . some people think that even those who lived far back in antiquity, long before the present age, and who were the first to discourse about the gods, held this kind of view about nature [regarding earth originally covered in water]. For they made Oceanus and Tythys the parents of all who had come into being, and said that what the gods swore by was water, which they called Styx: for what is most precious is what is most ancient." (4) This seems to be confirmed by Aristotle's learned predecessors Plato and Solon, the latter teaching and the former recording that there was more than one flood—". . . remember a single deluge, but there were many previous ones." Even before Solon the famous Hesiod 800 years before Christ wrote, "First came Chaos, and then broad-bosomed earth, the everlasting seat of all that is, and Love." In another part, Hesiod wrote, "From Chaos came Black Night and Erebos. And Night in turn gave birth to Day and Space." (5) The idea of cataclysm was conveyed also by early Hebraic scholars and renowned Church Fathers. The Hebrew Targum of Onkelos, the earliest Aramaic version of the Old Testament passages, translates Genesis 1:2 as ". . . and the earth was laid waste." Also did Origen [186-254 AD] in *De Principiis* write that Genesis 1:2 is after the earth had been "cast downwards."

The Sumerians and Babylonians too regarded water as the uncreated first principle and source of all from the primordial waste of waters. (6) That water was uncreated denotes that they recognized its preexistence, a former existence predicating the existence of a former world. We have here a confusing admixture of scientific observances cloaked in mythical garments so tangled as to have baffled even the ancients who recorded these events and scenarios. This confusion is also recorded in Vedic Hymn No. 129: "Darkness there was: at first concealed in darkness this All was indiscriminated Chaos. All that existed then was void and formless: by the great power of warmth was born that Unit . . . Who verily knows and who can here declare it, whence it was born and whence comes this creation? The gods are later than this world's production. Who knows when it first came into being?" (7) This very old Vedic description of earth in ruins is so informative and descriptive that we are left with the impression that the Genesis record is actually an abbreviated version of it. The "Unit" that was born by the power of warmth was the rotation of earth that restored the "evening to morning" motion of the planet's spinning as it rapidly thawed out.

Early Persian records tell that prior to the creation of earth was the First Creation, before the establishment of time, when ". . . the sun, the moon, and the stars stood still." (8) The Greeks believed that the world was inhabited before the creation of mankind by all male deities during a Golden Age before women had yet been made. (9) Also, Ovid's Metamorphosis holds that mankind was created using certain divine elements which had survived some preexisting catastrophe. (10) Philo wrote that ". . . the first beginning is quite half the whole," and later in the Christian apocryphal text entitled the Epistle of Barnabas we read, "I will show you, how He made us a second formation in the latter days." (11)

The history of humankind is fascinating and untold in Establishment literature. The history of the different types of races of humans is equally intriguing.

7. PreFlood Races Shocked by First Appearance of Caucasians

Thousands of historic and modern testimonies concerning extraterrestrial contact have witnesses describing the alien beings as tall, blue-eyed, blond humanlike entities that are usually accompanied by servile fetus-like aliens much shorter. (1)   This intriguing description is of the modern Nephilim, hybrids, genetically created by the fetus-like Grays that are building a race of semi-giants as they had done twice in biblical history both before and after the flood. Blond hair, blue eyes and tall features are descriptive of the Egyptian racial portraits and reliefs in the temples and traditions of the Sabeans, Amorites and Anakim giants, all partially descended from the Nephilim. These mysterious aliens witnessed by thousands of people are described by Raymond E. Fowler in The *Watchers* as tall, blond, robed human like entities. (2)   Interestingly, the gods Osiris and Orion [Nimrod] were regarded as being the same deity to the early Egyptians. (3)   This description calls to mind the Sumerian giant Gilgamesh whose name means Son of the Sun and the angelic Watchers that descended and taught men the secrets of God.

Concerning the strange physical characteristics of the gods of the mysterious Sumerians, Erich Von Daniken proclaims that the figures and statues of these people appear to fit no racial group known on earth, having goggle eyes, domed foreheads, narrow lips, and generally long, straight noses, (4) traits cited that belong to the Amorite and Anakim giants and the large Aryan mummies in the Chinese Takla Makan desert.   In *The Two Babylons*, by Alexander Hislop, we discover that the racial traits of gods and goddesses around the world from Babylonia, Egypt, India, Greece and Rome were of blue or grey-eyed, blond-haired entities with fair features. (5) This is confirmed by scholars. The statuary and anatomical remains from the royal graves and tombs of the ruling people of Sumer, India and Egypt as also supported by their portraits and sculptures is of a long-headed race with gray or blue eyes, a distinct Caucasian people. [*Egyptian Civilization: Its Sumerian Origin* IX]

In more contemporary times the high Nordic appearance of humans belonged to fairy children. Katherine Briggs in *An Encyclopedia of Fairies* writes that when fairies search for mortal children a golden-haired child was in far more danger of being stolen than a dark one. In *An Encyclopedia of Fairies*, page 62; Captives in Fairyland, we read that trolls derive from Nordic beliefs in fairies. These creatures were associated to the underworld and stole small children and sometimes even swapped troll babies for human infants. Some trolls were giants that guarded passes or bridges.

The motive assigned to fairies in northern countries is that of preserving and improving their race, on the one hand by carrying off human children to be brought up among the elves and to become united with them and on the other hand by obtaining the milk and fostering of human mothers for their own offspring.

Such traditions of fair-featured infants took on other forms in other cultures. In the Yaresan text of the 13th century CE, or Ajayeb ol-mayhluqat, the race of prehuman djinn were shapechangers that could appear as snakes or scorpions of men. (6)   The djinn were on earth before Adam, having been ousted from heaven. They were accused of switching infants of their own race with human babies. Muslim traditions hold that the children of the djinn had white European features. (7)

The Shahnameh, written by Arab poet Firdowsi, a Muslim of eastern Persia, composed the work based from older traditions. It is the Book of Kings, claiming that Zal (hero-Noah) was a "...son of the daevic race." (8) An ancient race of gods. As attested to the The Book of Enoch, the Dead Sea texts and the Arabic Shahnameh, Andrew Collins observed that, "...the antediluvian patriarchs of the Old Testament would seem to have had a very similar aversion to infants born with what appear to have been extreme white Caucasian features." (9)

The Flood hero Noah was born in 2839 BCE, the year 1056 of the PreFlood Calendar. In the Book of Enoch we find that at the birth of Noah his father Lamech was alarmed, for the infant was "...white as snow and red as the blooming of a rose, and the hair of his head and his long locks were white as wool, and his eyes were beautiful. And when he opened up his eyes he lighted up the whole house like the sun." (10) Lamech told Methuselah, "I have begotten a strange son, diverse from and unlike man, and resembling the sons of the God of heaven; and his nature is different, and he is not like us." (11) The fear of antediluvian people was that they were so small compared to the fair-featured figures they referred to as gods. To primitive, uneducated people these strangers with pale features and white skin were angels. The Ethiopian Kebra Nagast text reveals that children born to angels through the daughters of the Cainites were so large that women were ripped open. (12) Enki [Enoch] and his loyalists mated with the females of the civilized humans who gave birth to the first Caucasoid baby...Noah, in 2839 BCE.

The many Anunnaki "sons of God," took the many daughters of men and begat the Caucasian race rapidly. The first generation of infants born were Caucasians having dark recessive gene characteristics, white people with dark hair and eyes, but the second and third generation females were fair, appearing more and more like the Anunna themselves. The Anunna-human cross-breeding began some time after the start of the Contact Period in 3439 BCE but in 2839 BCE the project was completed with the birth of homo sapiens who were of the same DNA and appearance as Homo Anunna... Caucasians were very tall compared to the darker races before the Deluge, bearded which to other races was the mark of godhood, with white skin and eyes like gemstones. It was out of this genetic campaign that Enki took a fair female and fathered the famous Noah, an extremely white, blue-eyed blond child in the 600th year before the Great Flood. This began the Noachian Race, called in antiquity by other races as the Sons of the Sun and in ancient Egypt as Shemsu Hor and after the Flood as the Shepherd Kings. Zechariah Sitchin, writing of the birth of Noah, described him as "...white as snow his skin was, the color of wool was his hair, like the skies [blue] were his eyes..." (13)

Bearded Sons of the Gods

Unlike any other human type who were earlier created through Anunna females in birth-warrens, the stories of the Old World are consistent; these traditions are those of nonCaucasian peoples that together claim that white-skinned and fair-haired people were direct descendants of the 'gods,' and were NOT brought into this world through the older birth-goddesses scheme. The Sons of the Gods [God in biblical version] who were inventive, heroes, tall, giants compared to the indigenous moonborn peoples were Caucasians, the Children of the Sun. These are NOT Caucasian histories; yes the oldest Aryan texts relate that the gods were their ancestors, but it is nonCaucasian stories and writings from antiquity that explain that the NEW race of mortals to appear on Earth before the Flood were NOT like the people of Earth, NOT black-haired and eyed, not smooth-skinned with hairless faces, not with skins colored in Earth tones. The acadummies ignore these references because they fear being called racists, but it's NOT the white people who claimed these things. When Caucasians appeared they were Sons of Gods, mighty men of renown, of exceptional height and intelligence, wizards who knew secrets with white skin like snow, blue and green eyes, gold hair as Children of the Sun, red hair as descended from the blood of the gods and like the depictions of gods from China, India, Sumer, Egypt and ancient America- all places inhabited by smooth-faced people of short stature, the new race of white people were BEARDED just like their godlike fathers.

Sitchin's books are full of Sumerian reliefs showing bearded gods in the presence of smooth-faced humans. (14)   Sumerian depictions of themselves in reliefs showing soldiers, tradesmen, laborers, shepherds, leaders and kings clearly show that the Sumerians did not grow any facial hair. On the famous Royal Standard of Ur are 84 human figures and only one has a beard and he is the ONLY male depicted having hair on his head. (15)   He is clearly a foreigner. When Sumerians depicted their gods and goddesses they are bearded with straight, Caucasian noses and owlish round eyes of lapis lazuli (blue) [see cover art of Cradle of Civilization: Kramer]. The saucer-eyed pictures are how Asians have always represented Caucasians; even today Japanese art is full of examples of white people drawn or painted with overly large round eyes. Sumerians records depict the hunter-gatherers as smooth-skinned, dark-featured. Civilized men were bearded and white.

The story in antiquity of the first appearance of the New Breed of humans made by Enki was famous. Prior to this incidence humans were basically animals, naked before the Anunnaki, servants and slaves without education and writing. But Enki experimented and created Civilized Man. The other Anunnaki, who would accuse Enki of this trespass were fooled when Enki claimed it wasn't him, that he found the new human child so different than the others inside a reed basket floating on a river. (16) This is precisely why Sharrukin [Sargon I] of Akkad claimed to have been placed on a river in a reed basket and why the Jewish writers inventing the Moses Epic had their Giver of the Law placed in a reed basket on the Nile river in

Egypt...the baby-in-a-basket was the sign of DIVINE
PARENTAGE.

A stela excavated in Palestine shows the Canaanite god El
as a bearded Caucasian who is being served a beverage by
a smooth-faced adult male. (17)   In antiquity the ability to
grow a thick beard marked one as being a child of the
gods. It is why smooth-skinned Egyptian Pharaohs are
often depicted wearing artificial, ornamental beards of
wood on their chins and assumed the title Son of the Sun as
found on page 21 of Egyptian Civilization: Its Sumerian
Origin.   So much crossbreeding between races has
occurred through wars, migrations and marriage in the
passed four thousand years that the white race has absorbed
dark recessive gene characteristics like brown hair and
brown eyes just as many among the nonCaucasian peoples
have acquired fair eyes and facial hair. The Pharaohs
prided themselves as being descendants, or claimed scions,
of the earlier race called the Shemsu Hor.

In ancient Egypt the race of Shemsu Hor were sages, the
Followers of the Sun, called "ghosts," for their lightness
and the Turin Papyrus refers to the Shemsu Hor people as
the Akhu, which means "shining ones," according to
Ignatius Donnelly in Atlantis: The Antediluvian World on
 page 209, a racial description of white people from the
perspective of a dark race.

An entire article could be written about the Dragon Kings
of the Chinese prehistory, ancient founders of civilization
and bestowers of secrets, kin to the gods, giants who were
bearded. These rulers are why depictions of dragons in
Asia are with strange beards hanging from their chins.
Robert Temple wrote that "...the dragons of archaic China
were associated with the stars in a curious way." (18)   The

Dragon Kings may have claimed to have come from the stars or be descended from those who did.

Suddenly after the Great Flood [May 2239 BCE] fleets of bearded Caucasians sailed into all of the great river valleys- at Peru in Urumbamba Valley, South America, also in Central America, the Egyptian Nile, the Euphrates-Tigris of southern Mesopotamia, the Indus Valley of the Harappan Culture and Yellow River of China. These Caucasian mariners found at EVERY river delta and valley an indigenous population of non-Caucasian people, darker skinned with raven-black hair and eyes...the Adamu of the preFlood World.

Colin Wilson in From Atlantis to the Sphinx uncovers some stunning historical parallels concerning these racial characteristics. He finds that the South American gods accredited to having brought civilization and leaning to those cultures are named Quetzalcouatl, Viracocha and Kukulkan, gods that all had fair skin and blue eyes–as Osiris was represented in ancient Egyptian statues. (19) The native aboriginal races of South America were *beardless* but one of the colossal stone statues of Tiahuanacu is of a bearded figure, mentioned by Harold T. Wilkins in his Mysteries of Ancient South America on pages 48-49. The Inca version of the Great Flood was recorded between 1570-1584 CE by Christoval De Molina at Cuzco and reads- "In the life of Manco Ccapac, who was the first Inca [ruler], and from whom they began to be called the Children of the Sun...they had a full account of the Deluge. They say that all people and all created things perished in it, insomuch that the water rose above all the highest mountains in the world. No living things survived, except a man and a woman, who remained in a box...the wind carried them to Huanaco." [see Old Civilizations of Inca Land p. 86-87] Many researchers hold that Manca is a local memory of the foreigner Manu, the Vedic *Noah* or Hebrew Menahem who was the first of the Children of the Sun. The Deluge account is clearly not a memory of the Inca but was brought with the foreigners to South America.

Such a connection to Manu is intriguing, for in the Aryan literature in the Vedic text of the *Matsya Purana* we find that before the Flood a certain king named Manu was called a Son of the Sun. He was given a prophecy of the coming of the Great Cataclysm. [Atlantis: The Antediluvian World p. 73-74] He was the patriarch of a people who after the Flood filled the Earth.

Strangely, the oldest beliefs of the Peruvians of South America are little different than the Maya of Central America. The Mayan civilization was cultivated long ago by a strange group of light-skinned, blue-eyed people that wore serpent emblems affixed to their heads called Viracochas. (20) Braghine notes that the Maya employed the use of *false beards,* as documented by David Hatcher Childress in Lost Cities of Atlantis, Ancient Europe and the Mediterranean on page 270. Chichen Itza of the Maya has carvings of long-bearded men according to Dr. Le Plongeon and Ignatius Donnelly wrote- "On the monuments of Central America there are representations of *bearded* men. How could the beardless American indians have imagined a bearded race?" [Atlantis: The Antediluvian World pages 131-132]. More importantly, why build monuments with their statues and imagery if they were not highly regarded when those constructions were erected. In ancient Central America there were legends and traditions concerning Bochica who had come from the east over the sea, with a white beard, he taught them civilization and was called a Son of the Sun. [ibid p. 133]

In the mysterious city of Tiahuanaco the god Viracocha is discovered called Thunupa, the white god from the sea. (21)   A seven foot life-size statue of Viracocha clearly identifies this enigmatic god as being distinctly non-indian, having a thin nose, round eyes and facial hair, the last being a characteristic the Peruvians definitely did not have. (22) When the Inca saw the bearded, white Conquistadores of Spain they called them by an ancestral dynastic title-Children of the Sun. (23)

The Aztecs and earlier Maya shared a common belief. Dr. Thor Heyerdahl wrote- "The whole foundation of their religious beliefs was the assertion that there own royal families descended from certain white and bearded men resembling the Spaniards who had come from that sunken land and instructed their savage ancestors in the rites of sun worship and all the arts of civilization: writing, cotton cultivation, calendar system, and architecture, including the building of cities and pyramids." (24)   The Aztecs believed that long ago gigantic white men who came from somewhere in the sky once visited them. The Spanish explorers and Conquistadors learned that these giants were called the race of the sons of the sun who instructed mankind in all kinds of arts and disappeared again. (25) Legends of Central America concerning Tula claim a white, *bearded* race came from the east and became the ancestors of the Toltecs. They taught civilization, the calendar and arts. After a while the bearded race left in ships back eastward.

In Aztec Nahuatl traditions hold that the first settlers of ancient Mexico were white people who had been defeated later and driven from the land by a dark-skinned race. Many of the white people built ships and sailed away east. [*Mysteries of Ancient South America*; Wilkins p. 102] The Aztec tradition is supported by those of Guatemala and

Central America who told the Spanish Conquistadores that the race of Quetzalcoatl was very white but they were conquered by a dark race. Many escaped in ships eastward but others fled into the woods, who were captured and enslaved by the dark-skinned people. [ibid p. 103] The same story was related to Cieza de Leon in far South America who was told that after the fall of the bearded, white people the survivors fled to an island on Lake Titicaca where they lived a long time. [ibid p. 95]

North America is another story. North of Mexico in the United States there are NO ancient cities or pyramids. The Mound Builder civilization was NOT indians and a whole post will address these mysteries. The only archeological evidence of a great infrastructure of walled cities, paved roads and ornate stonework in North America has been found ONLY deep underground at multitudes of sites.

The native American presence of the red man in North America came rather late in antiquity; that the indians of America did not come from Asia is now proven by the genetic results and differences in blood types between Orientals and indians. The evidence of a non-Indian race occupying much of North America comes both from thousands of mound and burial sites and even from the testimony of the Native Americans today who claim that long before their ancestors walked the lands they were the home of *white* people. These references can be found in the hundreds in many pre-WWII publications but in more recent historical books the testimonies of the indians themselves has been sanitized, censored and often totally omitted. The picture of today's Native American is one of a single indigenous American red race from distant antiquity concentrated in South and Central America and only after a series of catastrophes did some fracture off to become independent cultures as they wandered farther and farther north. By the time Native Americans reached the present geography of the United States they found a vast frontier totally empty of civilizations...not realizing that under their feet lied the ruins of a buried civilization from before the Great Flood [2239 BCE].

Racial Conflict Became New Control Protocol of Anunnaki

Much of the confusion and disparities between elements of the same stories that have survived the ancient world, of legends, oral traditions, written records, are reconciled by acknowledging that we are today looking backward to the memories of two or three entirely different groups. The indigenous recollections of preCaucasian people who held that they were created by hideous reptoid beings does not nullify the later Caucasian records of Amorite-dominated Babylonia and Sumer that the bearded, white human race was created by bearded, white humanlike gods. Dark humans anciently recalled the Nordic appearances of "gods" and the unexpected births of the white babies, but Caucasian legends and lore have only remembered white Caucasian gods and predecessors.

Anunnaki-human unions continued for at least six centuries, the two separate races sharing the same gene pool. This history is considered today definitively racist but nonetheless true, and supported by nonCaucasian ancient testimony. The entire Genesis 6 passage concerning the sons of God and the daughters of men that created a mighty race of heroes, men of renown is the Old World's testimony of the birth of a NEW RACE into the world before the Flood, the Caucasian race, who inherited the height, intellect, physical characteristics, beards and eyes, the knowledges and technology of their Homo Anunna fathers. In the story of the Anunnaki we have the appearance on earth of ghost-white space-faring HUMANS from somewhere else who through a premeditated plan modified a small population out of the vast hordes of dark peoples on this planet and refined them to the point where they could easily procreate with them with no complications. These visitors bestow information and technology to their new genetic counterparts and then disappeared again in most part, though there is evidence that a faction of the Anunna remained on earth to eventually marry into, build family dynasties and die among their earthborn kin. Those-Who-From-Heaven-to-Earth-Fell were never gods, they were humans who had gone extremely pale with fair eyes and hair by living in a different biosphere. EVERY human on Earth today is in some degree Anunnaki-descended. Sumerians prided themselves as being the "black-headed people," and pictures on their reliefs show them as smooth-skinned with no facial hair but on their seals, statuary and reliefs the gods [Anunna] are always depicted with bearded faces. "Let us make man in our image, after our likeness," and "Behold, the man has become as one of us, to discern good and evil." This addendum about good and evil is not a part of the earlier Sumerian traditions but is a religionist addition to the story that totally ensnares humanity in a spiritual conflict that originally found fault and error only in the action of the gods [creators] in the manufacturing of humans [the created]. Not only were the narratives of Sumerian antiquity given as first person accounts, as also found in Genesis, told to the people by the Anunna themselves, but some Anunnaki never left earth-they remained marooned to live among the human family.

William Brambley in *Gods of Eden* wrote- "Human beings appear to be a slave race languishing on an isolated planet in a small galaxy. As such, the human race was once a source of labor for an extraterrestrial civilization and still remains a possession today..." (26) When modern homo sapiens served and lived among Homo Anunna [3439-2647 BCE] the concept of their world was more sophisticated than mankind a thousand years later. the threefold division of reality concerned the heavens, the realm of the gods [Anunnaki], what we call space, and Earth where men lived with many gods, and the underworld, or Deep, the Abzu, ruled by the Serpent, who was Enki, father of the Caucasian race. The Nordic division was similar to the Sumerian beliefs. Earth was Midgard and the underworld was Niflheim, the Land of the Elves [alien Grays], the Semitic Nephilim, being the Fallen Ones who fathered the Caucasian offspring of the sons of God [Anunnaki]. Long after the departure of the Anunna in 2647 BCE this threefold division took on the religious concepts of a heaven independent of interplanetary space, an Earth where gods did not physically exist and a Hell instead of a network of Deep Earth Biospheres, underground habitats occupied not by colonies of Anunnaki, Grays and humans, but by demons, elves and dwarves.

Enki violated the preFlood status quo...he led a benefactor sect of Homo Anunna who committed the ultimate treachery against their own civilization. By mating physically with their product, the "daughters of men," these rebellious Anunnaki fathered the ancestors of the Caucasian race, its Aryan and Semitic branches, who not only inherited the fair-featured characteristics of these benefactors, but also received some technology, written records, knowledges and the genetic traits of imagination, creativity, inventiveness, abstraction and colonial spirit. While all races have proven to be equally intelligent as Caucasians, the entire history of the world's past 5000 years demonstrates century-by-century that the Homo Anunna synaptic fail-safes have without fail retarded the ability, the growth and the prosperity of all races EXCEPT Caucasians.

The oversimplification of the Anunnaki as being strictly an extraterrestrial species of aliens ignores the great variety of types mentioned or alluded to in the ancient texts as pieced together by Sitchin and other authors: Anunna who-

> never left Nibiru [home]

> descended to Earth

> were born on Earth from offworld parents

> were born on Earth of unions between offworld and earthborn parents

> were born of parents both earthborn

These distinctions are mentionable because of the complexities of DNA, activation/deactivation of whole gene sequences or latent genes programmed to respond to certain environmental stimuli as cells transfer information at conception with the influence of various biospheres. We can add to this list the Anunna who were-

> stationed/born in lunar habitats

> born on Mars [Lahmu]; Igigi [Watchers]

> born on waystations in Sol system [asteroids/moons]

The variations in the Anunna genome due to these disparate environments may not have been so marked, however, when crossbreeding with homo inferiors and homo sapiens at different stages of genetic manufacturing, the changes barely noticed between Anunna of variant backgrounds actually produced drastic changes in homo sapiens descended from them. There are no ancient references to an Anunnaki crossbreeding with Negroid humans. In fact, homo sapiens [including Negroid] were not considered breeding stock until the upgraded Adamu were made, the red-skinned, black haired/eyed, smooth-skinned humans able to procreate on their own. Out of this Adamu stock were bred the Oriental black-headed people whose DNA was compatible enough for conception by Anunnaki male donors. The other races of the human species across the planet- Negroid, Mongolid, Amerindic and Dark Caucasoid [Iberic/Aboriginal] were the result of past Anunna gene development but as yet incompatible for conception. Once DNA compatibility was maintained the several different types of Anunna mated with the daughters of men producing homo sapiens sapiens who physically appeared in the likeness of their Anunna fathers. In the beginning of this interbreeding campaign there was great diversity between the produced Caucasian groups, all being bearded;

> very tall, blond, blue/hazel/gray/green-eyed

> average height, blond, blue\hazel/gray/green-eyed

> very tall, red-haired, blue/hazel/gray/green-eyed

> average height, red-haired, blue/hazel/gray/green-eyed

Caucasians today with brown and black hair or eyes is simply due to the same intermarriages, migrations and conquests that resulted with nonCaucasians today having blue, hazel, gray or green eyes and lighter, fairer features and facial hair. The Anunna born on Earth were not Nibiru loyalists. Earth-native Anunna had little in common with space-bourn Anunna, and the second-generation earthborn Anunna even less.

Rivalries in Anunnaki colonies probably transferred to rivalries between human workers of different regions also developing into human breeding programs left off at variant stages of racial maturation- the manufacturing of human workers was interrupted by conflict, hastened, altered to produce armies quickly. In the days before the Deluge a human's physical coloring and features marked him like a brand...designer DNA allowing Anunna overlords to know what product belonged to them or another. Ownership of worker-humans could not be argued when physical traits separated homo sapiens from other homo sapiens with totally different characteristics because they were owned by someone else. The common denominator between the antediluvian DNA-designer worker races was that of dark skin, black hair and eyes and smooth skin with no beards. The world was filled with millions of these Negroid, Mongolid, Amerindic, Dark Caucasoid peoples who all venerated the Mother Goddess and all claimed the Moon as the symbol of their race. The minority before the Deluge during the period of 2839-2239 BCE were the white-skinned, fair-eyed and featured race of Caucasians who were directly fathered by the Anunna, a race of patriarchal people who remembered their origin from male 'gods', a new race of fair-featured people that the dark races called Children of the Sun. This distinction, initially racial for the fiery golden color of Caucasian hair, quickly degenerated into complex solar and lunar dynasties that fashioned religions preserving the lunar goddess connection and solar All-Father relationship. Humans focusing on humans after the departure of the Anunna in 2647 BCE [final year of Contact Period] led to the stellar theologies of subordinate deities [Anunna] in service to a goddess [the Moon] or God [the Sun]. Sin, the name of the Moon was originally male in the Sumerian texts but this gender identity among goddess-worshippers fell into disrepute just as did the older solar-goddess associations in the far east.

The Caucasian Children of the Sun were worshippers of the All-Father, the patriarchal aspect of their cultured followed from the fact of their birth: Homo Anunna males with homo sapien females and NOT from the Anunna birth-goddesses campaign of those Homo Anunna who descended from their lunar habitat and genetically modified several darker races before Caucasians homo sapiens ever existed. From the beginning of the Contact Period [3439-2647 BCE] the distinction between the older matriarchal dark-featured people and the younger patriarchal, fair-featured people grew into whole societies purely based on race.

These two racial cultures separating the Caucasian civilizers from all the lunar-goddess venerating dark races manifested in a whole new unique way after the vanishing of the gods; end of the Contact Period in 2647 BCE. Two major cultural themes survived the preFlood world to be carried on after the destruction . Two competing ways of life clashed forging two distinct types of dynasties: the Hunter Kings and the Shepherd Kings. These divisions among the human family were at variance with one another and their ethnicities were markedly different. The great Hurrian, Aryan, Amorite, Syrian, Phoenician, Israelite, Ionian fair-featured, white descendants of Noah and Enoch [Enki] founded the powerful Shepherd King dynasties of the western Fertile Crescent- Egypt, Libya, Mitanni, Urartu, India, Anatolia, Syria, Lebanon in the Bronze Age 2nd millennium BCE. The Shepherd King civilizations were patriarchal with trade-alliance economies, all maritime nations, great builders, spiritual instructors, establishers of law codes and societies, mighty in war and expert navigators. As saviors of human communities victimized by raiding nomads and upholders of civilization, the Caucasian Shepherd King nations and occupying dynasties continued the legacy of the benevolent Anunna who had bioengineered the white, bearded people and then bred with them.

The Hunter Kings were aggressors, tyrants, destroyers of the harvest [humanity] opposed to the Shepherd Kings who protected the flock. In the Jewish narrative of Genesis this is found in the conflict between the gentle Jacob and his violent brother, Esau the Hunter. The major distinction between the nations having Hunter King and Shepherd King dynasties was entirely RACIAL- nomadic, Negroid, Mongolid, Amerindic and Dark Caucasoid hunter-gatherers made up the Hunter Kings of Dravidian India, Africa, Arabia that founded the early post-diluvian cultures of Egypt, the Indus, Akkad, Babylonia, Hittite Anatolia before the Shepherd Kings imposed their dynasties over many of them. The Shepherd Kings were not the only Caucasians but as descendants of Enki [Enoch] they were the fairest, having the most Anunna DNA. The Aryans were not hunters or nomads as collective ways of life, but dwelt in towns on highways. (27) They employed a decimal system of enumeration. Max Muller wrote that this was "...one of the most marvelous achievements of the human mind, based on an abstract conception of quantity." (28) In Hindu traditional histories the Asuras were a race of elder gods born of venerated mothers to Kasyapa, The non-Aryan Asuras were already established when a second race was born called the Adityas who quickly rose to dominance and were resented by the older Asuras. (29)

Sitchin notes that the non-Aryan name of Asuras was of Near Eastern origin akin to Ashur, Asar, Osiris and that in Hindu tradition the Asuras became evil gods, or demons, whereas the Adityas assumed the role of gods. Envy and contention between the first race and that which came after led to war during a time when earth produced food without cultivation, when a global famine occurred. The Satapatha Brahmana reads of a widespread conflict, wars fought for superiority and resources. The gods (Adityas) vanquished the Asuras, who later rose up and defeated the gods. Ultimately the gods finally put down the Asuras. (30)   We have in this Hindu tradition the preflood memory of the Asuras and the two distinct types of homo sapiens- those older dark humans venerating their mother-goddesses and the later patriarchal Aryan Adityas, the sons of the gods. In the *Mahabharata* the race of the Kshatriyas were red men who were at war with a white race- the Brahmans. [Atlantis: The Antediluvian World p. 147]   The famous Battle of Kuruksata was a race war.

That the Anunna were not gods is demonstrated in that Sitchin had found references to an Anunna belief in the Creator of All who influenced Enki [Enoch] to create humanity and again prompt him to warn humans of the coming Flood. (31)   After the Deluge, at seeing that pockets of humans survived the disaster, many Anunna concluded that it was the will of the Creator of All. (32)   It seems clear that the white, bearded Anunnaki race were entirely human; they are indistinguishable from the fairest of European Caucasians today.

Putting all the pieces together we have a world filled with humans after the fading away of Cro-Magnon, a world full of homo sapiens of four primary racial groups. Their world was interrupted by the sudden appearance of technologically advanced Caucasians that they mistook for "gods," people who came from somewhere else. In the early 1800s Alexander Humbolt wrote that the rare fragments of stories from the ancient world, when analyzed all together, paint a picture of a mass human migration that departed the hemisphere of the Americas to land upon the shores of the Mediterranean. Harold T. Wilkins believes from the evidence that this was a major Caucasian migration from the west to the east over the Atlantic. To a degree is correct but that's only half the story.

My own research on the 1687 BCE Phoenix Cataclysm that collapsed all of the dynasties of the Children of the Sun in Egypt, Sumer, the Indu Valley, China, Tiahuanaco, Guatemala and Easter Island has painted for me a more complete picture. In 2239 BCE The Great Deluge ONLY wiped out the center of a major, growing Caucasian civilization. From 1899 to 1849 BCE whole fleets of these Heliolithic mariners landed at the great river deltas of Egypt, the Euphrates-Tigris, the Indus, China two major river heads, the Urumbamba of South America and others. This was when the Caucasians arrived. It was centuries later in 1687 BCE at the Phoenix destruction in both hemispheres that the Caucasians fled back to their homelands, for EVERY Caucasian dynasty settled among foreigners collapsed in that year. In 1687 BCE the survivors began sailing into the Mediterranean and establishing colonies, becoming the Phoenicians, Philistines, Ionians, early Greeks, Sicilians, Latins, Libyans and many Canaanites, settlers of Ilium and the shores of Anatolia.

8. ADAMU...PreCaucasian Humans and Anunnaki Designer DNA Campaign Before the Flood

It is shameful in today's modern society so many take offense at any broach of the topic of race as if the subject is hallowed, not to be spoken nor explored. Our ancient masters wanted it this way. If you get offended at what you read why not analyze why? Emotional responses seem to be all that the majority are able to produce, and the reason for this is programming. The media takes great advantage of this, KNOWING that frenzied emotional reaction to troubling data is all most people are capable of. Don't be a victim anymore. We are who we are for reasons beyond our control. Race is not a subject to be shunned but to explore.

In prior posts it has already been explained that the exiled Jews in Babylonia misunderstood the many references to the Adamu in the records of the great libraries, changing Adamu from its original description of the human race before the Great Deluge to a pronoun for an individual's name, Adam. This is why after Adam was mentioned in Genesis he is then forgotten in the vast archives of the Old Testament. Only in the late rabbinical works after the Jews came back from Babylon did the writings of Adam surface, pure priestly inventions like the Book of Adam and Eve. The Father of Humanity should have been mentioned EVERYWHERE in the Holy Writ, but he is not because he was never a man but instead a designation for early MANKIND [Adamu].

The Chaldean account of the Creation shows that there was an original race of men at the beginning of Chaldean history, a dark race, the Zalmat-Qaqadi, who were called Admi and Adami, as opposed to the light-skinned race called the Sarku [Shar-KU]. (1) Shar is a title for ruler. Ignatius Donnelly wrote, "The name Adam is used in these legends, but as the name of a race, not of mankind." (2) The Jewish chronographers exiled to Babylonia invented the Adam-to-Seth lineage, making Enoch the seventh, misunderstanding the older Babylonian references to adamu for what they were- descriptions of early humans, a dark and red-skinned race with black hair and eyes and smooth skin with no facial hair who were created by the

Anunnaki. The Genesis and Sumerian accounts of Noah's lineage do not disagree. Enki created primitive humans from primate-Anunna DNA and then manufactured an upgraded type of humans by adding more Anunnaki DNA. Enki then used Anunna females to birth the upgrades which produced civilized humans that could procreate on their own. These were first the Adamu, and of this stock were Oriental people, the "black-headed people," a description used by the Sumerians to describe themselves over and over in their writings. The writings describing history before the Great Flood have the common theme that initially the entire world was populated by black-haired, black-eyed people of small stature and brown and red skin, smooth no no hair on their bodies and no beards. It was a world when Caucasians DID NOT EXIST (at least on the planet). As will be seen in this book, the first appearance of white people was a major theme of the PreFlood World.

Scientifically, the racial differences between Negroid, Mongolid, Amerindic and Caucasoid are inexplicable. (3) Skull thickness, cranial proportions and capacity, skeletal structure, musculature, blood types, pigmentation, dermal thickness, cerebral development, protuberance of features, the hair and eye color of the dark, preCaucasian humans are NOT the result of natural selection or evolution, but the product of genetic engineering using core primate DNA with infusions of their coding. Humans are the product of 30,000 genes, separated only by 300 genes from chimpanzees, a 1% difference. (4) But humans contain 223 genes that have no evolutionary predecessors (5), and with genes, even only a few genetic variations can result in vast differences. Where did these 223 genes come from, for they link EVERY human type on this planet together. Homo Anunna brought these genes here.

Geneticists know that over 98% of human DNA is identical to that of chimpanzees. Only 1-4% of modern human DNA is Neanderthalic, however, this 1-4% is NOT found in native African Negroid DNA. (6) The more we discover, the more evidence we find of different DNA designer programs effected in antiquity to populate the Earth. In tracking mitachondrial DNA back as far as it can go has revealed to geneticists that the modern human race is a family of 33 clans. (7) What makes the human species human is not our pedigree, but our spirituality; our bodies are but biological containers , DNA preservations housing lost-but-immortal spirits. The myriads of gene combinations are why life can exist in virtually every biospheric condition. Human DNA is extraterrestrial, interplanetary and quite likely, intergalactic.

The earlier earthborn races of Neanderthal and Cro-Magnon were long ago distinguished from the moonborn races of dark humans, linked culturally by their veneration of goddesses, matriarchal peoples before the Great Flood [May 2239 BCE]; Negroid, Mongolid, Amerindic and Dark Caucasoid, the Four Brother Races of remembered antiquity who existed on Earth BEFORE the white Caucasian race and their own patriarchal sun cultures- the bearded white Children of the Sun called Shemsu Hor in ancient Egypt. The moon-goddess cultures venerated the Mother-of-All-Living, her symbol for over 3000 years of both antediluvian and postFlood history being the crescent moon. The dark homo sapiens recalled their origin of Homo Anunna Birth-Goddesses who descended from the lunar habitats when the Moon was deliberately placed in its dead orbit by the Anunna in 4039 BCE. These Anunna, better known as Anunnaki, were rebels of their race who called the Moon by the name Sin. It was a title later attached to them by humans when they became known as the Sinners who birthed the first Adamu [men]. Hopi tradition tells that their ancestors arrived to the Fourth World by migrating through three previous worlds by the aid of Spider Grandmother. (8) Osages indians of North American Plains tell that they once lived in the sky way beyond earth. They were the Children of the Sun and Moon, told by their mother Moon to go live on Earth. (9) The Senecas were descended from Star Woman. (10) There are SO MANY recorded traditions of non-Caucasian peoples remembering that their origin was from a Creatrix or from the Moon that we can not possibly list them here.

While the dark races were programmed to obey, to follow, they were also heavily edited, their coding modified to impede creativity, genetic barriers erected, governors set in place to guarantee that upon their own initiative they could not knit together the requisite thoughts that would guide them toward any productivity that would result in erecting a civilization to rival the Anunna. The mistakes made with Cro-Magnon would not be revisited. These genetic parameters have functioned so perfectly for so long that every Negroid, Mongolid, Amerindic and Oriental people since the collapse of their ancient civilizations has continued for thousands of years as Neolithic farmers and hunter-gatherers unless they profited by contact with Caucasian people as in the 3rd millennium BCE Amorite/Hurrian/Aryan migrations into the Near East, India, Palestine and Egypt and again in these last four centuries with the global European colonization of the world.

The Establishment version of human racial evolution propagated today is extremely racist, proclaiming that modern humans descended from monkeys. The truth is occulted, that homo sapiens are the amalgamation of many parts and yes chimpanzee DNA is greatly a part of our genetic makeup. But the differences between human types is not from evolutionary development; the bull-crap passed off as history we are force-fed is wrong. Contrary to what is popularly taught, the Amerindian of North America is NOT Asian, they did not cross a frozen land-bridge over the Pacific or Atlantic. 0-blood type is the prevailing type of the Amerindians but Orientals are mostly B-types. (11) From the Mongolid stock further modification produced the High Oriental, civilized goddess-worshippers, the FIRST homo sapiens civilized culture after Cro-Magnon, the preFlood ancestors of the Chinese, Japanese, Koreans, Vietnamese and other oriental peoples today. These High Orientals were also the predecessors of the white Caucasian peoples who were not yet settled on Earth. That the goddess cults and matriarchal cultures are much OLDER than the appearance of Caucasians in the traditions of the world cannot be disputed. Beginning in 4039 BCE with the sudden appearance of Luna captured in Earth's orbit , the Anunna began a 144 year campaign inside lunar habitats creating colonies of Negroid, Mongolid, Amerindic and Dark Caucasoid peoples through the birth-goddesses scheme. These grew in population and were kept separated deliberately, kept inside the lunar habitats until the pass of the Phoenix Weapon in 3895 BCE. When Phoenix transited in 3895 BCE the Earth suffered a devastating pole shift, quakes, floods, volcanic fallout, meteorite rains as entire continents slipped under oceans and new seas appeared on what was formerly dry land. A new heavens and new earth were effected for the stars were no longer in the places they had been...the new pole star became Alpha Draconis [Eye of the Dragon] and the Moon Age began that would last 1656 years to the Great Flood. This Age is characterized by the appearance of the Vapor Canopy that hid the sun by day while diffusing light in a temperate-to-tropical world while magnifying the Moon and stars at night as the dark side of the planet's atmosphere became a nightly magnifying lense into the heavens. The anciently popular legends on the birth of the sun are memories of the collapse of this vapor canopy at the Great Deluge in 2239 BCE. During the preFlood world the entire day sky was well lit but the vapor canopy blocked out the circular orb of the sun. During the 3895 BCE poleshift destruction the last of the Neanderthal vanished and the Cro-Magnon population was decimated. The Anunna planted their new homo sapien colonies in different areas of the world, the invention of RACES a deliberate act of divisiveness.

To be led but not initiate, to comprehend but not conceive; the masses of humanity suffered a genetic programming of arrested development, designer DNA by Homo Anunna scientists who had figured out how to keep their human subordinates docile and ignorant yet teachable. The homo sapiens of all races from Negroid to Caucasoid were perfectly enslaved by masters who programmed synaptic fail-safes to switch off any time a human mind wandered beyond recognizable frames of reference. Because of this programming Negroid, Mongolid, Dark Caucasoid, Amerindic and High Oriental from the Neolithic to agrarian remained virtually unchanged until they experienced contact with a civilized people. Without civilized immersion into a more advanced culture their programming resets them right back in to their pre-civilized patterns. So effective was this genetic dampening that it was not until the European colonial period when Caucasians introduced modern civilization into China, India, the Middle East, Australia, the Americas and South Africa that these genetically damaged peoples around the world benefitted from, copied and began contributing to the modern infrastructure from their prior old primitive patterns.

The dark-haired white people called Iberians anciently inhabited Spain, Gaul, the British Isles, colonized Sicily and were the original settlers of Italy and Sardinia and even Libya. (12)   It is theorized that the dark-haired stock of early Sweden and Norway is of Iberian origin. Of the Turduli and Turdetani Iberians, Strabo wrote that they employ the art of writing, and have written books containing memorials of ancient times." (13) The last surviving population of Iberians not absorbed into the other Mediterranean races of today are the Basques of darker complexion than the Spaniards, with gray eyes and black hair. (14) This Iberian stock settled in the earliest times in Ireland, forming the base of the dark-haired population of Britain and Scotland. (15)   These darker, short Bretons are in stark contrast to the tall, white-skinned, blue-eyed Celts with their blond hair. (16)

There are no known written texts older than 2200 BCE, even the Sumerian records are post-2200 BCE though report to be copies of older writings and even depict events that date as early as 3800 BCE. The oldest writings in the world are not religious- they tell matter-of-factly of "gods" that manufactured humans both before and after major disasters.   The only architectural presence of humans known to archeology prior to 2200 BCE are town-sized settlements, many exhibiting evidence of advanced urban engineering and planning- the scattered survivors of a prior civilization destroyed by a cataclysm anterior to that of the Great Flood of 2239 BCE. Because of these facts we have had to rely solely on second-hand information and traditions. But we are fortunately, for out of this wealth of lore and legends has come forth common themes that cannot be denied for their remain intact in both hemispheres. They claim that "gods" came to earth, early humans worshipped, served and fought for them. The SAME gods that created the Four Brother Races: Black, Brown, Red and Yellow. during this period white people did not exist.

There are no Negroid, Mongolid or Amerindic traditions of a preFlood world, but ALL remember a Great Flood. Is this not unusual? Only the Oriental peoples preserved literary records with the Caucasians concerning antediluvian histories. The Orientals during the Contact Period [3439-2647 BCE] when the Anunna lived among mankind were the most genetically refined homo sapiens of the Anunnaki birth-goddesses program. Having the most modified DNA compatible with Anunna biology, in 2839 BCE the Anunna factions began a widespread breeding campaign that resulted in the birth of the Caucasian race and the Igigi-born Nephilim races. Enki and the Anunna loyal to him used Oriental females in birthing Caucasians instead of the older scheme of using Anunna females who conceived through artificial inception until the Adamus could conceive on their own. But the Igigi who had not participated in the Enki-led long term genetic refining process took the daughters of men [Mongolids, Amerindics, Dark Caucasoids and Negroids] and gave birth to other peoples, some small, others gigantic, mutants with six fingers and toes on their limbs, monsters.

2839 - 2647 BCE. Only the Oriental civilization of Asia maintains a culture and geography extending back to the antediluvian world. As the greatest creations of the Custodial Society of Anunna, the Oriental race is the older, half-brother to the Noachian white SONS of the Custodians. While even as late as the 20th century CE and today, five thousand years has not improved the Neolithic hunter-gatherer mindset of the Negroid, Mongolid and Amerindic people still spread across third world bushlands. If the infrastructure for civilization is not provided for them, they never invent one of their own. The nonEuropoid peoples have over and over through 42.5

centuries of recorded history since the Great Deluge cataclysm 2239 BCE been introduced to higher culture, values, living conditions, technology and maintained, even flourishing when living among Homo Anunna, Orientals or Caucasians, as long as the contact persisted. But when abandoned, when contact was severed or diminished, in every historical instance Negroid, Mongolid and Amerindic civilization collapsed back into base hand-to-mouth Neolithic patterns to totemic hunter-gatherers. World history is evidence alone of the long-standing dominance of the Oriental and Aryan civilizations, the far east and the west. The Oriental was programmed to stay in the Orient, Asians were very rarely colonizers outside of Asia. Many firsts belong to China, Japan, Korea and other Asians when explosions of intellectual brilliance manifested, but the overall genetic coding of racial, cultural, mental stability of the race over and over stamped out the achievements and discoveries. The Aryan, though originating in the far east, was specifically programmed to colonize, migrate, explore, build, invent and maintain a western movement. The Aryan breeding produced a Builder Race, innovators, creators of governments, religions, philosophies, agriculture and designers of vast infrastructures with great imaginations-the direct inheritors of traits formerly belonging only to Homo Anunna.

The Asian Oriental was the epitome of Anunnaki genetic invitro-fertilization engineering using Anunnaki birth-goddesses. The Oriental spirit of permanence, patience, humility, preservation of cultural institutions over millennia, explosions of brilliance only to be snuffed out by the masses programmed to maintain the status quo. The Anunnaki coded humans to obey, to carry out routines, to bear circumstances with little thought of altering their conditions. Orientals are fantastic culture bearers carrying their civilization virtually unchanged for over 4000 years until Caucasians arrived on their shores in the last 140 years and included them in the growing global industrial-technological complex.

With several Anunnaki interbreeding with Oriental females the Noachian white race was fathered by many Custodians while the mitachondrial DNA can be traced back to a small group or even a single female...the original Anunnaki birth-goddess Creatrix of the Oriental race. Thus, in a very short period of time the entire Europoid race was bred and allowed 600 years [an Anunnaki NER period from 2839 to 2239 BCE] to multiply in to a mighty population allied to their Oriental kin. Except for the distinguishing epicanthic fold [designer DNA coding] that gives the Mongolid/Oriental his almond-shaped eyes, it has been discovered that the shape and angle of the Mongolid/Oriental eye is the same as that of the Caucasoid. (17) This eye-placement structuring is not the same with Negroids but it is with the more ancient Cro-Magnon. Conclusion: Negroids are of the same genetic stock as all other homo sapiens, however, they possess more primate DNA. The Negroid race is the most terrestrial race with the least amount of Homo Anunna DNA.

There was a vast population of Nordic-featured people living in Asia from Japan and China to the Tarim Basin before the Great Flood. The Central Asia sea of the Tarim Basin, an ancient freshwater sea, burst out of its confines and floods the fertile plains richly populated by Caucasians inhabiting stone cities. The people who were drowned were the last surviving remnants of a prior ancient civilization where today lies the Gobi desert, which was before this flooding a lush land bordering an inland sea. The Pamir plateau to the west of this giant lake is believed to be the original Eden by many...the Oxus river is still called by the natives as the Dgihun [Gihon]. (18) David

Hatcher Childress wrote in his well-researched, Lost Cities of China, Central Asia and India, "A certain legendary evil aura hangs over the Gobi. The Gobi is called the 'Shamo' by Mongolians (Gobi being the word for desert) and this word may be related to the name of the god Shamos, who was worshipped in the Middle East as a 'Black Star.' Shamos is also the 'evil luminary' of the Arabs, probably based upon...some other heavenly body." (19) Childress knew nor published anything about planet Phoenix, the Phoenix Weapon. This Tarim Basin flooding occurred in 2239 BCE contemporary with the Great Mediterranean Deluge and Black Sea flood, all three a part of the global Great Flood of 2239 BCE caused in May by the Phoenix.

The Anunnaki themselves had sons and daughters and many took lovers from among the growing masses of humanity that were becoming more and more in their own likeness. By the time the Anunnaki departed Earth they had left behind human races in various gradations of development from primitive worker Negroid, Mongolid, Amerindic hunter-gatherers to the civilized Orientals [black-headed people] and finally the white, Indo-Aryan race of blond/red-haired and blue/green-eyed who served as genetic physical/intellectual replicas of the Anunnaki on Earth. All races have Anunna DNA, all are made in the image [coding] of the gods.

That the white, Aryan race is related to the older Asian Oriental race is also the conclusion of Lenormant- "All appearances would lead us to regard the Tauranian race as the first branch of the family of Japhath which went forth into the world; and by the premature separation, by an isolated and antagonistic existence, took, or rather preserved, a completely distinct physiognomy...it is a type of the white race imperfectly developed." (20) Winchell concludes that the Genesis 10 genealogical table is not intended to include the negroes, or the Chinese, the Japanese or American red men- it refers altogether to the Mediterranean races, the Aryans, the Cushites, the Phoenicians, the Hebrews and the Egyptians." (21)   The descendants of Noah were of a race whose homeland was destroyed by a flood. The flooding may have occurred globally but NOT in all areas; Chinese, Mongolid, Negroid and Amerindic peoples survived uninterrupted in hunter-gatherer totem societies, save for the sophisticated agrarian urban culture of China. The Table of Nations in Genesis was copied and amended as the Jewish priests saw fit, stealing the data from older Amorite records. In those days when the genealogies were drafted to include in the new 5th century BCE Genesis text they wanted to put at the front of their Holy Writ, the existence of these other races was unknown, therefore they were not included.

Caucasians are the very last to enter into the world scene in modern times post-Cro-Magnon. The MOST ANCIENT traditions and written records are from the perspective of nonCaucasian people.

9. A Flood Before Noah's...Enoch and the Gihon Flood 3439 BCE

3439 BCE is the only year in recorded history when one of the 600 year epochs known in antiquity as Great Years, or Anunnaki NER epochs, coincided with the exact year that NIBIRU either entered or exited the inner Sol system. That numerous traditions assert that it was at this time (1200 years before the Great Deluge: 2239 BCE) that the "gods" arrived to Earth is not without significance. One might argue that Sitchin wrote that NIBIRU caused the Great Flood but he was wrong. Planet Phoenix was responsible for the 2239 BCE destruction and it was Phoenix that was named in antiquity. Phoenix's orbit is different than that of NIBIRU and its chronology is firmly established by many proofs [see Phoenix Calendar]. Further, Sitchin conveyed that the Great Flood was way back during the last Ice Age which is ridiculous. That a flooding occurred during past Ice Ages is probably true, but the Great Flood of human memory and global fame throughout antiquity transpired toward the end of the 3rd millennium BCE (2239 BCE), an event dated easily in multitudes of ways that is scientifically verified by data exhibiting tremendous evidence of the worldwide destruction that ended the Early Bronze Age. These posts are already found in Phoenix Calendar.

In the Hebraic records the Watchers [Anunna] descend to earth in the days of Jared, whose name means descent, being in the 10th Jubilee, which was the first descent before the Great Flood. A second group of Anunnaki arrived later, also before the Flood. The descent of the Watchers is the central theme of the Book of Enoch and the name of Jared was a commemoration of the event.

This descent does not mark the first appearance of the Anunna but the arrival of the most important figure in the Old World human histories...ENKI. Even the Genesis chronology shows this to be the time Enoch is introduced into the biblical narrative. ENKI of Sumerian records is the same as Enoch of the later Semitic traditions.

The Sumerian text reads that Enki descended to Earth- "When I approached Earth there was much flooding..." (1) The Book of Jasher notes that at this precise year of 3439 BC in the chronological narrative that the Gihon flooded and killed a third of humanity. The Gihon is the Nile in

Egypt, its identity revealed by the Jewish historian Josephus almost two thousands years ago. Enki himself landed in the Snake Marsh among the Gizi reeds. (2) This was a marshland before the Flood, known today as Giza, where the Great Pyramid stands. This monument is also alluded to in the Sumerian text for it was there that Enki built his house, called E.ABZU (House of the Deep), his sacred precinct in Eridu. This links the Sumerian Enki to the biblical person of Enoch, for which many non-canonical and other documents assert was the builder of the Great Pyramid complex. Additionally, Eridu is the biblical Irad in Genesis that was built by Enoch.

The Book of Jasher reads that- "In the days of Enosh...the Lord caused the waters of the Gihon to overwhelm them, and He destroyed and consumed them, and He destroyed a third part of the earth...and there was no food for the sons of men and the famine was very great in those days." (3) This disaster in the time of Enosh is confirmed in the Jewish Haggadoth text which relates that this was a terrible flood before the Great Flood of Noah's day. (4) The Yezidas of Asia preserve traditions of a flooding more ancient than Noah's, stating that the world was flooded twice, the second flood far worse than the first. (5)

A long tablet series found in the ruins of the Sumerian city of Nippur is the source of the text which reads, "When I approached the earth, there was much flooding." (6) This is in a text narrated by Enki referred to as The Eridu Genesis Collection. We have here an ancient Sumerian narrative of the arrival to earth by ENKI that occurred 1200 years (432,000 shars) before the Great Flood, which would date his descent to earth in 3439 BCE. Coupled with this from independent sources like Jasher we have a terrible flooding (same ENKI witnessed) occurring in Egypt killing a third of humanity. Two separate sources telling the same story.

In the biblical chronology of Stephen Jones' work published in his book, The Secrets of Time, the flooding of the Gihon is perfectly dated at 3439 BCE, or 1200 years before the Great Flood in 2239 BCE. A Christian fundamentalist, Jones knew nothing nor published anything about NIBIRU or planet Phoenix. That the background of these Enochian/ENKITE traditions was ancient antediluvian Egypt is made more profound when we consider this next piece of chronological evidence which comes entirely from Egypt.

The 3439 BCE date is found perfectly in the chronometry of the Great Pyramid of Giza. Astronomer Royal for Scotland Charles Piazzi Smythe in the 1870s determined on-site at Giza that for reasons unknown to him the monument was designed using the descendant passage as a scope to point directly at the star Alpha Draconis (Eye of the Dragon) in the year 3440 BCE, which he said was the preflood pole star. (7) This 3440 BCE date is virtually a bull's-eye for 3439 BCE. The Great Pyramid was built by Enoch/ENKI which is the subject matter of my book, Lost Scriptures of Giza.

Using scripture to interpret scripture, a method of paramount import to the Christian apologist, we read in John 3:13 the very mysterious statement that, "And no man hath ascended up to heaven, but he that came down from heaven." We are led to believe this was Jesus, but it would be equally true of Enoch because the biblical records make it an important event that Enoch ascended into heaven and was never seen again. This is none other than a biblical admission that Enoch arrived to earth in descent before he again ascended to heaven.

Enoch/ENKI is a major player in the early affairs of civilized humanity and many more posts are coming concerning this fascinating individual. What is intriguing is that the apocalyptic Revelation prophecies record that in the Last Days a third of mankind shall die at the appearance of a celestial object in the sky it called Wormwood, though the 200,000,000 "demons" that scour the earth at the same time are perfect images of what the ancient Babylonians perceived the Anunnaki to be [not the Sumerians, who consistently exhibited the Anunnaki as tall, bearded Caucasians].

NIBIRU visited in 3439 BCE initiating an antediluvian apocalypse, the arrival of gods. NIBIRU returns in November 2046 to again kill off a third of the human race. This is the subject matter of my book, Anunnaki Homeworld, which is packed with charts just like these in this post.

The Fallen Ones Came From Somewhere Else

It is noteworthy that in the earliest records of the human race the gods are physical beings who created earth, and then visited it. No other deities are known, no primordial unseen Creator- the oldest texts leave no room for doubt...the only gods the preflood ancients knew fell from heaven. It was after the Great Deluge and after the disappearance of the Anunnaki did religionists invent the Fall of Man traditions by rewriting particulars that had only pertained to the Fall of the Gods. If there is a heavenly conflict, if there is an ongoing war in heaven, if there is to be a reckoning, a divine judgement executed against one or more groups, these have NOTHING to do with mankind. Humans are DNA-in-harvest, victims of offworld manipulation. An enemy manufactured humans with the unintended result of the designer DNA creating sentience enough that unconfined spirits outside the holosphere were pulled into physical bodies. Humans are biological spirit-prisons and this unintended consequence initiated a rift between opposing Anunna groups. A sufficiently powerful body of opposition rebelled against enslaving mankind and came to Earth as humanity's benefactors. These disobedient Anunnaki became the "sinners," or Those From the Moon [Sin] and it was their "fall" that disrupted Anunna plans to keep humans servile, cowed, ignorant and uncivilized. The Fall is predominantly a western religious theme popularized in Babylonia. It was later heavily borrowed and adapted with Jewish dressings for the biblical records.

Professor G.R.S. Mead in *Fragments of a Forgotten Faith*, wrote, "a persistent tradition in connection with all the great mystery institutions was that their several founders were the introducers of all the arts of civilization: they were either themselves gods or were instructed by gods- in brief; that they were men of far greater knowledge than any who had come after; they were the teachers of infant races...souls belonging to a more highly developed humanity than our own...a prior perfected humanity not necessarily earth-born." (1)

Andrew Collins in *From the Ashes of Angels* wrote, "The myths associated with these supernatural beings appear to be no more than the bastardized memories of the way in which survivors of a previous high civilization passed on their skills and capabilities to our own ancestors. If this is so we are dealing with neither the divine nor the supernatural, but with physical beings of flesh and blood communicating on a one-to-one basis with human kind. (2)

Jim Marrs in *Our Occulted History* adds that the Anunnaki found themselves marooned on a primitive world, without their infrastructure to manufacture their tools, but still possessing a superior knowledge. (3) The Fallen Ones, or Those Who From Heaven to Earth Came, were a small group of hundreds of survivors of a planetary cataclysm away from earth who were marooned on earth by other survivors who did not stay, still in possession of the vehicles of their technology. This is how high civilization-engineering, agriculture, writing and arithmetic suddenly appeared in the Neolithic during the Ubaid culture of southern Iraq- the birth of Sumer.

Will Hart in *The Genesis Race* wrote, what we "...find is an explosion of development, a quantum leap compressed into a mere fraction of humanity's existence as a species, a radically changed way of being, and an entirely new survival strategy based on the human engineering of plants and animals undreamed of by those of the Paleolithic Period." (4) These four popular authors were not the first to theorize these things. Charles Fort wrote about offworld manipulation of humans and history 70-80 years ago. The time when this was supposed to occur is best summed up by Hart. In *The Genesis Race* he wrote- "...a major developmental thrust between 3500 BCE and 1500 BCE...a sudden explosion of innovation in these distinct areas of the planet." (5) These six regions were Egypt, Sumer, Harappa [Indus Valley], China, Mexico and Bolivia-Peru. Hart asserts that at this time a superhuman race taught mankind how to be human. (6) Hart continues, "The fact that these ancient cultures do not take credit themselves for their achievements only supports the conclusion that indeed the gods were the source of the amazing explosion of growth and innovation that occurred from 3500 BCE to 3000 BCE..." (7) Also, "There is no traceable, step-by-step path leading to them from the hunter-gatherer way of life. Science has not explained the Sumerians sudden, unprecedented explosion of development." (8)

Almost a hundred years ago Lewis Spence wrote, "The histories of all peoples commence with a dynasty of god-kings, only shading later into real history as time proceeds. The Greek and Roman dynasties, the Egyptian, the Babylonian, the Mexican and Central American annals, all began with traditional notions of the lives and deeds of heaven-descended monarchs." (9)

Over 50 years before the Ancient Astronaut Theory began taking root many scholars concluded that at this time in history Egypt's civilization suddenly appeared. "The civilization of Egypt at its first appearance was of a higher order than at any subsequent period of its history, thus testifying that it drew its greatness from a fountain higher than itself." (10)

Ernest Renan wrote, "Egypt at the beginning appears mature, old, and entirely without mythical and heroic ages, as if the country had never known youth. Its civilization has no infancy, and its art no archaic period...it was already mature. (11)

Donnelly- "There is no evidence that the civilization of Egypt was developed in Egypt itself." (12) Citing *Blackwood's* magazine, Ignatius Donnelly continued- "...as soon as men were planted on the banks of the Nile they were already the cleverest men that ever lived, endowed with more knowledge and more power than their successors for centuries and centuries could attain to. Their system of writing, also, is found to have been complete from the very first...as we have not yet discovered any trace of the rude, savage Egypt...Our deepest researches have hitherto shown her to us as only the mother of a most accomplished race." (13)

Of early Egypt, Renan wrote- "It has no archaic epoch." (14) Osborn wrote, "It bursts upon us at once in the flower of its highest perfection." (15) Seiss wrote, "It suddenly takes its place in the world in all its matchless magnificence, without father, without mother...as if it had dropped from the unknown heavens." (16) Rawlinson wrote, "All the authorities agree that, however far back we go, we find in Egypt no rude or uncivilized time out of which civilization is developed." (17)

Anthropologists cannot account for the leap and the archeologist cannot help but find that the leap occurred anciently and everywhere. We understand this mystery as having its origin with Homo Anunna, passing on their knowledge to their own descendants after they had arrived from somewhere else; not a development but an inheritance. The beginning of this explosion of development at 3500 BCE according to Hart is an approximate that matches nicely with the 3439 BCE pass of NIBIRU through the inner Sol system, a date demonstrated in other posts and revealed in Anunnaki Homeworld. It was the appearance of Enki [biblical Enoch] and the Anunna who began preFlood Egyptian civilization in 3439 BCE.

The 432,000 Years Was 432,000 Days [1200 years] From 3439 BCE Descent of the Watchers to the Great Flood 2239 BCE

William A. Hinson in *Discovering Ancient Giants* wrote concerning the Sumerian histories- "In text after text, whenever the starting point was recalled, it was always this: 432,000 years before the Deluge, the DIN.GIR (gods) then came down to earth from their own world...NIBIRU." (1) Hinson's statement is mostly true save for the inflated 432,000 "years." For the misinformation that has saturated the genre of books published on Ancient Astronaut Theory, we have Zechariah Sitchin to thank.

Sitchin's belief that NIBIRU's orbit was 3600 years derives from a mistake. That the Deluge occurred in the 120th shar induced Sitchin to multiply 3600 years by 120 to produce 432,000 "years" from arrival of Anunnaki to the Great Flood, an error even Vedic chronographers made in determining the duration of the Yugas (World Ages). A preflood year was 360 days, the calendrical systems for ALL ancient 3rd millennium BCE civilizations was 360 days a year. Thus a decade was 3600 days. The shar was a term describing a day and a 120 year period. The historically-recorded ten shars from the descent of the Anunnaki to the Great Flood was simply 120 years times ten for a period lasting 1200 years. This 1200 years multiplied by 360 days a year is 432,000 days. Sitchin's mistake was a simple one but it expanded Anunnaki history from twelve centuries to almost half a million years, an untenable duration. Anything that is alive that lived as long as 432,000 actual years would be something totally different by the end of such a long period. It is a span of time that would make even major events within it to be of no significance. Sitchin's other error was assuming that NIBIRU had anything to do with the Great Flood cataclysm in 2239 BCE. It did not. That event was caused by the Phoenix.

Just as the shar was a unit of time measuring 120 of something, ten shars being 1200, so too did the gar measure distance and length. A gar was 12 cubits, so ten gar would be 120 cubits. (2) Sitchin knew this but still pushed the 432,000 "years" because it fit with his own belief in the evolutionary model, uniformitarianism and the Ice Age chronologies of Establishment academia.

Sitchin noted that the Sumerians held in high esteem the sum of 3600 shars, or perfect circles. (3) This shar term also meant completed cycle. He assumed that shars referred to years, but shar had also another connotation, that of a king or Supreme Ruler. This introduced the added confusion of the manifold traditions of the Ten Kings before the Flood. Babylonian historians wrote that the Ten Kings of the preflood world ruled 432,000 shars. (4) Berossus wrote that the Ten Kings reigned 120 shars. (5) The Babylonian priest-historian Berossus wrote that an amphibious figure called Oannes, a leader of the Annedotus [Repulsive Ones], appeared out of the sea in the first year [of Sumerian-Babylonian history] and taught mankind writing, counting, masonry, legal matters, agriculture, geometry and astronomy. Following Oannes, a succession of Ten Kings reigned until the Great Flood, the 10th being Xisuthrus, the survivors of the Deluge. This information comes from Andrew Collins in his *The Gods of Eden*, where we also learn that in the Royal Canon of Turin of the

19th Dynasty of Egypt dated about 1300 BCE, long ago a line of Ten Divinities ruled Egypt. Oannes was the later corrupted EA, which was another title for ENKI [Enoch]. The Ten Kings are associated by many with the Ten Patriarchs of the Genesis text from Adam to Noah, survivors of the Flood. The shar concept is preserved in Genesis where we learn that Noah was warned 120 years before the Deluge that it was going to transpire. The biblical Noah meets his parallel in the Phoenician Ouranos, the Greek Uranus, according to the 10th century BCE historian Sanchuniathon, was the son of Autochthon. In Plato's writings this Autochthon was one of the Ten Kings of Atlantis (6), a quasi-mythical realm that was destroyed utterly by a flooding cataclysm. The Ten Kings figure prominently on some versions of the Sumerian King-Lists.

These ten kings (shars being 3600 days) equaled 120 years, or a Great Shar.

A shar was 3600 days, or ten antediluvian years of 360 days each. To Sitchin's credit, Berossus as cited by Abydenus made the same mistake- "now, a shar is esteemed to be three thousand six hundred years..." (7) Sitchin used this as evidence. But Berossus wrote of things already lost to memory in the 3rd century BC, two thousand years after the shar-day system collapsed.

Puranic texts of ancient Vedic Sanskrit reads that there were Four Earth Ages totalling 432,000 years. (8) The actual composition of the Puranic records were circa 1500 BCE, so the misunderstanding between days-years in the older Sumerian shar system is understandable. It is remarkable that the Sumerian and the Vedic records cite the same number...432,000.

Sitchin further assumed that the 120 shars of Sumerian history to the Deluge was 432,000 years, a ridiculous sum, because Joseph Brady in 1972 wrote that a Jupiter-sized planet with a theoretical orbit of 1800 years (1/2 of 3600) would explain discrepancies in Halley's Comet orbit. Sitchin saw this as proof of his shar-year theory.(9)

My position is that the Anunnaki descended in 3439 BCE, which my books and posts will affirmatively demonstrate, which was 600 years after the Capture of Luna in 4039 BCE and 600 years before the start of the Anunna Dynasty in 2839 BCE, these 600 year periods being Anunnaki NER epochs so famous in distant antiquity. It is my contention that the 432,000 shars interpreted by Sitchin and mimicked by so many others are merely days on a 360-day annual calendar and in my books I offer the proofs that these 432,000 shars concern a 1200 year period marking descent of Anunnaki to Great Flood in 2239 BCE. Note just these few references-

The Vedic Puranas explain that the Kali Yuga Age was a period of 1200 years (10) The same records mentioned the 432,000 "years." This is evidence they preserved actual history while remaining confused as to the chronology;

Babylonian records of the Antediluvian world specifically refer to a distinct period of 1200 years involved the gods (11)

Early Arabians believed that they had an ancestor king before the Flood who lived 1200 years, King Shedd-Ad-Ben-Ad, the founder of civilization. (12)

In my other posts on the Phoenix we have seen numerous chronological proofs that the Great Flood occurred in 2239 BCE, the month of May. Simply adding 1200 years to

2239 gives us the date of 3439 BCE as the appearance of the Anunnaki. But there are other ways to date this event, as we will explore.

10. PreFlood Calendars, the Goddess & the Seven Anunnaki Kings

In 2011 my book *Anunnaki Homeworld* was published by Book Tree of San Diego, the year before 2012. All the craze was about speculating what was going to occur in 2012 at the end of the Mayan Long-Count Calendar. What happened to all those authors? In *Anunnaki Homeworld* I made it abundantly clear, with charts and detailed proof showing that 2012 was NOT the end of the Long-Count, an entire chapter packed with data revealing that the end of the Long-Count isn't until November 2046 CE. I'm not the first to know it either. Whoever built the Great Pyramid of Giza knew it too.

The bewildering Mayan Long-Count Calendar is not so mysterious once compared with the Annus Mundi system, or Year of the World chronology so popular in Alexandrian texts and afterward. Scholars have determined that this olden American calendar has a start-date of August 12th, 3113 BCE, a date that baffled Mayan scholars. The Mayan Calendar will end once 13 baktuns are completed, and incredibly, these baktuns are expansive units of time that are measured at exactly 144,000 days each. Thus the entire Mayan system concludes at 1,872,000 days, which reads 13.0.0.0.0. The fact that days were the prime unit of calendrical reckoning to the Maya is a common thread to the much earlier Sumerian civilization, a culture also counting their periods in days instead of years. 3113 BCE extends back to 782 AM [3113 BC] which is only 13 years prior to the date Sumerian scholars ascribe to Etana, the Enoch of the Sumerian King-lists; 11 years from the start of the Brahmanic Kali Yuga Age of India in 3102 BCE [793 AM]; and 8 years after the beginning of the Mayan Itza Temple of the Cross Calendar.

The Mayan system as well as the others noted here began during the reign of the prophet-King Enoch, the biblical figure merely a Hebracized version of the Sumerian ENKI. Its start date in conjunction with the building of the pyramids and reign of its principle architect [Enoch] and allusion to a time in the Last Days hints that this system was intended to start at a very significant date in the beginning that commemorated another time period in the end. And as Lost Scriptures of Giza clearly demonstrated, this was the chief purpose of the Great Pyramid—an apocalypse recorder and prophetic time capsule. Though antiquarians associate the Egyptian ruler Khufu with the Great Pyramid the actual title appears to be a Mayan Itza description meaning sacred area [K'UFU]. (1) Though this is not to be addressed until later in these posts, the author makes it very clear that he agrees with the start-date of the Mayan Long-Count in 3113 BCE, for reasons to be disclosed, but he is adamantly opposed to the modern scholarly interpretation that this system of 13 baktuns ends in 2012 CE because chronologists today assume that earth's 365.24 day orbital period making the year has always remained constant, and this is far from the truth. Recalibrating the Long-Count to 13 baktuns of Draconian days [360-day years] gives us 5200 years [52 being sacred to the Maya] and provides us an incredible date important to our study later in these posts. The Maya considered the 365.24 day-year to be vague, and they would never have adopted the vague year for their historic Long-Count. Even the greater sum of 144,000 days [baktun] exhibits the use of the lower denominator of 360 [360x4=1440].

But these facts and divisors do not only apply to the Mayan Long-Count. The truly remarkable Brahmanic system is even closer in synchronicity to the Sumerian system than the ancient American. The Kali Yuga age of India marks the beginning of mankind's degeneration into evil and has a start-date of 3102 BCE [793 AM], exactly 11 years after the beginning of the Long-Count. (2) The Kali Yuga age was predicated on the idea that the Age would come full circle to an end after 6000 years. Note that the Kali Yuga was the Fourth Age of India and did not start with the beginning of Brahmanic reckoning. The proximity of these start-dates is laden with implications. All four of these references, the Temple of the Cross, the Mayan Long-Count, Etana record and Brahmanic Calendar all fall within a 21 year period that perfectly averages out at 800 Annus Mundi [3095 BCE] if we conclude that the Mayan Temple of the Cross Calendar was designed to start contemporaneously with the Long-Count instead of seven years priorly. And this conclusion is not without further confirmation from the Maya themselves.

The Maya Itza Temple of the Cross Calendar has been assigned a start date of 3121 BCE [774 AM] and the Mayan records claim this system began with the ascension of a goddess from the earth who is represented by a rather grotesque glyph. The inscriptions in the Temple reads that Lady-Beast-With-Upturned-Snout was over 800 years old at the time of her ascension. (3). The ascension of a deity is preserved in the ascent of Enoch, however, an 800 year old woman was not uncommon during those days prior to the Flood. Before the Deluge the Goddess was the chief object of worship as attested around the world among the earliest sites. It was after the Flood that patriarchal societies became dominant and turned goddesses into gods. The 800 reference could refer to 800 Annus Mundi or the 800 could be a numerical disguise for the Eight Kings because the Lady-Beast is no doubt equated with the Sumero-Babylonian Dragon Tiamat, the seven-headed dragon that supports the Eighth. In the biblical apocalyptic Book of Revelation she is called MYSTERY BABYLON and the Harlot. Are we to delegate this as mere coincidence? Are we to assume Mayan records in the Temple of the Cross any less accurate than the scientific calculations in the Mayan Dresden Codex that contain Venus almanacs so precise they ensure an accuracy of within two hours in five hundred years of Venus calculations? (4) We are reminded here of a most truthful statement made by Robert B. Stacey-Judd in 1939 CE who wrote that beneath the stories of world mythology there is truth, veiled in various disguises and-

". . . by careful comparison with somewhat analogous accounts from widely scattered areas, fundamental charactorists frequently show remarkable parallels. If therefore, extraneous data disclose that a certain amount of fact underlies most myths and legends, let us, for the time being consider them as a medium of information, subject to the more definite acceptance of substantiation through other sources." (5)

Keeping this in mind we note that the Mayan and
Brahmanic histories are fused together by the goddess
motif, for the Kali Yuga was modeled after the Indian
Goddess of Destruction Kali. She had eight arms
(matriarchal memory of the Scorpion King) and was a
frenzied, bloody woman with weapons of war in each hand.
Other Native American cultures probably distantly related
to the Maya maintained traditions concerning Spider
Woman who was linked to the number 8 [arachnid having 8
legs] and the creative act of weaving webs. (6) In early
Mexico the spider was the surrogate of evil and cold,
known as the Arch-Deceiver and enemy of mankind. The
mother-goddess connection is prevalent everywhere in the
early Americas, the genitrix of a malignant race of Stone
Giants. These giants sought to exterminate mankind before
they were hurled over the great abyss. The Aztecs tell of
these giants during the reign of Tlaloc (Mexican Enoch), a
man who lived for 364 years until an evil goddess began to
rule and the world was destroyed in a Flood. This is a direct
memory of Enoch, who lived 365 years being translated
into heaven, the 364 recalled because it aligns the Mexican
calendar into periods of 52 years (52x7 is 364). This
goddess's name was Ixcuina and she is faulted for the
Flood, she further being remembered as being represented
by a constellation that fell from the sky.

This primordial woman that caused the Deluge is told of in
old Cornwall, Wales and Brittany as well as across the
globe in early Persia. The Hopi too remembered a wicked
goddess who had access to a ladder that reached the
world's axis. (7) These details are distinctly Euphratean in
origin. Ishtar of the Babylonians and Innana of Sumer also
were identified with ladders to reach heaven and were both
connected to flood myths involving divine necklaces with

beads that represented the Anunnaki. Another title for Innana was Aruru and she had a necklace of lapis lazuli beads similar to the divine necklace of jewels worn by the Japanese goddess Amaterusa. This Japanese story tells that after the passage of seven generations [which would be during eighth one] of gods appeared the Izanagi and Izanami. (8) These beings are no doubt a corruption of the Sumerian Anunnaki [A-NUN-NA-GE]: Iz[anagi]. Izanami is merely a Japanese female version of Izanagi. The goddess associated to the Seven in Egypt was called Sefket-Aabut, the Goddess of the Laying Down of the Foundation, of the repetitions of seven, the Guardian of the cycles of 30 and 120 years. Over her head was a seven-rayed star and about her neck was a rainbow scholars identify as the same symbol of Ishtar's collar of jewels. (9) The 7-pointed star as seen in Lost Scriptures of Giza was important to the architectural mechanics of the Great Pyramid for the 7-pointed star provides a perfect 52 degree angle and 120 is the Sumerian Great Shar in use when the pyramid complex was constructed upon the firm foundation in Egypt, its 52 degree angle slope making it the most unique pyramid in the world. Even in late Greek antiquity this mythos was still circulating. It was said that a god of forging made a wonderful necklace and it was given to Harmonia, a goddess. Despite its divine origin the necklace was to bring about the end of a later generation. (10) We will soon revisit this goddess of the antediluvian world.

The primordial Genitrix, the Goddess of all the antediluvian religions who reappears in the Last Days prophetic imagery of the Revelation, the Apocalypse, riding upon a seven-headed beast...she was the Matriarch, before those Seven Anunnaki Kings who claimed descent from her. Let us now explore who these regents were to the Ancient World.

1. Symbols, Sex and the Stars 293; 2. Early Man and the Cosmos 217; 3. Early The Histories, Herodotus Book II 4 pg. 87; 4. Man and the Cosmos 219; 5. Atlantis: Mother of Empires 71; 6. Herder Dictionary of Symbols 179; 7. Book of the Hopi 17; 8. Sun Lore of All Ages 23-24; 9. The Great Pyramid: Its Divine Message 173; 10. Mythology 255

Though Sumerian records tell of the Anunnaki and Seven Kings as having lived and ruled prior to the Flood they also reveal that these beings antedate the antediluvian world and even humanity, their existence having been archaic long ere mankind was created. They were originally a part of the hosts of the heavens that served a Godhead but they rebelled in pre-Adamic times. The Seven were from ancient heaven (1) and were cast down from their positions in a devastating war that destroyed the solar system, scarred the moon and pushed earth away from the sun to freeze until it returned to its present orbit centuries later. They made war against Enlil, the Chief of Old Time and were condemned by Enlil to enjoy their kingship over humanity [prophesied back in early heaven] for a period not to exceed 50 shars, or 6000 years [50x120]. Earth became the center of conflict between the Godhead and the rebellious Anunnaki before mankind was even created.

Sumerian, Akkadian and Babylonian stone tablets and stellar inscriptions describe the Anunnaki as having literally fell down from heaven. The tablet reads, "Those Seven, the evil gods, who swoop like the Deluge, swoop upon the world like a storm." (2) They are the seven serpents of death no doubt all connected to the Eighth, or Dragon. They are also constantly referred to as "Those who observe and see," or IGIGI, better known as the

Watchers (3) and in the Secrets of Enoch text the Watchers are called the "many-eyed ones." (4) Indra in the Indian epics wore a robe "covered in eyes," [fulfilling the office of Watcher] and incidentally in the Rig Veda he is called the 7-Slayer. (5) Watchers have long been connected to the serpent motif and those having read Lost Scriptures will know that the oldest root words in several archaic languages for serpent, snake and dragon were syllables all connected to seeing, observing and discerning. Enoch was commanded to testify against the Watchers, ". . . those that sinned with the daughters of men; for they had commenced to mix with the daughters of the earth, so that they were defiled; and Enoch testified against them all." (6)

The Babylonian historiographers and scribes were convinced that the Seven Kings came from the heavens and they designated these beings as the Children of Anu who rebelled (7), which is understandable because the older Sumerian writings tell that the Anunnaki were the Sons of Enlil [Lord Wind]. (8) To advance this position is the fact that the Hebraic texts of Jubilees, Genesis 6 and several extracanonical works convey that the Sons of God took [abducted forcibly] the daughters of men, fathering a race of giants. The Anunnaki, called Nephilim [Fallen Ones] in scripture descended upon the earth and created a counterfeit theology involving many "sons of God" rather than just One who was foretold in the Elder Prophecies to visit the earth to announce judgement. In the Old Testament books the Anunnaki offspring are a race of giants called the Anakim. The radical AK is found in both Anunn[AK]i and An[AK]im and is a syllable of great antiquity found in many languages and almost always meaning mighty or a variant thereof. (9) It is commonly found among the titles of rulers and kings like in the Sanskrit Ganaka [king],

Akbar [great] and Cormac, the High King of Ireland. Balak was king of Moab, Shishak of Egypt and Gwrnach was a female giant in the Arthurian legends and the syllable serves as the root for the strongest of all trees: the oak. O[AK]. (10) Anak was also a Philistine title of rank thought by some scholars to have come from the Mycenaean region of Anak. (11) It was also Phoenician for prince (12) and it was a part of many Graeco-Aegean titles and names: Anaxagoras, Anaxamander, Anaxidrides.

Because the Anunnaki were called the Children of Anu the later Babylonians misinterpreted the original and very old records of the Sumerians concerning these A-NUN-NA-GE [Anunnaki], for there is no evidence that NUN meant "heaven." (13) This was merely traditional etymology leading the later Babylonian scribes to interpret the epithet as "Offspring of Heaven and Earth." But the Sumerians did not convey this meaning at all. The Sumerian word NUN is synonymous with apsu, the Underworld, a common title used in many names of old. Apsu literally means the deep as in the mythical NUN-KI-GA, or City of the Deep. The Sumerian underworld was thought to be filled with water, the fountains of the deep and the idea and etymology can be traced back to Sanskrit as well where we learn that ap is the word for water. (14) The very earliest records held that the Anunnaki came from the Deep. (15)

Curiously the Deep has a dual meaning. To the credit of the Babylonians the apsu was not only the terrestrial oceans but was also a metaphor for the vastness of space, especially the lowest regions below the horizon that were alien to the Sumerians. Both were considered an abyss [bottomless pit]. In some writings the Anunnaki were seven Masters of the Underworld and Gloomy pit (16) and one

text reads: "In the Abyss of the Deep they are Seven . . ."
(17) The dual reference to the heavens and underworld are also seen in Akkadian hymns that read, "They are Seven, they are Seven! In the depths of the Ocean they are Seven! In the heights of the Heaven they are Seven!" (18) This dichotomy is also apparent in the Egyptian *Book of the Dead* concerning the Sons of Revolt: ". . . whether the fiends descend from out of heaven, or whether they come forth from the earth, or whether they advance on the waters, or whether they come from among the Star Gods . . ." (19)

The fall of the Anunnaki from heaven is often linked to a curious description given to them as Seven Mountains. (20) This imagery connects the Anunnaki to the Watchers of the Enochian and Hebraic traditions. Enoch traveled through heaven and came across a dreadful place between heaven and earth called the Prison of the Stars where in the Abyss he witnessed "Seven stars like great burning mountains," described later in the Book of Enoch as ". . . mountains burning with fire." (21) The imagery invoked in the texts is of a comet that hurls through the vastness of space [abyss] from the direction of the Deep [regions far below ecliptic in southernmost area of our solar system]. The Anunnaki/mountain motif link reappears in the book of the Revelation of the Last Days:

". . . and I saw a woman sit upon a scarlet colored beast, full of names of blasphemy, having seven heads and ten horns. . . the beast that thou sawest was, and is not; and shall ascend out of the bottomless pit [abyss] and go into perdition [ruin], and they that dwell on the earth shall wonder . . . and here is the mind which hath wisdom. The seven heads are seven mountains . . . And there are Seven Kings; five are fallen, and one is and the other is not yet

*come; and when he cometh, he must continue a short space.
And the beast that was, and is not, even he is the Eighth,
and is of the Seven . . ." (22)*

The *Lost Scriptures of Giza* disclosed ample evidence
exhibiting that motifs and symbols of the Revelation record
were not known to the Greeks and this is the case also with
the imagery of mountains identified as powerful
supernatural beings. The Revelation text had already been
recorded and seen by Enoch and later virtually lost into
fragments preserved within the scattered books and
traditions of cultures even thousands of miles apart. These
Seven Mountains are the seven Anunnaki of Sumer and
Babylonia, also called the Seven Kings, Sages and Igigi.
In India they were the Seven Avatars, the Maruts and the
Seven Rishis. The Egyptians remembered them as the
Seven Sons of Revolt, the Masters and Builder Gods. The
Hebraic traditions called them the Sons of God, the
Watchers and Nephilim while the Graeco-Aegean cultures
recalled these divinities as the Gygantes [giants], the
Cyclopes and the Titans.

Lost Scriptures served to show that the Enochian records
and the Revelation had come from the same source
material, a vast corpus of information abbreviated for
dissemination for both contain passages mirroring each
other laden with iconography and language unknown to the
Greeks and other civilizations extant at the time of the
second composition of the Revelation by John 2000 years
ago. However, these writings would have been perfectly
understandable to the average literate Sumerian. The
apocalyptic language of the Revelation and references to
the Seven indicate that the history of the Anunnaki did not
end with the Great Flood, but that these arcane beings have

yet another role to play in the Last Days. This is inferred in the riddle provided in the Revelation just cited about the Seven Kings, and then the Eighth who is a part of the Seven. The evidence suggests that the Eighth is the same as the Anunnaki King who never finished his rule because he was "cut off," the Flood bringing his kingship to a premature end in the year 2239 BCE, the 670th year of the Nephilim Dynasty. The seven-headed dragon of the Apocalypse is a symbol for this dynasty, the Seven Kings of the Anunnaki.

11. Before the Flood...A Caucasian Civil War

Books concerning the PreFlood World are rare indeed because of the immense amount of sources that must be searched. In fact, even the Bible only has scant data in a few chapters in Genesis and a couple verses in the New Testament about this vague time period. But the information is available, and now put together for you in *Chronicon Files* [Before the Flood] and free at www.nephilimarchives.com.

Learn the history of our binary solar system, the creation of the Dark Star and first recorded appearance of NIBIRU, the homeworld of the Anunnaki. Discover the antediluvian histories of the Phoenix object that brought ruin to the PreAdamic World, the oldest accounts of an Eden-like paradise and a revolt among powerful godlike beings...the

Daystar Rebellion. Ancient Gnostic records on the secrets of our solar system are herein and the construction of megalithic calendars specifically designed to survive millennia. The earliest records of the Anunnaki, or Homo Anunna, the scientific secrets of the Great Pyramid of Giza, constructed before there was an Egyptian civilization as we know it.

The orbital chronologies of Phoenix and Nibiru are outlined, Old World time-keeping systems and their relevance then and now, Sethite chronology, a dynasty before the Deluge of law-abiding people. The arrival of the Watchers, or Anunnaki, on Earth just days after a global disaster killed off a third of the human population...a flood more ancient than Noah's. Here is explained the day-count system of the Archaic Civilization that measured time not in years as we do but in the turning from night to day which gave rise to the method of recording for the Vedic, Olmec, Mayan, Sumerian calendars and is the reason why so many passages in the scriptures measure events in days rather than years...as in the days of Noah.

By understanding this day-count we make sense of all the Old World calendars that have start-dates before the Great Flood of 2239 BCE. The Olmec, Vedic, Mayan, Chinese, Sumerian calendars as well as the dated sequences on the Sumerian King-Lists and stunning chronolithic monuments like Giza, Carnac in Europe, Stonehenge and New grange, the Cursed Earth Chronology based off of the Phoenix orbit periods- the mysterious begins to make sense. We find proof the Mayan Long-Count was never designed to end in 2012 CE, that this was pure scholarly ineptitude. True end-date is in 2046 CE...29 years from the composition of this post. Mysterious geometry of the Great Pyramid identifies the date of its construction and the date for the end of Earth's present orbital chronology around the sun at 365.25 days a year. The fascinating monument is a literal three-dimensional series of calendars in stone, its angles and dimensions are actual space-time coordinates and prophecies of exact times coming when these dimensions we are familiar with will CHANGE.

Holospheric coding of time-space, the numbers of apocalypse, the mathematics that govern our existence, cross-calendrical parallels that provide direct evidence that the past histories are a predicate for the future and evidence of high technological sophistication- the records of the preFlood world are consistent. Our history books are very wrong. Technolithic methods of construction were so advanced they show proof of scalar boring, sound-levitation, smoothing rock to tolerances of .02 and the use of geopolymers at Giza is now proven.

The building of the Great Pyramid at the middle of the earth, the dreams that haunted the rulers before the Flood, great visions. A vast Enochian empire consisting of 130 kingdoms. Enoch (Enki) vanishes and the Nephilim Dynasty rules the world. Sphinx construction and her secrets, the evidence of a preEgyptian monument. A gathering of the antediluvian libraries for burial in preparation for the Great Cataclysm that is predicted. Enoch's (Enki) ministry among the giants/Nephilim (Anunnaki), the origin of demons, wraiths, unclean spirits, poltergeists, ghosts, specters.

The Nephilim Dynasty began by a female, remembered as a Mother Goddess, the regnal terms of the Seven Kings before the Flood. Uncanny parallels between preFlood historical traditions and the Chinese records concerning the first dynasty, the Dragon Kings. The abduction of human females by the Nephilim, widespread rape, the birth of mutants, , the hybridization of animals and different species of plants to create new variants. How the Dragon Kings corrupted the earth introducing forbidden knowledges. First recorded instances of abortion are from records citing the events of the preFlood world.

Identity of Noah, a king of the Sumerian city of Shurrupak, marriage of Noah to the daughter of Enki (Enoch), giants wars and cannibalism, the five years of Ark construction in preparation for the Deluge. Great Flood cataclysms detailed, collapse of the Vapor Canopy, appearance of the rainbow, volcanic resurfacing, 90% of global population dies, terrible meteoritic impacts, the transit of planet Phoenix and the darkening of the sun seven days before the Flood. PreFlood civilization collapsed when North America devastated by major Impact Object.

Chronicon has hundreds of independent facts and bibliographic sources cited, 98 dated entries of events that occurred before the Great Deluge in 2239 BCE, a history covering precisely 3000 years from 5239-2239 BCE. If I had time to freely research and write all of this material and provide it to you in Chronicon Files for free, YOU have time to read it. And if you hunger for even more knowledge on the world and conditions before the Flood and the origin of the most mysterious construction project on this planet, the Great Pyramid of Giza, then order my book [ebook or paperback], the *Lost Scriptures of Giza: Enoch and the Secrets of the World's Oldest Texts*, published by Book Tree. The book contains information you will NEVER forget.

The study of the archaic past is paramount because what transpired of old is destined to unfold again. The sociopolitical scenarios, environmental, spiritual are all a part of a patterned weave, a repetitive history. The evidence that our ancestors KNEW of the approach of a civilization-ending cataclysm and made efforts to prepare for it are found everywhere in the annals of antiquity. It would be foolish of us to ignore these traditions...warnings. We hold that we are the first technologically advanced civilization on this planet and we are very wrong.

One of the more controversial writers of our time, David Icke, in 1995 wrote- *"Planet Earth was highjacked...taken over by another civilization or civilizations, which are highly advanced technologically...it is from some of our neighbors in the fourth dimension that the interference has come...manipulation...via either thought control or direct intervention."* (1)

Of all the Anunna only Enki [Enoch] sought to preserve mankind. The Anunna had erred in their genetic engineering. Attempting to create docile halfwits, they introduced too much of their own DNA. Humans had become too wise, too intelligent and industrious so an attempt to destroy mankind with a plague was made, but Enki intervened. A famine was caused but again Enki intervened. In 1994 Dr. Arthur David Horn (Ph.D Physical Anthropology, Yale 1976) wrote that the Sumerian god Enlil's chance to rid the world of humans now came in the form of a FOREKNOWN catastrophe-what we call the Great Flood. Those familiar with my Phoenix Chronology posts will know that the antediluvian world's experts were not caught by surprise by the global cataclysm for the orbit of the Phoenix object was known. Enlil informed the

Anunna that a killing flood was coming, but humans were not told, and by humans I refer to ADAMU, the name of mankind in those days.

Horn wrote that "...it also makes sense that a long-lived race like the Anunnaki would be aware of the cycles of the Universe, such as movements of comets and other extraterrestrial bodies...he (Enlil) insisted that the news of this approaching calamity be kept away from humans." (2) All the Anunna were sworn to secrecy but Enki cleverly devised a way to inform Ziusudra. For this deception that benefitted humanity, when it was discovered by the other Anunna, Enki became known as the Serpent- a deceiver, not of humans, but of his own people. The Serpent in all the old tales was man's benefactor, an outlaw among the gods. This data further serves to identify Enki as the person of Enoch who predicted the Flood in all the pseudopigraphical and apocryphal writings. This also reveals that not all antediluvian writings and stories were recorded by humans (ADAMU), but after the cataclysm either someone from among the Anunna wrote these things down or dictated them to humans who later preserved them in writing.

The rift separating the Anunnaki from Enki was much more than their disapproval with a single person of Anunna pedigree. Enki led an entire faction of powerful Anunna. The oldest and longest enduring traditions agree upon an intriguing fact- IN THE BEGINNING, or, before the Flood, the gods were already divided in to two groups. The Vedic, Aryan, Hurrian, Amorite, Nordic, Germanic, Persian, Greek- all branches of the Caucasian race maintain traditions of two groups of gods in antiquity that were in opposition to each other and the source of contention was mankind. This fact necessarily leads us into another disturbing fact about the preFlood world that will be fully expounded up in a whole series of coming posts. The earliest cultures around the planet after the sudden demise of the Neanderthal and Cro-Magnon peoples were all river-dwelling people of short stature with black hair and black eyes and brown, olive or red skin, smooth skin with no facial hair. They were concentrated in the river valleys of the Nile, Tigris-Euphrates, the Indus Valley, great rivers of China and across the Pacific in the Urumbamba river valley of South America. These dark peoples all share a common belief system that is well-documented- when the gods appeared on Earth they were tall, blue and green eyed, grew long hair on their faces and had white skin. To the antediluvian peoples of a post-apocalyptic Earth many centuries after a prior civilization fell, the gods were Caucasians.

Two groups of Anunna...a civil war...both sides were Caucasians...both groups guilty of DNA manipulations in the creating of homo sapiens...designer DNA programs carried out to create separate homo sapien races...Anunna-supervised mining and labor settlements...homo sapien population explosion out of control...one group still able to move to and from the planet at specific windows of time sought to erase their trespass by killing off their product...the other group led by Enki were MAROONED on Earth to live among the humans they sought to save. An interesting theory? No. These facts will be proven many times over with verifiable source materials as these posts progress.

It was during the Contact Period [3439-2647 BCE] when both groups of Anunnaki abandoned the practice of using surrogate Anunna females [Birth-Goddesses] and began extensive Anunna-human interbreeding...but with totally different results. The Jewish author of the Genesis text in Babylonia read the archaic records of the Anunna and Igigi groups and modelled their antediluvian "history" into two prevailing lineages: Sethites and Cainites. The Cainite women were modelled from the Igigi (rebel Anunna not sanctioned to visit Earthside). These Cainite women gave birth to the Nephilim races of Anunna-human hybrid mutants, giants, monsters, demigodlike people, many having six fingers and toes on their hands and feet and a double-row of teeth. For actual skeletons found with these traits, see Giants on Ancient Earth: An In-Depth Study on the Nephilim. Highly intelligent, morally deficient, a wicked group.

Interestingly, red-haired giants, huge people found mummified with red hair still intact, double-rows of teeth and extra digits have been found all over the Americas. The Igigi-descended races survived the Great Flood of 2239 BCE at two prominent locations- North and South America and the second being the Levant regions all connected together: Lebanon, Syria, Canaan (Israel & Jordan) and Sinai. After the Flood the Sumerian name Igigi was recalled by the Pelasgian preGreek peoples as the Sons of Ge, or Mother Earth, who bore the Gigantes [Giants]. Prior to the Deluge the dark races all venerated goddesses, remembering the Anunna surrogate birth-mothers. Patriarchal gods were introduced strictly by Caucasians descended from the Enkite Anunna condemned to remain on Earth.

The Achaians of ancient Greece referred to the Land of the Giants as being in the Far West [origin of term Tartarus] over the Ocean in a place called Ogygia where the gigantes lived. Igigi. The Igigi-descended races of giants are listed in Genesis as the Rephaim, the Anakim, the Emims, the Zuzims and the Zamzummims. The biblical record names homo sapien races closely kin or descended from these giants as being the Avims, Horims and Amalekites, the latter led by a king called Agag [from Gog/Igig] who is described in scriptures as much taller than King Saul. This is remarkable, for the Bible clearly reads that Saul was two heads taller than other men. The Horims of Seir had intermarried with the Ammonites, Moabites and Edomites, from whom were descended the Jewish people. As will be shown in many coming posts, the offworld contention between the Anunnaki and their Igigi kin of antiquity has continued unabated through their DESCENDANTS into our modern world.

The progeny of Enki became "of Enoch" to the Jewish authors of Genesis in their Sethite genealogy to Noah who sanitized the clear references to racial distinctions that prevailed before the Flood. In Genesis the Hebrew word for generations [toledo] is about racial pedigree:

> ...these be the generations of Adam [ADAMU refers to black-eyed/haired people with no beards, red/brown skin...even the earliest Sumerians referred to themselves proudly as the "black-headed people."]

> ...these be the generations of Cain [Kan, a people of the ancient Americas created AFTER the ADAMU]

> ...these be the generations of Seth [of Set, a reference to preFlood Egyptian civilization]

> ...these be the generations of Noah [descendant of Enoch/Enki- all the extracanonical and Dead Sea Scrolls

texts describe birth of Noah as the FIRST time the preFlood people ever saw the birth of a white-skinned, blue-eyed homo sapien: more posts will cite these sources]

> ...these be the generations of Shem [Shemsu Hor, the Children of the Sun, a Caucasian preFlood race who inherited the sciences and knowledges of the Anunna of their parentage, who were the founders of the great post-Technolithic cities and global Heliolithic Maritime Empire of the Builders.

> ...these be the generations of Abraham [of Brahma, the Aryan patriarch of ancient Vedic-Caucasians whose consort was Saraswati just as Abram's consort was Sarah]

You MUST know this history. You have no excuse not to know it because my posts are FREE. Only by coming to terms with what occurred in antiquity, who altered these histories into what we have been taught, and why they sought to cover them up, will you gain great insight on our modern media fixation on RACE relations. The strife between the two opposing groups of Anunnaki, Homo Anunna and the Igigi, persists today and has completely saturated every aspect of our present life. I'll conclude with a quote from my favorite cynic who wrote this some time between 1919 and 1940-

"...beings from other places have come to this earth...some of the more degraded ones have felt at home here, and have hung around, or have stayed here...concealing their origin, of course; having perhaps only a slightly foreign appearance." (3)

CHARLES FORT

12. The Ten Kings of Atlantis, of the PreFlood World and Prophecy

It was the memory of the Great Flood and a dynasty of ten rulers that gave rise to the Atlantean mythos. Plato recorded the teachings of Solon of Athens who had visited Egypt and learned the histories from their venerable priesthood. The Egyptian scholars told Solon that the ancient world was sunk beneath the ocean in its tenth generation.(1) Atlantis is the collective embodiment of the preflood traditions.

The Ten Kings of Atlantis were venerated in a temple said to be on the Atlantic continent that had ten statues of pure gold of the ten kings and their wives. The original Atlantic tradition was a historic story from Egypt that Solon rewrote into an epic verse, according to Plutarch. Interestingly, the Egyptians told Solon that the world was destroyed periodically at long intervals of time because the bodies moving around the earth deviate from their courses. (2) Aside from the Atlantean beliefs, the biblical ten-king dynasty before the Great Deluge seems to have been remembered universally. Iranian legends recall a ten king dynasty in antiquity, called the Men of Ancient Law. In India were remembered the Ten petris, or fathers. The old Germans and Arabs had ten patriarchal fathers in the beginning of their histories, all kings and the Chinese begin their ancestral annals with the Ten Emperors, men that lived before the dawn of historical times. The Chinese stories tell that just after the reign of the Ten Kings, after the Creation, mankind struggled against fierce and gigantic monsters back when people lived unusually long lives. (3)

Unlike the more peaceful memories of the ten kings or patriarchs the Eight Kings of Sumer are remembered as a dynasty of iniquity, the cause of the Flood itself and the catastrophic events that collapsed the earlier heavens [firmament], pushed earth out of its place and ruined the perfect Draconian calendrical system. These Eight Kings are also dissimilar to the ten patriarchs because they are not historically identifiable outside the King-List, being commemorated over and again only within the Sumerian, Akkadian and Babylonian fragments that mention the Seven [or Eight] Kings. The patriarchs have the entire biblical and extracanonical records stemming from them and their descendants but the Seven Kings as well as the Eighth do not return to the world's literary scenes until the apocalyptic text known as the Book of Revelation. In Revelation they are described as demonic and this corresponds with their Sumerian identities. The very first king was Alulim, an epithet denoting one who is possessed with an evil spirit [alu]. In Sumerian the designation for this demon is A-LA and it was noted for its ability to change its form at will. (4)

The records of the past concerning these Eight Kings are prolific in the surviving Mesopotamian annals, and all contain one startling fact. From the start there were only Seven Kings, the Eighth was one of the Seven who returned to rule again. In these texts these Kings are referred to as the Anunnaki. There are seven deities named in the most ancient texts but the lists contain eight kings, the last never named, but the ideograms indicate only seven regents. (5) The later Babylonians considered the Eighth to be the Dragon of Chaos named Tiamat, a Goddess of the Deep (6) and the Akkadians before them held that the Seven Gods were merely heads on the Great Dragon who is the Eighth. (7) In the Vedic texts the Rishis were Seven Sages immortalized in the stars according to the Vayu Purana who were numbered as Eight. (8) The Rishis visited earth when humanity was in its infancy, thus identifying these Sages as the Anunnaki. Incidentally, the Anunnaki are specifically called the Seven Sages who built the walls of Uruk in the Epic of Gilgamesh. Even an obscure fragment in the Bible concerns this arcane enigma. In Ecclesiastes we read ". . . give a portion to seven and also to eight, for thou knowest not what evil shall be upon the earth."

A female was often associated to the Seven Kings. She was called Dingir-DAM-NUN-GAL-E-NE or Damkina. (9) These seven were also called the Sons of Isharra (10) that intriguingly maintains a root word pertinent to this study: I[shar]ra. Antiquarian Gerald Massey in the 1880s wrote in his Ancient Egypt Light of the World that the goddess may have been the originator of the Seven, a primordial Genitrix who is mysteriously also identified as a masculine deity. He also addressed this problem in his epic The Natural Genesis, writing that the Seven Kings were the sons of Anu, Babylonian god of heaven. (11) This confusion between a male and female originator may simply be due to preferential ideologies between patriarchal and matriarchal cultures over time, also by historians and redactors handling newer copies of older texts. The goddess link may be due to the fact that the Chaos known throughout antiquity was also personified as a female, even the word for deep in Genesis 1:2 is in feminine tense. Either way the belief in seven deities having their beginning with an Eighth is not exclusively Mesopotamian. The Egyptians, later Gnostics and others as will be shown recalled their kingship. (12) In my book Descent of the Seven Kings to be released in the fall of 2017, it is shown that the belief in the Seven Gods and a mothergoddess before a cataclysm was a prominent tradition far across the oceans in the lands of ancient America.

The theme of the Ten Kings vanished from the writings and beliefs of the world for about a thousand years and then suddenly were resurrected about 96 CE with the enigmatic text of the Revelation that suffixes our Bibles, a writing highly reminescent of the Sibylline writings and those of the Gnosis. This strange apocalyptic text, Revelations, concerns many themes from the Ancient World that abruptly reappeared with the appearance of this prophetic text.

My new book, *Return of the Fallen Ones*, is packed with chronological data on the antediluvian world, research necessary because the histories detailed mathematically and conceptually presage everything you are about to read. The past indeed repeats itself and after reviewing the following material it will be blatantly obvious that there is vast gulf between what is taught and what is KNOWN.

Unfortunately, science at its best seeks most to keep us in this simplified, thoroughly artificial, falsified world. This author is absolutely convinced that a Greater Intellect beyond human comprehension has been long at work behind the scenes of world history. It is because of this that historical analysis has predictive value, caused by a Grand Designer whose intention from the start was to end His world by the same mechanics extent at its beginning.

Our analysis of the Anunnaki history will be a two-part review. We will now isolate the themes attached to the events. The first part of this study concerns the beginning, which would encompass the preflood histories, a span of 3000 years from 5239 BCE or 2239 BCE. The history of the beginning sets the stage for the end, the Last Days, which is confirmed by the prophecy of Jesus who said that the End Times would ". . . be as the days of Noah." In the construction of our thesis we began with the Anunnaki as co-creators and 3000 years later the Great Flood resulted with their imprisonment. Thus we see in the Last Days the Anunnaki coming as destroyers after they are released.Here are the elements of the beginning that will reoccur in the end times. The Anunnaki—

contribute to ruination of earth

create a nonhuman sentient species

create hybrids of this species and humans (transgenics)

enslave their own minions

war against own minions to deceive humanity

cause Apocalypse altering Earth's orbit (NIBIRU Passover)

conspire against man

descend to Earth during catastrophe

appear after one-third mankind killed

trade knowledges for human females

abduct human females

father the Nephilim (Giants)

fill a power vacuum after human government falls

oppose Ten Kings (10-Ruler Government) and subdue them

Eighth King will reign, one of the Seven Kings

world destroyed by falling of two stars

This is the framework of Apocalypse, and as readers of this author's other works have found, this is precisely how the Last Days unfolds. The Anunnaki Chronology merely validates what has already been discovered through studying biblical prophecy, calendrical isometrics, comparative timelines and cross-calendrical parallels as clearly revealed in *Chronicon* [Members Only ARCANA Files]. This 3000 years is five NER, 600 years each. This means the pattern is firmly established, being five pentagons of our dodecahedron, the pentagonal dodecahedron geometry of our space-time structure detailed in *Return of the Fallen Ones*. But there is 4200 years of events (lines, angles and planes) remaining until this chronological solid is formed in 1962 CE. These Anunnaki chronological markers provide us additional details illuminating our dodecahedron of Apocalypse. Here are these elements gleaned from the timeline.

planet Phoenix will enter the inner system

planet NIBIRU will pass close to earth

Mayan Long-Count will end (Time Collapses)

natural disasters and calamities

North America depopulated

Dark Satillite will pass close to Earth

"Kingship" will be "lowered from heaven."

Anunnaki artifact discovered-interpreted

major architectural project venerating Anunnaki

new dynasty founded in Iraq

new Order founded in Iraq

"Throne of David" set up

major war won by Anunnaki

the West subdues the Kings of the East

nations descended from Israel (10 Kings) in peril

major rift in Jewish world

global persecution of innocents

state-church sanctioned genocide

By combining these two categories of motifs together a synthesis emerges that startling synchronizes with modern contemporary events. Because this is a synoptic review of the End Times we cannot possibly reiterate this timeline, which has already been done in minute detail within this author's other works. The following dates and events are proven in Chronicon and demonstrated thoroughly in *When the Sun Darkens* and *Anunnaki Homeworld*. Astonishingly, this Last Days timeline was already complete in manuscripts prior to this author's discovery of the Anunnaki Chronology's future-past themes priorly listed. The uniqueness of the Revelation record cannot be overstated. When it was allegedly composed about 19 centuries ago it was written employing motifs and symbols alien to the Greek and Roman mind. Revelation contains imagery that antedates the Greeks by a thousand years, the text packed with Sumerian ideas, symbols and imagery.

13. Annus Mundi Calendar, Abraham & the Secret Records of the Great Pyramid

The earth is very old. Of all the chronologies and calendrical systems of long ago that have survived and those used today very few, if any, claim to span all the way back to a creation event. Most of them stretch back in time to the supposed beginning of mankind or some major event in early history that depopulated our planet. One of the dating systems thought to go back the furthest and with the best accuracy is the Annus Mundi Chronology [Year of the World]. Alexandrian scholars in Egypt were familiar with Annus Mundi dating but even then there were varying versions and just as the Egyptian priestly classes altered their own sacral calendars to suit their socio-religious purposes so too did Alexandrian scribes and Christian writers modify AM [Annus Mundi designation used throughout this book] dates to correspond with assumed calendrical points in other dating systems. Over time this dating has resurfaced, been lost again, reverse-researched to again put it back together up until the present.

The Greek astronomer in charge of the Library at Alexandria during the reign of Ptolemy III was Eratosthenes [276-196 BCE]. He interpreted Egyptian dynasties as containing periods derived from Genesis dating and was familiar with the Annus Mundi dating. (1) Flavius Josephus who gave us his Antiquities was acquainted with AM system, even claiming that Solomon became king circa. 3100 AM. (2) The Egyptian Book of Sothis preserved by Syncellus [800 CE] recorded events in AM years and Geoffrey of Monmouth, celebrated author of Historia Regum Brittanae [History of the Kings of Britain] also used the Annus Mundi Chronology to ascertain that the city of Londonum was founded 1004 years before Christ's birth. Even texts from secret societies like Masons published in the past three and four hundred years date events by Annus Mundi reckoning, principally the Inigo Jones Document and Wood Manuscript.

Unlike the Julian/Gregorian system the Annus Mundi Calendar is without a break or merging with any other calendar. The greatest and most accurate reconstruction of the AM system was performed by Stephen Jones and published in his Secrets of Time. He began Year 1 with Adam's expulsion from Eden, which corresponds exactly with the start of the Hebraic Chronology prior to its rabbinical corruption. The Genesis narrative for this year, the first of 1656 year to the Deluge, is of mankind banished from Paradise. But the darker reality was that Year One was a total restart of the world's civilizations and calendars, this being 3895 BCE, the year of a devastating poleshift, lithospheric displacement that created the continents we know today. For some perspective let the reader understand that as of this writing in 2017 AD [Anno Domini] it is the Year 5911 Annus Mundi. Next year, 2018 CE, will be 5912 AM, or 88 years short of 6000.

The Giza Complex was finished at 2815 BC [1080 AM] after 90 years of construction that started in 990 AM [2905 BCE]. Construction began 60 years after the death of Adam, the patriarch of mankind, who died in 2965 BCE [930 AM], and while Lost Scriptures of Giza provides the full account of the building of the pyramid complex and Sphinx by the instructions of Enoch who had received them from heaven, the following account was not elaborated. This Egypto-Coptic history amazingly aligns with Sumerian chronology. This ancient Coptic manuscript was found in a tomb in the Monastery of Abou Harmeis. The text was translated into Arabic by a monk of the Monestary of Al Kalmun:

"In the first year of King Diocletian [3rd. cent. AD] an account was taken from a book, copied in the first year of King Philippus. from an inscription of great antiquity written upon a tablet of gold, which tablet was translated by two brothers—Ilwa and Yercha—at the request of King Philippus, who asked them how it happened that they could understand an inscription which was unintelligible to the learned men of his capital? They answered, because they were descended from one of the ancient inhabitants of Egypt, who was preserved with Noah in the Ark, and who, after the Flood had subsided, went into Egypt with the sons of Ham, and dying in that country left to his descendants (from who the brothers had received them), the books of the ancient Egyptians, which had been written one thousand seven hundred and eighty-five [1785] years before the time of Philippus, nine hundred and forty-six [946] years before the arrival of the sons of Ham in Egypt, and contained the history of the two thousand three hundred and seventy-two [2372] years; and that it was from these books that the tablet was formed. The contents of the books were:

'. . . we have seen what the stars foretold; we saw the calamity descending from the heavens, and going out from the earth, with the inhabitants and plants . . .'

"The two brothers calculated what time had elapsed from the Flood to the day when the translation was made for King Philippus; and it appeared to be one thousand seven hundred and forty-one years [1741]." (3)

This translation was made for King Philippus in 498 BCE, or 1741 years after the Flood in 2239 BCE [1656 AM]. The text goes on to explain how and why the Great Pyramid was constructed before this catastrophe, which is largely the focus of Lost Scriptures. Interestingly though, Ilwa and Yercha conclude their translation for this king with—

". . . in this manner were the Pyramids built. Upon the walls were written the mysteries of science, astronomy, geometry, physics and much useful knowledge, which any person, who understands our writing, can read . . ." (4)

This passage further supports this author's contention that the Great Pyramid was indeed covered in myriads of writings that had over millennia faded to obscurity. According to the appendix in the book Origin and Significance of the Great Pyramid, "This statement was translated from the Coptic into Arabic 225 AH [After Hijrah]." (5) This was 839 or 840 CE.

Annus Mundi reckoning and Hebraic records reveal that Egypt was settled 341 years after the diluvian catastrophe. This would be 1899 BCE [1996 AM]. Remember, this is the post-flood occupation of Egypt. There was also a civilization centered there prior to the Flood that was Sethite, having little connection to the ancient Egypt we know about today. 1899 BCE was during the reign of Anam of Sumer who occupied Egypt and is remembered by the earliest Egyptians as Mena [Menes] or Min according to Herodotus in Book II of his Histories. (6) This was during the life of Abraham and only a few years before the excavation of Giza from flood sedimentation that half buried the site. The Coptic record holds that the pyramids were built and inscribed with the knowledges from which their information derived 946 years before the arrival of the sons of Ham to Egypt. This would be 2843 BCE [1052 AM], only four years difference from the Sumerian King-List regnal year of 2839 BCE [1056 AM] when the Seven Kings began their reign the same year Noah was born. Due to the expanse of four thousand years in these calculations a variance of 4 years is virtually precise. But this may have been a deliberately contrived disparity. As shown in Lost Scriptures of Giza there were once 144,000 white polished limestone casing blocks upon the surfaces of the Great Pyramid, the lower courses with minute inscriptions, and there are four years between these two dates which under the preflood Draconian System would be exactly 1440 days [360x4].

The Sethite builders of the monument had a direct descendant who would visit the site, a man remembered by many nations even today. His name was Abram, later to be renamed Abraham in the Hebrew traditions.

To discover fascinating information of the Great Pyramid of Egypt not found anywhere else, see *Lost Scriptures of Giza.*

Abram and Giza in Egypt

The Giza, or Achuzan Complex of the Great Pyramid in Egypt, was completed after 90 years of labor in the year 1080 Annus Mundi [2815 BCE] and the beginning of Giza's construction before the Flood in 990 AM [2905 BC] began a 1080 year countdown to the year 2070 Annus Mundi [1825 BCE] which was the time when Abraham was living among the Philistines of Gerar spending several years at Giza in Egypt translating the antediluvian Sethite texts [origin of concept of Egyptian Set deity] found inscribed upon the surface casing stones of the Great Pyramid. Abraham's translating and appearance before the Egyptian Court is fully detailed in Lost Scriptures.

Abraham's association to the Great Pyramid is the subject of much Vedic esoterica. The Vedic writings of India venerate Brahma as the Creator and a god of remote antiquity, but he is not the oldest in the pantheon. Nor could he be, for Brahma, renowned for wisdom and knowledge of the past and future was A[Brahma]m, translator of the Giza texts known in Vedic literature as the Altar of Agni. The chief characteristics given to Brahma were as Creator, Preserver and Destroyer which is unusual because

Brahma was assigned a very minor role. (1) This disparity is understood by realizing that these characteristics were later attached to Abraham after he had translated the preflood texts that did contain the histories and prophecies from an elder civilization. Lost Scriptures of Giza serves to show how all of the oldest writings, including Brahmaic, are abbreviated versions of a vast corpus of ancient texts all taken from the surface stones of the Great Pyramid which explains the uncanny similarities in content and syntax of historic cosmologies and apocalypses from cultures thought to have never experienced contact.

The Altar of Agni is a mine of revelations. The word altar comes from a root meaning knowledge just as veda means knowledge. (2) This altar is akin to the Great Pyramid, called by the prophet Isaiah the altar in Egypt at the border to the Lord. The Altar of Agni had 10,800 bricks (3) corresponding to the 10,800 stanzas of the ancient Rig-Veda text, each stanza containing 40 syllables each. (4) The Giza Complex is located at what was long ago called Siriad and was a structure built to warn of the Flood and to warn of an even more remote future apocalypse involving fire. Incidentally, the ancients called the Great Pyramid a pillar of fire that contained upon its stones instructions for mankind, which links it to the Tree of Life/Knowledge motif as well as the pillar of fire by night and pillar of smoke by day the Israelites followed out of Egypt. Agni was the Brahman god of Fire worshipped as Surya [Siriad].

The confusion over Brahma and Agni both relate to Abraham and his contact with the Great Pyramid's inscriptions after the Flood. The Vedic books tell that Brahma was at the bottom of the ocean [abyss] during the Flood (5) and that Brahma had four faces. What was a deity doing at the bottom of the sea? The imagery conveyed is actually of the four-faced Great Pyramid under the waters of the Flood. Depictions of Brahma from India are directly related to Giza correspondences. Four-headed Brahma supports a triune glyph [identifying Brahmanic trinity] and rests atop a seven-petalled lotus [symbol for creative power] with a long stem [planetary axis] that descends to the navel [middle] of Vishnu, who lays on top of a seven-headed dragon in the abyss of waters [ocean and space]. (6) Vishnu covered the Deep much in the same way the Great Pyramid covers the entrance to the underworld. Brahma, Vishnu and Shiva made up the Hindu trinity, Brahma appearing with four faces identifying him as the Great Pyramid, Vishnu was the coverer who covered the Deep [which was the symbolic function of the Sphinx] and Shiva is merely a number anciently personified into a deity . . . seven. Scholars of Sanskrit literature assert that the number assigned to Agni was 7. (7) *Lost Scriptures* heavily focused on this number and its relation to the Great Pyramid's interior and exterior angles of 52°. Interestingly, the god Shiva was also represented as having five faces, the fifth facing upwards and was usually identified with the world axis! (8) The fifth face [surface] would link this imagery with that of the Sumerian AR UB symbol of judgement.

There can be no doubt as to the identity of the Vedic Brahma being the prominent historical figure of Abraham for his consort was Saraswati just as A[Brahma]m's wife was his half-sister Sarah [Sara-swati]. Indian traditions claim that Brahma committed incest with his consort because they were related, the same accusation levied at Abraham. (9) The archaic syllables AR and UB are contained in the names [AB]raham and S[AR]ah, the latter also expanded to construct the Sumerian word shar [SARah]. Abraham was a man who profoundly impacted the entire ancient world of the Near East and Africa from Persia [Elam of Genesis 14], Sumer, Akkad and Babylonia, to Canaan, Aram [Syria and Lebanon] as far as Egypt. There is every chance that Abraham is the reason why the Great Pyramid complex is remembered as Giza. Abraham was a Chaldean from Haran, a city right next to the city of Gozan in northern Babylonia (10) and he later moved and lived among the Philistines at the city of Gaza which was the chief city of the Philistine Pentapolis of the Five Lords of the Philistines. Gaza is pronounced GAY-zuh (11) and could easily be the origin of the present Giza. One of the cities of this Pentapolis was called Gath and was home to the famous giant Goliath. Abraham is especially venerated by the Hebrews, Christians, Muslims and indirectly by other names by the Persians as Zoroaster and many other titles by as many cultures. His actual name, Abramu, has been found in some Assyrian writings according to Smith in his Chaldean Genesis (12) and in the Egyptian Sheshonq

List mention is made of a Fortress of Abram. (13) Having spent the majority of his lifetime in Canaan we are not surprised to discover his name inscribed within Canaanite Ras Shamra stone tablets of the 2nd millennium BC. (14)

Abraham and his connection to the Great Pyramid and ancient Egypt is well documented in the literature of the ancient world and is the subject of *Lost Scriptures of Giza.*

The Great Pyramid Measured in Phoenix Orbits

The old history books from around the world contain many references to the Great Pyramid of Giza in Egypt like this Arabic tradition preserved by Abou Balkhi once located in the Bodleian Library-

"The Wise Men previous to the Flood, foreseeing an impending judgement from heaven...built upon the tops of the mountains in Upper Egypt many pyramids of stone...two of these buildings exceeded the rest in height...so well put together that the joints were scarcely perceptible. Upon the exterior of the building every charm and wonder of physic was inscribed." (1)

2000 years ago Diodorus Siculus expressed his own amazement at the site of the Great Pyramid, which during his day still has the sheath of white gleaming limestone casing blocks before the Muslims stripped them off to rebuild Cairo-

"It is said that the stone was conveyed over a great distance...they [The Great Pyramids] do not have the appearance of being the slow handiwork of men but look like a sudden creation, as though they had been made by

some god and set down bodily in the surrounding sand."
(2)

My book, *Lost Scriptures of Giza,* is packed with scores of these obscure references to ancient secret knowledges written on the surfaces of the monument or hidden inside its recesses. The prevailing belief among our ancestors that the Great Pyramid possessed a secret vital to human survival is shown through Lost Scriptures, but the following material is NOT found in the book. I had to research for and write four more books before I learned the following material.

Before the Flood in the period from 2905-2647 BCE architects built fantastic massive structures by carving and boring into living rock, using blocks of immense size of natural hewn stone, sawn rock, quarried and excavations out of basement rock. But one superstructure was erected before the Deluge, totally unique, constructed of geopolymer manufacture, a discovery that would not be made for 48 centuries when humans were finally able to recognize this species of sophistication. After the Flood [2239 BCE] this knowledge of geopolymer manufacturing of synthetic stone was lost. Builders of the post-diluvian Heliolithic Period again produced megalithic masonry, natural boulders of great size cut into polygonal shapes-cyclopean constructions- in their efforts to 'earthquake-proof' their buildings. Initially after the Deluge stone was quarried for these projects but soon after the cataclysm some cultures began employing kiln-fired mud brick manufacturing in molds to provide their building materials.

The blocks of the Great Pyramid in Egypt are made of geopolymers; made through a process in which artificial stone is created that is virtually indistinguishable from natural rock. (3) The limestone casing blocks of the Giza structure contain opal, CT, hydroxy-apatite, a silico-aluminate not found in the quarries, blocks containing numerous trapped air bubbles. (4) Organic fibers having accidentally fallen into the mixture have been found in the stone blocks of the Great Pyramid. (5)

Sir Flinders Petrie found abundant evidence of a drilling and boring technology employed in the structure that was beyond his ability to understand- but a century later Christopher Dunn recognized that these builders used ultrasonic drilling with diamond-tipped bits. (6) Petrie's measurements are published in his book, *The Pyramids and Temples of Gizeh*. His measurements are accepted by Egyptologists and especially by Zawi Hawass, head of Egypt's Antiquities Department. Hawass calls Petrie "The Father of Egyptology." (7)

Graham Hancock and Robert Bauval in *The Message of the Sphinx* in Appendix 3 come very close to understanding the purpose of the Great Pyramid's holospheric function [not its engineering purpose]. They wrote that- "...the function of the Giza blueprint is to provide a virtually indestructible 'holographic' apparatus...'living' man is the result of a holographic union between matter and spirit. It would very much appear that the 'Followers of Horus' understood the cosmic mechanism to somehow re-separate the two...the construction of the amazing 'holographic' star/stone apparatus of Giza." (8) The Giza interior is definitely a blueprint, that it is linked to an interface with the holosphere we are immersed inside is true, that it serves a "cosmic mechanism" is correct...but Hancock and Bauval do not even know anything about the Phoenix chronology nor the internal measurements of the Great Pyramid "blueprint" that are scientifically accepted today. The following data is unknown to them, which only makes me appreciate their observations even more.

The earliest traditions of the Great Pyramid of Giza are not Egyptian and assert that it was designed to endure through a cataclysm...that to provide a basis of knowledge for a future generation was its purpose. Internal measurements scientifically conducted by Sir Flinders Petrie of the rectilinear subterranean passage widths, chamber heights, passage length in Descendant and Ascendant passages easily provides a uniform unit of measurement that was used by the constructors throughout the monument. These measurements were discovered over a century ago and were conducted to disprove the wildly popular Pyramid-Inch theories of the time. These measurements are scientifically acceptable today, absolutely precise, and they are arranged in rectilinear lengths of 138, 552, 1518, 1656, 2070, 3036, 4140 and 5796- EVERY single number is divisible by 138...the orbital period of planet Phoenix. Petrie knew NOTHING of Phoenix. These numbers as orbital lengths are proven in my books *When the Sun Darkens* and in *Nostradamus and the Planets of Apocalypse*. On the website www.nephilimarchives.com go to Chronicon Files and read *Chronotecture: Lost Science of Prophetic Engineering* to see the actual illustrations showing these scientific measurements.

We must conclude that the builders of the Great Pyramid of Giza were aware of the Phoenix Object and this awareness allowed them to know when it would return over and over again. We also conclude that the world of the Sethites, of Enoch and later Abraham, was not the primitive society we have been led to believe. The Great Flood of 2239 BCE did not catch them unaware, they prepared for it. These measurements PROVE the Phoenix Object will return to visit great destruction on our modern world in May 2040 CE...less than 23 years from now.

14. The Giza Deception & Sphinx Enigma... Architectural Misdirection

Continental Europe and Asia, Australia, the continents of Africa and North America all share a common characteristic largely unknown to antiquarians...except for the Great Pyramid complex at Giza and the Osireion at Abydos, both in Egypt, there are NO PRE-CATACLYSM [2239 BCE Great Deluge] STRUCTURES found above ground. All of the ancient walls, citadels, mound-defense systems, canal works and stone cities spread across these continents were erected by Post-Technolithic engineers after the Deluge of 2239 BCE or by Heliolithic builders from 1899 BCE to about 1650 BCE. Britain, not a part of the continent, boasts of one technolithic structure in that of Stonehenge I, an antediluvian chronolithic calendar. The interior of the island of Britain [ancient Albion] was little affected by the Flood disaster. There are about 60 underground cities each having numerous sublevels and precision-bored air shafts of technolithic design beneath the surface of Turkey. Hittite inscriptions and art on the first couple of levels reveals that they did not build these subterranean cities but had found them and only occupied the closest levels to the surface. One continent stands out as having technolithic archeological remains deep in its underground, spread across its surface and at the highest altitudes of its mountains…South America- in the opposite hemisphere from Giza.

Antiquarian James O'Kon coined the term "technolithic." Technolithic civilization employed scalar boring, quarrying, levitation and transportation of blocks. Homo Anunna employing cerebral-interface technologies were able to tunnel out and excavate whole underground cities, bases, connecting subterranean roads and accesses, ventilation shafts through thousands of feet of bedrock and raise laser-precision monuments comprised of millions of separate lithic components like the Great Pyramid of Giza. A chief accomplishment of this technolithic civilization was the use of synthetic stone for building materials, geopolymers in the Great Pyramid that had until recently not been discovered. Over 60 underground cities have been found in Turkey-Asia Minor and the corridors underground that connect them all are similar to those found EVERYWHERE beneath South America. Technolithic examples of architecture and vast areas of shaped rock show evidence of people PRACTICING with these technologies. The Phoenix transit and cataclysms of May 1687 BCE [see Phoenix Calendar posts] thoroughly broke apart the basement rock of the Andes mountains thrusting South American cities like Tiahuanacu over 12,000 feet above sea level…a city that just moments before the upheaval was a PORT. The books of David Hatcher Childress and others have greatly examined the historical findings of a vast network of underground tunnels in South America, precision cut and OLDER than the native populations who have no recollection of them.

There are NO technolithic architectural remains ANYWHERE in the lands of Sumer, Akkad, Babylonia,

Assyria, the whole of the Near East, the Levant, the entire Mediterranean and none to be found anywhere in continental Europe or Central Asia. The Great Pyramid of Giza is entirely technolithic, as is Puma Punka in Bolivia, South America and Stonehenge in southern Britain. There are hundreds of examples of post-Technolithic structures and practice molds found all over South America demonstrating that the technology had been passed on but not the technical skill to use it. 99.% of all the megalithic structures found around the world are Post-Technolithic [2647-2239 BCE] and Heliolithic [2239-1687 BCE]. Technolithic architecture dates strictly to the Contact Period [3439-2647 BCE], during the 792 years that Homo Anunna were present on Earth among homo sapiens. Technolithic architecture was devoid of stylized facing-all utilitarian 90 degree angles, very smooth planed surfaces, precise...austere. It was after the Flood that the descendants of Homo Anunna from before the Cataclysm, called now the Heliolithic Culture of the Old Bronze Age, the Shemsu Hor or Children of the Sun famous in antiquity, adorned EVERY facade of every structure with reliefs-artistic expressionism of humans long after the contact with Homo Anunna was broken.

The Great Pyramid was built by Homo Anunna from 2905-2815 BCE. No humans were involved. After it was completed, humans were trained and allowed to aid in constructing the Second Pyramid, which is connected by a causeway to the Sphinx, a Dog-Human hybrid representing the domestication of humankind that was later arbitrarily altered into a Heliolithic lion image. Men learned pyramid-building but the Second Pyramid and then the Third Pyramid are inferior constructions. Trained to use Anunnaki technology, humans were not nearly as skilled.

The Great Pyramid is truly unique of all pyramids. Not only was its 51.51 degree angle NEVER replicated, but its construction was precise and has never been matched; the epitome of technolithic engineering. Additionally, while hundreds of pyramids around the world all have subterranean tunnels leading to chambers, and some even to well shafts resembling the Great Pyramid, ONLY the Great Pyramid of Giza has ASCENDANT PASSAGES AND CHAMBERS AND A GRAND GALLERY AND STAR SHAFTS. No other pyramids in the entire world replicated these features because humans of the Post-Technolithic Period [2647-2239 BCE] and Heliolithic Period [2239-1687 BCE] did NOT KNOW about them. Homo Anunna sealed off access to the ascendant passages and chambers of the Great Pyramid by a cleverly concealed granite plug system disguised as a ceiling block like any other in the Descendant Passage. Humans crawled into the depths of the Subterranean Chamber during the Old and Late Bronze Age periods, the whole duration of Egyptian civilization, the entire length of the Roman Monarchy, the Republic and then the Empire and NEVER did mankind discover the hidden entrance until Al Mamoun tunneled into the Great Pyramid in 820 CE when his men accidentally shook loose the concealed ceiling block with all their hammering in another area 36 centuries after it was sealed.

The Second and Third Pyramids at Giza only have descending passages and chambers because they did not know that the Great Pyramid had been constructed with ascendant passages and chambers, a Grand Gallery and shafts. In this way Homo Anunna protected the secret of the interior of the Great Pyramid. Humans were deliberately involved in the construction projects of the

Second and Third Pyramids to safeguard this secret. This is why hundreds of pyramids found around the world in both the Old and New Worlds all have descending passages leading down to underground chambers or caves. Homo Anunna added the ultimate architectural piece of misdirection…the Sarcophagus. In the event that humans ever did find their way into the upper interior of the edifice, the Sarcophagus was placed to give them an explanation for the monument. A burial, though no body was ever interred. When DIRECTED what to believe humans would not SEARCH for the actual engineering function of the structure. That the monument served as some sort of facility that performed a specific function can not be doubted. Anyone who has seen the inside of the Grand Gallery with its precision-niches and overlapping wall surfaces can easily ascertain that something large moved up and down the gallery.

The rituals and ceremonies carried out blindly by the ancient Egyptians are not known today; Masonic degrees may or may not have derived from the older Mystery Schools. Masonry, if at all, preserves practices of antiquity only in pieces. What homo sapiens observed of Homo Anunna's activities was definitely not of esoteric doings. The precision, permanence and immensity of this 41-storey edifice called the Great Pyramid is evidence of an important function. The precision-aligned observation shafts infer that this function could only occur at a specific TIME OF YEAR. Meaning, whatever was occurring inside the pyramid happened only when the northern hemisphere was facing a certain region of the sky. Homo Anunna may have harnessed a technology allowing for the drawing, storing and transference of directed energy into orbit to power vessels, or, as so many believe today, the technology functioned as a teleport/transdimensional station only when Earth was in position. Perhaps the Kings and Queens Chambers were sending and receiving ports for interplanetary-dimensional materials...cargoes. There is evidence of high energy presence in the Kings Chamber. Sir Flinders Petrie's scientific analysis of the Kings Chamber found that the room of stone had been subject ot a violent internal disturbance that had shaken it so badly that the entire chamber had EXPANDED BY AN INCH. Engineer Christopher Dunn notes that this immense pressure ONLY affected the Kings Chamber.

The Pyramid Texts are thousands of verses combined into hundreds of utterances embossed or painted in hieroglyphic writing of ancient Egypt on the walls, passages and chambers of the pyramids of five Pharaohs- Unas, Teti, Pepi I, Merenra and Pepi II. The Pyramid Texts preserve the Great Lie of Homo Anunna. Sitchin wrote that the texts when taken together describe a journey to a realm that begins above ground [Giza Complex], that leads underground [Descendant Passage of pyramids] that ends with an opening to the skies through which the gods were launched heavenward. The Anunna geniuses had humans help them build the Second and Third Pyramids KNOWING their misinformation would be replicated. The secret of the existence of the Ascendant Passage and Kings Chamber was UNKNOWN TO ALL pyramid-building cultures...the FALSE pyramid with only a Descendant Passage was copied by all as civilizations exhausted themselves attempting to build a pyramid satisfactory enough to BRIDGE heaven and earth to induce the return of the gods [Anunna]. Sitchin notes that the Pyramid Texts hieroglyphic connotation combined the concept of a subterranean place with a celestial function. Humans were given a puzzle they were meant to figure out but were not given all of its components. These texts concern the operation of the Ladder to the Sky, a Stairway to Heaven, a concept that is repeated in the Book of the Dead, but the ideas of the Pyramid Texts were vague because the Egyptians themselves were preserving a concept for which they possessed no technical knowledge. Scholar J. H. Breasted wrote of the Pyramid Texts- "…they abound in pictures from the long-vanished world of which they were a reflection."

The placement of the Sphinx before the Second Pyramid, which appears to be of equal height but is actually standing on an elevated platform, the causeway connecting the Sphinx enclosure to the Second Pyramid and the layout of the entire Giza Complex is an elaborately planned DECEPTION designed to draw attention away from the Great Pyramid, to visually lessen its importance…to invoke the perception that it is but a part of the whole rather than the hidden truth…that it is the central secret of Anunnaki technology. For this reason the Sphinx requires a bit more of our attention.

One of my strongest passions concerns the Great Pyramid of Giza and I've spent a lot of my life and resources uncovering its secrets, which you can learn at merely a fraction of the cost I expended in purchasing the hundreds of books in my bibliography to acquire this knowledge. Check out *Lost Scriptures of Giza: Enoch and the Secret of the World's Oldest Texts.*

The largest statue to survive the Ancient World is the Sphinx at the Giza Complex in Egypt. It is 240 feet in length and 66 feet high, or 792 inches, paralleling the 792 year orbit of Nibiru that the Anunna use as a ferry for their travel to and from the inner solar system. This 792 years is also the duration of the preFlood Contact Period [3439-2647 BCE] of the Anunna from their arrival to departure. Strangely, this colossus has NO HISTORY. Egypt nor any other civilization has left us records on when the Sphinx was constructed or who built it. In fact, it was a persistent transcultural belief in antiquity that the Sphinx was the work of the gods themselves.

The Sphinx is not mentioned in any Old Kingdom texts. (1) Hancock and Bauval note that Selim Hassan in 1949 wrote that "...there is not a single ancient inscription which connects the Sphinx with Khafre." (2) Selim Hassan in 1926 led an expedition underground below the Giza plateau into a hall connecting the Sphinx to the Second Pyramid that was riddled with precision-cut shafts with depths up to 125 feet long and large chambers with huge niches. The main hall is flagstoned at 72 feet wide [864 inches] and 1476 feet in length, truly heroic underground dimensions, with gigantic blocks. shafts lead out and down hundreds of feet further to large sarcophagus-like crypts, one venerable sarcophagus made of polished white limestone. (3) In 1926 the Sphinx was excavated down to its foundation for the first time since the same excavations were conducted by Pharaoh Thutmose III in 1515 BCE using Israelite laborers 3440 years earlier.

The earliest surviving texts concerning term Hor-em-Akhet [Sphinx] date from the New Kingdom. (4) Jaromir Malik of Oxford University cited by Hancock and Bauval wrote, "Old Kingdom sources are strangely and surprisingly silent about the Great Sphinx of Giza." (5) The Egyptian New Kingdom began about 1650 BCE as civilizations around the world all together began stirring back to life after just having suffered through a 25 year Winter and famine that began in 1687 BCE with a planetary cataclysm caused by Phoenix [see Phoenix Calendar]. Hancock and Bauval, on the Sphinx, wrote- "They [Egyptians] did not mention it because they did not build it- but rather inherited it from a far earlier epoch." (6) A particularly old root [ack] attached to the Sphinx is found in the term Hor-em-Akhet in the New Kingdom references, the prototype of the ancient Egyptian AKER, or Guardian of the Way. Later the Greeks preserved this archaic root and belief in their Acheron, which was the Realm of the Dead. (7) This is the root preserved in the Enochian texts for the sacred site of Enoch, called Ach-uzan...the Giza monuments believed to cover over the Gate of the Deep.

As with the pyramids, information about the Sphinx is also heavily censored by the Establishment authorities. The excavations of the subterranean metropolis below the Sphinx and Great Pyramids of Giza conducted by Selim Hassan are not generally known. The findings get diplomatically buried. In 1978 ground-penetrating radar was used to map what was described as *"...an extraordinary subterranean complex beneath the Egyptian pyramids...a vast metropolis...reaching several layers beneath the Giza plateau."* (8) In 1991 seismic soundings of the bedrock beneath the Sphinx enclosure conducted by Dr. Thomas Dobecki revealed presence of a large rectangular room some 5 meters under the Sphinx. The discovery was made public in 1993 (9) and this was the first time people outside of academic insiders were ever made aware that underground discoveries were being made at Giza. In 1996 geophysicists detected presence of nine tunnels and chambers under the Sphinx at Giza, equipment readings detecting presence of metal in all of them. (10)

Before the Flood [2239 BCE] Egypt was founded by the Custodial Society [Homo Anunna/ Anunnaki] during the Contact Period I [3439-2647 BCE]. Its original, oldest monuments were all megalithic in scope and devoid of hieroglyphic writings or any art that would reveal their culture. At this time in history Alpha Draconis [preFlood pole star] and Sirius [Dog Star] were the most important stellar bodies, with not a hint of the existence of the Zodiac. The Dog-Sphinx was the symbol of the DOMESTICATION and BREEDING of the human race, mankind's cultivation by the Custodians and the responsibility laid upon humans to protect the Giza complex until their return. After the Flood the sun took preeminence in the cosmic theater with the collapse of the vapor canopy in 2239 BCE. Prior to this collapse cataclysm the sun had its light diffused. Condensation at night did not obscure the moon, but magnified it. Before the Deluge the cultures were goddess-worshipping and the moon crescent was the most prominent religious symbol. With the vapor canopy gone the sun was BRILLIANT [as we know it today] and the Heliolithic Maritime Culture of the Early Bronze Age began with new civilizations venerating the Sun as conqueror over the world and the Goddess. The antediluvian canine sculpture of Giza was altered into the heliolithic Lion and the Zodiac was created to subdue the stars in the Sun's passage. The preFlood stellar calendars were no longer viable and solar calendars were born. The archaic time-keeping methods of counting evenings to mornings [days] was altered and soon after the Flood many cultures began counting years instead. The Canine Sphinx was changed into the likeness of a Lion by Bronze Age Egyptians.

Robert Temple's observations on the Sphinx bear
mentioning. The statue animal does NOT resemble a lion:
the straight back, shape of the rear legs and tail are those of
a dog, not a feline. Lion's tails have tufts on their ends.
Further, the Sphinx has no mane. Temple is also of the
opinion that the Sphinx was originally fashioned in the
likeness of Anubis, the dog-headed deity. (11) The links
the Sphinx withy the Dog-Star, Sirius, and is probably
correct, for it is known that long ago the Queen's Chamber
shaft pointed directly at Sirius, and as late as 2000 years
ago the Jewish historian Josephus called Egypt the Land of
Siriad. Additionally, the lion was not early on regarded as
a guardian- such has ALWAYS been the role of the
domesticated canine. Temple quotes the learned
Egyptologist Wallis Budge- *"...in ancient times the
Egyptians paid the greatest reverence and honor to the
dog."* (12) The star Sirius is in the constellation Canis
Major [Great Dog].

The origin of our every day common domesticated dog is
truly a mystery. The genetic history of the domestic canine
is just as enigmatic as that of modern homo sapiens. It is
believed that the wild wolves were bred into a subspecies
by humans circa 3500 BCE [3435 BCE was descent of
Anunna/Watchers- see other posts]. But how? Domestic
canines are very different in hereditary characteristics.
Wolves molt, dogs do not. Wolves breed only once a year,
dogs can breed at will. Wolves have erect ears, dog's ears
droop or are flattened. (13) Wolves do not have the
upturned tails of dogs and wolves are much stronger,
having the jaw-crushing power of 1500 lbs. per square
inch. Yet despite these differences, geneticists know that
all domesticated breeds of dogs are genetic descendants of
wolves- not coyotes, jackals, hyenas or dingos. (14) This

genetic manipulation was NOT GRADUAL, but occurred suddenly, was abrupt- man's best friend appears to have been a gift.

In my researches published throughout my books and posts I have made note of the numerous parallels between ancient Greek traditions and those found in the early Americas. This tradition of the Aztecs is no less fascinating. Aztecs maintained a belief that the souls of the dead must pass over a river called Chicunoapa, or The Nine Rivers, where the deceased must pay a toll to a DOG. (15) The ancient Greeks too believed they dead had to cross the river Styx and pay a toll for safe passage. These ancestral beliefs concern fragmented memories of the Great Pyramid where the head of the Egyptian Nine Bows [Delta of the Nile] is where the Giza complex is located, where sits the proud Sphinx [Anubis Dog]. The Egyptians claim that Anubis was from the Old World and wrote annals before the Great Cataclysm. (16) The black-haired, black-eyed Amerindians share the same characteristics as the early Iberians and the river folk peoples who all maintains variants of this belief.

PostFlood Egypt was populated by the same kind of black-eyed, black-haired river folk that lived in the Urumbamba river of South America, the Indus of Pakistan/India, the "black-headed people" called Sumerians at the Tigris-Euphrates river valleys and the Chinese river valleys. It was in 1899 BCE, 340 years after the Cataclysm known as the Great Flood that sank Giza that civilizers arrived in Egypt just months after a series of earthquakes thrust the north African plate back into its antediluvian position. The Great Pyramid Complex drained, as did the surrounding land creating the Delta [Nine Bows: Goshen area] as the Mediterranean receded to its present boundary 108 miles north of Giza. The pyramids remained half-buried in silt, sand and shells for centuries. The civilizers came from the Near East, a ruling dynasty of Caucasians whose skeletal remains have been excavated and studied. PreDynastic tombs and burials reveal these colonizers to be of a much larger and very different race than the shorter, smaller, dark-featured indigenous peoples who learned from them. Egypt became just one of many colonies of the Heliolithic Maritime Empire, a civilization of Caucasian mariners who built Easter Island, Tiahunacu [NOT Puma Punka which was built by Homo Anunna 3439-2647 BCE], Cuzcu, Mohenjo-daro, the earliest Sumerian cities, Baalbek, the pyramid-city of Xian in China, the rock cities of Bashan in Syria and a host of other sites around the world before their own transoceanic empire collapsed in the 25-year Winter that began with the worldwide earthquakes and sun darkening of 1687 BCE when planet Phoenix transited initiating a planet wide destruction. The Heliolithic civilizers were patriarchal sun-venerators unlike the preFlood indigenous people of Earth who worshipped the Moon, goddesses and employed the use of stellar calendars, assigning animals and concepts to the regions of space the moon traversed at night.

After the Cataclysm of 2239 BCE the Heliolithic Caucasians who had prepared for the disasters were supreme and the collapse of the vapor canopy that had before diffused the sun's light during the day now had the sun shining brilliantly, blindingly, as we see it today. The zodiac was changed from a lunar system to a Sun-Ascendant system with now the SUN passing through the houses of the zodiac and conquering them. Alpha Draconis had fallen, the Eye of the Dragon and Sirius was forgotten. The Sun took the throne from the stars and the symbol for the Sun, the Lion, usurped all the significance of the antediluvian canine. The Egypt we know of from the history books was founded by these Heliolithic civilizers whose own home was flooded and destroyed. They arrived in fleets of reed ships just after 1899 BCE and settled northern Egypt which was just months earlier reclaimed from below the Mediterranean. These people immediately set out to excavating the Great Pyramid complex and it was they who altered the Dog-Sphinx to that of the Lion.

The silt-buried Giza pyramids, temples and Sphinx were thrust upward through hundreds of millions of tons of water to break the surface as the north African plate elevated back into its present position. The pyramids, protected in glass-smooth white limestone casing blocks only provide internal evidence of having been submerged in saltwater for a long period of time, pressure fractures and salt-encrusted walls and tunnels as if the trapped sea waters too centuries to evaporate through the shafts after the structures were raised out of the sea. The casing blocks that were later removed by Muslim engineers for building materials anciently protected the interior, softer limestone core blocks from weathering. The temples too had been protected by casing blocks or deeper burial but the softened limestone of the Sphinx was unprotected. The grooves on the Sphinx misinterpreted by so many as being from long-term rainfall were actually created in minutes as the soft rock was thrust upward rapidly out of the Mediterranean to again bake in the hot sun after 340 years undersea. It has long been a most unusual tradition from early Egypt that after a period of chaos and desolation, the god Ptah visited the world and dried away the waters to create land. This was only done in Lower Egypt [northern Egypt] which was then called The Raised Land. (17) Southern Egypt [Upper Egypt] was populated when this occurred and it is said that after raising the land to the north out of the waters the god Ptah then went to Upper Egypt and lived.

The mystery of the weathering on the Sphinx compared to the Great Pyramids is simply because during the preCataclym period before May of 2239 BCE when the vapor canopy was intact all of the Giza monuments were protected in smooth casing blocks EXCEPT the Sphinx, the Sphinx Temple and the Valley Temple. It is an established fact that these two temples, also unprotected, exhibit the SAME water erosion damage as the Sphinx. (18) this clearly reveals that they were constructed together.

Graham Hancock and Robert Bauval believe that this damage was precipitation-induced, a theory that advances the age of the Sphinx to thousands of years BEFORE the Contact Period [3439-2647 BCE], far back into the 10th millennium BCE. Their theory stretches the age of the Sphinx to an impossible date. Robert Schoch also advances this theory of long-period rain damage, none considering that the saltwater alluvium caused the damage to the Sphinx giving it its badly weathered appearance. The Sphinx gazes east but temple complexes erected in the Near East and ancient Americas in the 3rd millennium BCE are not aligned cardinally with later temples built from 1100-500 BCE demonstrating that the obliquity and motion of the Earth has not remained as it is now. Assigning the Sphinx an origin in the 10th millennium BCE means the statue was NOT meant to look eastward. Additionally, magnetite readings and a whole host of other evidence reveals that poleshifts have occurred much more recently than the 10th millennium BCE. The Sphinx gazes east along the 30th parallel, which means that Earth's motion has NOT changed fundamentally since its construction. This further establishes an origin for the Sphinx MUCH later than the 10th millennium BCE...some time after 3895 BCE.

Stick with me folks. We are far from finished concerning the pyramids and Sphinx. If you have a genuine interest in the secrets of the Great Pyramid complex at Giza and the Sphinx monument and want to learn fascinating information not found in any other books on the subject, read my book, *Lost Scriptures of Giza: Enoch and the Secrets of the World's Oldest Texts*.

15. The Great Pyramid's 4900 Year Old Secret

The calendrical significance of the Great Pyramid involves the cycles of Phoenix destructions, the subject of my books *When the Sun Darkens* and *Nostradamus and the Planets of Apocalypse*, as well as my prior post, Great Pyramid Holographic Blueprint of World Destructions. These knowledges were hidden. But there is an engineering function, some anciently powerful TECHNOLOGICAL purpose for the physical structure of the Great Pyramid that much misdirection was employed to conceal it. Let us look deeper into this layering of mysteries.

Upper Egypt was settled and developed AFTER the Flood [2239 BCE] at a time when EVERYTHING north of Abydos was underwater, beneath the Mediterranean and Red Sea which were conjoined. This is why the Red Sea mariner kingdoms of Magan had flourished- they

controlled traffic and trade from the Upper Sea to the
Lower Sea. The great quake of 1899 BCE uplifted the
north African plate and the seas were separated, dry land
appearing. Magan vanished in the days of Menes [Narmer]
who was a royal officer of Sumer named Anam [more posts
on Anam/Menes in future]. The Egyptian civilization from
2239 to 1899 BCE [340 years] was all preDynastic and all
situated in Upper Egypt [Southern Egypt], at Abydos,
Thebes, Karnak, Luxor, Hierakonpolis and Edfu. (1)

There are NO megalithic preDynastic architectural ruins in
all of Upper Egypt and most importantly, these earliest of
Egyptian settlements and ALL of Upper Egypt contains NO
PYRAMIDS. In all the reference works by Egyptologists
these deceitful scholars gloss conveniently over the fact
that ALL of Egypt's over 70 pyramids are 300 miles north
of the cities of Upper Egypt, all located in Lower Egypt at
Giza, Abu Roash, Saqqara, Dahshur and Hawara. The
textbooks describe pyramids "...as far south as Hawara," (2)
knowing the readers probably won't look at a map and see
that Hawara is in the NORTH far away from the Egyptian
cities of Upper Egypt. Hawara is 50 miles south of the
Great Pyramid and 290 miles northwest of Upper Egypt's
ancient cities. There is no ancient evidence from Thebes,
Luxor, Karnak or anywhere in Upper Egypt that they knew
of the Great Pyramid and Sphinx of Giza because ALL OF
LOWER EGYPT was underneath the Mediterranean when
Upper Egypt was settled. In fact, Will Hart in The Genesis
Race notes that the Egyptians NOWHERE left any records
of having built the Sphinx or Great Pyramid of Giza. (3)
The complete absence of records concerning the origin and
construction of pyramids in Egypt is what led Zechariah
Sitchin to conclude- "There is nothing left to contradict our
contention that these three pyramids were built by the

"gods." On the contrary: everything about them suggests that they were not conceived by men for men's use." (4)

Standard Establishment Egyptology books are packed with disinformation, and deliberately. Example- Gordan C. Baldwin's ridiculous statement in Pyramids of the New World on page 17- "Inside the Great Pyramid, as in other pyramids, there is a network of passageways and shaft and subterranean chambers, with a room called the Kings Chamber near the center of the pyramid." Everything in this statement is true about the Great Pyramid of Giza but the inclusion of "...as in other pyramids," is a deliberate lie. The Great Pyramid of Egypt is the ONLY pyramid in the entire world with an Ascendant Passage, Grand Gallery and Kings Chamber. The long, cramped Descending and Ascending Passages in the Great Pyramid were NOT made for men to traverse...they are too small. The moving through the structure is tedious, always stooped over and crawling. These passages performed some other function. Strabo described his entry into the interior of the Great Pyramid 21 centuries ago through the north face of the structure passing through a cleverly hidden hinged stone. He passed down the long Descending Passage to reach the Subterranean Chamber and well-pit in the bedrock. (5) Even as late as the 1st century BCE the Egyptians still knew nothing about the secret Ascendant Passage system, the Grand Gallery, Queens and Kings Chambers and shafts.

The three Giza pyramids contain hard Aswan granite quarried nearly 600 miles to the south. (6) Menkaure Pyramid, or Third Pyramid, the smallest of the three at Giza, was built using granite, not limestone like the other two Great Pyramids which only have this granite in their interiors. The granite blocks of Menkaure are of inferior masonry, a lack of skill, less precision. (7)   With a limestone quarry right across the Nile , why go to the trouble of quarrying, moving and dressing granite unless its dense crystalline structure was needed for a purpose?

Egyptian Chronology is contorted due to the obvious high antiquity of technolithic architecture. Claiming all artifacts as Egyptian, scholars erroneously stretch true Egyptian civilization 12 centuries backward into Homo Anunna's technolithic civilization [3439-2647 BCE]. Because scientific data demonstrates that the Giza Complex temples, Sphinx and Great Pyramids date to 2900-2800 BCE Egyptologists arbitrarily stretch Egypt's First Dynasty to circa 3100 BCE, also assigning lesser pyramids to impossible anachronistic dates, as with Zoser's Stepped Pyramid. Imagine scholars claiming that the Spanish culture of Central America dates back 12 centuries as proven by the presence of pyramids in the jungle ruins. As the Spanish language has fully spread throughout North, Central and South America, this contact was initiated not even 5.5 centuries ago. All over the world people have settled in previously-occupied lands containing old ruins erected by unrelated cultures. The Egyptologists claiming that all relics in north Africa being Egyptian or Libyan in origin is simply ridiculous. Academia is not bereft of morons.

Zoser's Step Pyramid was an improvisation of Imhotep, who built a mastaba and then constructed a succession of mastabas over it, one over another. Still, the structure is only slightly above 200 feet. (8) To the Establishment archeologist this is evidence that the Stepped Pyramid of Saqqara is older than the Giza pyramids, a formative period of learning how to build. However, this is actually proof

that by Zoser's time architects in Egypt did not have a clue
how to replicate the pyramids they saw. At Maidum
architects attempted to construct a 52 degree angle pyramid
slope like that of the Great Pyramid, but the structure
collapsed. At Dahshur the news of the collapse led
architects to correct their sloping angle to 43 degrees,
resulting in the famous Bent Pyramid. The third pyramid
attributed to Sneferu also at Dahshur, a 43.5 degrees, led to
the first classical pyramid. (9) Sneferu is dated at the 4th
Dynasty, which was NOT circa 2600 BCE as is so
popularly taught. Egyptologists have grafted standard
Egyptian history onto a much older nonEgyptian
civilization that dated before the Cataclysm of 2239 BCE
[Great Deluge]. The Great Pyramid complex at Giza was
built from 2905-2815 BCE and ALL other pyramids in
Egypt were constructed AFTER 1899 BCE when the quake
drained the Mediterranean off creating the Delta. The
appearance of Menes, a foreigner, and his rule was from
1898 to about 1875 BCE and this dating is demonstrating in
my Chronicon and will be proven in a later post concerning
the identity and history of Menes [Mena is Anam of
Sumer].

The Great Pyramid of Giza is the largest megalithic
structure in the world. A few other structures, also
pyramids, do have more mass, but they are NOT
constructions. These structures, in the Americas are filled
with rubble and the debris from earlier structures filled in.
Not true pyramids but more like mounds faced with stones.
To make the matter even more mysterious, the Great
Pyramid of Giza was not built on a planed flat foundation
of natural bedrock, but atop a small limestone mound

which bears most of its immense weight. Its lower courses were shaped onto this mound, allowing the gigantic artificial mountain to resonate with the natural energies and vibrations coursing through the bedrock. This mound is mentioned in the Edfu texts of Egypt concerning the Seven Sages- "...divine beings who knew how the temples were to be created...they who initiated construction work at the Great Primeval Mound." (10) The Edfu Building Texts preserved the only references to the Seven Sages from ancient Egypt, these being the same as the Seven Sages of the Sumerian texts who were admitted to be the Anunnaki. As shown numerous times in my book Anunnaki Homeworld, the orbit of Nibiru is exactly 792 years. The Contact Period before the Flood was 3439-2647 BCE, a total of 792 years that Homo Anunna were on Earth before most of them departed. This 792 years was the distance in time between two different orbital appearances of Nibiru. Perhaps coincidentally, or not, the same unit of measurement employed in the Great Pyramid was also used in designing the Sphinx. The Sphinx stands at 66 feet high, or 792 inches.

In 2239 BCE the entire valley system now submerged below the waters of the Mediterranean was flooded by the Atlantic Ocean when the land bridge at Gibraltar broke apart, this caused by subsidence of the entire North African plate. The Giza Complex with its pyramids and temples sank about 600 feet, 02 240 feet deep inland at far as Giza so that only the upper half of the two Great Pyramids could be seen above sea level. There was no Egyptian Delta or Nine Bows region. From 2239 to 1899 BCE, exactly 340 years, the pyramids were underwater and the coast of the newly created Mediterranean that had flooded hundreds of preFlood communities and stone cities [now located below

Mediterranean; many discovered] was during this time almost to Abydos where the Osireion lied. Because the cardinal orientation of the Great Pyramid's four sides with north, south, east and west is still accurate today in 2017 CE we conclude that there has not occurred any lithospheric displacement permanently altering the poles since this date. For 48.3 centuries the polar axis has been stable. Several times during this period the planet has moved erratically in temporary poleshifts, stabilizing back within hours. Even the duration of the solar year has changed from 360 days to 365.25.

In 1899 BCE the Giza Complex emerged out of the sea by quake to be found by men after it was submerged 340 years. In a strange parallel, in 1899 CE the enormous underground labyrinth and galleries under the Great Pyramid complex was rediscovered by Professor Emery. (11) Joseph Jochman wrote that when the pyramid was first entered there were salt encrustations an inch thick. Chemical analysis in modern times showed that some of this salt had a mineral content consistent with salt from the sea. (12) He also wrote that the medieval historian Biruni, writing in his treatise, The Chronology of Ancient Nations, noted, "...the traces of the water of the Deluge and effects of the waves are still visible on these pyramids half way up, above which the water did not rise." (13) Here we have a clearer picture of what occurred in 2239 BCE. The northern African plate was submerged and only people from SHIPS could see the Two Mountains so renowned in the traditions of the Old World. This also answers for us why so many archaic traditions concerning the Holy Mountain at the center of the world was once surrounded completely by water. Even half submerged for 340 years from the Deluge in 2239 BCE to the quake of 1899 BCE that drained the Delta into the Nine Bows we know today the two Great Pyramids would still have been about 240 feet above the water and IMPOSSIBLE to ascend. Only ships could near them and the 51.51 degree angled slopes of glass-smooth casing blocks were unclimbable.

Three Temples in Egypt Date From Before the Flood

Two of these temples are at Giza and the third is located at Abydos. For most of ancient Egyptian history, all three of these structures were buried. Entire dynasties passed without any Pharaoh being aware they were there. The Sphinx Temple and the Valley Temple are both at Giza and were both constructed from 200-ton stacked blocks that were every bit as much of an engineering feat as that of the Great Pyramids. All of the blocks are gigantic, the least of them weighing 50 tons. (14) The area was hewn, excavated out into a large horseshoe. The excavated rock around the Sphinx enclosure has been proven by geologists to be the 200-ton blocks of the Sphinx and Valley Temples, (15) thus, the area surrounding the mass of limestone that became the Sphinx IS THE QUARRY used to material the adjacent temples, proving, as Hancock and Bauval wrote in The Message of the Sphinx that the Sphinx, Valley Temple and Sphinx Temple were all BUILT AT THE SAME TIME. They write, "What we may be looking at here are the fingerprints of highly sophisticated and perhaps technological people capable of awe-inspiring architectural and engineering feats at a time when no civilization of any kind is supposed to have existed anywhere on Earth." (16)

The Temple of the Sphinx [the Granite Temple] was uncovered in 1853 CE for the first time by French archeologist Auguste Mariette. Scholars are convinced that its unusual cyclopean masonry and complete lack of hieroglyphs confirmed its immense antiquity. (17) Here, at Giza near the foot of the Great Pyramid was a mysterious structure that during the entire Age of the Pharaohs was UNDERGROUND and unknown to the Egyptians. The Egyptian Antiquities Authority officially began with viceroy Said Pasha's appointment of Frenchman August Mariette, to head the service. This Authority put to an end all unauthorized excavations. (18) This year, 1857 CE, began the academic and political campaign to search only for evidence of an Egyptian indigenous origin for the anomalies throughout Egypt rather than that of a much older nonEgyptian civilization. Egyptology is a science of censorship.

Temple of the Sphinx is devoid of hieroglyphs. (19) The Valley Temple next to the Sphinx has no inscriptions of any kind and the giant blocks are perfectly fitted together in a curious jigsaw pattern interlocking the blocks. (20) It is also called the Upper Temple at Giza, and contains colossal stones weighing 468 tons. (21) The Valley Temple has a precision-cut technolithic corner block fitted into the two walls, a most unusual architectural feature found in the later Heliolithic buildings at Machu Piccu in South American Peru, a corner block in the same position adjoining two megalithic walls. (22) The Valley Temple and Sphinx Temple attached by causeway to the Middle Pyramid of the three Great Pyramids is entirely MISDIRECTION. Homo Anunna in secret constructed the Great Pyramid with its interior ascendant corridors, gallery, chambers and shafts without mankind knowing of their existence. We will return to this in a moment.

In 1902 CE the buried megalithic temple complex called the Osireion was discovered by Sir Flinders Petrie and Margaret Alice Murray, its floor located 40 feet below ground level, a massive complex of red granite in a deep swamp. Its blocks were 60 tons and more, a temple 100 feet long and 60 feet wide, the enclosure wall being 20 feet thick. It has two casings, the outer of limestone roughly worked, the inner being of beautiful masonry of red quartzite sandstone with very fine joints...architecture similar only to two other megalithic constructions devoid of any Egyptian writing or artifacts- the Sphinx Temple and the Valley Temple- both at Giza. (23) The Osireion at Abydos is of unknown antiquity, officially, but it dates to the same period of construction at Giza. It is constructed of immense blocks of gigantic posts, blocks being 15 feet in length and its construction parallels that of the Sphinx Temple. (24) In 1912-1914 CE Naville also noted that the Osireion was similar to the Valley Temple at Giza. (25) He published data showing architectural similarities between the Osireion at Abydos and the Temple of the Sphinx at Giza. On some of the megalithic blocks was a thick knob, a feature noted by David Hatcher Childress to be found on the great stone blocks at Cuzco in South America. Childress wrote that the architecture of the Osireion "...is completely different from anything Egyptian." (26) Seti I of the 19th Dynasty built his own Temple of Osiris at Abydos right next to the much older and impressive Osireion structure, called the Tomb of Osiris by the ancient Egyptians who found the building. In his inscriptions, Seti I never claimed to have built the Osireion. (27)

The Giza Complex pyramids and temples and the Osireion at Abydos are devoid of Egyptian hieroglyphics because they date from 2900-2750 BCE when hieroglyphics DID NOT YET EXIST. There is no evidence nor proof of the existence of hieroglyphic writing in Egypt until AFTER 1899 BCE and this proto-hieroglyphic writing is remarkably similar to early Sumerian pictographic writing. All of the artifacts, like the Narmer Stele, assigned to 3100 BCE are done so arbitrarily simply because Egyptologists need to "create" a formative period when "Egyptians" had to learn pyramid and temple construction in order to convince themselves and the world that the monuments of high antiquity found in their country today are of "Egyptian" origin and not relics of a pre-Egyptian civilization.

The focus of the Giza site temples, causeways, lesser pyramids and Sphinx geometrically is clearly the Middle Pyramid, the second of the two Great Pyramids. So much misdirection was employed that even the subterranean levels reinforce the importance of the Middle Pyramid...which is of lesser height, though built upon a platform and is much shorter than the Great Pyramid. The Middle Pyramid has none of the refinement of the Great Pyramid, is of inferior construction and has no Ascendant Passages, no Grand Gallery, no Queens Chamber, no Ante-Chamber, No Kings Chamber, no upward shafts and is merely the most perfect "typecast" pyramid known to the ancients in both hemispheres...people who never once attempted to build a structure to mimic the Great Pyramid's unique upper features simply because they did NOT KNOWN ABOUT THEM. Campbell's shaft is a 15 ft. square pit that descends about 100 feet on the Giza plateau located between the Sphinx and the Second Pyramid. Again, deliberate deception intended to mislead later generations into believing the importance of the Second

Pyramid. The entire Giza Complex has a geometrical focus NOT on the Great Pyramid, but on the Second, inferior pyramid. The Great Pyramid is to the perimeter of the entire complex and given the impression that it is merely a part of the whole rather than the most important part. Clever misdirection. Men were NEVER intended to know of its true interior. Imagine...the greatest structure in all of Egypt, far away from the most ancient Egyptian metropolis cities, far from the Valley of the Kings...not built by Egyptians at all. Blasphemy they say. A desert full of dullards mistaking mirages for history.

Misdirection was employed inside the Great Pyramid as well. The Empty Sarcophagus in the Kings Chamber was a bit of genius, a successful tactic to induce its discoverers to conclude that the chamber was for burial, hence the monument was merely an elaborate sepulchre. Zechariah Sitchin has found some internal misdirection as well. The mysterious shaft connecting the lower end of the Grand Gallery to the lower end of the Descending Passage was an ORIGINAL part of the construction. Like the whole layout of the exterior of the Giza monuments, it was architectural misdirection. This well shaft is about 200 feet, twisting and turning in seven distinct segments. (28) Most of its length is a uniform 28" bore but for over 37 centuries its existence was unknown because of the ingenious ceiling blocks in the Descending Passage that concealed it. This shaft was not discovered until 820 CE when the Caliph of Baghdad, Al Mamoun, tunneled passed the newly discovered granite plugs of the Ascendant Passage to enter a Grand Gallery covered in fine white powder. (29) The Muslims found the shaft and lowered themselves all the way to the Descending Passage by busting through the hidden ceiling block from above. (ibid p. 205) Sitchin cites evidence that the shaft was bored DOWNWARD from the Grand Gallery and stopped and likewise it was bored UPWARD from the Descending Passage and also stopped short of connecting to the upper bore. The clever ceiling block was emplaced to hide the lower bore. The Great Pyramid was complete, the upper infrastructure concealed. But the upper and lower bored shafts terminated several feet from one another. Sitchin claims accurately that the unbored, rough and irregular section connecting the two bored shafts was tunneled through AFTER the pyramid was complete and the upper tunnels and chambers sealed off from the Descending Passage, hidden from discovery. (30) A wedge-like ramp stone originally concealed the upper shaft entrance in the Grand Gallery but the Arabs in 820 CE found only a gaping hole, the gallery covered in fine white dust. Sitchin cites references claiming that the ramp was blown outward by someone ascending through the bored shafts after they were connected.

Zechariah Sitchin's penchant for absolute genius and vision in reconstructing archaic puzzle pieces is again overshadowed by his profoundly stupid, insupportable position that the god Marduk was imprisoned inside the Great Pyramid and the concealed shafts were used and tunneled together to rescue him. Ridiculous. For these hidden shafts to have been a part of the original construction executed between 2905-2815 BCE then it was the ORIGINAL PLAN to enter the Ascending Passage, Grand Gallery, Queens and Kings Chambers IN SECRECY for the act of REMOVING MATERIALS after construction was complete...materials that were NOT present when the Muslims explored the upper interior of the Great Pyramid 37 centuries later...the FIRST humans to enter those passages and chambers since the unidentified materials were removed.

We are a long way off from understanding the function of the Great Pyramid, engineering beyons our present comprehension. Continued discoveries made public bear this out. In 1993 CE Rudolph Gantenbrink sent up a specially-invented robot up one of the mysterious shafts extending up through the courses of masonry from the Queens Chamber where the robot discovered a photographed a mysterious and virtually inaccessible tiny door with a copper handle. This sensational find dispels the view that the shafts were intended for viewing the stars or were air shafts. The door is closed and the shafts would required tiny mirrors because they do not open straight out nor extend to the exterior faces of the monument. The Gantenbrink discovery contributes to the fact that the Great Pyramid, the ONLY structure with such unique shafts, had a specific technolithic function, an engineering purpose. There is no telling how many discoveries like this have NOT been made public.

So what was removed? What could possibly be so important that decades were spent in designing and fabricating an edifice that would cover their tracks? Perhaps we know already and have not put all the pieces together. Let us return to the studies of Sitchin, a profound researcher and thinker who knew absolutely NOTHING about the Phoenix Object, its orbital period or purpose. Sitchin was a man who led us many times to a portal but never entered it himself.

Sumerian Traditions of the Great Pyramid of Giza

Sitchin relates that the Oriental religious beliefs of the early Central Asian steppe, from India to China, Japan, that at the Navel of the Earth was a mountain called Sumeru where gods of heaven and earth were, where the bond that connected heaven to earth was in the form of TWO PYRAMIDS, one inverted atop the other. (31) This is a memory of the Great Pyramid of Giza, that it is the ONLY monument with Ascendant and Descendant passages and chambers that internally resembled a pyramid inverted atop another pyramid.

In the ancient Sumerian tradition, the E.KUR at Nippur, was considered the Navel of the Earth. (32) At Nippur, at the center, stood a "Heavenward pillar reaching to the sky...as a platform that cannot be overturned," according to ancient Sumerian texts. (33) This was Giza, the Great Pyramid, the Pillar of Heaven, also Irem of the Columns, the Axis Mundi. From here Enlil would send his word out and "...abundance would pour down on Earth." (34) Sitchin believes it was a communication device to call spacecraft. Enlil's "lofty house," had a mysterious chamber called the DIR.GA. (35)

Sitchin was aware of the similarities between the Great Pyramid site and the preflood E.KUR temple of Enlil, he believing the E.KUR was merely Enlil's ziggurat in Nippur. (36)   This E.KUR housed the DUR.AN.KI, or Bond Between Heaven and Earth. (37)   Inside was located the DIR.GA, which contained a dark chamber possessing orbital data. (38) Sitchin also recognized that Sumerian texts described the E.KUR [House Which is Like a Mountain] as also being located "...in a distant place." (39) He admits a belief that the Anunnaki constructed the Great

Pyramids of Giza and even notes that scholars have been puzzled by reference of an E.KUR far away from Sumer. (40) But Sitchin errs in promoting that the Anunnaki had anything to do with Sumer or its own E.KUR [ziggurats] which were merely human constructions attempting to emulate earlier Anunnaki concepts from far away. Sitchin further makes the serious chronological mistake of claiming that the Giza artifacts were built after the Flood (41), a dating he asserts in contradiction to every ancient source of information on the subject. This dating is equally ludicrous as his belief that the Great Flood was about 11,000 BCE...87 centuries before almost every archaic writer claimed the Deluge occurred.

In Nippur the E.KUR stood "clad in awesome brilliance." (42) White limestone casing blocks on Great Pyramid. An enigmatic Sumerian poem reads, "E.KUR, House of the gods with pointed peak; for heaven-to-earth it is greatly equipped...men cannot understand it." (43) But can we? In prior posts I demonstrated the holographic nature of the Giza Complex, which extends to its traditions as well. Take this for example.   The E.KUR was located at the place of A.ZAG, the Great Serpent. (44)   Enki. Sitchin relates that many Sumerian words retain their meaning when read in reverse, like anagrams. A.ZAG thus becomes GAZ.A [Giza]. The DIR.GA was the most restricted chamber, where celestial charts and orbit data was kept...the Tablets of Destinies, according to Sitchin. It was located inside the Great Pyramid. Interestingly, as we view the Sumerian facts through the lens of reality's reflective holosphere we see that DIR.GA mirrors the English phrase A.GRID.

 In the story of ZU, he entered Enlil's sanctuary and stole the Tablets of Destinies, whereupon "...the hallowed inner chamber lost its brilliance...stillness spread...silence prevailed." Sitchin asserts that the Sumerian concept of "destinies" concerned PLANETARY ORBITS. (45)   He links the Tablet of Destinies with the "bond" between heaven and earth. Interestingly, the internal arrangements of the Great Pyramid form orbital periods for planet Phoenix, rectilinear distances in the architectural features all divisible by 138...reflecting the 138 year orbit of Phoenix, as I have PROVEN in Chronotecture: Lost Science of Prophetic Engineering. The Great Pyramid is indeed A GRID [DIRG.A], a holographic one that depicts two major planetary "destinies." Phoenix returns in May 2040 CE to begin a major depopulation of the earth by cataclysm, and Nibiru follows in November 2046 CE to finalize the depopulation protocol.

That Enki was identified here is not surprising as he is the later biblical Enoch. In the noncanonical texts Enoch was the builder of the Great Pyramid, the prophet against the Watchers and giants, the doomsayer over the Nephilim. He predicted the Great Flood and he is prominent in the traditions of the Phoenix. The Sumerian traditions concern a place BEFORE Sumer, far away. There are NO Technolithic [3439-2647 BCE] or Post-Technolithic [2647-2239 BCE] ruins anywhere in Sumer or Babylonia. The entire Near East contains only Heliolithic [2239-1687 BCE] architectural remains of the Old Bronze Age. The stories of the E.KUR, of A.ZAG and the cities of Nippur and Eridu [Irad of Genesis 5] are memories of a period BEFORE Sumer at a place distant from the region of Sumer-Babylonia. Proof of this is also found in the stories of Enki.

Another body of archaic Sumerian records holds that Enki designed a sacred temple structure called the EN.INNU, built by a ruler called Gudea. This structure is believed by scholars to have been a ziggurat, a type of pyramid, but the details concerning Enki and EN.INNU specifically relate to the Great Pyramid of Giza [A.ZAG]. The EN.INNU was a structure with its cornerstone embedded by Ningishzidda [the master builder], said to be kin to Enki. Ningishzidda was the Egyptian Tehuti, or Thoth...Enoch. (46) He was Lord of the Artifact of Life according to Sitchin. It was a temple...a Heaven-Earth mountain (47), its head reached heavenward, its brickwork was faced with bright stone of a certain thickness. (48) Sitchin notes that this was NOT a Sumerian architectural feature, but an Egyptian one. The Great Pyramid had 144,000 white limestone blocks, very bright, that weighed 20 tons each and were 100 inches thick. For this reason the Sumerian text reads- "Like a bright mass it stands, a radiant brightness of its facing covers everything, like a mountain which glows..." (49) The pyramid structure is associated to a goddess called Nisaba who possessed a stylus of Seven Numbers. Nisaba knew the secret of numbers [same thing said of Thoth and Enoch] and Sitchin compares Nisaba to the Egyptian goddess Sesheta, the goddess of construction and the calendar who wore a smooth-sided pyramid hat...a Sumerian goddess exhibiting an Egyptian-style pyramid. He also notes that the depiction of a god wearing a monument as a hat was also a Sumerian innovation. (50)

EN.INNU was the name of the sacred place before the Flood built by gods [Anunnaki] as told by the people of the Sumerian city of Lagash. But the people of Uruk [biblical Erech of Genesis] called it E.ANNU. It was also considered a ziggurat by the scholars unaware of its connection to the Giza structures. Sumerian temple traditions were fragments from an earlier period concerning the mystery surrounding the monument built ONLY by the "gods," the Great Pyramid of Egypt. Sitchin notes that E.ANNA was "the pure sanctuary," and that "...the gods themselves had fashioned its parts." (51) E.ANNA'S purpose was as the "House for Descending from Heaven." (52) The temple of Anu [heaven] was called E.ANNA [House of An], similar to On, a city named Annu in Egypt, later called Heliopolis. (53) It was this holy sanctuary before the Deluge at a place called Eridu that- "...no one uninvited can enter...in its sanctuary, from the Abzu, the Divine Formulas Enki had deposited." (54) The Tablets of Destinies, Divine Formulas...what was stored in the Great Pyramid was something of advanced scientific or technological value, something that was REMOVED deliberately by its designer.

Sitchin spent a prodigous amount of energy trying to create an antediluvian Sumer, a civilization of Sumerians before the Deluge who lived in cities in the Near East that they repopulated after the cataclysm. But he got so much wrong. There was a world before the Flood, there were cities, a thriving civilization long before Egypt existed...the Sumerians recorded fragments concerning a world that was not their own.

16. Great Pyramid Holographic Blueprint of World Destructions

The old history books from around the world contain many references to the Great Pyramid of Giza in Egypt like this

Arabic tradition preserved by Abou Balkhi once located in the Bodleian Library-

"The Wise Men previous to the Flood, foreseeing an impending judgement from heaven...built upon the tops of the mountains in Upper Egypt many pyramids of stone...two of these buildings exceeded the rest in height...so well put together that the joints were scarcely perceptible. Upon the exterior of the building every charm and wonder of physic was inscribed." (1)

2000 years ago Diodorus Siculus expressed his own amazement at the site of the Great Pyramid, which during his day still has the sheath of white gleaming limestone casing blocks before the Muslims stripped them off to rebuild Cairo-

"It is said that the stone was conveyed over a great distance...they [The Great Pyramids] do not have the appearance of being the slow handiwork of men but look like a sudden creation, as though they had been made by some god and set down bodily in the surrounding sand." (2)

My book, Lost Scriptures of Giza, is packed with scores of these obscure references to ancient secret knowledges written on the surfaces of the monument or hidden inside its recesses. The prevailing belief among our ancestors that the Great Pyramid possessed a secret vital to human survival is shown through Lost Scriptures, but what follows herein is NOT found in the book. I had to research for and write four more books before I learned the following material.

Before the Flood in the period from 2905-2647 BCE architects built fantastic massive structures by carving and boring into living rock, using blocks of immense size of natural hewn stone, sawn rock, quarried and excavations out of basement rock. But one superstructure was erected before the Deluge, totally unique, constructed of geopolymer manufacture, a discovery that would not be made for 48 centuries when humans were finally able to recognize this species of sophistication. After the Flood [2239 BCE] this knowledge of geopolymer manufacturing of synthetic stone was lost. Builders of the post-diluvian Heliolithic Period again produced megalithic masonry, natural boulders of great size cut into polygonal shapes- cyclopean constructions- in their efforts to 'earthquake-proof' their buildings. Initially after the Deluge stone was quarried for these projects but soon after the cataclysm some cultures began employing kiln-fired mud brick manufacturing in molds to provide their building materials.

The blocks of the Great Pyramid in Egypt are made of geopolymers; made through a process in which artificial stone is created that is virtually indistinguishable from natural rock. (3) The limestone casing blocks of the Giza structure contain opal, CT, hydroxy-apatite, a silico-aluminate not found in the quarries, blocks containing numerous trapped air bubbles. (4) Organic fibers having accidentally fallen into the mixture have been found in the stone blocks of the Great Pyramid. (5)

Sir Flinders Petrie found abundant evidence of a drilling and boring technology employed in the structure that was beyond his ability to understand- but a century later Christopher Dunn recognized that these builders used ultrasonic drilling with diamond-tipped bits. (6) Petrie's measurements are published in his book, The Pyramids and Temples of Gizeh. His measurements are accepted by

Egyptologists and especially by Zawi Hawass, head of Egypt's Antiquities Department. Hawass calls Petrie "The Father of Egyptology." (7) To fully appreciate the magnitude of my discovery of the Phoenix holography encoded in the Great Pyramid, a little history leading up to Petrie's analysis of Giza is in order.

In 1646 CE the monumental research of John Greaves was published, titled Pyramidographia, Or, A Description of the Pyramids of Egypt, in England. He was then made the Professor of Astronomy at Oxford. (8) This was the scientific world's first true examination of the Egyptian relics and Great Pyramids. Over two centuries later, in 1859 CE John Taylor completed his work, The Great Pyramid: Why Was It Built and Who Built It? The book was published and became a sensation in 1860, the first book to theorize that the Great Pyramid was of biblical import, that it was a prophetic calendar erected by the biblical patriarchs. Unfortunately his work was scoffed at by the Royal Society. (9) Because the structure was located near ancient Egypt they assumed it must be Egyptian. Taylor was the editor of the London Observer.

Inspired by John Taylor's work on the Great Pyramid mysteries, Astronomer Royale for Scotland, Charles Piazzi Smyth, travelled with his wife at his own expense to Egypt where he took careful measurements of the Great Pyramid in late 1864 and early 1865. During his study of the structure Smyth became convinced of the Great Pyramid's biblical import. His findings were published in 1880 in Our Inheritance in the Great Pyramid. At this same time Robert Menzies developed the theory of the Pyramid Inch and it's length representing a single year in world history, every measurement of the monument made in these pyramid inches. Smyth adopted this view, even producing evidence to support it, however, Taylor, Smyth, Menzies and those thereafter like Davidson all employed inaccurate chronologies of world history or inaccurate measurements of the Giza structure which caused the Pyramid Inch theory to fall into academic disfavor. In 1883 Richard Proctor, English astronomer, verified ancient claim of Proclus that earlier traditions referred to Great Pyramid's function as an astronomical observatory. (10) In 1900 Moses Cotsworth studied the Great Pyramid, finding that its shadow was a marker of time. From York he was a brilliant scholar interested in calendars who believed that the monuments of antiquity were astronomical in nature, devices for time-keeping, having also studied Avebury for the same reasons.(11)

David Davidson was an English engineer who sought to prove Robert Menzies wrong, that the Great Pyramid was not a prophetic calendar or historical timeline in stone. He extensively studied and measured the monument and completely changed his mind. His own mammoth book, The Great Pyramid: Its Divine Message, ended up supporting Menzies, Smyth and Taylor but added a wealth of new supporting evidence. By 1926 his book was famous. Adam Rutherford came next releasing his 4-volume work Pyramidology in 1957 CE that also added much more evidence of the pyramid calendar theory. All these men were correct in their theory but corrupt in their calculations. The most precise measurements ever made and scientifically accepted by academia and by Egyptologists alike are those of the meticulous analysis of Sir Flinders Petrie whose own instruments made measurements to a thousandths of an inch...and it is ONLY these measurements that exhibit PROOF of the Great Pyramid's rectilinear calendar of world history and the future. This is the subject matter of my research in Chronotecture: Lost Science of Prophetic Engineering.

The criticism these pioneers of pyramidology received has guaranteed that today's generation of popular pyramid researchers totally avoid the whole Pyramid Inch concept. Instead they advance the most ridiculous and insupportable theories and the publishing houses mass produce this idiocy. But what you are about to read is found in NONE of the modern or older books. ONLY Petrie's measurements are employed. That's not to say some authors have not come close. The following two writers have impressed me with their vision [I assure you my compliments are uneasily obtained] though it is obvious they grasp at a shadow from its periphery.

Graham Hancock and Robert Bauval in The Message of the Sphinx in Appendix 3 come very close to understanding the purpose of the Great Pyramid's holospheric function [not its engineering purpose]. They wrote that- "...the function of the Giza blueprint is to provide a virtually indestructible 'holographic' apparatus...'living' man is the result of a holographic union between matter and spirit. It would very much appear that the 'Followers of Horus' understood the cosmic mechanism to somehow re-separate the two...the construction of the amazing 'holographic' star/stone apparatus of Giza." (12) The Giza interior is definitely a blueprint, that it is linked to an interface with the holosphere we are immersed inside is true, that it serves a "cosmic mechanism" is correct...but Hancock and Bauval do not even know anything about the Phoenix chronology nor the internal measurements of the Great Pyramid "blueprint" that are scientifically accepted today. The following data is unknown to them, which only makes me appreciate their observations even more.

The earliest traditions of the Great Pyramid of Giza are not Egyptian and assert that it was designed to endure through a cataclysm...that to provide a basis of knowledge for a future generation was its purpose. Internal measurements scientifically conducted by Sir Flinders Petrie of the rectilinear subterranean passage widths, chamber heights, passage length in Descendant and Ascendant passages easily provides a uniform unit of measurement that was used by the constructors throughout the monument. These measurements were discovered over a century ago and were conducted to disprove the wildly popular Pyramid-Inch theories of the time. These measurements are scientifically acceptable today, absolutely precise, and they are arranged in rectilinear lengths of 138, 552, 1518, 1656, 2070, 3036, 4140 and 5796- EVERY single number is divisible by 138...the orbital period of planet Phoenix. Petrie knew NOTHING of Phoenix. These numbers as orbital lengths are proven in my books When the Sun Darkens and in Nostradamus and the Planets of Apocalypse. On this website go to Chronicon Files and read Chronotecture: Lost Science of Prophetic Engineering to see the actual illustrations showing these scientific measurements. Four meticulously illustrated charts of the interior of the Great Pyramid exhibit precisely multitudes of measurements all divisible by 138, all four found at end of the book. It's free to look at.

We must conclude that the builders of the Great Pyramid of Giza were aware of the Phoenix Object and this awareness allowed them to know when it would return over and over again. We also conclude that the world of the Sethites, of

Enoch and later Abraham, was not the primitive society we have been led to believe. The Great Flood of 2239 BCE did not catch them unaware, they prepared for it. These measurements PROVE the Phoenix Object will return to visit great destruction on our modern world in May 2040 CE...less than 23 years from now. You can be sure many more posts on the Great Pyramid and Phoenix are coming.

These numbers encoded again and again suggest a holographic nature of space-time structuring, that the builders or at least the chief architect was aware of the existence of our holosphere. The following material will demonstrate more evidence of this holographic aspect of the Great Pyramid.

2815 BCE Date of Great Pyramid Completion Imprinted in Holosphere

2905 BCE was the year 990 Annus Mundi, or Year of the World, the first year of Giza construction, 990 years after a poleshift created a new heavens (star canopy) and new earth (ocean basins dried as urban centers slipped under the seas). The patterns of today's constellations in the Zodiac do not fit their descriptions at all because the animals and concepts of the Zodiac houses are not of the stars now seen in those places. When the pole star fell the entire stellasphere moved out of place as well. This rearrangement of the heavens and earth was Year One, our 3895 BCE, or 1656 years before the Great Flood in 2239 BCE. Employing technolithic methods and technology Homo Anunna tunneled out several subterranean levels of galleries, corridors and chambers below the Giza plateau. The four cornerstones were laid first of the Great Pyramid and the distances between their corners, the sides of the monument, were 756 antediluvian feet, or 108x7. The 203 courses of blocks to its apex platform 481 feet above the plateau were set at a sloping angle of 51.51 degrees for a apothem (sloping distance) of 612 feet (7344 inches, or 108x68). The sum of 7344 is 2448x3, and 2448 is the ancient number for "cataclysm" in Egypt as well as the year, 2448 Annus Mundi which was 1447 BCE when plagues struck Egypt depopulating the country and the Israelite branch of the Amorites escaped into Canaan as the surviving Egyptians blamed the Semitic gods for the disasters. The Great Pyramid was completed in the year 2815 BCE, or 1080 Annus Mundi after 90 years of construction, being 1080 months of labor.

Edgar Cayce, known popularly as the Sleeping Prophet, is accused by many of being a medium, of witchcraft, God-touched, demon-possessed, a formerly illiterate simpleton whose mind is in touch with transdimensional beings that divulge to him secrets...whatever the case he has been right many times and wrong even more. Concerning the Great Pyramid mysteries he has been uncannily correct. Quoting Cayce in 1972, Lytle Robinson wrote, "The Great Pyramid of Gizeh is generally believed to have been constructed about 2900 BC." (1) Also, :...it was one hundred years in the building." (2) "The Great Pyramid is a record in stone of the history and development of man...to the end of the present earth cycle, in 1998. Its records are written in the language of mathematics, geometry and astronomy, as well as in the kinds of stone used...after the end of the cycle, there is to be another change in the earth's position, with the return of the Great Initiate for the culmination of the prophecies. All changes that have come and are to come are shown there in the passages from the base to the top.

Changes are signified by the layer of stone..." (3) Cayce's dating of the Great Pyramid at about 2900 BCE is precise, and about 100 years of construction is accurate too, the 90 years of building being 1080 months of work from 2905 to 2815 BCE. I demonstrate in my work, Chronotecture: Lost Science of Prophetic Engineering, that the monument is indeed a calendar of world history in its internal dimensions and a countdown of years involving the Last Days in its external features, each course of stone representing a year of time from 1902 to 2106 CE. Additionally, Cayce's notes the import of the year 1998 [666x3], which is exactly 108 years to the END of the Annus Mundi Calendar in 2106 CE. These dating systems are also detailed in my books When the Sun Darkens, Anunnaki Homeworld and Chronicon. Of course, we need not take Cayce's word alone for dating the monument. In 1984 CE a total of sixty-four samples taken from the Great Pyramid were radiocarbon dated to produce a consistent date of about 2900 BCE. In 1995 another 353 samples were taken and radiocarbon dated to again produce the result of about 2900 BCE. (4)

The three-dimensional geometry of a pyramid is of four lower corners and one high corner, or five points to make the solid pyramid. When the 3D form is rendered in one dimension, a flat plane, the five points form a pentagram. The pentagram, or five-pointed star, in ancient Sumer was the DIN.GIR, or the symbol not only for a "god," but also the AR.UB, denoting something that falls from the sky to break up the ground. The five-pointed star in geometry is made up of ten perfect 108 degree angles, comprising of the sum of 1080.

 John Mitchell wrote that 1080 was a unique number representing prophecy and intuition. In Greek the term "fountain of wisdom," has the gematrical value of 1080, as does "realm of the dead." [Tartaros] (5)   Mitchell wrote that 1080 was a lunar number opposite of its solar counterpart, 666. Though Mitchell did not know it, the completion of the Giza Complex in 1080 AM [2815 BCE] was exactly 666 years to the Great Flood cataclysm in the year 1656 AM/Hebrew Reckoning [2239 BCE] when according to the ancients the SUN WAS BORN, the Water Sun Age began with the collapse of the vapor canopy. Before this collapse of the marine firmament the whole earth was like a greenhouse and the entire sky was lit up but with no round sun visible.

In the archaic Vedic beliefs of the Aryan people of India there existed a holy place at the center of the earth constructed of 10,800 bricks containing the knowledges of the past, present histories and sciences and the future. It was the Altar of Agni [Fire deity: pyramid word contains root for FIRE]. In my book Lost Scriptures of Giza I show proofs that the Great Pyramid was considered by the ancients to be a gigantic altar. In the Vedic traditions the Altar of Agni was drowned in the sea. The oldest of all Sanskrit texts is the Rig Veda, it is divided in to ten books containing 10,800 stanzas, or 1080 stanzas each. (6)   So many interesting coincidences. In 2239 BCE the Giza Complex and entire northern coastlands of Africa plunged beneath the newly formed Mediterranean Sea and remained underwater for 340 years till 1899 BCE when another quake uplifted the region, draining it off to create the ONLY Delta in the world emptying a river that runs from south to north making the Great Pyramid to be located 108 miles to the newly formed Mediterranean coast. That the

Giza site is associated to cataclysm is all of its traditions is widely acknowledged. Of further coincidence is that Heraclitus taught that the world is destroyed every 10,800 years. (7) He was an Ionian scholar of Ephesus about 503 BCE, nicknamed The Obscure, for the difficulty of his writings. Heraclitus opposed polytheism and idolatry, declaring there to be One Eternal Reality and he believed that the Self in man was a part of the Divine Intelligence. He is quoted as saying to the men of Ephesus- "Your knowledge of many things does not give you wisdom." (8)

What are we to make of so many parallels? Egyptian Heliopolitan-influenced Coffin Texts preserve the fact of the presence of something of extreme importance beneath the Great Pyramid plateau according to Andrew Collins. (9) Amazingly, the Coffin Texts preserve this secret as Spell 1080-

"This is the sealed thing, which is in darkness...put in Rostau. It has been hidden since it fell from Him, and it is what came down from Him onto the desert of sand..." (10)

Collins believes that Spell 1080 parallels a portion of the Book of Enoch (11). The famous Egyptologist Wallis E. Budge wrote that the Egyptians who copied older hieroglyphic texts often did not understand what they were transcribing. Spell 1080 is a mistake of translation which in its original form meant YEAR 1080. It was the year 1080 Annus Mundi [2815 BCE] that the Great Pyramid [the Sealed Thing] was finished by the gods [nonEgyptians]. Rostau was a gate-land of the Dead one travelled to get ot the next life. Later Arab traditions are little different than the Aryan and Egyptian memories.

Arabic pre-Islamic tradition holds that there is a Preserved Tablet from of old, a writing of stone dating from the Beginning of Time that contains all the histories, knowledges and prophecies. The Angel of Death is there with 1080 eyes searching continually through the records making sure no one dies before their time. (12)

Thousands of books in passed three hundred years have sought to show that the Great Pyramid contains the mysteries of Earth, the Moon and planets, the sun, orbital data, distances, velocities. People conceive of concepts they ordinarily can not prove, yet the evidence is ever there. At the Earth's equator, the rotation of the planet is moving at 1080 mph. (13)   Further, because of the distance and velocity of the Moon and Earth's own rotation, the lunar umbra, the Moon's shadow of total darkness during an eclipse, travels across the face of the earth at a mean average of 1080 mph. Also 1080 pixels is the highest resolution the human eye can perceive, anything advertising more or better clarity is just marketing. Concerning pixels, one of the most controversial photographs ever taken was satillite photo 70A13 taken of the Mars' surface that depicts the famous sphinxlike face in the Cydonia region, a monument staring upward into the sky positioned close to the unique pentahedral pyramid known as the D & M Pyramid. Perhaps coincidentally this amazing photograph happened to have been taken when the satellite camera was exactly 1080 miles away.

The search for synchronicity will never end. We exist submerged in a flowing hologram governed by initiatives and protocols that serve to keep humanity ignorant, enslaved and depopulated. Our existence is the desert and all perceptions are mirage. The coding for apocalypse was preserved in stone inside the dimensions of the Great Pyramid. All of the Phoenix data is found therein. We are pawns in someone else's game, made to believe in fictions to keep our minds away from facts.

17. The Great Flood...Ancient & Modern Science on the Phoenix Cataclysm

In 2007 I believed my research on the Phoenix Calendar was concluded, that I had mined the records of history and found everything possible to discover on this fascinating and harrowing subject. My book, *When the Sun Darkens: Orbital History and 2040 AD Return of Planet Phoenix* was published by Book Tree in San Diego in 2009. Like all humans I am subject to many illusions and like all men I fall prey to them as well. No sooner had the work been released than eleven different books written about Nostradamus come to my attention. I then found reference-after-reference to more Phoenix-date disasters and soon had so much new data on Phoenix visitations that I wrote another book, *Nostradamus and the Planets of Apocalypse*, released in 2012.

But reality again threw me a curve. Book Tree published my Nostradamus book, which contained a lot of new Phoenix material not in *When the Sun Darkens.* And again I thought I was done. As soon as the second work was released I came into contact with the 75-year old writings of Harold T. Wilkins. Reading his two books took the air out of my tires. I was elated to be validated by correct information put together on my part but distressed that such important Phoenix-related facts were not included in my own books. What he wrote will be disclosed in this post.

Concerning the 1687 BCE disasters remembered in ancient Greece as the Ogygian Flood, in *When the Sun Darkens* I provided a solidly dated reference from The Book of Jasher. Twice in the Old Testament the biblical records directly cite The Book of Jasher. In my own work, Lost Scriptures of Giza, I explain how this book has survived in only a few copies while others have tried to nullify it by the deliberate act of publishing forgeries. In the Jasher text we find that in the year Dinah was raped by the men of Shechem, her brothers, the Israelite sons of Jacob, gathered for war against the Canaanites. This event is dated by biblical chronologist and author Stephen Jones who knows nothing about planet Phoenix or its orbital chronology. Jones used Jasher, Genesis and the Jubilees text to date the following event at precisely 1687 BCE: "And when Jacob ceased praying to the Lord the earth shook from its place, and the sun darkened, and all these kings were terrified and a great consternation seized them. And the Lord hearkened to the prayer of Jacob, and the Lord impressed the hearts of all the kings and their hosts with the terror and awe of the sons of Jacob..." (1) Not only did biblical chronologist Stephen Jones in his book *The Secrets of Time* accurately date this sun darkening of Phoenix in 1687 BCE, but he also dated in perfectly as 2208 Annus Mundi, the calendar of the Old World which the Hebrew Chronology was originally designed from before it was corrupted by rabbinical redactions. It can not be said enough- Jones knows nothing of the Phoenix object nor its orbital chronology. He simply adhered to biblical and extracanonical writings. Does the Israelite sun darkening episode sound familiar? The Phoenix darkening aided the

Israelites just as the darkening of the sun in 1135 BCE
aided their Danaan descendants in the invasion of archaic
Ireland against the Firbolgs.

In *When the Sun Darkens* and *Nostradamus and the Planets
of Apocalypse* we are confronted with the appearance in
2239 BCE of a gigantic intruder planet passing close to
earth and darkening the sun, major continental earthquakes,
oceans swelling over landmasses, islands disappearing,
whole cities and civilizations erased and the terrible fact
that this worldwide destruction occurred again in 1687
BCE. These conclusions are based off of modern and old
chronological studies that are independent from the source
materials used by Harold T. Wilkins in his own books
released in the 1940s.

Wilkins' penetrating research in to ancient American
traditions and texts has him specifically connect the ruin of
Eastern Island to the Ogygian Flood of 1687 BCE. He
wrote- "The whole island shook... mountainous waves of a
ocean infuriated and maddened by some tremendous force
swept right over the tall cliffs and crashed onto the feet of
the colossal images. The light of day went out. The night
of total eclipse had come. A heavy black pall covered the
vault of the heavens. Strange rains of blood-red water and
white ash...cascaded onto the causeways...the terrified
slaves in the quarry workshops threw down their tools..."
(2) Wilkins wrote this having no knowledge of the Phoenix
history or chronology and yet accurately connected the
timing of Easter Island's ruin in the Southern Hemisphere
with that of the destruction that transpired at the Ogygian
Flood in the Northern Hemisphere. He further wrote that
"...a black cloud seemed suddenly to cover the face of the
sun. It spread very rapidly to the horizon. The ground

heaved violently in tremendous tremors that lasted many minutes..." (3) He wrote that whole country sides that had never seen the sea were drowned as sky flames descended to set ablaze great primeval forests. The earth "...behaving very much like a planet that has been forced out of her orbit..." The light of the sun vanished to return as a ball of blood. The penumbra darkened all the air, as in time of eclipse. "Then an immense cloud of reddish powder filled the air...followed by a rain of fine cinders..." (4) The object approached the earth- "...it shown with a brilliant light reflected from the sun, falling on a thick coating of ice- the glaciosphere. This split and fell on the earth, exposing a layer of red earth, which in turn, fell on the earth like a rain of blood." (5)

Citing information provided by Diodorus Siculus of Carthage who wrote over 2000 years ago, Wilkins wrote- "...some cosmic body...approached our own planet, the earth, after the sun had vanished behind vast clouds into a night of blackness, and brought on an appalling cataclysm- the Great Deluge of the Old World myths and Genesis..." (6) "...the light of the sun appeared to have gone out...for many days, indeed, night and day could hardly be told apart...the sun hung like a ball of blood, but the penumbra soon darkened all the air, as in time of eclipse...when the pall of smoke had partly cleared, two moons rode in the sky..." (7)

Wilkins in his 1947 work titled *Mysteries of Ancient South America* documents the many parallels between the Great Flood of 2239 BCE and the later Ogygian Flood disaster of 1687 BCE- similarities in the historical record and traditions that he ventures to propose that these two traditionally separated events may have been the same cataclysm. He is wrong, they being 552 years apart. But Wilkins knew nothing of planet Phoenix and still his penetrating insight understood that these catastrophes were brought upon our world by the same intruder planet mechanism. He wrote- *"When the Great Deluge of Noah and Ogyges happened...convulsions of the shuddering earth and sea stretched right around our globe from the Pacific across South America to the shores of Africa...right into the Mediterranean, till they shook the Old Levant and a more ancient Greece. In the skies of terrible night shown a giant comet, or wandering star, or planet...but which brought such destruction on the earth that those who survived the disasters regained sanity only slowly, and in some cases, never."* (8)

Since reading Wilkins' work I have continued my studies and found an abundance of Phoenix-related discoveries not included in my published books.

...Ancient & Modern Science

The prestigious periodical British Archeaology in 1997 in the article titled Comets and Disasters in the Bronze Age reads- "At some time around 2300 BC, give or take a century...a large number of the major civilizations of this world collapsed simultaneously it seems. The Akkadian empire in Mesopotamia, the Old Kingdom in Egypt, the Early Bronze Age civilization in Israel, Anatolia and Greece, as well as the Indus Valley civilization in India, the Hilmand civilization of Afghanistan, and the Hongshan culture of China-the first urban civilizations in the world-all fell into ruin at more or less the same time. (1) This article lists the reasons as abrupt climate change, sudden sea level changes, catastrophic inundations, widespread seismic activity and evidence for massive volcanic activity. (2) G. Ernest Wright wrote that the Early Bronze Age destruction was so violent "...that scarcely a vestige survived." (3) The scientific estimate of approximately 2300 BCE +/-100 years is a bulls'eye for the well-documented Deluge date of 2239 BCE. This major cataclysm and its dating is the conclusion of investigators who did not rely on old books, chronologies and traditions, but excavated their evidences and and successfully extrapolated whole pictures from mere pieces. We can easily match their conclusion with our own.

The thorough and impressive author, Frank Joseph, one of my personal favorites, in his *The Destruction of Atlantis*, cites several traditions claiming that at the Great Flood the sun was darkened. (4)   But one such text escaped him. This is our cherished Book of Jasher (not to be confused with its forgeries). The text of Jasher perfectly preserves a Phoenix fragment though the author of the book did not know it, nor did biblical chronologist Stephen Jones who in his book *The Secrets of Time* accurately dated this passage as describing events that occurred in the year 2239 BCE- "The Lord caused the whole earth to shake, and the sun darkened, and the foundations of the world raged, and the whole earth was moved violently, and the lightning flashed, and the thunder roared, and all the fountains in the earth were broken up, such as was not known to the inhabitants before; and God did this mighty act , in order to terrify the sons of men, that there might not be more evil upon the earth...and at the end of seven days...the waters of the Flood were upon the earth." (5)   This extrabiblical text is cited twice in the Old Testament as a credible source and it relates that this 2239 BCE destruction was worldwide. The scientist has his own independent conclusion supported by an old Rabbinical text copied from more ancient sources formerly based off oral traditions but accurately dated by a chronologist using source materials unknown to the scientist.

Over a century ago Ignatius Donnelly wrote, "The world might relapse into barbarism...but the memory of the cataclysm in which the center of a universal empire instantaneously went down to death would never be forgotten; it would survive in fragments, more or less complete, in every land on earth; it would outlive the memory of a thousand lesser convulsions of nature; it would survive dynasties, nations, creeds and languages; it would never be forgotten while man continued to inhabit the face of the globe." (*Atlantis: The Antediluvian World* p. 324) He is correct, for there are more than 500 documented flood myths belonging to over 250 peoples. (6)

An Egyptian priest-historian 26 centuries ago told a Greek statesman, Athenian Solon, at Sais in Egypt these words concerning the Old World- "When the gods purge the earth with a deluge of water, the survivors in your country are herdsman and shepherds who dwell on the mountains. But those who, like you, live in cities are carried by the rivers into the sea...just when you and other nations are beginning to be provided with letters and the other prerequisites of civilized life, after the usual interval, the stream from heaven, like a pestilence, comes pouring down and leaves only those of you who are destitute of letters and education, and so you have to begin all over again like children and know nothing of what happened in ancient times...you remember a single deluge only, but there were many previous ones...you and your whole city are descended from a small seed or remnant of them which survived. And this was unknown to you, because, for many generations, the survivors of the destruction died, leaving no written word." (7)

Over 2000 years ago the libraries of Alexandria, Pergamum and Carthage possessed far more records about Phoenix and past catastrophes than we have available to us today, no doubt many copied from older Egyptian temple libraries. The surviving writings of two special men demonstrate this truth. Pliny the Elder was a prolific writer and reader. His epic work Natural History is still internationally esteemed and published today, his source materials including 147 Roman writers and 327 foreign authors. A bibliography of 471 different writings was astounding in those times. He was known to write down excerpts from all the books he studied. Pliny's penetrating study of history led him to conclude that throughout the span of human history there has transpired "...ominous and long drawn-out eclipses of the sun," and that "their cause was hidden by the rarity of their occurrence, and for this reason they are not understood." Pliny added that these strange darkenings of the sun were by natural but unknown causes and that they occurred at fixed times. (8) Doesn't this sound a lot like the Egyptian priest's description- "...after the usual interval..." The educated idiots of our universities swear Pliny was simply writing about regular eclipses, just as they say the same about Thales in 583 BCE. But as with Thales they stay silent about the fact that Pliny wrote quite a lot about regular eclipses and definitely knew the difference. Eclipses in Pliny's day were well understood.

Just a few decades before Pliny lived the erudite poet-philosopher, Lucretius. His work is preserved in a 7400 line poem titled On the Nature of the Universe still published widely today. Lucretius is most famous for his theory that the entire universe is composed of infinitely tiny atoms, a position now widely accepted. He wrote that the history of the world was one of earthquakes that caused entire cities with their citizens to sink to the bottom of the seas, and that the Great Flood that destroyed whole races of men was only one cataclysm in the cycle of quakes. (9) But Lucretius' most incredible statement is that some unknown body, not the moon, passes over the surface of the sun and darkens the earth at a fixed time. (10)

Arnobius, a Christian apologist in Sicca of Africa in the 4th century CE, in his First Book, wrote, *"...ransack the records of history written in various languages, and you will find that all countries have often been desolated and deprived of their inhabitants. Every kind of crop is consumed, and devoured by locusts and by mice: go through your own annals and you will be taught by these plagues how often former ages were visited by them, and how often they were brought to the wretchedness of poverty. Cities shaken by powerful earthquakes totter to their destruction: what! Did not bygone days witness cities with their populations engulfed by huge rents of the earth?"* (11) This is a remarkable passage because Arnobius infers here that even after all the book burnings at Carthage, Pontus, Asia Minor, Alexandria, Gaul and Rome, by his day in the 4th century CE there were still enough historical accounts preserved for him to make this statement.

I conclude by citing a passage in my own book, *When the Sun Darkens*- "That the future was never meant to be known is a modern fiction perpetuated by those who don't know it. Knowledge filters have been cast over the truth by our greatest institutions of learning, and history has been concealed by those invested with the responsibility to reveal it. Our learned predecessor Pliny lamented this condition when he remarked that nothing is being added to the sum of knowledge as the result of original research and that today's researchers ignore the findings of those who preceded them." (12)

Stick with me, dear reader. You'll find that I ignore nothing.

Phoenix Returns in 23 Years...in the Month of May 2040

My books on the Phoenix and posts demonstrate that the object Phoenix darkened the sun, caused earthquakes and in two instances caused global cataclysms in its transit across the ecliptic between the earth and the sun in the years 2239, 1687, 1135 and 583 BCE. The chart above is one of those published in *When the Sun Darkens*, which explains that these four transit episodes are the origin of the Vedic and Greek Four Ages belief system and the ancient American concept of the Four Suns of traditional chronology. These four dates and the recorded events that transpired reveal to us today the Phoenix Cycle of 552 years, being four orbits of Phoenix at 138 years each. These orbital histories maintain a mathematical precision far superior to what is today considered scientifically acceptible, and the following facts demonstrate just how incredible these histories are:

a.   Thousands of libraries throughout history with millions of texts have been accidently or deliberately   destroyed and we no longer have these accounts. This is evidence from fact that Thales, Aristarchus, Anaxagoras, Lucretius, Pliny and others provided information about Phoenix they had gathered from the books of their time;

b.   Many witnesses throughout antiquity were either illiterate or their writings were transmitted on perishable media (paper, leaves, bone, bark, wood tablets, parchment, skins, etc.);

c.   Inclement weather, thick overcast or even daylight would have prevented anyone from seeing and recording the transit of Phoenix, or for that matter, any astronomical body;

d.   Many appearances of Phoenix, comets or astroids that would ordinarily affect Earth in a direct transit go unnoticed because these celestial objects pass over the ecliptic on the other side of the sun or too far to be seen from Earth position;

e.   We know that Phoenix is responsible for the violent death of millions of people, maybe even hundreds of millions and many of those who perished, had they lived, would have left us records of what happened. That we still have so many records is amazing.

When the Sun Darkens is the first (and still the ONLY) published book about planet Phoenix, being entirely original research. The book's chapters cover information found nowhere else: Existence of Planet Phoenix...Age of the Phoenix and Cycle of Cataclysm...A Planet of Two Calendars...Phoenix Cycles Demonstrated...Cursed Earth Periods...Modern Cursed Earth Periods...Orbital

Chronology of Planet Phoenix...Secret Calendar of the Great Seal of the United States of America...2040 AD Return of Planet Phoenix...The Joshua Comet Group...Vials of Phoenix Comet Group...Appendix A: Effect of 2040 AD Phoenix Transit...B. Legends and Myths of the Sun Darkening...C. When the Sun Stood Still.

So much information about the Phoenix phenomenon has survived that is analyzing all the data in When the Sun Darkens I was able to affirmatively conclude-

> Every 138 years planet Phoenix passes through the inner solar system between Earth and the sun on a north-to-south trajectory;

> The 138 year orbit was known to the ancients and transmitted to us through legends and old texts;

> As 138 years is 1656 months and the PreFlood World's history was 1656 years from start to ruin at the Great Flood, there seems to be some   intelligent design involved in this cycle;

> The Phoenix orbits pinpoint 3895 BCE as Year One of Ancient World's calendar;

> The Cursed Earth system is predicated upon fact that three Phoenix orbits of 138 years each is 414 years;

> The Phoenix Cycle is predicated upon fact that four orbits of Phoenix at 138 years each is 552 years;

> The Age of the Phoenix in antiquity was from 2239 to 583 BCE, known in the New World as the Four Suns Ages;

> When Phoenix directly transits between Earth and the sun, the solar orb darkens and the moon appears red as blood;

> Planet Phoenix is surfaced with a glaciosphere of frozen red earth, mud and dust that constantly fractures off when in proximity of Sol sending immense dust clouds careening toward Earth, detritus, astroid trains;

> Planet Phoenix is currently realigning for a direct transit between Earth and Sol, first noticed by Hoffman in May of 1764 and confirmed when 138 years later in 1902 Earth was blanketed in red mud and dust;

> Planet Phoenix will return in May 2040 and is the subject matter of the prophecy concerning the sun darkening and moon turning to blood in the Apocalypse texts of the biblical record-especially the Sixth Seal judgement...global catastrophe.

As my readers know, When the Sun Darkens merely opened a floodgate in my understanding of Phoenix. New discoveries and data are covered in the sequel, Nostradamus and the Planets of Apocalypse. As of this writing, May of 2040 is only twenty-three years from today. This is a disturbing notion, that the Revelation text, which we know was heavily borrowed from the older Sybilline prophecies of the Ionians, remarks that the following will kill 25% of all humanity-

And I beheld when he had opened the Sixth Seal, and lo, there was a great earthquake; and the sun became black as sackcloth of hair, and the moon became as blood [Phoenix transit]. And the stars of heaven fell unto the earth...and the heavens departed as a scroll when it is rolled together, and every mountain and island were moved out of their places.

Revelation 6:12-14

If you think 23 years is a long time, what were you doing 23 years ago in 1994? Further, the prophetic text of Revelation is very clear that the Sixth Seal cataclysm that kills a fourth of humanity is at the END of a Seven Seals judgements period or war, starvation, disease and death. Its going to get real bad before 2040. Perhaps 23 years from now the Phoenix will be welcomed...

18. Mysteries of Easter Island and the Flood of Ogyges 1687 BCE

Today Easter Island is thousands of miles away from any civilization, yet on this small island are megalithic structures and statues of weight and size too large for engineers today to quarry and move in to position. Hundreds of books have explained these megalithic enigmas, and they will be explored in more detail later. This post concerns astronomical-calendrical knowledge preserved by those who erected these statues. Easter Island met the same fate as Tiahuanacu in Bolivia, and at the same time. This devastating end to the Heliolithic Maritime Empire was by transit of planet Phoenix in 1687 BCE. As will be shown in other posts, Tiahuanacu and Easter Island were constructed by the same people, using the same building techniques.

Easter Island in the southern Pacific is a small island packed with mysteries. Historian Harold T. Wilkins notes that the island's peculiar megalithic statues numbered about 550 relics, with only one statue being of a female and another is of gargantuan dimensions still lying in the quarry. Some of the masterwork statues exhibit "...the wrinkled lip and sneer of cold command," while others have a merciful, or contemplative look. (1) Wilkins asks- "Who were these strange people who left the amazing number of 550 colossal images in Easter Island?" (2) It is my own theory that I will set out to prove in these posts that the archaic architects were following a grand design to complete 600 of these statues, each sculpture representing a solar year of the Heliolithic period marking an older calendar system known during the antediluvian time as a Great Year. Each of these gigantic 551 statues identified a year from 2239 BCE cataclysm which itself occurred at the conclusion of a major 600 year period before the Deluge, to the year 1639 BCE, which would have ended another Great Year of 600 years, called the NER in Sumer, a system employed by the Anunnaki. But something unanticipated happened in 1687 BCE that halted all work on the island. The gigantic statue still lying in situ in the quarry was for the 600th year, a calendrical monument, but their labor was cut short by 48 years by the sudden appearance of Phoenix in 1687 BCE and the global chaos it wrought in the month of May.

Wilkins' penetrating research in to ancient American traditions and texts has him specifically connect the ruin of Eastern Island to the Ogygian Flood of 1687 BCE. He wrote- "The whole island shook... mountainous waves of a ocean infuriated and maddened by some tremendous force swept right over the tall cliffs and crashed onto the feet of the colossal images. The light of day went out. The night of total eclipse had come. A heavy black pall covered the vault of the heavens. Strange rains of blood-red water and white ash...cascaded onto the causeways...the terrified slaves in the quarry workshops threw down their tools..." (3) Wilkins wrote this having no knowledge of the Phoenix history or chronology and yet accurately connected the timing of Easter Island's ruin in the Southern Hemisphere with that of the destruction that transpired at the Ogygian Flood in the Northern Hemisphere. He further wrote that "...a black cloud seemed suddenly to cover the face of the sun. It spread very rapidly to the horizon. The ground heaved violently in tremendous tremors that lasted many minutes..." (4)

The volcanic crater known as Ranu Raraku on Easter Island serving as a natural amphitheater is the most peculiar site on the island. Seven chairs are hewn out of natural rock and the rim of the crater has 193 statues complete and another 83 unfinished deliberately placed. (5) Again we see the calendrical significance, for the rim being a circle embodies the concept of the cycle. The unfinished statues only reveal that the work was interrupted, but the total number of statues on the rim is 276...or two Phoenix orbits of 138 years each, or half a Phoenix Cycle of 552 years. The majority of these statues are at least 40 feet tall and weighing 200 to 300 tons so their significance was indeed weighty with their architects. The Great Deluge cataclysm in 2239 BCE was 552 years before the Phoenix catastrophes of 1687 BCE, which was 552 years before the return of Phoenix to ruin kingdoms in 1135 BCE which in turn was 552 years before Phoenix darkened the sun again in 583 BCE as predicted by Thales of Miletus. The seven chairs may symbolize the Seven Kings of the Anunnaki, the Seven Sages, or ancient preflood Builder Gods.

The Heliolithic civilizations of the Indus Valley, Tiahuanacu, Easter Island and others of the Early Bronze Age are thoroughly studied in the 551-page book by historian W.J. Perry called *Children of the Sun* published in

1923. Perry provides a wealth of information on Archaic Period cultures and their ruling dynasties who referred to themselves as Children of the Sun, a trans-oceanic people who founded megalithic colonies all around the world. Perry knew nothing about planet Phoenix nor the Phoenix chronology, made no connection in his work to any Phoenix-related traditions, yet he documented that all around the world suddenly the Archaic Civilization collapsed ending in warring states and violence "...about 1688 BC." (6) From this year on the rulers ceased referring to themselves as Children of the Sun. Perry does not know why, he merely records the fact. It is my contention that those dynastic rulers lost their faith in the sun's power when it was darkened by Phoenix. Perry concluded by writing- *"The destruction of the Archaic Civilization revealed fresh potentialities in man; mother-right gave way to father-right, military aristocracies came into being, war gods emerged, and the world began to take on a shape that we all recognize."* (7)

We are not finished with Easter Island's mysteries. Much more will be disclosed. My message is so profound I cannot afford to lose any readers in a myriad of details. Easter Island's connections to Tiahuanacu in South America and Mohenjo Daro in the Indus Valley of Pakistan-India as well as other very old Heliolithic sites will be detailed in coming posts. The destruction of Easter Island's archaic civilization in the southern hemisphere occurred at the same time the Phoenix wasted the northern hemisphere as well, which was remembered in the Old World of the Mediterranean as we will now examine. The disaster was recorded in the annals of antiquity as the Ogygian Flood of 1687 BCE.

The vast global destruction of 1687 BCE that ended the
Heliolithic Maritime Empire that built Easter Island is
further explored in *When the Sun Darkens* and
Nostradamus and the Planets of Apocalypse.

The Flood of Ogyges

Plato's writings in Timaeus admit that the oldest Greek
memories of their historical period date back to the reign of
Phoroneus, when occurred the Ogygian Flood. Pausanius
wrote that Ogyges was king of Boeotia, of Attica. (1)   He
is credited with founding Eleusis, reigning there as king
when his own lands were flooded. The megalithic remains
scattered throughout old Boeotia mark his preflood domain.
(2) His origin is a mystery still, Aeschylus writing long ago
that Ogyges was from Thebes in Egypt. (3) This may be
true, for Velikovsky is convinced that Ogyges is a
rendering of the Amalekite king Agag, a Hyksos ruler over
Egypt. Agag was a title for the ruler of the Amalekites as
found in the biblical records when an Amelakite king called
Agag was killed by Solomon about the 10th century BCE.

In the chronological records of Marcus Varro as
conveyed by Augustine the land of Argos in southern
Greece was ruled by Phoroneus, son of Inachus of
Mycenaea. Ancient writers claim that this was the time of
the Ogygian Flood. This disaster afflicted the region that
would later be known as the Peloponnese. Citing Varro's
Of the Race of the Roman People we read, *"There occurred
a remarkable celestial portent; for Castor reports that, in
the brilliant star Venus, called Vesperugo by Plautus, and
the lovely Hesperus by Homer, there occurred a strange
prodigy, that it changed its color, size, form, course, which*

never happened before nor since. Adrastus of Cyzicus, and Dion of Naples, famous mathematicians, said that this occurred in the reign of Ogyges." (4) The planet we call Venus today was not originally known by this name, which is actually an etymological relic of the word phoenix [ph-enus]. The planet Venus never altered its course, nor changed colors or grew in size. What appeared was Phoenix which approached earth and was anciently mistaken for Venus either by witnesses or those writing about this event much later. Proof this was Phoenix and not Venus is found in that the Flood of Ogyges was accompanied by a great darkness. (5)

The confusion between Phoenix and Venus may have been due to the fact that Phoenix transits between earth and the sun in the region of Venus's orbital belt, passing the ecliptic on a north-to-south trajectory. The Venus confusion was commented on by Frank Joseph in his *Survivors of Atlantis* where he writes that this disaster happened in the 9th year of reign of King Amaziduga of the Hittites, when the king describes in a stone tablet a great celestial body he called NINSIANNA that other researchers pass off as Venus. (6) Joseph goes further in citing the conclusions of scientists who met in 1997 representing the fields of archeology, archeoastronomy, geology, paleobotany, climatology, astrophysics and oceanography who reported that the ancient world suffered a series of cataclysmic impacts and disasters in or about the year 1628 BCE. (7) This dating derived from tree ring samples of California's very old bristlecone pines, from sea deposits and ice core samples. (8) While relative dating methods do not impress me due to the assumptions that must be borne in accepting them, it must be recalled that the 1687 BCE cataclysm began 25 years of darkness, an ash-filled atmosphere and decades-long winter. This leaves us with 1662-1661 BCE before plants and trees made full recovery and the science of dendrochronology can aid our dating. Considering that this was 3679 years ago from today, the 1628 BCE dating of the scientists is close enough, only 34 year variance [1662-34=1628 BCE].

Harold T. Wilkins in the 1940s wrote concerning the Ogygian Flood- "...*some great stellar body of a lost or dead world...which approached our sun on a parabolic, or hyperbolic course...having caused a grave catastrophe on earth, vanished...*" (9) "*The wandering planet streamed into our earth's skies...tremendous earthquakes shook the ground. The blazing sky turned to night- a rain with terrible lightning flashes and a rain of vast meteorites upon the stricken earth...aloft, the planet Venus seemed hourly changing her color, course and size. Our earth was receding into space backwards from her old orbit, nearer the sun.*" (10) Wilkins is careful to attribute the destruction to an unknown celestial body and not to Venus.

Archbishop James Ussher in his *Annals of the World* dated the Ogygian Flood in the year 2208 Annus Mundi, which is precise. Ussher's attempts to date events using the BC calendar erred greatly but it is amazing to find that Ussher had access to old records that accurately dated this cataclysm in the year 2208 of the Old World's calendar, which is exactly 1687 BCE. In fact, 2208 is four Phoenix Cycles of 552 years each, demonstrating that Year One of the Annus Mundi Calendar (3895 BCE) marked a year when Phoenix transited passing through the inner solar system.

Ogyges arrived during the reign of Phoroneus the Argive, son of Inachus, grandson of Oceanus and Tethys, progenitors of the Pelasgians, or Men of the Sea. (11) Inachus was the Greek rendering of Anak, son of Arba of Argos, giants mentioned by name in the Old Testament record. Julius Africanus wrote, *"After Ogygus, by reason of the vast destruction caused by the flood, the present land of Attica remained without a king up to Cecrops, a period of 189 years."* (12) These traditions seem to paint a picture of the arrival of a fleet led by someone remembered later as Ogyges who landed in southern Greece after both his own homeland flooded as well as Greece. Further fragments seem to bear this out.

Plutarch in Morals wrote that Ogygia was an island about five days sail west of Britain. (13) We know that only Ireland lies that close to Britain. It was in ancient Ireland where the traditions of Tir Nan Og were more prevalent. The Ogygian island was a secluded place from antediluvian times, (14) this being from a historical time anterior to this 1687 BCE flood. Ogyges is claimed to have been a son of Neptune (Poseidon, god of the Sea), related to the Titans. (15) But this merely identifies Ogyges as one who arrived from the sea. The ancient pre-Greek population seems to have remembered a cataclysm that devastated the far west, for they were informed of it by the newcomers from Ogygia. This Ogygia was an island of Calypso according to Homer who composed his epics about 800-750 BCE. (16) Destroyed in the upheaval, the island's name serves as the root word in apo(calypse).

For a long time many believed that the enigmatic dolmans and rings of ancient Stonehenge was an eclipse-predictor of some kind. Sir Norman Lockyer, the father of archeoastronomy, visited Salisbury plain in Wiltshire and studied Stonehenge extensively. His remarkable conclusion was that Stonehenge was built at about 1680 BCE. (17) He was mistaken. Stonehenge II was toppled in the 1687 BCE quakes and Stonehenge III was erected, with changes from the original preflood plan. Still, his dating is astute. A connection between Ogygia in the far west of Greece and Stonehenge in ancient Briton (Albion) is unknown, however, Ireland is nearby and it was Ireland that according to early writers was called Ogygia. Ireland was also the island the Danaan invaded in 1135 BCE when Phoenix darkened the sun.

Our study of 1687 BCE is far from concluded. The worldwide catastrophe is further detailed in my works *When the Sun Darkens* and *Nostradamus and the Planets of Apocalypse.*

19. From Thales of Greece to the Olmecs of Ancient America...Phoenix Disasters

The education of the masses is a business; the commerce of Establishment historians is censorship. Morally bankrupt, the authorities govern over what materials they deem the many worthy to know. Your own college professors don't know history because they were not taught it. Knowledge filters are passed off as facts and our teachers are unwittingly perpetuating this vast censorship by teaching a fixed syllabus of historic events that are largely untrue, edited or sanitized beyond any semblance with reality.

My name is Jason and I have dedicated my life, resources and time to educating those who will dare to pierce the veil, to venture outside their comfort zones and know truths others will never attain. In this series of blogs I will educate you on the history, identity and future significance of an celestial object that terrified the ancients remembered as the Phoenix.   I have already had two book-length studies published about the Phoenix phenomenon, titled *When the Sun Darkens* (2009) and *Nostradamus and the Planets of Apocalypse* (2013). That you do not already know this material is proof that you are a victim of Establishment censorship. We shall begin this startling study with a man who travelled the world 24 centuries ago.

Herodotus of Halicarnassus, renowned as the Father of History, wrote an enormous book filled with facts about the ancient world. He wrote that after five years of war between the nations of Lydia and Media their armies met again on the field of battle when something unexpected and unusual occurred. Just as the two hosts were about to clash the sun darkened causing both sides to give pause, Herodotus writing that "...day was suddenly turned to night." (1) He mentioned three times that the sun darkened and not once referred to the moon nor a regular eclipse in this passage. However, elsewhere in the Histories he clearly relates that an eclipse occurred in 481 BCE as Xerxes of Persia marched toward Greece prior to the Battle of Salamais.

The sun darkening during the Medo-Lydian battle in 583 BCE according to historian Vandenberg in The Mystery of the Oracles (2) occurred in the month of May; May is also the dating mentioned in the massive The Encyclopedia of World Facts and Dates (3). Solar and lunar eclipses continued to terrify the Greeks for centuries. In 413 BCE the Athenians delayed an assault to an unexpected omen, a regular eclipse (4). Another unanticipated eclipse transpired in 357 BCE (5). In the whole of Greek and Roman history not one eclipse of the sun by the moon was ever predicted with any accuracy or recorded for prosperity.

Thales dared to claim that earthquakes and the deep rumblings of the earth were not caused by the god Poseidon, but were instead natural phenomena. (6) Despite this fact our scholars today will try to convince you that Thales merely predicted a regular eclipse, conveniently omitting any reference to the fact that Thales went on record predicting a darkening of the sun two years before it happened, and that the annals show that he predicted the year not the day. Thales predicted an unusual event, not an eclipse. The sum of Thales' knowledge was carefully preserved through his students but posterity has never received from Thales any science of eclipse prediction. This knowledge would never have been lost.

The much vilified Immanuel Velikovsky mentioned the discovery at Yazilikaya of a monumental relief depicting two ancient kings concluding peace while grasping between them an eclipsed sun. (Ages in Chaos.) Yazilikaya in Turkish means inscribed rock. (7) The monument correctly reveals that something darkened the sun in 583 BCE. A vast object transited between the earth and the sun occulting the solar light and the obvious assumption would be that it was the moon. But no eclipse occurred in May 583 BCE over Lydia by any model of computation.

Thales began the Ionic school of philosophy, his intellectual pupils and their students in order being famous men- Anaximander, Anaximenes, Anaxagoras, Diogenes, Archelaus and Socrates who gave us our Atlantis account.

(8) Thales lived from 640-546 BCE and is believed to be the first of the Greeks to travel to Egypt to receive formal scientific instruction. Thales was accounted as one of the Seven Wise Men of Greece, believed to be the originator of algebra and he taught that the stars were solids, knowing that the moon's light was borrowed from the sun by reflection. Thales was aware that earth was a sphere that cut off sunlight on the surface of the moon to create an eclipse. (9) He was the teacher of the famous philosopher-mathematician Pythagoras. (10) Thales' genius was demonstrated when in Egypt he calculated the height of the Great Pyramid by calculating the ratio between his own shadow and the shadow cast by the enormous monument.

Concerning the integrity of Herodotus' writings, Frederick Schlegel wrote, "The deeper and more comprehensive the researches of the moderns have been, the more their regard for Herodotus has increased." And Buckle wrote, "The more he is understood, the more accurate he is found to be."

King Alyattes was the father of the world famous Lydian king, Croesus, and it was during his reign according to Pliny the Elder that Thales predicted the darkening of the sun, in 585 BCE, in the 4th year of the 48th Olympiad, two years before it occurred (11)   Pliny's book was published widely over 19 centuries ago.

With the rich heritage of Israelite-Amorite migrations filling the cities of Asia Minor for over seven centuries basically being the backbone of Ionian culture it is not surprising to find that Herodotus claimed that Thales himself was "...a Phoenician by remote descent." Ionians, Milesians, Phoenicians, Israelites and Amorites were all of the same ethnic stock, no different than Canadians are from the English or colonial Americans. In fact, the Ionic name Anax prefixing many names of people 25 centuries ago was derived from the older prestige of the family of Anak considered to be a race of giants compared to other peoples, known as the Anakim in the Old Testament records. The undisputed authority of Greek antiquities, Robert Graves, wrote that the ancient Greek memories of Anax are those of the biblical Israelite traditions of Anak. The associations between Ionian-Greek culture and the older Israelite-Amorite civilization will be more evident as these blogs continue because the biblical record and the traditions of the Bronze Age Mediterranean world agree on many points concerning the existence of the Phoenix phenomenon and unusualness of these darkenings of the sun. Thales was little different than any biblical Israelite. He believed in the soul's immortality and he completely rejected the Homeric and Hesiod cosmologies borrowed from the east. (12)

Thales was a scientist having records from the Old World concerning Phoenix destructions and the cyclic pattern of its visitations. Concerning the shocking history and existence of planet Phoenix, censorship ends here.

From Thales to the Dead Sea Scrolls

Having put forth the chronological proofs that the same object appeared in the inner solar system and caused global disasters in 2239, 1687, 1135 and 583 BCE, and also showing that all four of these episodes were precisely 552 years apart occurring only in the month of May, it is necessary to demonstrate that this object did not vanish into obscurity. The Phoenix that so terrifed the ancients by 31 BCE was already relegated to a ridiculous memory of a giant space bird that darkened the sun by immersing in to it. The Phoenix was a celestial bird that resurrected, a theory of the ancients invented to account for the fact that the Phoenix was said to die when it darkened the solar orb and then come back alive after it moved away from the sun as the solar light returned in the day sky.

It is obvious from the historical accounts found in my two books, *When the Sun Darkens* and *Nostradamus and the Planets of Apocalypse*, the two earlier visitations were catastrophic on a global scale while the two later ones in 1135 and 583 seem to be hemispheric events lesser in scale. The Phoenix object is falling out of synch, the transit times not aligning perfectly as they did of old. But the Phoenix still returns on the exact years of its orbital cycle. Counting 552 years after 583 BCE when Thales predicted the darkening of the sun caused by Phoenix was 31 BCE. So the natural question any critic should have is- What evidence can you show that Phoenix appeared in this year? The answer: quite a bit. Let the reader be the judge.

In May 31 BCE the naval and ground forces of Octavian of Rome were locked in combat with the armies of the Roman Marc Antony and his lover Cleopatra of Egypt in the Battle of Actium in what was a major Roman civil war. It was during the naval conflict of the Battle of Actium off the coast of Greece that a sudden earthquake instantly killed 10,000 people in the Aegean but injuries that festered and disease in the days that followed resulted in 30,000 fatalities. (1) The earthquake was also destructive in Judaea where Archbishop James Ussher wrote that it was said by writers of the time that it was the most devastating quake in the history of Jerusalem. (2) That Jerusalem and

Judaea were severely affected links us directly to a Phoenix culprit. The following is astonishing.

The Dead Sea Scrolls were written a few decades before 31 BCE, copied from more ancient documents. The scholar Gaster relates that the scrolls belonged to a people who were expecting the end of a Great Year, and great cycle of the ages when terrible upheavals occur. The very learned Acharya S. in her book The Christ Conspiracy refers to this cycle they were waiting on as the Phoenix Cycle. (3) The Dead Sea Scrolls were abandoned and buried by the earthquake and not found until 1947. Clearly by this time in Judaea the Phoenix calendar was lost but a general sense of timing was partially preserved. Of interest is the fact that Acharya S. offers no evidence that she was aware of the existence of planet Phoenix or its particularly destructive cycle of 552 years in antiquity. The academic opinion as put forth in Canaanite Myth and Hebrew Epic is that the Dead Sea Scrolls were preserved because the buildings of the Qumrum settlement collapsed upon them by an earthquake. (4)

That the Essenes of the Dead Sea community had an incompletely preserved tradition of the Phoenix by 31 BCE is also what we discovered with Pliny and Lucretius as previously posted. Remember, Lucretius was alive at this time and he wrote that some unknown body, other than the moon, darkens the earth at a fixed time. (5) Also just shortly after this period in the first century CE Pliny the Elder wrote the world suffers mysterious long, drawn-out eclipses of the sun and that their cause was hidden by the rarity of their occurrence. (6) It is surprising that these two fragments were allowed to survive through the countless book burnings and censorship of the Roman Church that plunged the western world into the Dark Ages. Equally surprising was the survival of Cassius Dio's account of the strange rain that afflicted Egypt at this exact time (dated 31-30 BCE) that was mixed with blood. There were odd flashes in the skies seen even through the clouds as this red rain bathed the land. It was followed by what was described as a red dragon of incredible size accompanied by comets. (7) As any reader of my books knows, Phoenix was often described as a dragon devouring the sun and it many times resulted in red dust, mud or rain storms.

Greece, Judaea and Egypt are concentrated close together in one hemisphere so we are very fortunate to have found these next two pieces of evidence from ancient America. Scholars of Central American antiquities believe that the Olmecs, called more modernly the proto-Maya, disappeared into obscurity, depopulations, caused by disasters that ended the Late Olmec III Period.

Archeologists excavated a relic monument known as Stela C in the ruins of Tres Zapotes in the Yucatan, a calendar in stone with the final year recorded by the Olmecs as being 31 BCE. (8) This date, 31 BCE, is the official end of the Olmec civilization as recorded is history books everywhere.

The Yucatan is in North America, but further north in Drip Rock, Kentucky an odd petroglyph was discovered in March of 1994. It was studied by Harvard professor Barry Fell who determined that the charactors were ancient Libyan of North Africa. This is not really incredible as Roman and older Carthaginian and Phoenician artifacts and writing have been found at many locations in North America. What is astounding is that Fell concluded that the Drip Rock petroglyph concerned an historic eclipse. (9) As an expert epigrapher, actually one of the world's leading epigraphers, Fell determined that the Libyan script was over 2000 years old, which would place this sun darkening event recorded by Libyan sailors far from home as being around the 31 BCE date. This is not proof, but interesting evidence. Someone from the Old World was in the New World when an event occurred monumentous enough for him to sit down and carve it on a rock. Would that be a normal eclipse?

This sums up my 31 BCE evidence of continued visits by Phoenix into the inner solar system, but I am not through with the subject. You have a lot more coming.

I conclude with a quote from a smarter man than I-

A careful analysis of the historical facts shows that the scholars of ancient times had a great deal more accurate information available to them than most historians have judged and the scientific traditions preceding them were of a much higher level. (10)

20. How Jesus Stole the Phoenix

In today's commercial society we are made to believe all sorts of things that are untrue. Eighteen centuries ago the social engineers of ancient Rome were no less designing and deceitful than those now operating in corporate America, our government agencies and the media. They know that in the creation of mass deception there is a fundamental that must be adhered to in order to be an effective deceiver- the fiction must be introduced along with a series of facts.

Absorbing whole ethnic groups, foreign populations, their languages, creeds and beliefs, the government of Rome had become too overspread, plagued by civil unrest. Though the political structure faltered and collapsed, Roman religious authorities did not fail to perceive a common thread of belief among all of the diverse groups throughout their empire's vast provincial domains.

In deepest Africa to the battlefields of the Germans and from Gaul and the kingdoms of the Celts in western Europe to the civilizations of the Near East and abroad, all mankind knew of and feared the Phoenix. Many are the ancient chroniclers who left us records of the Phoenix. Some claimed that it was a great round object in the heavens that drew close to the sun, darkening it, while others referred to it as a huge red star or fiery sword. When the Phoenix appeared it always brought earthquakes and the moon turned blood red. In fact, the Greek antiquarian Robert Graves in his *The Greek Myths* translates Phoenix as meaning blood red.

It was this history of Phoenix disasters that the early Christian mythographers used to link fact with fiction. By the emergence of earliest Christianity the knowledge of the orbit, the timing of Phoenix appearances, was lost. The terrible disasters that all occurred 552 years apart from the Great Flood in 2239 BCE, the Ogygian Flood of 1687 BCE and 25 year darkness and starvation that killed the Old Bronze Age civilizations, the disasters of 1135 BCE and Phoenix transit of 583 BCE were remembered in a variety of ways though by 31 BCE when Phoenix passed again causing major earthquakes in Greece and Judea the knowledge of its periodicity was lost.

Over 140 years after the story of Jesus was alleged to have occurred, the account received an added dimension claiming that the Phoenix appeared in the form of the darkening of the sun and an earthquake at the death of Jesus. By introducing an element of fiction on a background of fact the Church stole the Phoenix to authenticate their religious design.

By the majority of Christian authorities Jesus was crucified in 33 CE. The earliest documents belonging to Christianity make no mention of the darkening of the sun or earthquake, however, in 180 CE the four gospels texts suddenly appeared- Matthew, Mark, Luke and John. Prior to the appearance of these accounts no Church fathers left any records of the sun darkening. Matthew 27:45 reads-

 Now from the sixth hour there was darkness over all the land unto the ninth hour.

Suddenly this is reiterated in the Gospel of Nicodemus- "...a terrible darkness covered the whole land when the Christ was crucified." (1) In fact, with the appearance of the Church's official version of events, the four gospels, many Christian writers openly claimed that at the crucifixion of Jesus the Phoenix made an appearance. (2) One of the most widely known and easily proven forgeries from early Christianity is called Pilate's Report to Tiberius Caesar wherein we read-

...the sun was altogether hidden, and the sky appeared dark while it was yet day...wherefore, I suppose, your excellency is not unaware that in all the world they lighted their lamps from the sixth hour unto evening. And the moon, which was like blood, did not shine all night long, although it was at the full...so dreadful were the signs that men saw both in the heavens and on the earth that Dionysius the Areopagite is reported to have said, 'Either the Author of Nature is suffering or the Universe is falling apart." (3)

Dionysius neither wrote or said any such thing nor was he the only early authority to have their observations stolen and words added to their accounts. Church officials destroyed all known copies of earlier records to conceal their misdeeds. The Dionysius account was of a Phoenix event of the past contorted to suit their purpose. The same was done by Eusebius three centuries after the alleged crucifixion event. He wrote that a pagan historian named Phlegon of Bithynia wrote a book called Olympiads, that the sun darkened and a terrible quake transpired that destroyed the city of Nice in Bithynia. But scholars have found no trace of Phlegon, no ancient writers mention him, cite him, nor are the books called Olympiads known to the multitudes of ancient authors who would have cited them. Either Phlegon was purely a Church invention three hundred years after the fact or the Phoenix event preserved by Phlegon was a real, authentic account but from an earlier time period not corresponding to the 33 CE crucifixion timing so the Olympiad text had to be destroyed allowing Eusebius, a known forger and liar, to use the account with impunity.

By adopting the Phoenix into their version of events the Church authorities gave people pause, many accepting the divinity of Jesus simply because his death was visited by the celestial Phoenix. And history unveils how truly effective this common denominator was in bringing so many into the Christian fold. The legend and story of the Phoenix was one of the greatest told in the ancient world simply because it was relevant to human survival. The

Church had stolen this concept to empower their position knowing well what ideas were attached to the memories of the Phoenix.

The Phoenix appeared to die as it collided into the sun, darkening it, casting the world in shadow much longer than an ordinary eclipse. But the sun and the Phoenix resurrected to repeat the drama all over again after 552 years. Life after death was a Phoenix motif. In the archaic Egyptian city of On [Annu/Heliopolis] was located the Mansion of the Phoenix where a holy relic stone called the benben was protected, an old fragment of a meteorite. The Phoenix was known as the Divine Bennu Bird and its disappearances and reappearances were "...linked to violent cosmic cycles and to the destruction and rebirth of world ages." (4) An Egyptian papyrus written in Greek but dated as a copy of an older text from the time of Amenhotep reads, "...for in the Typhon time the sun is veiled." (5) This would refer to the sun darkening at the appearance of Ty-Phoen, or Phoenix. In Egypt the date-palms were called phoenix-palms, these trees held sacred to the reckoning of the times.

Manly P. Hall in his *The Secret Teachings of All Ages* wrote that it was the testimony of early writers that the Phoenix returned every 500 to 100 years. Its appearance in the sky was taken for a standard for measuring the motion of the heavenly bodies and the duration of the cycles of time. (6) Clement in the second century CE wrote that when Phoenix appeared "...the priests then inspect the registers of the dates, and find that it has returned exactly as the five hundredth year was completed." (7) Five centuries is wrong. By the time of early Christianity the knowledge that Phoenix appeared every 552 was lost. That it was known precisely in distant antiquity is proven in the predictions made by Atreus and Thales of Miletus.

Stories of the Phoenix at the inception of the Christian movement were deeply embedded within the human psyche. Cycles of global disaster die hard. For this reason the power of the early Christian gospel accounts came from its borrowed materials, the facts that were used to support the fiction. By adding the sun darkening and quake effect of Phoenix to the story of Jesus's crucifixion the Church brilliantly provided itself an historical touch to an imagined event. But this only worked because it was contrived centuries after it was supposed to have occurred. Anyone who has taken serious consideration of the alleged evidences of the gospel narratives will note that-

> Paul nor any other New Testament writer mentioned the sun darkening or earthquake at Jesus's crucifixion;

> the gospels were composed over a century and a half after the time period they allege to relate;

> many of the parables and sayings of Jesus were taken straight out of Buddhist and eastern texts;

> Jesus was the last popularized version of over two dozen crucified saviors;

> no Christian documents antedating the gospels mention the sun darkening or quake and the Church Fathers writings are extensive;

> none of the historians, naturalists or chronographers of Jesus' day mentioned him or the crucifixion, no authentic records exist concerning the sun darkening or quake. Cassius Dio, Pliny the Elder, Seneca, Tacitus, even the

Jewish writers Philo Judiacus and Flavius Josephus are silent on the crucifixion, darkening of the sun and quake;

> eliminating all of the contrived historical statements in the gospels leaves us with a narrative too similar to a Greek drama to be coincidence, a stage play production moving rapidly from scene to scene, a production of Galilee condemning the Jews for the murder of Jesus that took a life of its own in Antioch, the cradle of Christianity.

The secret to the allure of Christianity lies in the antiquity of its elements. The Roman religious authority attempted to bring together all people under its influence and power choosing many symbols to perfect its purpose. The literal meaning of "symbolic" is to bring things together. (8) Through the act of gathering, a religion is formed, the word religion meaning "to bind." (9) The word church itself is quite revealing, for it is a word derived from the name of a goddess or enchantress named Circe. She deceived men when they approached her and turned them into pigs (unclean animals) (10) The Christian story is of extreme antiquity antedating the biblical Christian movement by over a thousand years and the history of the Phoenix is far older.

We have had to put together the pieces to unravel the deceit because the hundreds, perhaps thousands of texts from antiquity stored at the Pergamum Library, the Alexandrian Library, at Carthage and abroad were purposefully burned by Church officials in a series of purges designed to empower their own version of history by removing the true records that would have exposed their schemes. The historical records concerning the Phoenix are found in the books *When the Sun Darkens* and *Nostradamus and the Planets of Apocalypse.*

There was long ago an ORIGINAL Christianity, a core belief system before Church officials introduced so many mythical fictions, a profound faith that is fully expounded upon in my newly revised and updated book, *Lost Scriptures of Giza: Enoch and the Secrets of the World's Oldest Texts*. The antiquity of the Phoenix knowledge is very real, and detailed, as we will now see.

Danaan Invaders Predict Darkening of the Sun...1135 BCE

Phoenix appears as a red planet.   In 1447 BCE the eruption of Santorini on Thera devastated the Cyclades and Crete ending the Mediterranean power of Knossus. The master shipwrights and navies that survived were absorbed into the surrounding nations and Mycenaea quickly filled the power vacuum, rivalled only by the Trojan state of Ilium. It was during this 218 years from 1447 BCE to the Fall of Troy in 1229 BCE that another major naval power emerged. The Danaan. An Amorite people, a subgroup called by later writers as Danites of the Israelite stock. This mariner race departed the ancient Canaanite coasts and founded colonies in Asia Minor, Ionia, the coasts of the Mediterranean and a large fleet carrying their families landed in Argos. The Danaan quickly became the ruling elite over the Argives and Achaeans of early Greece. The inclusion of the Danaan fleets instantly made Mycenaea the maritime superpower of the Mediterranean though Ilium continued to block access to the Black Sea trade ports (true cause of the Trojan conflict and Fall of Troy).

In 1411 BCE the Israelites (Amorite Hyksos-Hurrian group) overran the kingdoms in Bashan territory of the

Rephaim giants named Og and King Sihon, defeating the sixty cities of Argob. The Danaan, referred to as Dan in the biblical narrative, failed to oust the giants from the Valley of Rephaim and the whole group took to ships and sailed out of the pages of the Bible and right into the pages of the Iliad. Homer's epic has the race of Danaan ally themselves to the Argives and Achaeans to overcome Ilium and Troy. In the Bible, Dan could not defeat the giants, but in the Irish traditions the descendants of Dan, the Danaan, not only followed the Anakim and Rephaim giants that fled to ancient Ireland, but also defeated them. The Bronze Age institution of the Heroic Code, a challenge of one warrior to a warrior in the opposing army for single combat is found prominently in the biblical record in Goliath's challenge of the Israelite host with David accepting. The Homeric epic has several instances of the Heroic Code, especially between Hector and Paris. The Irish annals also contain instances of the Heroic Code employed and the common denominator between all three (Bible, Iliad, Annals of Clonmacnois & Book of Invasions) is that the Amorite group of Dan, Danaan, Tuatha de Danaan participated in them all. After centuries of absorption the Irish people themselves came to call themselves Tech Donn, or House of Dan. (1)

Ancient Irish traditions are from the perspective of the then-indigenous Iberian stock peoples, a dark-eyed, short of stature race. They claim that the invading Tuatha de Danaan were believed to somehow control the light of the sun. At the First Battle of Magh-Tureidh, "They won by smothering the land in darkness and hiding the light of the sun." (2) Concerning this widespread Irish tradition, Knight and Lomas in Uriel's Machine wrote that this "...seems to suggest that they were accomplished astronomers who possessed the ability to predict eclipses." (3) Magh-Tureidh means The Field of Towers. (4) This indicates that the mysterious round towers of old Ireland were already there. The prediction of the sun darkening is made more interesting by the fact that the Irish records have the Danaan landing their ships on May 1st and then spending some time negotiating with the Fir Bholgs before the first battle when the sun darkened. As the Phoenix researcher knows, Phoenix always darkened the sun from May 14th to the 17th. Many posts will bear this out. For additional Phoenix information, see this author's published books, *When the Sun Darkens* and *Nostradamus and the Planets of Apocalypse.*

Tuatha de Danaan in the Second Battle of Magh-Tureadh ended the 37 year reign of the Firbolgs. (5) They are described as blue-eyed metalworkers who fled Greece and the Aegean due to a Syrian invasion. (6) The Danaan arrived with an organized body of surgeons, a bardic and also a druid class. (7) In a later study it will be shown that the religion of the druids was identical to the religion of the whole host of Amorite families of Canaan/Syria. So identical are the early invaders of Ireland with those of Canaan/Syria that Abbe Brasseur de Bourbourg confidently wrote, "We should bear in mind that Ireland was colonized by the Phoenicians (or a people of that race)." (8) Phoenicia was situated in Canaan.

When the Danaan landed on the shores of Ireland the Firbolgs were in power, having driven the Fomorii into the hills. The remnants of the Fomorii were too strong to oust from the Hebrides and were left alone. (9) To the Iberian natives of Ireland the earliest invaders, the Fomorians, were giants. So were the later Firbolgs ruling over them at the time of the Danaan landing. Then the Tuatha de Danaan appeared. The Danaan fought against the Firbolgs valiantly and in the war it was found that the occupying Firbolgs and the invading Danaan spoke the same language. (10) The Irish lore is entirely from the perspective of the short, squat Iberic people but later preserved by those that absorbed them. The three successive invasions, Fomorii, Firbolg and Danaan represent three distinct migrations of Amorite-mariner peoples who landed in early Ireland from the Mediterranean waters. The Amorite family were pale, Caucasian and very tall, represented as Tammahu on Egyptian monuments and better known as Northern Canaanites, Syrians, Mitannians, Phoenicians, Israelites, Ionians and once called Hyksos by Egyptians who hated them. In the Near East they were feared and highly regarded, called Amurru, or westerners. The focus in these blogs on race and identity of early peoples is because the ancient knowledge of Phoenix appearances seems to have belonged solely to one people. As with Thales in 583 BCE who was a Phoenician by remote descent, the pages of history demonstrate over and again that the foreknowledge of sun darkenings was guarded by the learned of the Amorites family of nations...Israelites.

The Fomorii were descendants of Chem, of early Egypt. (11) In the Second Battle of Magh-Tureidh the god Lug Samildanach defeated the Tuatha de Danaan. (12) This name is from the east, being Sham-il and Anak, indicative of a sun-god chief or giant. This is recorded in the ancient Irish Annals of Clonmacnois. (13) The Danaan fleets reaching Ireland are remembered because the island was already occupied, but at this time natural disasters had driven fleets from the Amorite countries of the Old World onto newer Mediterranean shores and islands, whole fleets even vanishing over the Atlantic into the Americas. (14) 1135 BCE earthquakes separated Morocco, Algeria and Tunis from mainland Africa sinking cities into the sea.(15) Athens, Tiryns, Pylos and Mycenaea collapsed in a wave of destruction, the palaces of megalithic blocks falling to ruin, cities wasted and emptied. Life continued in the countryside but the Aegean was ruined. Huge populations of Danaan, Argives, Achaeans disappeared by ships into the sea. In Anatolia across the Aegean citadels of immense blocks fell down as did the fortified constructions of Cyprus, Canaan and Mesopotamia as cities became ruinous heaps. The widespread evidence according to Barry Strauss is of earthquakes which he dates to approximately 1180 BCE. (16) A good guess, being only 45 years off from 1135 BCE which was over 3150 years ago. Scholars also date the collapse of the Mycenaean Trade Empire at approximately 1150 BCE. (17)

In the traditions of the Fall of Troy there is an account of the sun darkening that was widely popular during classical antiquity, however, this was not a Phoenix transit for Troy fell by many reliable sources in 1229 BCE. The darkening of the sun promoted so much confusion with the traditions of the Phoenix darkenings long ago that Ephoras in the 4th century BCE actually accidently dated the Fall of Troy in exactly 1135 BCE. (18) This mistake is profound because it reveals that there were records available to Ephoras that the sun darkened in what translates in our calendar as 1135 BCE and he used them to wrongly date an unrelated event.

To conclude, we have in the Irish records an account of an invasion that took place in 1135 BCE when suddenly the sun darkened. No mention of the moon or a regular eclipse. The event was linked to major earthquakes that destroyed the infrastructure of whole civilizations. If this was the only account from this time then it could easily be ignored. But it is not as will be shown. What makes this history so profound is that all the Seven Churches of the New Testament that were the focus of Paul's letters and the Book of Revelation were in the Bronze Age all in cities occupied or founded by the Danaan, a people having knowledge of the Phoenix visitations throughout antiquity.

21. The Moses Epic a Jewish Invention by Ezra...The Great Deceit [Part I]

The religions of the world ascribe to humanity a false beginning- as assumption of original sin, that mankind is a fallen being. This fiction empowers religion requiring humanity to seek a Savior. This diabolical scheme was designed as a control mechanism allowing an elite minority to rule over a vast majority. The Sumerian records of the ancient Near East are OLDER than the religious systems of the world and they tell an entirely different story of mankind's origins. All religious faiths and writings from distant antiquity were conceived by Anunnaki deceivers and their lackeys, ultimately stemming from Babylon, including both the Old and the New Testament collections of books. The earliest Sumerian records are nonreligious and provide us the histories before the Flood of the physical descent to Earth of a race called Those Who From Heaven to Earth Fell, or the Anunnaki, Homo Anunna, who genetically manufactured mankind.

The historical and archeological records appears to support the stories of Genesis of a pre- and postFlood world, of giants, of the Tower of Babel [ziggurat] story, of an

Enoch/ENKI, of a Flood survivor and his sons, a Nimrod [Sargon I/ Amarudaak], an Abram [Brahma] and Sarah [Saraswati], of cities called Nineveh, Babel, Sodom and Gomorrah, of migrations of whole peoples and a Great War in the Near East involving the Elamite Empite. Much of the Genesis text prefixing out Bibles seems to have a lot of historical support.

But with the second book of the Bible, the Exodus, the historical evidence is lacking. Archeology is silent. The ancient chronographers say nothing. There is no hint anywhere that a Moses-type figure existed, or a Joshua, or ANY of the judges. Confounding this is the abundance of evidence that Saul, David and Solomon are figures borrowed straight out of Canaanite lore.

A disturbing fact is that no Old Testament books, the Torah, books of the Chronicles, Kings, Prophets or any others have ever been found outside of Judah in the 8th-4th centuries BCE. Why? Israelite groups are known to have departed Palestine in wave after wave of fleets immigrating to the shores of the Aegean, the Black and Caspian Seas, the Mediterranean as far as the Atlantic- but none of these people took their holiest writings? Or carried with them oral traditions heard by locals who would have preserved them secondhand like so many other stories have been remembered through the history of the world. This dearth of ancient texts and silent traditions is evidence of a LATE AUTHORSHIP for the Old Testament books. In fact, scholars provide much evidence that EVERY single book of the Old Testament has been redacted, edited, altered and that none are actually written by those names they have been given. (The Christ Conspiracy p. 90)

In the year 2448 of the Old World's calendar, or our year 1447 BCE, the Anunnaki initiated a catastrophic series of disasters that afflicted humanity around the world- a global depopulation. The Israelites, or more properly those Amorites who stayed in Egypt after their Hyksos kin returned to Syro-Phoenicia, were under the Brahmic Covenant [Abrahamic] and they used this disastrous episode to escape Egyptian slavery. The Anunnaki used a pawn to spiritually enslave the Israelites and lay the foundations to two false religions that would forever impede human development- Judaism and Christianity, which by themselves would spawn hundreds of cults and hundreds of thousands of fanatics.

A new god unknown to Abram, called YHVH, brought a totally new covenant. Masquerading as holy and just, YHVH had no capacity for love or compassion. He is the Arch Deceiver, the bloodiest of all the gods. Though the biblical records reveal YHVH to be an unholy god, a demon, we have been deceived through misinterpretation to regard YHVH in a favorable light despite the clear warnings in the Old Testament...YHVH was an imposter. He first enslaved the Israelites and then deceived the world.

Here is an analysis of the Moses story as recorded in Exodus. This analysis spans all 39 books of the Old Testament and considers the following key terms of the Exodus account:

Moses	Sinai	brasen serpent	fiery bush
manna	law(s) of Moses	burning bush	
Pharaoh	book of the law	Red Sea	
Jordan	Og of Bashan	flood stood upright	
Miriam	Sihon of Amorites	ten plagues	

Aaron   ark of the covenant   signs and wonders
Joshua   Caleb

Moses is named 705 times in the five books covering his life: Exodus, Leviticus, Numbers, Deuteronomy and Joshua. He is named 290 times in the book of Exodus alone. Moses is mentioned only 4 times in Judges and Ruth, 25 chapters covering 300 years of history. Moses is mentioned 2 times in 1 Samuel and in Daniel. Disturbingly, references to the name Moses after the book of Joshua are all repetitious variations of-

> ...as my servant Moses

> ...book of the law of Moses

> ...as the Lord commanded Moses

These are repeated over and over in the 62 times Moses' name appears in books after Joshua. In the 66 chapters of the book of Isaiah, Moses is found only once (63:11-12), and only once in the 52 chapters of Jeremiah (15:1), only once in Micah 6:4 and once in Malachi 4:4. Moses is NOT mentioned at all in 2 Samuel, Esther, Job Proverbs, Ecclesiastes, Song of Solomon, Lamentations, Ezekiel, Hosea, Joel, Amos, Obadiah, Jonah, Nahum, Habakkak, Zephaniah, Haggai, Zechariah...18 books.

YHVH revealed himself to Moses not as a living tree but as a burning bush. In the entire Old Testament this story of how God met Moses is UNKNOWN outside the Exodus text. The incredible parting of the Red Sea after the book of Joshua is only found in Nehemiah 9:9-25 and in 4 passages in the Psalms (66:6, 106:7-9, 22, 114:3-5, 136:13, 15. So miraculous of an event is not mentioned in 31 books of the Old Testament. The term "signs and wonders" as a description for what transpired in Egypt before the Exodus first appears in scripture in Nehemiah 9:10, with a second reference in the Psalms (78:43) and a third in Jeremiah 32:20-21. Bear with me dear reader, I do not want to tell you what to see. A pattern will soon emerge.

The fascinating story of the Ten Plagues visited upon Egypt depicted in Exodus is NOT found remembered ANYWHERE in the entire Old Testament- it is strictly an Exodus account. That a disaster in ancient Egypt occurred is historical, and alluded to in the Psalms. (105:26-45, 136:10-21, Deut. 4:34, 7:19, 26:8, 2 Sam. 7:23, 1 Chronicles 17:21) But the Ten Plagues narrative is unknown. Mount Sinai where Moses received the law is not in Joshua, and only once is Sinai mentioned in Judges. In the remaining 32 books of the Old Testament, Sinai is found ONLY in Nehemiah 9:13 and Psalm 68:8, 17. Also, the extraordinary account of manna, or Bread of Heaven, [angel food] feeding the Israelites is found nowhere in Old Testament after Joshua EXCEPT Nehemiah 9:20 and Psalm 78:24, 105:40. Pharaoh oppressing the Israelites is mentioned in 4 books after Deuteronomy- 1 Samuel 6:6, 2 Kings 17:7, Nehemiah 9:10 and Psalm 135:9, 136:16. The Jordan river appears 60 times in the Old Testament after Joshua, many times with armies passing over it without any supernatural assistance. God stopping flow of Jordan to allow Israelites to pass is found once after Joshua- in Psalm 114:3-5.

Miriam, the first female of import in Exodus is found twice in entire Old Testament after Joshua- 1 Chronicles 6:3 and Micah 6:4. Aaron was the patriarch of the Israelite priesthood. He is NOT mentioned in the first 76 Psalms, Ruth, 2 Samuel, 1 & 2 Kings, Esther, Job, Proverbs,

Ecclesiastes, Song of Solomon, Isaiah, Jeremiah, Ezekiel, Lamentations, Daniel, Hosea, Joel , Amos, Obadiah, Jonah, Nahum, Habakkuk, Zephaniah, Haggai, Zechariah and Malachi. In 1 Samuel Aaron is only mentioned briefly in 12:6-8. There are over 350 references to Aaron in Exodus, Leviticus, Numbers, Deuteronomy, Joshua and 1 & 2 Chronicles, but of all the other Old Testament books Aaron is found only in EZRA 7:5...NEHEMIAH 10:38, 14:27 and in Micah 6:4.

The infamous giant kings defeated by the Israelites called Og of Bashan and King Sihon of the Amorites are only mentioned in the Old Testament after Joshua in 1 Kings 4:19, in NEHEMIAH 9:22 and Psalm 135:11, 136:19. Joshua, the hero of the Conquest of Canaan, nation-builder, giant-slayer, appointed by Moses, endorsed by God, has his life and exploits detailed in Exodus, Leviticus, Numbers, Deuteronomy and Joshua with mentions in Judges. Except for one mention in 1 Kings 16:34 and NEHEMIAH 8:17, the hero Joshua is NOT mentioned in any other Old Testament books. This is the man who commanded the sun and moon to be still, and the stopping of the sun and moon is mentioned in Habakkak 3:11 but no mention of the hero is made. Another hero, Caleb, after the book of Joshua is found only once, in 1 Chronicles (2:50, 4:13-15). The remaining 26 books of the Old Testament do not know of Caleb or his career.

For the Old Testament adherent the terms "law(s) of Moses," "books of Moses," and "book of the law," are of paramount import. It is the Law that provides the entire foundation for the Judaic faith and it was the Law that had to exist in order to give credence to Christianity which was supposed to be a newer covenant that replaced this law.

Unfortunately, these terms do NOT appear in Judges, Ruth, 1 & 2 Samuel, Ecclesiastes, Song of Solomon, Joel, Obadiah, Jonah, Nahum, Esther, Proverbs, Isaiah, Jeremiah, Lamentations, Ezekiel, Hosea, Amos, Micah, Habakkuk, Zephaniah, Haggai, Zechariah...it is clear that the prophets of Israel knew NOTHING about the laws of YHVH or his messenger Moses. That 23 Old Testament books do not reference anything about these laws or the Lawgiver causes us to pay closer attention to those few books where they are found.

Law of Moses is found-

> 1 time in 1 Kings (2:3)

> 2 times in 2 Kings (14:6, 23:25)

> 2 times in 2 Chronicles

> 4 times in EZRA

> 3 times in NEHEMIAH

> 2 times in Daniel (9:11, 13 but in 1 passage)

> 1 time in Malachi 4:4 at very end of Old Testament record, believed by scholars to be an interpolation.

It is to be noted that Daniel appears to be the only prophet that knew of any Laws of YHVH or Book of the Law. Daniel lived in Babylon among the Jewish exiles, not in Judah.

The Psalms has 3 references to the Law of Jacob and 36 references to Law of YHVH, but NOT ONE reference to law or books of Moses is to be found anywhere in the 150 Psalms.

Job is dated preMosaic at about 1520 BCE and in Job 22:22 we find Law of the Almighty, which is same as Laws of God found in Genesis referring to Abrahamic Covenant that dates 4 centuries before Moses [Genesis 26:5]. But Law of the Almighty is English translation but in Hebrew the actual rendering is "instruction of the Almighty."

In the scriptures, once Moses died, the term law of Moses is only found 15 times in the entirety of the Old Testament record- 7 times in EZRA and NEHEMIAH. Because of their content, syntax, subject matter, scholars have long known that the books Ezra and Nehemiah were a joint work. In this analysis the book of Nehemiah stands out as the only book outside of Exodus-Joshua that mentions ALL of the elements of the Moses Epic-

> Israelites in Egypt, oppressed by Pharaoh

> signs and wonders in Egypt

> escape through the Red Sea

> Mount Sinai

> law of Moses

> high priest Aaron

> the hero Joshua

> giants named Og and Sihon

> manna from heaven

Every one of these elements in the book of Nehemiah are virtually unknown in the rest of the Old Testament outside of the Moses Epic. This analysis would be incomplete without an understanding of who Ezra and Nehemiah were, where they came from, what they accomplished and what the scriptures ADMIT as true.

Ezra and Nehemiah are joint works as they cover the exact same historical period involving the same events (450-440 BCE)- introducing the scriptures to a people who did not have them...the Jews. In Ezra and Nehemiah is told the story of how the book of the law of Moses was first read to the locals and Jews returned from exile in Babylon and Persia in about 446 BCE, according to its own account that was written during King Artaxerxes' reign. This makes Ezra and Nehemiah the LAST books included in the Old Testament canon, about 139 years after the fall of Jerusalem to Nebuchadnezzar II in 585 BCE, 91 years after the fall of Babylon to Persia. The books of Ezra and Nehemiah are chronologically last but these books are hidden in plain sight placed deliberately toward the middle of the Old Testament to conceal this fact.

The book of Nehemiah is the ONLY Old Testament book attributed to a POLITICIAN. It concerns itself with explaining that at the direction of the priest Ezra the books of Moses were reintroduced to the Jews who had not only lost them, but had no traditions of ever having known them. It is the opinion of most scholars that Ezra and Nehemiah introduced the Moses Epic for the FIRST time, that the story was pure invention. It is no coincidence that virtually 50% of all references to book/laws of Moses are grouped together in EZRA and NEHEMIAH. The book of Nehemiah contains all the same interpolations as those found in the redacted Psalms, often word-for-word. By his own account, Nehemiah was a wealthy, powerful Persian administrator, a Jew in service to Artaxerxes and Ezra was a priest.

Early on removed from the Old Testament canon was another book by Ezra now called 1 Esdras. The use of his Greek name is an attempt put some distance between Ezra of the scriptures and Esdras of the apocrypha. In 1 Esdras we learn that Ezra came from Babylon (1 Esdras 8:1) claiming descent from Aaron, the high priest of the Moses Epic of which no one had ever heard. This was 950 years after Aaron allegedly died. 1 Esdras reads that Ezra was "...a scholar with a thorough knowledge of the Law." (1 Esdras 8:3-4), but this knowledge came AFTER it was REWRITTEN as admitted in 2 Esdras 14:21-22 where we read the prayer of Ezra to YHVH-

Your Law has been destroyed by fire, so no one can know what you have done in the past or what you are plannin to do in the future. Please send your Holy Spirit to me, so that I can write down everything that has been done in this world from the beginning, everything that has been written in your Law.

The simple exiles were impressed by Ezra and his story. Ezra claimed that YHVH took him up to Mount Sinai and spoke to him with a voice from a burning bush (2 Esdras 14:1-4). For 40 days Ezra dictated to 5 men who REWROTE the Old Testament books in a language they had not known before...Hebrew. (2 Esdras 14:42-44). Ezra was indeed a scholar-made-priest who INVENTED the Jewish people by giving the locals of Edomite/Hebrew stock a ruling body of Judahites returned from exile, an invented history to be proud of and a totally fictitious body of writings he passed off as holy. Nehemiah organized this new people into a nation-state . In this way these Hebrews kin to the ancient Israelites [Amorite Syro-Phoenicians] totally assimilated with local Edomites and descendants of

Judahites to become the fanatical Yawist culture of the Jews. The biblical records had been lost for at least 139 years and the scriptures admit that Ezra recomposed them. But he was NOT the first.

Over 175 years before Ezra and Nehemiah, in the reign of King Josiah, the biblical account of 2 Kings 22-23 admits that the scriptures , the Law of YHVH, had been rediscovered in Jerusalem by the high priest Hilkiah and a scribe named Shaphan in 619 BCE. According to the text the scriptures had been lost for CENTURIES, since Egypt sacked the Temple in 927 BCE three hundred years earlier. Many scholars hold this story to be a fiction too, that the first version of the Torah was invented at this time or that the Josiah-period rediscovery was added to the Kings account as an explanation for the obvious lack of any knowledge of a Law of Moses prior to the time of Ezra and Nehemiah. It is damning that the most fundamental foundation of the Mosaic Law was the TEN COMMANDMENTS..."Thou shalt not-" echoing NOT ONCE in the entirety of the Old Testament. NONE of the Ten Commandments are quoted by any other biblical writer of the Old Testament because the Ezra-Nehemiah fiction was INVENTED after the Babylonian exile.

Twice in recorded Jewish history the books of Moses were "lost" and had to be rewritten. In the former account of King Josiah an old copy of the Book of the Law was supposedly found during Temple renovations by a priest. In the latter account Ezra rewrites the scriptures and passes them off as the Word of YHVH to justify the building of a Temple in Jerusalem. Because the high priest Hilkiah "discovered" the book of the law and King Josiah used this to centralize all worship [offerings of property/money/animals to priests] in Jerusalem, most biblical scholars assert that no book of Moses was ever found by the Judahites...it was invented by the Jews. This is merely the first post on this fascinating topic of biblical deceit.

22. Ezra's False Scriptures and the Serpent Code in the Old Testament...The Great Deceit [Part II]

In the prior post, The Great Deceit [Part I], it is revealed that the biblical record claims that the entire body of the scriptures was lost not once, but TWICE, the Bible rewritten two times by Jewish priests. By biblical records we are only referring to the Old Testament. When the second rewrite occurred as admitted in the apocryphal Esdras texts and the book of Ezra at about 445 BCE it would still be another six centuries before the New Testament books would be in the form we know them now. It was shown that Ezra and Nehemiah together invented the Moses story we have become familiar with in Exodus.

Our analysis of the Old Testament record is far from complete. If the books of the law, Genesis, Exodus, Leviticus, Numbers and Deuteronomy were so important, how were copies not made and safeguarded both times these scriptures were lost, and how is it that no other Israelite-descended people known to be scattered in Lydia, Phrygia, Ionia, Phoenicia, Syria, the Aegean, Carthage, through the vast Mediterranean, Spain, Gaul and ancient Briton not know of these writings and stories? How did it occur that Moses' incredible story of the Exodus was totally unknown outside of Judea?

Interpolations are new additions to an older text. When we look back over a list of the terms we analyzed from the Moses story as found in the Old Testament books, this is what we see:

Judges & Ruth..........................Moses (4 times)

1 Samuel................................Moses (2 times), Aaron (once)

2 Samuel................................0

1 Kings...................................law of Moses (x1), Joshua (x1), Og & Sihon (x1)

2 Kings...................................law of Moses (x2)

1 Chronicles............................Aaron (x1), Miriam (x1), Caleb (x1)

2 Chronicles............................law of Moses (x2), Aaron (x1)

EZRA......................................law of Moses (x4), Aaron (x1)

NEHEMIAH............................law of Moses (x3), Joshua (x1), Aaron (x1), Red Sea parting (x1), signs and   wonders (x1), Sinai (x1), manna (x1), Og and Sihon (x1)

Esther.....................................0

Job...0

Psalms....................................Red Sea parting (x1), signs
and wonders (x1), Sinai (x1), manna (x1), Og and Sihon
(x1), Aaron (x1), Jordan crossing (x1)

Proverbs...................................0

Ecclesiastes.............................0

Song of Solomon......................0

Isaiah.....................................Moses (x1)

Jeremiah................................Moses (x1)

Lamentations...........................0

Ezekiel...................................0

Daniel....................................law of Moses (x2)

Hosea, Joel, Amos, Obadiah, Jonah- all 0

Micah.....................................Moses (x1), Aaron (x1),
Miriam (x1)

Nahum, Habakkuk, Zephaniah, Haggai, Zechariah- all 0

Malachi...................................law of Moses (x1)

There are 18 Old Testament books left virtually untouched
by the biblical redactors/copyists as seen above that include
no supporting material knowledge of the Moses story. But
when recognizing the interpolations for what they are we
see other texts touched hardly at all. Isaiah is a large book
with only one reference introduced, Jeremiah also lengthy,
but with two interpolations. Malachi's interpolation is
obvious for it is located at the end of the book and 2 Kings
had only two interpolations.

The books 1 Samuel, 1 Kings, Micah, 1 Chronicles and 2 Chronicles all have 3 interpolations. Judges and Ruth combined contain 4 (they were written together). Because the biblical interpolations are all only short terms or phrases, and because the added materials are often stacked together in a book, this immense corpus of biblical narrative spread across 33 books was barely even touched by the lying copyists as they rewrote older scrolls into newer manuscripts. All forged interpolated passages combined do not add up to even .01% of the content of these 33 books. In 500 pages of Old Testament scripture all of the added terms and passages deceitfully introduced into unrelated books to support the fictitious Moses Epic would easily fit ON ONE PAGE. Not only was it easy for the redactors to insert fictitious "history" in to older Hebrew manuscripts AS THEY WERE BEING COPIED, but they did a poor job doing it. In fact, the repetitive syntax hints that it was all the work of a single man.

Eleven of the books were barely touched by the copyist, who added only 25 interpolations including references to the formerly unknown Moses story, all 25 found in less than 20 passages because introduced material sometimes appeared together in the same passage. The deceitful scribe inserted these additions into the existing Hebrew writings to bridge them to the new forged false histories of Genesis, Exodus, Leviticus, Numbers, Deuteronomy and Joshua that were largely written in Babylon by Jews exiled there who visited the great Near East libraries.

As the Israelite origin from Egypt is prevalent in Old Testament texts we can surmise that Exodus through Joshua was composed using now-unknown sources and oral tradition, though Moses was an invention modelled after an old king of Akkad called Sargon I whose baby-in-a-basket-on-the-river was a famous story in Babylonia that was dated at least 500 years before Moses was supposed to have lived.

What makes Nehemiah so suspicious an account is because it literally lists all of the Moses story interpolations that are spread thinly in the other books. But Nehemiah NEVER once mentions the Ten Commandments, the Ark of the Covenant which alone appears 121 times in just 1 and 2 Samuel, 1 Kings and 1 and 2 Chronicles. Nehemiah is also silent on Moses making the Brasen Serpent staff. It appears that Nehemiah purposely avoided mentioning two of the actual REAL elements of ancient Bronze Age Israelite religion. The ark is now known as a popular ceremonial object from Egyptian antiquity and the caducaeus [serpent-twined staff] was Israel's first national standard, a religious emblem signifying their allegiance to a God. Unlike the Moses interpolations, the other Hebrew books maintain many whole passages full of historical data on the ark of the covenant. And if one were to assume that the serpent staff was not of paramount import to the message of the scriptures and identity of the imposter god YHVH, he would be terribly in error.

Nehemiah's silence on the Ten Commandments and serpent staff was deliberate, as they completely contradict one another. Moses is commanded by YHVH in the second commandment- THOU SHALT MAKE NO GRAVEN IMAGE OF ANY BEAST OF THE FIELD and reconfirms this later in Deuteronomy 4:23-

Take heed unto yourselves, lest you forget the covenant of the Lord your God, which He made   with you, and make you a graven image or the likeness of any thing, which the Lord thy God hath forbidden.

Verse 25 says that the making of such an image is evil in the sight of the Lord. A glaring contradiction, that the ancient Israelite scriptures prohibited the fashioning of a brasen serpent that YHVH commanded Moses to fashion.

In their journey away from Egypt conditions became harsh and many complained to Moses, whereby YHVH killed them, using fiery serpents. Moses prayed about this and YHVH replied- "Moses, make thee a fiery serpent, and set it upon a pole: and it shall come to pass, that every one that is bitten, when he looketh upon it, shall live. And Moses made a serpent of brass, and put it upon a pole." (Numbers 21:5-9) Thou shalt NOT and thou shalt are synonymous in regards to the serpent.

The greatest evidence for exposing Moses for a myth is from the biblical record itself. In 2 Kings 18:4 King Hezekiah did "...break in pieces the brasen serpent that Moses had made: for unto those days the children of Israel did burn incense to it; and he called it Nehushtan." This admits that the ancient Israelites prayed [burned incense] to the Brass Serpent for OVER 700 YEARS, something they would NOT have done had they knew of the law of Moses. Why the text mentions Nehushtan is not known but what is clearly known is that this is merely a masculinization of the Syrian sea-serpent of Kadesh called Nehushta. (The Christ Conspiracy p. 187) To worship the Brass Serpent for seven centuries means there was no Mosaic Law to know, or that the laws of Moses were absolutely unknown to the Israelites, which of course is true, for they were invented by Jews of the 6-4th century BCE.

The identity of YHVH who did not deliver the Israelites but enslaved them is found out by examining the passages of the Old Testament containing references to the Serpent. To those who disbelieve the biblical records contain codes and ciphers, the next part, the Serpent Code, will change your mind. The Brasen Serpent of Moses is linked to a stunning series of passages that will enlighten even the most stringent critic.

Here in the second part of The Great Deceit concerning the deceitful additions added to the books of the Old Testament by 6-4th century BCE Jewish scribes, we come in contact with a cipher spread throughout the older biblical texts. This is a code concerning the TRUE identity of the deity who appeared in the form of a burning bush and in the narrative gave Moses the Law. This is a unmistakable code deliberately placed in the Bible and what you are about to read is no accident. Too many coincidences exhibits evidence of no coincidence at all.

Moses was commanded to make a graven image of a SERPENT and to hold up this forbidden image which VIOLATED the Law so the people could look up to it and be SAVED. Christian fundamentalists have little difficult saying that this serpent was merely a prophetic foreshadowing of the Christ, raised on the Cross. Well then, why not a dove? A sheep? No, it was a BRASEN SERPENT and this term is a puzzle lock deciphered by ALL of the passages in the Old Testament referencing SERPENTS and DRAGONS. Together these passages IDENTIFY the personality behind the burning bush who gave Moses the Law and enslaved the Israelites.

Biblical fundamentalists, especially Christians, normally do not entertain secular materials that criticize the biblical texts. Christians staunchly adhere to the method of using only SCRIPTURE TO INTERPRET SCRIPTURE, thus allowing them an intellectual bastion against nonbiblical facts that assault their beliefs.. So as not to offend our well-meaning Christian seekers of truth, we shall employ their own cherished method to unveil what the Bible teaches is YHVH's true identity.

The term serpent(s) or brasen serpent is not mentioned in 26 of the 39 Old Testament books, meaning, that our study is confined to merely 13 books, or a third of the Old Testament writings. EVERY fact you are about to read is easily proven by a casual glace into a Strong's Concordance of the Bible.

> Genesis..........serpent is mentioned 6 times, 5 times as a DECEIVER in Eden, once in reference to Dan, a FALLEN tribe later removed from the Israelite roster.

> Exodus...........Moses' and the Egyptian magician's staves became serpents in a demonstration of SORCERY (4:3, 7:9-15).

> Numbers.........Moses commanded by YHVH to make brasen serpent 3 times (21:5-9).

> Deuteronomy...fiery serpents were symbol of AFFLICTION (8:15, 32:24).

> 2 Kings...........the brasen serpent was BROKEN IN PIECES after Israelites prayed to it for 700 years (18:4).

> Job.................the crooked serpent is astronomical designation for former preFlood circumpolar constellation Draconis [the DRAGON] but it had FALLEN in antiquity; Alpha Draconis no longer the pole star, today it is Polaris in Ursa Minor (26:13).

> Psalms.............serpent associated to LIES (58:3-4), and WICKED SPEECH and VIOLENCE (104:1-4). Hezekiah broke the brasen serpent in pieces, and in Psalm 74:14 God "...BREAKEST the heads of LEVIATHON IN PIECES."

> Proverbs..........serpent associated to DRUNKENESS (23:30-33) and ADULTEROUS WOMAN (30:19-20).

> Ecclesiastes......serpent associated to EVIL, ERROR PROCEEDING FROM A RULER, FOLLY, BABBLING (10:5-11).

> Isaiah...............serpent becomes a FIERY, FLYING SERPENT [dragon] in Palestine (14:29). God will punish LEVIATHON THE PIERCING SERPENT, THE CROOKED SERPENT, THE DRAGON IN THE SEA. (27:1). Serpent associated with rebellious children OUT OF EGYPT (30:1-6). Serpent symbol of JUDGEMENT, ACCURSED (65:24-26).

> Jeremiah...........Serpent associated to VOICE OF VIOLENCE AND WAR (46:21-23). Serpents associated to God's anger over Israel's GRAVEN IMAGES and STRANGE VANITIES (8:17-19).

> Amos...............Serpent associated to JUDGEMENT, DARKNESS, FALSE SECURITY THAT HARMS sent against Israel for their HATED FEAST DAYS, this referring back to Israel's 40 years in wilderness and their TABERNACLE TO MOLECH and CHIUN- "the star of your god." (5:18-26). The ONLY tabernacle in the Old Testament was that of YHVH built by Moses, which Amos declares here was a tabernacle to a FALSE GOD associated to a STAR [Alpha Draconis/ Eye of the Dragon]. Serpent associated to JUDGEMENT CONTROLLED BY GOD (9:3).

> Micah................Serpent a symbol of THOSE GOD JUDGED (7:16-19).

These are all of the references to serpents in the 39 books of the Old Testament. In every instance we are confronted with a symbol representing evil, lies, deception, sorcery, affliction, idolatry, a false god, impurity, drunkeness, violence and judgement. By the Judeo-Christian exegesis of using scripture to interpret scripture we MUST conclude that the Mosaic covenant was instituted NOT by the Creator, but by the Arch Deceiver...YHVH. The Old Testament is the product of a diabolical mind bent on leading mankind astray.

It is to be noted that the ancient Levites revered the serpent and were called Sons of the Great Serpent. (The Christ Conspiracy p. 187) In fact, Levi is from a root meaning TO TWINE [3867 Strong's Concordance] like a serpent; the same root in LEVIATHON [3882 Strong's]. The brasen serpent of Moses was TWINED around a pole. In the Hebrew context the serpent was a symbol for OMENS, WHISPERINGS and later to the Greeks it was the symbol of the Pythian Oracle [snake divination].

Again, using scripture to interpret scripture YHVH's true identity as a DEMON is shown in the Bible. The prophet Amos called YHVH by the title of a popular Canaanite god- MOLECH. In Exodus 6:2-3 YHVH said to Moses-

"I am the Lord. And I appeared unto Abraham, unto Isaac, and unto Jacob, by the name of God Almighty, but by my name YHVH was I NOT KNOWN to them."

Not only was YHVH not known, nor did the prior Abrahamic covenant have anything to do with the covenant of the law. In writing Exodus the redactors originally left

Genesis untouched, these older writings not naming YHVH for at that time God was referred to as Elohim which is consistent with Genesis' true origin as a Babylonian document later Hebraicized. Elohim is literally "gods," but as evidenced in Exodus 6:2-3 the redactors later changed many Elohim words to that of YHVH when Genesis went through a revision. As any Hebrew lexicon shows, God is El Shaddai many times in Genesis, though often translated in English as simply God. But this title identifies a GOD DESCRIBED AS A DEVIL, the epithet being a deification of the word "shedu," which means DEVIL. Near East scholars know that the shedim were DESERT DEVILS as they are found in this form in Psalm 106:37 (The Christ Conspiracy p. 92) Like Molech, another anciently popular Canaanite god was Baal, and YHVH claims through Hosea in 2:16 that the Israelites long prior to Hosea' day called YHVH by the names of Baal.

That YHVH is the great deceiver is again learned by using scripture to interpret scripture. In 1 Samuel 4:4 the term Lord of Hosts appears in the translation but the Hebrew text reads, "Sabaoth, who sits above the cherubim." This is important. To sit above is TO COVER, and in scripture the evil one was also formerly the "anointed Cherub that COVERETH..." It was a weapon-weilding cherub who in Genesis prevented mankind from going back to Eden. Ezekiel in 28:13-19 identifies this imposter god who sat between the cherubim on the ark-

"Thou hast been in Eden the garden of God...thou art the anointed cherub that covereth...thou wast perfect in all thy waysfrom the day that thou wast created, till iniquity was found in thee...I will destroy thee O COVERING cherub...I will cast thee to the ground..."

In this passage in Ezekiel the evil cherub is likened to a merchant, and in Hosea 12:7 we read that "He [YHVH] is as a merchant; the balances of deceit are in his hand; he loveth to oppress." This Ezekiel passage parallels Isaiah 14:12-20 where we find that he is called LUCIFER, who had fallen from heaven, whose goal was to "...be like the Most High," who was guilty because HE SLEW HIS PEOPLE.

In the Old Testament God is both good and evil and Judeo-Christianity has invented many justifications to explain why a loving God could be so venomously murderous. But here we shall only attribute to YHVH what the scriptures admit. It was the prophets who had much to reveal about YHVH, writings that know next to nothing about Moses or the Law. In Isaiah 45:7 we read- "I form the light and create darkness. I make peace, and I CREATE EVIL. I, the Lord [YHVH] do all these things." In Jeremiah 4:10 we read- "You [YHVH] have greatly deceived this people." Ezekiel 14:9 reads- "If a prophet is deceived, I the Lord [YHVH] have deceived that prophet." Amos 3:6 reads- "Shall there be evil in a city, and the Lord [YHVH] hath not done it."

A god or man who delegates to others evil deeds is no less guilty than the doer. YHVH in Judges 9:23 sent an evil spirit to influence the men of Shechem to deal treacherously with Abimelech. In 1 Kings 22:21-22 YHVH sent a lying spirit to give a prophet a false prophecy to deceive King Ahab which lead directly to his death. In 1 Samuel 16:14 an EVIL SPIRIT FROM YHVH troubled King Saul. Later in 18:10 this same evil spirit provoked Saul to attack David with a spear, which is mentioned again in 19:9.

It was a book written by Gnostic minister and publisher
Paul Tice that really opened my eyes to diligently study this
figure called YHVH. He showed me that many important
Old Testament stories are narrated two and three times
spread throughout different books, similar to the synoptic
Gospels. In 2 Samuel 24:1 we read that "The anger of
YHVH was kindles against Israel, and he moved David
against them, to say, Go, number Israel and Judah." This
passage concerns a census and the exact same story
IDENTIFIES YHVH by using scripture to interpret
scripture for in 1 Chronicles 21 the SAME passage reads-
"And SATAN stood up against Israel, and provoked David
to number Israel."

Oh I hear the howling! The faithful are offended that my
simplemindedness can not understand that God USES
Satan to perform His will...indeed. I'm using scripture to
interpret scripture and it tells me here that the figure YHVH
is ALSO known as SATAN. Religionist beware! If these
two posts on The Great Deceit have not convinced you that
the Moses story is a fiction and that YHVH is an imposter,
you don't have long to wait. Part III is more convincing
than the first three parts combined.

23. YHVH the God of Murder...The Great Deceit [Part III]

It has long troubled biblical scholars that not one Old
Testament book outside of the Moses Epic uses the Moses
story as a teaching point or borrows anything from the life
of Moses to illustrate a point. If the Bible is the Word of
God then why are historical figures deemed important in

antiquity later allowed to be forgotten? If Moses was so popularly known to the ancient Israelites, then why didn't any of them name their children Moses? Israelite names are found in abundance in the Assyrian Horse Lists and other records, including the Old Testament canon itself, the pseudopigraphical works and apocryphal books...but Moses only becomes a popular name after the Babylonian exile of the Jews and not a trace of earlier Israelite evidences has ever surfaced demonstrating they had any knowledge of a Moses or his amazing life.

The reason there is not one single account of an Israelite named Moses is because the northern kingdom of the Israelites fled or were deported by the Assyrians between 745 and 721 BCE, almost 280 years before the politician Nehemiah with the Jewish priest Ezra invented the Moses Epic. Most Christians have no idea that the oldest biblical manuscripts only go back as far as 100 BCE (The Gospel Truth p. 25) and they are different than the Bibles they hold today. Christianity was a New Covenant. The old covenant required the plunging of as knife into a living, terrified and innocent animal so its blood can cleanse wicked humans of their sins (not the animal's). That ritual was barbaric and evil. Animal sacrifice never made Israel holy, the entire notion is ridiculous for the WHOLE ancient world performed this as a global Bronze Age institution. Additionally, the Word says that this covenant with YHVH would NEVER be superseded (see Leviticus 26:44-45). So what is Christianity then?

Thomas Paine called the Bible the Word of a Demon (Jumpin' Jehovah p. 35), holding to the tenet of Euripides, "If the gods do evil then they are not gods." Paine and others realized that YHVH was an imposter, that NOT

ONCE in the entire Old Testament did YHVH ever promise the righteous any kind of AFTERLIFE. Every benefit he offered was of power over enemies, wealth, food, increase- the immortal souls of men were not a concern of YHVH.

YHVH is not a God of love, there is no capacity for compassion found in him. His covenant with ancient Israel was a blackmail list of demands with promises of punishments for the slightest disobedience. YHVH was a bloodthirsty tyrant, a master of ambiguity and deception and he imprinted his nature on the Jewish people but not on the other Israelites who rebelled again YHVH over and over and were scattered around the Earth in fulfillment of the Abrahamic Covenant, not the Covenant of the Law. YHVH commanded the Israelites to slay all men, women and children of enemy cities, but the Israelites departed and assimilated with other peoples while the Judahites continued in service to a racsist, murderous God. The Jews steadily followed YHVH despite the fact that every promise YHVH made to them has either been broken or unfulfilled. From Judea we have inherited nothing buy bigotry, misogyny, religion-justified racsism and confusing texts. But lasting works of historical, artistic, scientific and philosophical value have been passed down from the older Greek works (biblical writings all date AFTER Alexandrian period), the Vedic, Sumerian, Egyptian, Near Eastern, Chinese, Persian and Roman cultures. The Jewish scriptures are the only writings from classical antiquity so fixated on elevating their own race above all others.

The majority of believers in the Christian faith and its factions and denominations are good people who just haven't searched beyond the safe parameters their spiritual leaders have set out for them. Accusations and assertions by me will never change someone's mind, especially when having been born into a faith or finding nothing disagreeable with its positions. So now I will cite the Word itself. The Word of a God. The Word of the Old Testament, of a deity who claimed his covenant will NEVER be superseded (meaning-Christianity is a false). Here are the scriptures of what we are told is a loving God.

"Thou shalt save alive nothing that breatheth; but thou shalt utterly destroy them." (Deuteronomy 20:16-17, also in Numbers 31:17-18) In Deuteronomy 3:6 we find that the Israelites went forth and killed all the men, women and children of the 60 cities of Argob.

"Go and smite Amalek, and utterly destroy all that they have, and spare them not, but slay both man and woman, infant and suckling..." (1 Samuel 15:3)

Jews in reference to YHVH make it a happy occasion to murder Edomite babies. (Psalm 137:8-9)

Israelites killed all 12,000 men and women of the city of Ai. (Joshua 8:25)

YHVH commands Israelites to make siege and war against foreign cities who will not agree to be slaves. (Deuteronomy 20:10-11)

YHVH promises to force Israel's enemies to commit cannibalism- "And I will feed them that oppress thee with their own flesh..."

Many, in fact the majority, of the Israelites were appalled by the atrocities of YHVH and they revolted over and over against Moses and this imposter god. According to the scriptures they were dealt with by YHVH. The Covenant of the Law initiated by YHVH through Moses was only accomplished by force and violence, executions and threats. Israel did not enter this covenant willingly, but were brutalized and intimidated in to submitting. Even YHVH says it was MY covenant, not "ours." (Leviticus 26:15) If an agreement is made and broken the parties are no longer bound to its terms. Buy YHVH is not satisfied with a nullification, he threatens to become Israel's ENEMY-

"I will even appoint over you terror, consumption and the burning ague, that shall consume the eyes, and cause sorrow of heart; and you shall sow your seed in vain, for your enemies shall eat it. And I will set my face against you, and you shall be slain before your enemies: they that hate you shall reign over you..." (Leviticus 26:16-17)

As publisher Paul Tice of Book Tree in San Diego put it-
this wasn't an agreement, it's blackmail.

YHVH had no problem with killing off the innocent with the guilty. In Deuteronomy 32:21-26 YHVH promised those who disobeyed him that he would consume the earth, heap mischiefs upon Israel, spend his arrows on them, burn them with hunger, devour them with burning heat and destruction. Send beasts and poisonous serpents against them and the sword to kill "both the young man and the virgin, the suckling also with the man of gray hairs."

Fundamentalists have so many hypocritical explanations for this genocide. "Oh, the Jews are God's chosen people..." "The Jews were allowed to exterminate their enemies because it was God's will." Or, "God allowed the Israelites to exterminate man, woman and child because the Jews were the only ones allowed to live in the Promise

Land." The fictions so easily accepted by religionists are maddening. These same morons would be offended if Hispanics of native American descent suddenly butchered an entire Arizona town of Caucasians simply because it was the land of their nativity.

YHVH was never silent about his priorities.

> "I kill and I make alive, I wound and I heal..." (Deuteronomy 32:39)

> "I will choose their delusions, and will bring their fears upon them; because when I called, none did answer..." (Isaiah 66:4)

> "Behold, I frame evil against you, and devise a device against you..." (Jeremiah 18:11)

> "I gave them also statutes that were NOT GOOD, and judgements whereby they should not live." (Ezekiel 20:24-25)

> "Behold, I am bringing such evil upon Jerusalem and Judah that whosoever heareth of it, both his ears shall tingle." (2 Kings 21:12)

> "Yet he [YHVH] is wise, and will bring evil, and will not call back his words." (Isaiah 31:2)

> "I frame evil against you..." (Jeremiah 18:11)

> "...I have brought all this great evil upon this people," and "...hear all the evil which I purpose to do unto them..." (Jeremiah 32:42, 36:3)

> "Ye have seen all the evil I have brought upon Jerusalem," (Jeremiah 44:2)

> "I will bring evil upon all flesh..." (Jeremiah 45:5)

> "Out of the mouth of the Most High proceedeth not evil and good?" (Lamentations 3:38)

Such a wonderful, loving god to follow and adore, and according to Christians this deity is the same one who had a son who was allowed to bring forth a new, formerly prohibited covenant. The duplicity gives me pause. Old YHVH summons evil against the Israelites in Jeremiah 1:14-16 and again in 11:11- "I will bring evil upon them, which they shall not be able to escape; and thought they shall cry unto me, I will not hearken unto them," and in 11:17 we read that YHVH "hath pronounced evil against thee." In 11:22-23 YHVH will kill by famine and the sword, and "...will bring evil upon the men of Anathoth." Not bring JUSTICE, nor vengeance...evil.

In Psalm 78:49 "He cast upon them the fierceness of his anger, wrath, and indignation, and trouble, by sending EVIL ANGELS among them." In Isaiah 19:13-14 the errors of Egypt for which YHVH later judged the nation in a series of disasters was caused by a PERVERSE SPIRIT FROM YHVH. In 2 Kings 2:23-24 YHVH slays 42 children using two bears simply for calling a prophet "thou bald head." Later in 17:25 he uses lions to kill people. In Judges 3:20 YHVH uses an Israelite to murder someone- "I have a message from YHVH unto thee," said Ehud just before plunging a dagger into Eglon, King of Moab.

In Numbers 11:1 YHVH burned to death a group of Israelites discontent with him. The Israelites were fed up with Moses and the tyrant YHVH, openly complained and were as a result BURNED ALIVE (Numbers 16:32-35), then YHVH burned alive 250 more of their leaders, the smartest men, those the rest of Israel followed and then killed a total of 14,700 Israelites to effective cower the rest into submission. ((16:44-49) Again the Israelites rose up against the tyrant and his prophet and YHVH killed 24,000 more Israelites after impaling their leaders. (25:1-9).

YHVH from the beginning was a Taker of Life. In Genesis 38:7 YHVH slew a son of Judah, and then a second one. (38:10) He slew 50,070 Israelites for just looking inside the Ark of the Covenant after the Philistines had returned it. (1 Samuel 6:19). Perhaps there was nothing inside and this could not be let out. When the Ark was about to fall over Nathan reached up merely to steady it and YHVH slew him. (2 Samuel 6:6-7) In Numbers 1:51 YHVH commanded that if any man approached too close to the Tabernacle he was to be executed. Why? What would a god have to fear? In Leviticus YHVH killed both sons of Aaron the high priest for their offering "strange fire," and then orders Aaron not to grieve. Moses ordered the execution of anyone by arrows or stones who ventured too close to Mount Sinai. (Exodus 19:12-13)

Moses and Aaron were the greatest servants of YHVH but Moses was NOT allowed to enter the Promise Land. YHVH burned alive Aaron's sons Nadab and Abihu and Aaron was discarded, left to die on a mountain. However, Joshua and David found favor with YHVH, the two MOST BLOODIEST, murderous men in all the Old Testament.

First, Joshua reiterated the threats of Moses- "And Joshua said unto these people, 'Ye cannot serve the Lord; for he is a holy God; he is a jealous God; he will not forgive your transgressions nor your sins. If ye forsake the Lord, and serve strange gods, the he will turn and do you hurt..." (Joshua 24:19-20) Joshua spearheaded the assault against the seven nations of Canaan and led the genocidal war, city after city killing men, women, children and sometimes even all the livestock. Joshua died of old age.

In 2 Samuel 5:8 we find that David exhorted his men to kill the LAME and the BLIND hanging around Jerusalem for they "...are hated of David's soul." David killed Goliath, led many military campaigns, stole the city of Urusalim from the Gebusites, murdered his friend Uriah to steal his wife Bathsheba, committed adultery with the married woman before the husband was dead and this same David was a man after YHVH's own heart. This is what scripture says. David too died of old age.

A loving god who promises that you will be so hungry that you will eat your own children. "If ye will not...hearken unto me...ye shall eat the flesh of your sons, and the flesh of your daughters...I will...cast your carcasses upon the carcasses of your idols...I will make your cities waste..." (Leviticus 26:29) In 2 Kings 6:27, 29, 33 the Israelites who are starving resort to eating their own sons, and they were told- "Behold, this evil is of YHVH." In Jeremiah 19:9 YHVH ranting- "And I will cause them [in Jerusalem] to eat the flesh of their sons and the flesh of their daughters, and they shall eat every one the flesh of their friend..." In Lamentations 4:9-11 the prophet Jeremiah wrote that in causing the Israelites to eat their own children, "YHVH hath accomplished his fury." Even Jeremiah admits that something is terribly wrong, "O YHVH, thou hast deceived me, and I was deceived." (Jeremiah 20:7)

Having considered these passages we can better interpret the real meaning behind these biblical passages.

> "For the Lord Most High is terrible..." (Psalm 47:2)

> "Knowing therefore the terror of the Lord, we persuade men..." (2 Corinthians 5:11)

> "It is a fearful thing to fall into the hands of the living God." (Hebrews 10:31)

Burning alive...impalement...plague...starvation...cannibalism...butc hered by weapons- these be the rewards to those who do not follow his dictates, commands that very specifically have you to agreeing to MURDER others. YHVH was an imposter god as shown clearly in The Great Deceit Part I and II, he is NOT the God of the Abrahamic Covenant adhered to by the Israelites and all those nations today descended from her. YHVH is the god the Jews chose. Christianity is a continuation of the ABRAHAMIC covenant and has NOTHING to do with this hateful, racist, murderous demon called YHVH.

"Cursed be he that keepeth back his sword from blood." (Jeremiah 48:10)

24. Giants on Ancient Earth & the Origin of Nephilim Theory

Giants on Ancient Earth: An In-Depth Study on the NEPHILIM is a paperback and ebook I wrote after many years of exhaustive research on the Nephilim. This work is over 320 pages packed with data on giants, ancient texts and little-known histories concerning the races of gigantic peoples that once lived on this rock and the Establishment censorship employed to silence news of these modern discoveries. For this post I will give you a sneak peek of the book's contents.

Table of Contents

Prologue-**Vast Gulf of Missing History...Some Discoveries of Note...Origin of Nephilim Theory...Antediluvian Giants and the Flood...Post-Diluvian Giants...Giants in the Promise Land...Conquest of Canaan...The Last Bible Giants...Giants in Ancient Egypt...The Giant of Babylon...The Giant Wars...Albion: Isle of the Giants...Epics of the Giants...Relics of the Gods...The Bones of Giants...Birth of the Great Lie...Epilogue-As in the Days of Noah**...Bibliography

Chapter One

Some Discoveries of Note

Writing of events before his own time when he finished his monumental book The Histories about 440 BC, Herodotus wrote that an excavation of what was believed to be the crypt of a Trojan War hero, Orestes, yeilded forth the remains of a giant who had stood 10 feet high.(1) This book of world history was written over 24 centuries ago and as will be shown in this work, it is but only one of the multitudes of ancient texts that mention an historic race of giants. In 170 AD Athenagoras wrote the book Of Angels and Giants. It was the accepted history of the time and had been for two millennia with wicked angels long ago before the Deluge copulated with human females who then gave birth to monstrous giants. These angels were gods, djinn, demons, fairies, each culture painting them with their own brush. Only later did official Christianity stamp out the belief by declaring it pagan similarly to how the modern scientific community censors all discoveries concerning giants from the public domain.

After the Romans conquered Jerusalem in 135 AD the rabbi Johnanan ben Zakkai led Hadrian into the deep underground catacombs beneath the Temple. He was shown the bones of enormous men who had stood over nine feet tall and told they were Amorites.(2) About the same time over 17 centuries ago Sertorius in Spain was shown the crypt of a giant named Anteaus, the skeletal remains of a man who stood six cubits high.(3) This measures to a height of 108 inches, or nine feet. It was during Hadrian's reign sea waves at Rhoeteum washed open an ancient tomb containing a giant's skeleton. Its knee caps were the size of a large discuss. Hadrian ordered that the bones be reburied.(4) In 240 AD Mani the Persian wrote The Book of Giants, a text not to be confused with the Dead Sea Scrolls text of the same name that is almost three centuries older. Mani was a religious reformer but was killed by the religious authorities of his time. He believed that Christianity had become corrupted by the influence of Judaism.(5) He founded the Gnostic sect of Manichaeism. Mani may have derived much of his material from the various writings in circulation at the time attributed to Enoch. Texts explored in this work.

Some of the more unusual information from ancient writings have now been verified in chance finds. In the Babylonian Talmud called the Berakthoth we learn that giants before the Flood had double rows of teeth.(6) Such large human skeletons have now been found that prominently exhibit these double rows of teeth. In 1822 at Lompcock Rancho, California soldiers excavated among carved shells, huge stone axes and blocks of porphyry adorned in an unknown script containing the skeleton of a man who once stood 12 feet tall with a double-row of teeth.(7)   Later more gigantic human skeletons were found with double dentition inside a mound near Clearwater, Minnosota.(8)   In 1872 at Seneca Township, Ohio were excavated three human skeletons 8 feet tall with double-rows of teeth.(9)   In 1880 giant skeletons with double-rows of teeth (hyperdontia) were found in Clearwater, MN.(10)   In 1892 a gigantic human skeleton was found with a double row of teeth at Proctorville, Ohio(11).   The ancient race of giants occupying Ireland of old called the Fomorii had a double row of teeth.(12)   More will be discussed on the Fomorii later in this work.

I have hyperdontia. Even today I have a double row of teeth, my lower jaw, though I've grown extra adult teeth time and again along my uppers. This genetic increase of anatomical traits is also found in Nephilim studies in the six-fingered and six-toed skeletal remains unique to gigantic human skeletons. In 1891 at Crittenden, Arizona was discovered a stone sarcophagus of a giant who once stood about 12 feet high having six fingers and toes on his hands and feet according to the carving of the giant on the stone.(13)   In 1895 a 12 foot tall fossilized giant was found in County Antrim, Ireland. It had six toes on its right foot.(14)   In 1949 in New Zealand it is reported that gigantic human footprints with six toes were discovered in volcanic ash (petrified), giants once standing at least 12 feet tall.(15)   At Tiahuanacu in South America were excavated statues of great age with men having six fingers on their hands and six toes on their feet.(16)   In the area of

Braystown near the headwaters of the Tennessee river were found fossilized footprints of six-toed giants, one being monstrous, the heel impression 13 inches wide.(17) Petroglyphs found near Three Rivers, New Mexico are of hands with six fingers.(18)

A strong link between the official censorship between Nephilim discoveries and extraterrestrial/UFO studies has been noted by many researchers. In May of 1947 a six-fingered alien was autopsied on film, the extraterrestrial body said to have been taken from the UFO crash site near Roswell, New Mexico.(19) This case is famous and only mentioned here because of the obvious correlation to six-fingered specimens. But the censorship is relevant. In 1999 a washout unearthed humanoid skeletons about 7 foot tall with six fingers and six toes on their limbs, with human teeth but no canines. Extra large molars and incisors, large skulls, larger than proportional eye-sockets and fingers too long for such small hands. Skeletons had been buried with beautiful pottery and baskets of fine weave. They were unearthed at Arizona's Canyon de Chelly National Monument. All Park Service personnel were pressed into service to box up the artifacts and remains as they were directly overseen by personnel from the Smithsonian Institute and FBI who conducted full body searches. All involved were forced to sign nondisclosure secrecy documents.(20)

Extra teeth, extra fingers and toes and now this. In 1899 near Mexico City was unearthed a human skeleton having two extra ribs- 26 ribs in all.(21) The whole human race has 24 ribs...how did that happen? Sorry folks, a teaser. Giants on Ancient Earth quotes from over 140 sources not including the biblical books, many of these sources being out-of-print texts other Nephilim researchers are unaware of. The ebook version is only $2.99 and contains the exact same information.

Origin of Nephilim Theory...Daughter of Men

The only place in Scripture that the term daughters of men can be found is in Genesis 6:2-4, mentioned twice, both in direct reference to sons of God.

And it came to pass, when men began to multiply on the face of the earth, and daughters were born unto them, that the sons of God saw that the daughters of men that they were fair; and they took them wives of all which they chose.

It is unfortunate that so many Bible-believing Christians have fallen prey to the misleading theologians and scholars that have misinterpreted these two verses of history as referring to how ancient men and women married. They contend that the sons of God is a title for those of the righteous bloodline of Seth, while the daughters of men were the women of the evil Cainite lineage. But this is completely untrue and without merit.

Another indication as to the identity of the sons of God is discovered in that all through the Bible the phrase sons of men is used when speaking about large populations of people. Here, daughters of men are not wives of sons of men, but rather they are wives of the sons of God. Scripture differentiates between the sons of God and the sons of Adam (Deuteronomy 32:8). It is not an accident that both of these terms, describing angels and humans, are found within the Torah, the first five books of the Bible.

Other references to sons concerning angels are found in the Jewish apocalyptic literature found among the Dead Sea Scrolls. One reference made is in the War Scroll. It foretells of a last days war in heaven between the sons of light and the sons of darkness. (1)   Lucifer was called son of the morning, and in Psalm 89 it calls angels of the host of heaven sons of the mighty.

The Hebrew meanings and definitions from which our English translations derive offer us a clearer picture as to the events described in these two verses in Genesis detailed earlier, 6:2 and 6:4. First, the word fair in Genesis 6:2 is tov, which means good, pleasant, and beautiful physically while also implying good, right, and beneficial morally and ethically. The daughters of men could not be described as such if they were truly a reference to the females of the Cainite lineage. Another word in the same verse is chose. The passage reads: and they took them wives of all which they chose. The word for chose in this Hebrew context is bachar, and it has a deeper meaning that no word in the English language could have been provided for in proper transliteration. Bachar means chose, but more precisely, to select after keenly observing and is used in Hebrew texts where choices that have eternal consequences are made...and the fact that the angels that sexually trespassed against mankind will suffer eternal consequences is taught all throughout Scripture.

In fact, all contention between good and evil in the Bible is focused in between the sons of God, former holy angels now fallen, the present sons of God that still remain holy, and the future sons of God they are commanded to protect, humans often referred to in the Bible as sons of men until the First Resurrection takes place and believers receive their sonship. Thus we shall be like the angels (Luke 20:35-36). This contention will one day end between the fallen sons and holy ones when the children of the kingdom will be cast out (Matthew 8:12).

In 1 Corinthians we find that Paul retained some knowledge about the former sins of angels and their lusts.

Neither was man created for the woman, but the woman for the man. For this cause ought the woman to have power on her head because of the angels. But if a woman have long hair, it is a glory to her; for her hair is given her for a covering. (1 Corinthians 11:9-11, 14)

Paul is suggesting that women have long hair because of the angels, that women should cherish long hair for its serves as a covering. In these modern days this is difficult to comprehend. Today's culture dictates otherwise by fashions and traditions, but during the days of only a hundred years ago and beyond through thousands of years, it was universally held that all women have long hair. To view a woman's fleshly beauty was by removing her hair from her body, something only husbands had the right to do. Today this is rarely practiced. By mentioning the angels here, Paul reveals that he was aware that the angels had at one time in history or still did lust after human women, and his suggestion is to hinder this by having women grow long hair.

In Jude 6-7 the apostle writes that the angels sinned even as Sodom and Gomorrah, giving themselves over to fornication, and going after strange flesh. The Greek phrase strange flesh also translates to sexual abominations; thus, the angels were guilty of sexual relations with women when they were not permitted just as the people of Sodom and Gomorrah were guilty of homosexual abominations.

He gave me the signs of all the secret things in the book of my great grandfather Enoch.5 Noah studied Enoch's writings. These texts are prophetic and very informative concerning the geographical, social, spiritual and celestial conditions from Eden to the Flood. The patriarchal bloodline family of Genesis from Adam to Noah knew that the world would be destroyed, and this knowledge was preserved through Enoch's books that were inherited by his own son:

Preserve, my son Mathusalah, the books of the hand of thy father: that thou mayest transmit them to future generations. (Enoch 81:2)

Evidence that the Book of Enoch was available to the writers of the Bible is unveiled in that a portion of Enoch 99:2 is quoted five times by Bible prophets (2) and millions of times by people all around the world. Enoch says, "The apple of my eye," a phrase no doubt connected to the Edenic sin of eating the apple from the accursed tree of knowledge of good and evil. James Kugel in his book The Bible as It Was commented that the writings of Enoch seem to be the oldest Jewish writings that have survived outside the Bible itself.

These ancient and often debated writings were a part of the universal canon of Scripture, in the Bible for five centuries! (3) Later it was decided that only the book of the Revelation of John would remain canonical. Meetings and disputes raged as the early church selected and deleted various books and writings for the Bible. The writings of Enoch were accepted as Scripture by Jesus and Paul, and the whole Christian church for several centuries, and quoted by the apostle Jude as well.

The daughters of men in the Enochian text are described as elegant and beautiful. The Enoch writings also make it very clear that there is a difference between sons of God (or of heaven) and sons of men. In this story the sons of heaven assembled and said, "Come, let us select for ourselves wives from the progeny of men, and let us beget children." (Enoch 7:2) In the Hebrew commentary called the Book of Jasher cited twice in the Bible itself (Joshua 10:13, 2 Samuel 1:18) we learn that the rebellious angels shift their authoritative capacities from guardians or Watchers to judges and rulers over men.

And their judges and rulers went to the daughters of men and took their wives by force from their husbands according to their choice. (Jasher 4:18) In Baruch 56:12-14 the angels descended, and mingled with women. And then those who did so were tormented in chains. But the rest of the multitude of angels, of which there is no number, restrained themselves.

Among the Dead Sea texts is the Lamech Scroll. This preflood patriarch had a son so beautiful and radiant that he accused his wife of adultery with the angels! (4) This story of Noah's birth is ancient and was not regarded as myth by the Hebrews, nor should it be today. It is evident that Lamech's wife was referring to angels when she said sons of heaven, which is greatly supported by the fact that the Greek version of the Old Testament, the Septuagint, translates bene Elohim in the Hebrew as angels of God instead of sons of God like the Masoretic text.

The Greek rendering is not to be regarded lightly; even Jesus and the apostles accepted its authority and quoted from it extensively. Though the Masoretic text was the original Hebrew version of the Bible, it was the Greek Septuagint that was most widely used during the first century churches and Jewish people. In fact, there is no historical or textual evidence from antiquity that the Jewish version of the Old Testament is any older than the Greek version. Concerning the Nephilim, attempts from all avenues of scholarship and theology have attempted to refute the existence of literal giants. Just a few generations ago there existed no proof of the existence of Nephilim. But today the evidence is piling. Archeologists are confounded the world over as they dig up artifacts and relics that do not fit into their preconceived beliefs of ancient history. The prophecy of Daniel that knowledge shall be increased in the last days is coming to pass.

In keeping with the spirit of the scriptures I quoted the sources as they were, referencing angels and sons of God but my own personal belief is more complex. These are religionist versions, primitive attempts to make sense of the unusual knowledge our ancestors maintained, memories of visitors who came to Earth and found that they were DNA-compatible with the human population here. Noah's birth, porcelain skin, sky blue eyes- traits of the "angels" and Sons of God merely demonstrates that these visitors appeared more Caucasian than the indigenous humans. For more on the Sons of God, the Daughters of Men and Nephilim histories and the ancient records that discuss them, see my book, Giants on Ancient Earth: An In- Depth Study on the Nephilim.

25. Epics of the Giants

Giants are the most common and thoroughly ignored presence in the vast majority of ancient literature. From the four thousand year old *Epic of Gilgamesh* to the late one thousand year old poem *Beowulf*, giants are discovered in fascinating accuracy when compared to the biblical accounts of the Nephilim. Between these two historic epics are the famous Homeric epics called the *Odyssey* and the *Iliad*, both extremely lengthy stories about gods and giants that archeologists and historians marvel over even today. The Roman poet and writer Virgil continued this art form of epic preservation in his articulate collection called the *Aeneid* and his contemporary in the first century B.C. named Ovid also wrote about the giants and their conflicts with the gods and mortals.

It is in the epic poem titled *Beowulf* that we learn the most stunning and intricate insights into giant history and beliefs. This ancient poem was truly preserved by a miracle, for only one burnt copy of the thousand year old epic remains and it is located today in the British Museum.[1] Under Catholic persecution long ago all known copies of *Beowulf* were burnt and their owners punished severely.

Beowulf is the sole survivor of what may have been a thriving epic tradition, but it is great poetry. Approached as an archaeological relic, it is fascinating. Taken as a linguistic document, it is a marvel, a mine of revelations and controversies. It gives us vital information about many things that scholars would like to have much more information on. [2]

Long ago, as far back as a few decades after the flood bards and sages would tell stories, weaving their history into a poetic cadence often using harps or other instruments for effect and entertainment. Entire stories line by line were memorized and told with great effect. Later these traditions passed from being solely oral to written epics that preserved the human experience and beliefs people maintained in artistic forms that earned their tellers high esteem and a good living.

Even today these poems are hauntingly vivid despite that their translations no longer have the effect of rhythm. Like the power experienced within the pages of our Bibles these ancient epics echo of times magically familiar to us deep within our being.

These are stories of folklore and romance which run back from the medieval courts through Celtic legend and minstrelsy to archaic Sumer, and perhaps further, to the very beginning of story-telling. [3]

William Cooper has put together a very scholarly and convincing argument for the historicity of the ancient Old English epic *Beowulf*, identifying named in the poem in archaic Danish and Anglo-Saxon genealogies, including the Geatish warrior Beowulf himself. This research is found in William Cooper's book *After the Flood*, a fascinating and new look at ancient and modern Anglo-Saxon history.

The Anglo-Saxon race, along with the Geats, Swedes, Gauls, Norse, Celts, and Scythians among others of European ancestry are all more recent descendants of people who trace their bloodlines directly back to

Mesopotamia, to the patriarchs Japheth and Noah. The Norse remembered the giants as enemies of the gods, evil Frost giants that terrorized their ancestors during an ice age long ago. The Celts recorded their battles with the last Firbolgs and Fomorian giants and then later Tuatha de Danaan, all huge and violent peoples. And now, in *Beowulf* is discovered a knowledge of evil giants by the ancient Danish and Geatish people. The author of this famous poem is no longer known, lost in the mists of history and Catholic oppression, but his belief in the existence of giants and their *biblical* history is unquestionable. In Burton Raffel's creative translation of *Beowulf* we read;

He was spawned in that slime, conceived by a pair of those monsters born of Cain, murderous creatures banished by God, punished forever for the crime of Abel's death. The Almighty drove those demons out, and their exile was better, shut away from men; they split into a thousand forms of evil-spirits, and friends, goblins, monsters, giants, a brood forever opposing the Lord's will, and again and again defeated.[4]

It is interesting to us today that the author of this poem believed that monsters and giants were born of *Cain* and were banished by God, a parallel found in Genesis when Cain himself killed Abel and was banished by God to depart form Eden. Before the flood when the *sons of God* rebelled sexually against God and impregnated women, this hybrid union gave birth to the giants. The Nephilim. It was probably through Cainite women that angels abducted when fathering the giants. Also of immense interest is the fact that the author made the connection between giants and the Bible, to times before the flood, identifying the fathers of these giants indirectly as *demons*.

The belief of old that giants and demons are one and the same has incredibly ancient origins. The writings of *Enoch*, another epic-like collection of stories, revelations, and prophecies concerning angels and giants confirmed this connection long ago. The book of *Enoch* explains that when giants die *evil spirits shall proceed form their flesh, because they were created form above, form the holy Watchers was their beginning...evil spirits shall they be upon the earth, and the spirits of the wicked shall they be called.*[5]

John Milton reflects this archaic belief in his modern epic of the seventeenth century entitled, *Paradise Lost,* in which we read that the original fallen angels became fairies, having sons of enormous stature long ago that in more contemporary times have become diminutive;

...in bigness Earth's Giant Sons, now less then smallest Dwarfs...[6]

William Cooper's genealogy of the Royal Geatish House has Beowulf living from A.D. 495-583. The members of Beowulf's family and ancestors as listed in the poem are also discovered in the genealogy and traced directly back to Noah by ancient chroniclers such as Geoffrey of Monmouth in his *History of the Kings of Britain*. Having a definitive place in northern European history the writings in *Beowulf* thus strengthen the writings of Enoch concerning the giants and their demonic relations. In Burton Raffel's translation of *Beowulf*, in the back of the book is an Afterword by Robert Creed. In this Afterword we read many more proofs this epic contains many verifiable events, a work of true history. Concerning *Beowulf* Dr. Paul Carus wrote in his book *The History of the Devil and the Idea of Evil:*

There are innumerable legends which preserve the old conception and simply replace the names of giants by devils...[7]

The entire plot of the *Beowulf* epic concerns these giants. Already by the time of this saga the giants were no longer existing as a civilization. Beowulf traveled to help the Danes kill Grendel, a fierce beast that haunted the fens and swampy moors. Before his famous stand against the creature he boasted, "*I drove five great giants into chains, chased all of that race from the earth.*"[8]

Here is evidence that the early Anglo-Saxon people regarded the giants as a *race* and not regarded as random mutations caused by inbreeding. This is not unusual and nor would it have been contended by the first millennium BCE and CE Britons, Celts, and Norse, all who incidentally trace their ancestry to post-diluvian patriarchs who had lived long ago when giants were a much more common threat. Beowulf kills a monster called Grendel, a beast that lived among reptilian creatures with sharp claws and teeth. William Cooper cites evidence and provides photographs of archaeological relics of stone and clay figurines of prehistoric-like creatures. Dinosaurs. In his book, *After the Flood*, he reveals astonishing historical proofs and records of these and other creatures now extinct that evidently lived in the swamps and lakes of Europe over a thousand years ago. A complete list of 71 zoologically applied terms in *Beowulf* is in this fascinating book.

After the defeat of Grendel in a wrestling match where Beowulf tore off the monster's arm, bards immediately compose songs and poems of Beowulf's bravery, weaving their lyrics into older songs about heroes long ago. The unknown narrator states:

...There were tales of giants wiped from the earth by Siegmund's might.[9]

The writer of the poem describes these verses of Siegmund as being from *old songs*, revealing that the giants were a part of their distant history. Just as the people alive during the epic's story have been identified in early genealogies so also has Siegmund been discovered in the genealogy of the East Saxon kings as *Siegmund,* fifth descendant of Sledd.[10]

This archaic race was believed to have been born of Cain before the flood. Speaking of Cain, the writer states: *And he bore a race of fiends accursed like their father.*[11]

To the author all demons became monsters, fiends and giants. After Beowulf killed Grendel the monster's mother ate a Danish warrior in King Hrothgar's renovated hall, beginning her revenge. One of Beowulf's soldiers was eaten the next night as well. Beowulf meets the *fog-giant Grendel and defeats him...he then encounters Grendel's mother, the giantess of the marsh whence the fog rises...*[12] Traced back to early Briton we find many parallels concerning the giants in Beowulf and the giant remnants detailed in the previous chapter, *Albion...Isle of the Giants.* There were hill giants, mountain giants, storm and fog giants, all related to the Firbolgs or Fomorians. In *Bulfinch's Mythology* are found huge mountain giants allied to the Frost giants that warred against the Norse gods. Grendel is also described as being very large in the Time-Life Books collection called *The Enchanted World...Night Creatures*:

Although manlike, that being was no man. Huge and hairy, it shambled through the night mists of fell and fen...[13]

Beowulf hunted the mother of Grendel (a female giant) in a swamp and found her among the ruins of an ancient hall that the creature was using for a lair. His own sword useless against the she-beast, Beowulf wrestles her as he had done her son. Unlike any woman today, this monster had incredible strength and pinned Beowulf to the stone floor of the dilapidated building.

Squatting with her weight on his stomach, she drew a dagger, brown with dried blood, and prepared to avenge her only son...[14]

Beowulf had entered the swamp with the mindset of defeating the giant without a weapon as he had done her son. Or so he boasted. But during the unique conflict Beowulf frees himself from her grasp and sees-

Hanging on the wall, a heavy sword, hammered by giants, strong and blessed with their magic, the best of all weapons, but so massive that no ordinary man could lift its carved and decorated length.[15]

This passage calls to mind the many citations in this book concerning the metallurgical practices of the giants, of the Anakim of the Bible and Anunnaki of Babylonian antiquity both of which have their name derived from ancient words for *metals* as expounded upon in earlier chapters. These giants mined rare and precious metals and were smiths that incorporated vast intelligence, alchemy and adept metallurgical skills into their weaponry. Today people regard giants as being clumsy, unintelligent and mythical but no long ago they were perceived as agile, malicious and highly skilled, their workmanship of *magic*.

Another unique connection we see in the person of this giantess in relation to the old Celtic and British beliefs in giant hags and witch-giants expounded upon in the previous chapter is the fact that in the epic *Beowulf* this female giantess is also called *a monstruous hag*[16] And she is called *a horrible hag, fierce and wild.*[17]

After slaying Grendel's mother in the ruins, the hero returned; *...but all that Beowulf took was Grendel's head and the hilt of the giant's jeweled sword...*[18]

Grendel was not a single creature but the name of the mysterious giants known to hide in the swamplands away from human civilization. The *Beowulf* epic makes careful mention of other monsters, great beasts that fit perfectly into today's versions of prehistoric creatures. In *After the Flood* we discover that many prehistoric animals became extinct because of climatic conditions after the deluge were more frigid compared to the global tropical weather before the flood that promoted the growth of such great beasts as the dinosaurs. The flood caused global cooling, an ice age where Frost giants became the greatest threat because the enormous reptiles were dying.

The *Book of Enoch* indicates that the rebellious angels called the Watchers were imprisoned during the flood as a foreshadowing of the eternal imprisonment these sexual angels will suffer. After the flood these angels were again released. *And when the angels shall ascend, the waters of the springs shall again undergo a change, and be frozen.*[19]

The global cooling effected by the flood and the collapse of the aquatic atmosphere that entrapped earth's geothermal heat and magnified the sun's light initiated an ice age in which the northern and southern poles and regions for thousands of miles became desolate *frozen* glacial wastes. Only the equatorial lands were habitable for nearly five hundred years after the flood, which is why most archaeologists concede that the cradle of civilization was in Mesopotamia which was merely the land where the descendants of Noah multiplied and became nations that eventually began wandering away as the ice melted and earth became a warmer place.

Because of these colder climates the reptiles and creatures no longer grew to their former sizes nor lived as long. But remnants of these creatures survived and dispersed to areas around the world more suitable to their nature. And the warm lakes, fens, swamps and marshes of Finland and Denmark were one of these havens. It is a possibility that the Loch Ness Monster is more fact than fiction because of this historic occurrence. Grendel was personified as a demon by the author of *Beowulf*. Being an early Christian writer this is not unusual, however the word *grendel* was used in the English transliterations to describe such phrases as *terrifying ugly one*[20] *solitary walker*[21] *terrible*[22] *evil doer*[23] *devil*[24] *accursed outcast*[25] *fierce in battle*[26] and *giant.*[27] The word for giant is found in line 426 of the epic, *Thyrs*, which refers to the *male* Grendel Beowulf killed first.

Earlier in this book we learned that the Fomorians (Irish giants of old) were hideous in appearance and could easily be described as *terrifying ugly one(s)*. Since no good giants are found in Scripture it is not surprising that giants have been universally associated with the devil and evil-doing by scores of historical texts and traditions. The description of Grendel being *terrible* fits perfectly with the biblical giants called Emims, for *terrible* is the translation of their name. All the giant nations, the Anakim, Rephaim, Emims, Zamzummmims and Zuzims were warlike, *fierce in battle*. No Nephilim people ever knew peace.

There is little description of Grendel except for these and other literal translations of the creatures called *Grendel*. In fact, in the *Beowulf* text we discover that Grendel is described to walk *like a man*, an attribute very rare save for humans. This proves Grendel was no ordinary monster. Speaking to Beowulf, King Hrothgar said,

"I've heard that my people, peasants working in the fields, have seen a pair of such fiends wandering in the moors and marshes, giant monsters living in those desert lands. And they said to my wise men that, as well as they could see, one of the devils was a female creature. The other, they say, walked through the wilderness like a man-but mightier than any man..."[28]

This description of the beasts gives forth the image of a giant humanoid creature. Although other fierce reptilian animals are described in *Beowulf* it appears that the Grendel beasts slain by the hero were giants that lived in some ancient ruins in a swamp. The peasants mentioned by the king could discern that one of the creatures was female from a distance. If truly reptilian this would never have been so easily noticed. Also, reptiles or amphibian creatures have no *hair*.

After slaying the first Grendel's mother, Beowulf then decapitated her and *carried that terrible trophy by the hair*.[29] Admittedly, Beowulf had killed giants before, but this Grendel was the first giantess he's slain.

If these Grendel beasts were descended from ancient Nephilim giants then they would have been intelligent. The giants were forgers and metallurgical masters that definitely retained the intelligence to have a written language. Here, in this archaic Old English poem is found astonishing historical accuracy in what is regarded today by the intellectual elite as mere myth. Beowulf used a *mighty old sword[30]* to kill the giantess in the ruined hall where Grendel dwelt;

He gave the golden sword hilt to Hrothgar, who held it in his wrinkled hands and stared at what giants had made, and monsters owned; it was his, an ancient weapon shaped by wonderful smiths...[31]

This inspiring rendition by Burton Raffel calls to mind the biblical stories of trophies kept in remembrance of the giants so popular in Bible history. Earlier in this book is cited the Scriptures where the giant named Og was killed and his 13½ foot bed was kept as a trophy by the Ammonites. And then David killed Goliath with his own giant sword after knocking the Philistine giant unconscious with a stone. The sword of Goliath was kept in a temple and many years later was welded by David again.

The old king bent close to the handle of the ancient relic, and saw written there the story of ancient wars between good and evil, the opening of the waters, the flood sweeping giants away, how they suffered and died, that race who hated the Ruler of us all and received judgement from his hands. Surging waves that found them wherever they fled. And Hrothgar saw runic letter clearly carved in that shining hilt, spelling its original owner's name...[32]

This enormous sword given to King Hrothgar of the Danes was called an *ancient relic* almost fifteen hundred years ago! The Sumerians and Akkadians of Babylonia remembered the smith-giants of old, calling them A_nunaki and Anakim. Goliath was a descendant of the Anakims that fled Canaan and found refuge in Philistia away from the conquests and bloody campaigns of Joshua and the invading Israelites.

When David killed Goliath he took the giant's sword as a trophy of his feat as Beowulf had done also. Both heroes also gave these relics away. The amazing aspect of this giant sword hilt is the *runic* letters. The runes were used only by initiates in the Celtic mysterious Druidic worship and practices. As cited earlier in this book the Celts and Druid beliefs migrated from greater Canaan and ultimately from the regions of Chaldea in Mesopotamia. The runes were called *moon letters* long ago, specially imprinted with light wax, invisible unless held up to the moon or candle to be read *through* the paper, thin vellum or parchment. Runes developed from the ancient Akkadian cuneiform letters, crescent shaped letters resembling little moons. Remarkably, Chaldea is translated *the moon*. This runic inscription upon the hilt of the sword was probably inscribed by Tuatha de Danaan people, enormous in stature and from Canaan and Philistia as cited throughout this book.

The details in *Beowulf* concerning the flood are uncanny in their biblical accuracy. The flood was issued by God because of the utter chaos wrought by the giants. If the rebellious angels had not sexually integrated with humans and the giants were not a hostile presence among God's people during the days of Jared, Enoch and Noah then the Creator might have judged the earth in a very different way. But He did not. Nor is there any biblical evidence that Noah was told to warn anyone of the coming flood. Earth was corrupt and God washed her clean.

Also, the *Beowulf* text reads that the flood was caused by *the opening of the waters*. This unique phrase is descriptive of the collapse of the firmament above detailed in the Genesis creation account. This marine atmosphere rained upon earth, sending *surging waves* over the planet. This abundance of water caused global cooling. A drop in temperature around the world caused the north and south poles to accumulate ice rapidly because they are the farthest distances from the equator. To relieve the immense stress and weight at the poles, the arctic regions fragmented and still continue to do so, sending glaciers and icebergs toward the equator.

A roman epic writer and historian named Ovid also wrote about the giants, metallurgy and a flood that destroyed them with their wicked practices;

Then comes *the Age of Iron, and the day of evil dawns...man tore open the earth and rummaged in her bowels. Precious ores the Creator had concealed...were dug up...So now iron comes with its cruel ideas. And gold with crueller...But not even heaven was safe. Now came the turn of the giants...They coveted the very throne of Jove.*[33]

Ovid lived over forty years before Jesus and may have still been alive at the age of eighty or so during Christ's ministry. Being a Roman citizen and being a scribe, Ovid had access to many ancient archives and traditions recorded by former scribes. His information is eerily aligned to the biblical records concerning the giants and their rebellious nature. According to Roman and the earlier Greek beliefs God destroyed these giants with thunderbolts, and then later the Creator flooded earth to kill men. Ovid wrote that Jove addressed the other gods, saying, "*When the giants, whose arms came in hundreds...reached for heaven, I was less angered. Those creatures were dreadful but they were few-a single family. But no...I have to root out, family by family, mankind's teeming millions.*"[34]

At the end of Burton Raffel's translation of *Beowulf* are two sections of interest, an Afterword and Glossary of names. The Afterword is a detailed study of the historical applications of *Beowulf* by Robert P. Creed. This research provides many insights into the people of ancient Denmark, Sweden and other relative European people mentioned in the poem. Like William Cooper in *After the Flood* he puts forth very persuasive evidence in the historical accuracy of *Beowulf.*

In the Glossary of Names at the very end of the Raffel translation is a list of the characters in *Beowulf* and their relationships to each other as well as information that historians have gathered about these ancient people.

In the Glossary we find Grendel. The text states that the etymology of this title *is perhaps related to the Old Norse word grindill* (storm). This comparison is interesting because of the Norse belief in Frost Giants. The icy realm of the dead to these archaic Icelandic people was called *Niflheim*, a word directly derived from Nephilim, *the fallen ones*. The giants of Bible antiquity were known as the *Dead Ones*, being the Rephaim which is plural of *rapha* [dead; very tall] a unique Hebrew word having a dual meaning. So Niflheim of Norse memory could very well be the icy realm of *Rephaim*, the dead. Remembered as Frost giants, the Norse also associated these giants as storm-bringers, akin to *grindils*. Storm giants. Even the word giant in Old English, *gawr*, is comparable to the Hebrew word for *huger man* which is gibbar, found in Genesis 7:4; *might men which were of old, men of renown.*

The Anglo-Saxons and Norse were racial cousins, their ancestry sharing distinctive parallels along with many other European peoples such as the Gauls, Celts and Danes.

In modern occult lore found extensively in adult fantasy role-playing games and other fantasy books is discovered the Frost giants, Fomorians, Firbolgs and ogres, all giants driven out of ancient Canaan and Europe by the early Britons, celts and Norse invaders. This same occult lore that very explicitly details the appearance and traits of these Nephilim-kin nations also features the enormously feared Storm giants. The Grendels.

Their ancient civilizations lost to the judgements of God the giants migrated further west, to Gaza, Gath and Ashdod in the thirteenth century BCE.[35] These giants and giant-kin peoples are identified in Homer's *Odyssey* as revealed earlier in this book as the Phaistos [Philistine-Phoenicians and the Danaans who allied with the Greeks under Agamemnon at the destruction of the Trojan states and capital city of Troy. The Danaans migrated to ancient Albion where they battled Nephilim refugees from Canaan and possibly remnants of giant Rephaims, Emims and Zuzims who fled from Chedorlaomer who tried to eradicate their race in the days of Abraham. These giants were called Firbolgs by the early Trojan colonizers under Brutus and Corineus who'd fled from the Greek invasion of Ionia. For a complete historical account of the Tuatha de Danaan's arrival to Ireland and battles with the Firbolgs, read *Gods and Fighting Men* by Lady Gregory.[36]

By the first millennium A.D. the giants as a civilization anywhere on earth were no more, reduced to *solitary walkers* like the Grendels, vagabonds and swamp recluses so degenerated they were incapable of reading the runic inscriptions on the old relic hilt given to Hrothgar, a weapon made by their own ancestors. Like the Yeti of Tibet's mountains and desolate reaches and the Sasquatch of northwestern America and British Columbia the Grendels were a forlorn, bestial remnant of an ancient and powerful race cursed by God best described in *Beowulf* as an *accursed outcast.*[37]

Like Beowulf of the Anglo-Saxons a hero lived long ago among the Sumerians, Babylonians and Akkadians named Gilgamesh. And not unlike Beowulf this royal figure has been identified as being a real personage of distant antiquity, the king of biblical Erech ruled by Nimrod, called Uruk in the *Epic of Gilgamesh*. Also, just as the Geatish hero slew a giant at the edges of human civilization, Gilgamesh killed a giant much larger than himself even though he himself was of partial giant ancestry. The giant slain by the Sumerian hero was named Humbaba, the *Guardian of the Cedar Forest*.[38] This Cedar Forest has been located by archaeologists as being in Lebanon, but interestingly the *Epic of Gilgamesh* has been discovered in fragments as far as Canaan near Megiddo, a land once inhabited by enormous people.

What makes the *Epic of Gilgamesh* so much more unique than *Beowulf* is the archaic symbolism discovered throughout the ancient text that corresponds beautifully with biblical passages. Unlike *Beowulf* which does not contain many parallels with biblical history, the *Gilgamesh* tablets not only reflect Bible history but reveal astonishing revelations through symbols found only in our Bibles. It unveils a lost language, a form of communication preserved by the Bible's writers but lost to contemporary civilization.

My son, in Uruk lives Gilgamesh; no one has ever prevailed against him, he is strong as a star from heaven.

The term *star of heaven* is representative of more than one idea. In line 107 of the first tablet of *Gilgamesh* the hero is said to have strength *as mighty as the meteorite of Anu*. This word *kisru* was translated *meteorite* in the text but this Akkadian noun could also be accurately rendered–*lump of metal*.[39]

This phrase hints again at the heavenly metallurgical practices taught by the Watchers and their giant offspring. To be compared with a *star of heaven* was an honor akin to being called *god-like*. On old Sumerian and Akkadian texts and monuments *every symbol of a god was also connected with a star.*[40]

In previous chapters we discovered intriguing passages in the Bible located in both testaments that describe and associate *stars of heaven* with angels, which are revealed to be *greater in power and might* than ordinary humans. Gilgamesh is herein compared with supernatural being, which is further seen in the *Gilgamesh* epic; *He will come in his strength like one of the host of heaven.* The art of conveying vital information through unobtrusive symbols permeates throughout Scripture. In the epic si found that Humbaba was also called *watcher of the forest.* The title *watchers* is found in the very old books of Enoch, Jubilees and even the Bible in the book of the prophet Daniel. The Watchers were guardians and this Humbaba was doing just that. This rebellious order of angels fathered the giants, which is reflected in the *Gilgamesh* text;

In the forest lives Humbaba whose name is hugeness, a ferocious giant. Symbols were used by ancient writers to reveal things often misunderstood or not believed, and protected the writers from criticism when others openly defied them. Having written in symbols the authors could easily apply another meaning to thus appease any dissidents. Dr. Paul Carus most articulately explains the usage of symbols and encrypted writing;

Symbols are not lies; symbols contain truth. Allegories and parables are not falsehoods; they convey information; moreover, they can be understood by those who are not as yet prepared to receive the plain truth.[41]

Humbaba is killed by Gilgamesh, the giant being *identified as a north Syrian, Anatolian or Elamite god.*[42] The parallels found in this ancient Sumerian epic that correspond with the Bible go deeper. The biblical giants called the Anakim are the same Nephilim race as the Babylonian *Anunnaki.* Like the Philistine-Anakim giant Goliath in the Old Testament, we discover that Humbaba the giant had a *sword of eight talents.* As David kept Goliath's sword and Beowulf the giant sword hilt of Grendel, Gilgamesh took this enormous sword. The fact that Humbaba was a giant guardian conveys that he was keeping post for others or something of value, and this is what is discovered by Gilgamesh. After slaying the giant the Sumerian hero came across the *sacred dwellings of the Anunnaki.*[43] *Anakim* giants of the Bible renowned for their height and metallurgical skills. Gilgamesh later travels to visit Noah, named Utnapishtim in the Babylonia-Akkadian version and hears a story about antediluvian life and the flood. The *Epic of Gilgamesh* is fascinating and should be studied by all serious Bible students.

He was wise, he saw mysteries and knew secret things, he brought us a tale of the days before the flood....

26. Trojan Exiles of Albion...Isle of the Giants

The most ancient historical evidences of Britain and Ireland's history derive from the oral traditions and myths of these and other European people. It is within these legends that pieces of actual history are found and where we also find information solidly in support of the biblical history of giants. Long before any humans attempted to colonize the isles of the present day United Kingdom of western Europe the Nephilim were already there.

The Greeks of the early ages knew little of any real people except those to the east and south of their country, or near the coast of the Mediterranean. Their imagination meantime peopled the western portion of this sea with giants, monsters, and enchantresses.[1]

But was this imagination? The whole of Greek society thrived hundreds of years after Israel conquered and drove out the Anakim and Rephaim of Canaan and Philistia. The Bible reveals that the giants fled *west* from Canaan, to Gaza, Gath and Ashdod (Joshua 11:21-22), to coastal cities and regions in Philistia. This maritime nation was already in ruins by the time of the Greeks. The Philistines were worshipers of Dagon, a fish god, and Ashtoreth, a mother goddess from the stars. There exists many clues that these Nephilim-kin people had fled Philistia by sea and migrated to the ancient island of Albion. Briton of old.

According to the earliest accounts, Albion, a giant and son of Neptune, a contemporary with Hercules, ruled over this island, to which he gave his name.[2]

This giant established his kingdom long before the Philistines reached the Briton shores. But Albion the giant, if factual must have dwelled in the isles after the greatly remembered flood that initiated the Ice Age that the Norse believed the Frost giants ruled. In the Bible the five giant nations were the Emims, Zuzims, Anakim, Rephaim and the Zamzummins, but in the *Encyclopedia of Fairies* by Katharine Briggs[3] we discover that *the first unnamed inhabitants had perished in the great flood*, but after this the fierce giants called the Firbolgs and the Fomorians were the first inhabitants of the British Isles. Where did these two giant nations come from? In the *Encyclopedia the Highland Fomorians were a race of giants.*

Evidently the Fomorians were a different clan of giants than the Firbolgs, the former inhabiting Briton (Albion) and the latter residing in Ireland. The giant Albion himself, according to the evidence was a Fomorian. A third giant clan was present on the Isles called the *Foawr*. This name closely resembles the Old English word for giant, *gawr*. In the *Encyclopedia of Fairies* they are described as *stone-throwing giants* and could be an ancient lineage of the Fomorians. The origin of these three nations of giants must have been in Canaan, Babylonia or the older Mesopotamian city-states that Nimrod ruled over after the flood. These are where the Bible indicates that the Nephilim occupied until driven out by other nations who descended from Noah.

It is possible that *Albion* and Anak the giant are one in the same, or related. These Fomorians and Firbolgs might have migrated war-torn Canaan in the days of Joshua and the Israeli conquest. They possibly arrived to the Isles around 1400-1200 B.C., or and more probably, these giants are Emims that were driven out of ancient Moab sometime between 2000-1700 B.C. It is possible that King Chedorlaomer in Genesis 14 did not eradicate them all, but they fled.

The first inhabitants of Ireland, according to ancient traditions, were the Firbolgs, who were conquered and driven into the western islands by the Tuatha de Danaan. The Firbolgs became the first fairies of Ireland, giant-like grotesque creatures.[4]

The Tuatha de Danaan invaded by ship. They were a warlike nation of people of inhuman stature. Dagda was their High King, the battle-lord of this great **race of Danu,** the Tuatha de Danaan. Danu is described as a *mother goddess* which further links these mysterious maritime people to the ancient Philistines and Anakim exiles. The Canaanites and Philistines worshiped Anat, Antit, Istar, Ashtoreth and the most ancient Mesopotamian goddess *Inana*, all known as mother goddesses, called Queen of Heaven or Mother of the Gods. After killing King Saul and his sons years after David killed the giant Goliath, the Philistines worshiped *Ashtaroth* (1 Samuel 31:10).

Anu and Danu are one and the same mother goddess. Like many other deities they come from different origins and are the result of a cultural merging of people who combined their gods. her previous personages worshiped in Canaan and traced back to Sumer and Mesopotamia descend through cultures of old back to the *Annuna*:

The ancient Sumerian records confirm the astral lineage of the descendants of Anak, for ancient tablets repeatedly speak of "The Annuna, Gods of heaven and earth."[5]

Danu was recorded to be the ancestress of the Tuatha de Danaan. The majority of cultures past traced their descent from a great male historical figure, an archaic yet well remembered patriarch like Albion or Anak of the giants. On the surface it appears to be that the Danaanites find their origin with a female, Danu,[6] and being Philistines with a history found in the Bible this would be an oddity, however, when traced back to Canaan the male counterpart to the Danaanite's ancestry emerges. While the Philistines trace their descent from Ham and then Noah, so did the Fomorian giants![7]

In the ancient Sumerian belief the Annuna were also called the Annunaki. *Ki* is the Sumerian word for *earth* and *Anu* was to them long ago a male divinity who had once lived among them but was originally from heaven. The Annunaki of Mesopotamia back then (biblical Anakim) were considered to be resulted from a union of heaven (anu) and earth (ki). The Annunaki were giant offspring of the gods.[8] A perfect example from the *Book of Jasher* of these mysterious beings is found in the name of a sage in Nimrod's court in Babylonia named *Anuki*.[9] Even in the archaic epic of *Gilgamesh* the god Anu lived at one time on earth. This giant boasted that "Gilgamesh is my name, I am from Uruk (biblical Erech) *from the house of Anu*."[10]

It is true that after the conquest of Canaan by the Israelites that the Philistines remained in Philistia even until today, being called the Palestinians[11] or the biblical *Pelishtim*[12], however, once David and his men killed Goliath and four of the giant's sons the Philistine families that were larger from intermarriage with the Anakim exiles fled, knowing that they were being specifically targeted for extinction.

The male divinity worshiped by the Philistines was Dagon, a merman, half fish and half man. Living so much of their lives at sea and on coastal cities it was important to them to pay homage to an aquatic deity. Evidence of the ancient Philistine presence in Briton and Ireland exists strongly in that merman and mermaids were believed to exist by the early inhabitants of the Isles. Though tainted by tradition we can see how these fantasy creatures originated, being they the children of Dagon. Dagon was worshiped in Philistia and Canaan as early as 1900 B.C. In the chapter in this book entitled, *The Giant Wars* is cited historical texts proving that even the early Assyrian tyrant Sargon I worshiped Dagon. In these lands a goddess named Anu was also worshiped.

As time progressed through the centuries Dagon and Anu became synchronized into Danaan. Tuatha de Danaan literally means *peoples of the goddess Danu*, but the relationships between the deities are more complex. Anu in a feminine tense is *Ana*, the base word found in the roman goddess Diana Di[ana]. She was a *moon goddess* called Ashtareth in Palestine. She was Canaan's supreme female divinity.[13] Illustrations of Diana in *Smith's Bible Dictionary*[14] depict her with conjoined legs and fish fins over her feet. Other images of her have her wearing fins instead of feet. A mermaid. Dagon was also worshiped in a female form named Derceto.[15] Fascinating historical information about this fish god can be found in *The Rephaim* by Miss Fanny Corbeaux. The center of Diana's cult was in Ephesus in Asia Minor, the ruins of her temple being one of the *Seven Wonders of the Ancient World* called Aysaluk, the *city of the moon*.[16]

Powerful evidence that the Philistines migrated to early Ireland and Briton is discovered in the name of the Tuatha de Danaan's High King. *Dagda*. This king's name derived from Dagon, their national fish god. In fact, the Hebrew word for fish is *dagah,* or simply *dag*.

The Philistines and many other Canaanite peoples were astutely pagan. They worshiped nature and sacrificed to Ashtoreth to ensure human and agricultural fertility. These places of worship were wooded areas on hills and mountains, *high places* forbidden by God where the powers of nature in a feminine sense were deified and the stars in a masculine sense were consulted and followed after the pattern of Zodiacal ritualism. The name of the primary fertility goddess was Asherah, the Hebrew word that likewise means a *grove*.

The paganism of Canaan extends far into human history into the realms of the ancient Euphrates civilization under Nimrod and then the later great Sargon I who took these regions by force and adopted their beliefs, especially in *Dagon*.[17] Further evidence is found in the early Britons in the Celtic priesthood that have *traced to ancient Chaldea*[18] the system of their beliefs. From Chaldea (Old Babylonia) spread the occultic observation of worshiping *Baalim and the groves* in Judges 3:5-7.

Initially practiced by the pagan Canaanites and then adopted by many Israelites as recorded in the Bible, these tree-altars and groves were imported to ancient Briton by the Philistines and were discovered throughout the Isles by the early Trojan settlers. Later this pagan practice was incorporated into the nature worship of the early Druids and Celts who religiously regarded oak trees as sacred, thus making oak groves *holy ground*. This remnant tradition finds its origins not with the Philistines but form the Anakim and Rephaim giants who worshiped the *oaks of Bashan*, gigantic trees in southern Canaan. In the Bible the giants later became symbolized by these enormous trees, the oaks of Bashan.[19] An old British proverb cited by Katherine Briggs is *"Fairy folks are in old oaks."*[20] An interesting link between oak trees, fairies, and giants in Canaan that lived in Ashtaroth [The Star] is the fact that fairies in all the old tales among the Isles were *starworshipers*![21] The mythical Dryad, a female spirit called a nymph or fairy was believed by the Druids to live only in oak trees. The appearance of deified oak trees and pagan groves permeated through continental Europe as the Celtic and Druid influence spread abroad. It was Moses who led the Israelites through Bashan, killing the giants and then Joshua destroyed the *high places* throughout Canaan. Og of Bashan was slain in the Conquest, a giant king descended from the Rephaims and Amorites that fought against Chedorlaomer in Genesis 14 and lost. The Anakim giants fled to Philistia, seeking *refuge* in Gaza, Gath and Ashdod on the Mediterranean Sea, but it was the Philistine worshipers of Dagon that carried the pagan oak beliefs to early Briton.

Incredibly, discovered on a rock in southern Ireland is this inscription: *"We are Canaanites who fled from Joshua the son of Nun, the Robber."*[22] But aside from all this proof there are yet other pieces of evidence linking the seafaring cultures.

Another clue as to the Anakim-Philistine presence in historic Ireland lies in the intriguing facts that both nations were sea-faring, both were giant or giant-kin peoples, and both spoke the same *language*![23] The answer to how the Philistines spoke the same language as the island Firbolgs and Fomorians can only be discovered in the Old Testament. The Philistines were mariners long before they colonized the southern coasts of Canaan and northeast Egypt. In fact, Philistia is translated *land of sojourners*. The origin of the Philistines has been traced back to old Crete, called Caphtor long ago. Caphtor was an island nation in the Mediterranean Sea. In Genesis 10:14 the Philistines are said to come from the *Caphtorim*. In Amos 9:7 it reads, *the Philistines of Caphtor*. These people were already of great stature long before they migrated to Canaan. Nephilim influence in their ancestry derived not from the giants of Canaan but from the giants of much older times called the *Avims*. In Deuteronomy 2 is an extensive history of the geographical regions inhabited by the giants and giant-kin peoples of old. Explained therein is the Emims, Zuzims and Zamzummims' defeat by the descendants of Noah, the Ammonites, Edomites and the Moabites. This eradication was actually begun hundreds of years earlier in the days of King Chedorlaomer of Elam in

Genesis 14. Also mentioned are lesser Nephilim nations of giants, but ones smaller than the pure Nephilim-stock giants like the Anakim and Rephaim. These are the Horims who lived in the ancient caverns that the city of Petra was hewn from by the early descendants of Esau. The other race were called the *Avims*. The Avims were a mysterious race of giant-kin people that lived on the coast of Canaan until the Philistines sailed from Caphtor and invaded their land, *destroyed them, and dwelt in their stead* (Deut. 2:23). The land of the Avims was then called Hazerim until their defeat by the early Philistines.

The Philistines then established Philistia in the land of the giants called Avims. These Avims then lived among the Philistines, submissively, as the Anakim and the Rephaim exiles of Canaan who fled from the hosts of Israel in the fourteenth and thirteenth centuries B.C. Other Avims may have fled by ship to Albion, becoming the Firbolgs. Whatever the case, the language of the giants was the same, a language known by the Philistines because of their complex history of coinhabiting cities and regions with giants. The Firbolgs must have originated from Canaan somewhere, be they former Avims, Anakim, Emims, Horims or Rephaim to have spoken the same language as the Tuatha de Danaan (Philistines). Even Homer in his *Odyssey* uses the names *Danaanites* and *Phaistos* interchangeably as allies of the Greek invasion of Ionia and the Trojan enemies.

Centuries after expelling the Avims it appears that the Philistines then *followed* them to the western frontiers, away from human civilization. To Albion, a safe haven and land of refuge. Just as the Philistines conquered them in the past, the Tuatha de Danaan then again conquered the Avims who were known to the ancient Irish and Britons as the Firbolgs. Twice destroyed, the Avims disappeared or were merged into the Danaanite culture since both spoke the same language and it was customary for the Philistines to *absorb* their enemies rather than eradicating them.

In reference to the Isle of Albion Frederick Haberman cited evidence in his book *Tracing Our Ancestors* that *mining and smelting operations were carried on by an eastern superior race.* This write further provides ample proof that such a race came from the east which is *proved by the ancient stone circles and alignments, which are identical to those of Syria, Persia, and the highlands of Tibet.*[24] Also, megalithic dolmans called *Giant's Beds* are found in India, east Asia, Canaan, South Sea islands, in Europe and on into Britain, indicating a *great mass migration in early times.*[25]

This mysterious race abruptly appears as a southbound trek of ancient Philistines that appeared on the northernmost edges of civilization as a massive migration by land and ships along the coasts of the Mediterranean. The Hittites fell along with every other Canaanite nation that opposed their presence. There is considerable evidence in Homer's *Odyssey* that the Greek-allied *Phaistos* warriors under Agamemnon were Philistines who aided in the fall of Troy and Ionia.

Terrifying reports heralded the approach of these alien people...a trail of burning houses, ruined cities and devastated crops.[26]

These Philistines marched and settled into the Hinterlands between Canaan and Egypt, provoking the Pharaohs to build their border defenses. The Egyptian historian Manetho wrote that Egypt fell dramatically when *unexpectedly from the regions of the east, came men of unknown race.*[27]

Once a vassal-state of Egypt, the city of Ezion-geber was later occupied by Philistine-Phoenicians. This port city is just a few days walk from the Anakim and Amorite cities of southern Canaan and the borders of the land of Philistia on the Mediterranean. Among the ruins of Ezion-geber are earthenware smelting-pots that have *the remarkable capacity of 14 cubit feet.*[28] An enormous furnace for refining metals, this industrious place once produced copper. *Nowhere else in the Fertile Crescent, neither in Babylonia nor in Egypt, was such a great furnace to be found.*[29]

In *The Bible as History*, Werner Keller reveals that similar furnaces, smaller replicas were excavated in the Philistine city of Gaza. But still, Mr. Keller asks the obvious question:

How was copper refined in this ancient apparatus? Smelting experts of today cannot solve the mystery.

Ezion-geber was on the coast between Egypt, Midian, Philitia and Canaan on the northern Sinia waters of the Red Sea called the Gulf of Aqaba. Its metals were exported by land and sea.

From Ezion-geber the ships set sail on their mysterious voyages to distant and unfamiliar shores.[30]

Early Albion could have been visited and surveyed by early Philistine-Phoenicians, and even colonized. The fact that prehistoric mines and quarries have been discovered support this. Being a sea-faring nation these people knew Albion was an ideal land to settle. Perhaps there is truth that the metallurgical practices of creating alloys, mixed metals began with the giants, men of *mixed* lineages. The ages-old *Book of Enoch* has dozens of references to this.

The Nephilim infiltrated Philistine culture because they chose to settle off the coast of Canaan in giant-infested lands. They learned the techniques of mining and the making of alloys from the giants they conquered and lived among them. This is greatly supported by the intriguing fact that Ezion-geber literally translates to *backbone of a giant*! What fossilized relic was found there by the Israelites to cause them to name this city in such an unusual way?

True to their Canaanite nature the Philistines, or Danaanites began building their warriors through selective breeding, attempting to produce larger and more powerful offspring like Goliath. In an *Encyclopedia of Fairies*[31] we find that after defeating the Firbolg giants the Tuatha de Danaan began a widespread program of *interbreeding with the Fomorians*. The Danaanites were initially inferior to the Fomorian race, a people described as *monsters and giants that were frequently sacrificed to*.[32]

Just as these Philistines had done with the Anakim giants, they grew larger and more powerful warriors by sexually uniting themselves.

Beat into submission and heavily outnumbered, the Firbolgs allied themselves to their Danaanite masters when war broke out in Albion. With remnants of Firbolgs in their army the Tuatha de Danaan waged war against the indigenous Fomorians for full dominion of the Isles. After years of contention the war was ended in the famous and often thought legendary battles of Moytura.[33] Dispersed but not extinct the Fomorians became roving bands of nomadic giants, hermits and scarcely seen.

Many years later the Isle of Albion was a quieter place. Only in the hills afar off and the mountains did small gangs of giants, Firbolgs, Fomorians and Foawr roam, and in the dark fens and marshes lurked solitary giants that were seen hardly at all by those who lived to tell about the. The descendants of the powerful Philistines, these Tuatha de Danaan peoples ruled Albion but they themselves were a weaker strain than before. Without enemies the Danaanites softened, their communities no longer advanced, but tribal. It was then that the first purely Human invaders arrived to the Isles.

The Tuatha de Danaan were defeated and driven underground by the invading Milesians. They retreated to an underground realm.[34]

This fantasy underworld realm inhabited by the defeated Danaanite giants was long ago called Tir Nan Og, the *Land of Og*. Here is startling proof in the Canaanite origin of the Danaanites, for Og was king of Bashan and a once renowned giant in Canaan. The Celts remembered him as Ogmius, a type of Hercules who put down many giants. Other traces of Canaanite history and memory are found in the names of Dagda's (Dagon of the Philistines) sons. Angus Mac Og is one, a giant and god of ancient Ireland of the Tuatha de Danaan,[35] and Ogme the Champion who is detailed in one of the most ancient books of Ireland entitled, *Lebor Gebar*.[36] Interestingly, Goliath the giant is called a *Champion* in the Bible and Gebar derives from the Hebrew word Gibbar which means *giants*. This dateless time of Ireland's history is literally translated the *Book* [Lebor] *of giants*!

Tir Nan Og was called the Land of the Young[37] because of the incredible longevity of the Danaanite people. This magical land was also reckoned as a *Land of the Giants*,[38] their long lives bolstered by magic, *for by their enchantments they could resist the power of death*.[39]

These Milesians are mysterious in that little is known of their attack. However, Miletus was an ancient seaport in Ionia, an area occupied by the Trojans. It is most likely that these Milesian invaders were refugees of Troy after the city was burned by the Greeks. Frederick Haberman in his book *Tracing Our Ancestors* cites proof that an expedition of adventurers from the Trojan Ionic state of Miletus set out on a voyage *at an early date in the annals of Miletus.*[40]

As cited earlier the first fairies of Ireland often regarded as evil fiends and spirits were the Firbolgs when the Danaanites defeated them. Now, suffering defeat themselves these people are then driven underground, allegedly becoming fairies. This old belief in the origin of fairies is fully supportive of the ancient Enochian account that the spirits of the giants were cursed by God to roam the earth as demons and foul spirits until the day of Judgment.

Danu was the ancestress of the Tuatha de Danaan, who later dwindled to the Daoine Sidhe, the fairies of Ireland.[41]

The giants were the offspring of sexually disobedient angels and mortal women, taken by force or given in sacrifice to these angelic beings then regarded as *gods.* The Daoine Sidhe were the demons, ghosts, wraiths, spectres, goblins, trolls and other fiends that the giants had become when their physical bodies were destroyed. Katharine Briggs states:

Various theories of the origin of fairies are presented; fairies as the dead, or alternatively as "of a middle nature betwixt man and angel, as the daemons thought to be of old."[42]

This middle nature is what this entire book is about. The Nephilim, *fallen ones* from heaven who thought to wrest the throne of God. A hybrid race of heavenly and earthly origins. The union of *Anu* and *Ki*. Satanic creatures that now continue their war against the Creator through men. When contemplating the origin of fairies it is often suggested by the early Britons and Celts that fairies were the *souls of those drowned in Noah's flood*.[43] This comment and belief is accurate, since giants lived before the flood and were killed in the waters. Without the guidance of biblical texts in the first millennium B.C. these early Britons and islanders knew that the giants were fathered by angels and associated their presence with the flood. The *Daoine Sidhe* according to Lady Wilde in *Ancient Legends of Ireland*[44] were the remnants of fallen angels;

Some fell to earth, and dwelt there, long before man was created, as the first gods of the earth, others fell into the sea.[45]

The history of the peoples now living in the United Kingdom once called Albion goes back over three thousand years and is directly related to the Milesians. Just like the giants these people find their origin in the Bible. In this excursion into the fascinating past of the British people we will find how the Milesians came about.

The eighteenth descendant of Japheth, son of Noah in *Alanus*, who is recorded in ancient genealogies to be the great grandfather of Dardanus. This man built a city and named it Troy after his son *Trous*. With Trous begins the Welsh genealogies and Geoffrey of Monmouth's *Historia Regum Brittanae*.[46] The Dardanians initially settled *around the area of Troy whose coastal regions are known today as the Dardanelles.*

312

It was with Trous that the Trojans came about in their famous and now excavated city of Troy. This city's history is old and complex. In fact, Werner Keller in his bok, *The Bible as History*, states that *a second Troy had long been standing upon the ruins of the first*.[47] These ruins were discovered by Prof. Schiemann at Hissarlik in Asia Minor (ancient Ionia). He successfully shocked the world by breaking through the facades of Greek myth by digging up the Trojan city-state of Troy. These most renowned people were written about over 2,500 years ago in Homer's *Odyssey* and *Illiad* and then hundreds of years later by Virgil in the *Aenied*. The founding of the city of Troy *must have occurred in 1520 B.C. at the latest*.[48] The actual fall of Troy was told by Eratosthenes of Alexandria, Egypt, to have taken place in 1183 B.C.[49]

More recent research from diverse sources agrees that Troy fell in the year 1229 B.C.

The Trojan war is a story of immense passion and sorrow, of a great people driven out by the Greeks, of Achilles and Agamemnon and their involvements with the Olympian gods who overcame the gigantic Titans. Many of these gods were actually men of historic prestige like Dardanus. This ancestral founder of the Dodanim (the ancestors of the Trojans) *was deified by his descendants and worshiped under the name of Jupiter Dodanaeus. (Here we have a mingling of the names of Japheth and Dodan)*.[50] The Roman name Jupiter derives from the name Iupater, which in turn finds its beginning in *Iapetos*, the Greek name for Japheth of the Bible.[51]

The Trojans trace their lineage through Tiras back to Japheth, son of Noah. They worshiped the deified version of their forefather Tiras, calling his name **Thurus** (i.e. Thor) *the god of war*.[52] Thor is the prime deity of the

Norse, recognized by the old Celts and highly regarded
throughout the entire ancient and modern European
pantheons. Thor fought against the Frost giants, protecting
Asgard, the realm of the Norse gods and Yggsdrasil, the
tree of life. William Cooper in his thought provoking
research *After the Flood* finds evidence that Thor is
uniquely connected to the ancient Trojan city of Troy.[53]

After the destruction of Troy in Ionia the Trojan survivors
fled to a predetermined location:

*On arriving at the place of rendezvous, numerous fugitives
of both sexes, were found, who put themselves under the
guidance of Aeneas.*[54]

Troy was burned to the ground, the capitol of the Trojan
state. Aeneas was a valiant warrior and descendant of
Trous, listed as one of the *principal leaders of the Trojans*.
He led the Trojans to Italy where they remained for several
decades. Aeneas' great grandson was named Brutus. He
was considered to be a Trojan noble, but born in Italy.

From Italy, Brutus led an armada of *320 sails* to a *certain
island, which they found destitute of inhabitants, though
there were appearances of former habitation.*[55] Other
accounts have Brutus' fleet at 324 ships.[56] Knowing that
this was not a place to colonize he sailed further west,
happening upon another colony of Trojans ruled by a man
named Corineus. Corineus is listed in the early British
genealogy as a possible cousin of Brutus around 1100 B.C.,
which remarkably coincides with the traditional date of the
fall of Troy, being 1193 B.C. This is over ninety years
when the two colonies merged to become one body of
exiles, a small nation. The Milesians mentioned earlier
were from Ionia also, from the city of Miletus, a Trojan
city-state. Miletus was a port city and it is more likely that

Corineus was raised among the Trojan exiles of Miletus after the Greeks burned Troy. Corineus is famous in history for destroying a race of giants so it is he that probably led the Milesians to Albion where they defeated the Tuatha de Danaan. *The name of their commander was Duke Corineus...who could overthrow even gigantic opponents.*[57] Unfortunately, because the giants were not completely gone from the Isles, Corineus retreated to a lesser island where Brutus found his colony. Corineus fathered Gwendolen (1081 B.C.) who became the wife of *Locrinus, son of Brutus.*[58] This was after Briton was established and Albion was no more. After joining forces with Corineus, Brutus led the ships to the shores of France where they were violently attacked by settlers on the shore. Sailing on, Brutus followed the instructions of a mysterious prophecy. In *Milton's History* is cited a quote from a Trojan goddess recorded by Geoffrey of Monmouth:

Brutus! Far to the west, in the ocean wide, beyond the realm of Gaul, a land there lies, seagirt it lies, where giants dwelt of old.[59]

In the research of Frederick Haberman we are given an alternative translation of this prophecy, reading. . . *giants once possessed, now few remain* instead of "where giants dwelt of old."[60]

Brutus searched for a *seagirt* land, an expansive island good enough to build a kingdom. Gaul was mainly Germanic so Brutus knew his destination was further north along the coast of Europe. But before arriving to this ancient giant realm they passed another island, not dissimilar to their destination.

The Cyclopses were giants, who inhabited an island of which they were the only possessors. . .They dwelt in caves and fed on the wild productions of the island.[61]

The Cyclopses were giant sons of the sea god Poseidon, named Neptune by the Romans. These are the giants that the Greeks claimed inhabited the western islands. The primeval giant Albion may have been a Cyclopse. Homer described the Cyclopse as being *a brute so huge, he seemed no man at all.*[62] Albion was also a *son of Neptune.*[63] Herodotus described a community of people where far north of the regions of the Scythians, dwelt men among them who had but one eye.[64] Pliny also cites a most archaic tradition about a race of one-eyed people called the Arimaspi who lived beyond Palus Moeotis.[65]

In the *Odyssey* and the *Illiad* we discover Cyclopean islands but they are not the island home sought by Brutus. Albion is also pictured as a Cyclopse because these giants were also called ogres in Virgil's *Aeneid*. In traditional Irish lore the ogres are giants called Formorians.[66] The *Odyssey* refers to one of the giant sons of Poseidon as *Eurymedon, commander of the Gigante_ in the olden days, who led those wild things to their doom and his.*[67] Detailing his travels at sea among the western islands, Odysseus says, *"In the next land we found were Kyklopês [Cyclopses] giants, louts, without a law to bless them... Kyklopês have no muster and no meeting, no consultation or old tribal way, but each one dwells in his own mountain cave...*[68]

The Titans are the Gigantês who warred with the *gods* long ago. Homer wrote his epics with haunting accuracy in chronology and geography. A number of antiquated sources told of islands that harbored giants. So prevalent was this belief that even to this day walls and edifices constructed of enormous boulders of various shapes form-fitted together are still called *Cyclopse walls.*

After sailing many days north of the Cyclopean islands, Brutus anchors his fleet on the enormous island of Albion.

Albion was in a manner desert and inhospitable, occupied only by a remnant of the giant race whose excessive force and tyranny had destroyed the others...And there the hugest giants dwelt, lurking in rocks and caves, till Corineus rid the land of them.[69]

Upon arriving to the island Brutus became king and named it Briton. According to William Cooper in *After the Flood* the Britons (former Trojans) did not establish themselves until 1104 B.C., approximately 300 years after the end of the Ice Age caused by the Flood Cataclysm in 2239 BCE. Other than the Frost giants, no one lived on these isles before the Fomorians, Foawr and Firbolgs because of the inhospitable conditions and glacial terrain of prehistoric Briton. The polar ice caps extended dramatically closer to the equator during the Ice Age, a freezing epoch that endured for almost a thousand years. This frozen land is what preserved so many of the giant megalithic relics still standing today in Ireland and Briton.

Knowledge of these large western islands was not new. Throughout the first millennium B.C. Phoenician sailors told stories of the giants that darkly mirrored the mythology that told of these cyclopean savages on the isles of the Great Sea. Aristotle wrote: *In this ocean, however, there are two islands, and those are very huge, and are called Brittanic, Albion, and Ierne...*[70] Brutus knew that an enormous island existed somewhere out there beyond the edge of the know world. Even in the ancient Hebrew Torah commentary called the *Book of Jasher*[71] the isle of Brittania was known and inhabited as far back as the fourteenth century B.C.

In a most incredible work of research containing evidences of both ancient and modern giant remains called *Giants, Dwarfs and Other Oddities* by C.J.S. Thompson, M.B.E. is a confirming statement concerning Corineus; *"There are many other stories of giants in Cornwall, a county which abounds in legendary lore, and is still the home of fairies and the "Spriggins," who are believed to be the ghosts of giants who guard hidden wealth."*[72]

Brutus built Trojanova (New Troy) while Corineus organized hunting parties that fed the people and occasionally fought off *remnants of the giant race.* Corineus had already been to this island and defeated the Tuatha de Danaan a decade or so earlier, but no, reinforced with younger and more Trojans from the ranks of Brutus he renewed his campaign against the giants and Danaanites and almost drove them to extinction. This intensity was most likely motivated because the Danaanites themselves were a part of the forces that aided the Greeks in destroying the Trojan states on the Mediterranean in Ionia. Also called the Phaistos in Homer's *Odyssey*, these epic Danaans were the Philistines of Canaan.

Those who followed Corineus became known as the Cornish people. They settled part of the isles known today as Corinea. It was there that the giants *were in greater numbers there than in all the other provinces.*[73] He did not put an end to the giants on Briton though, or giant-kin people, but he did succeed in decimating their populations and driving them deeper into the wilderness that they no longer posed a threat to Trojanova's sovereignty. *They forced the giants to fly into the caves of the mountains.*[74] Trojanova was known by several names over the millennia as the britons lost their past and history over the expanse of time. However, the historians of old did not forget and have made us aware that Trojanova is none other than London, England today.[75]

As centuries passed the Britons, Celts, Norse and other European peoples began warring against each other, the threat of marauding giants nigh forgotten. But they still were lurking out there. Reports filtered into the cities from distant stretches of the country of large beasts, monsters and even giants even as late as the sixth and seventh centuries A.D. Occasionally encountered by hunting parties was the dreaded *Athach*, which means monster or *giant*. This large humanoid beast *haunted lonely lochans or gorges in the Highlands*. Like Grendel's mother in the epic poem *Beowulf* some of the athach beasts were female.

Akin to the Athach was the hideous *Direach*, a giant descendant of the Fomorian cyclopses. It had *one eye in the middle of his forehead* and was known by locals long ago as the *desert creature of Glen Eiti* in J.F. Campbell's *Popular Tales of the West Highlands*.[76] As we will find shortly, the Direach was not the only *one-eyed* giant residing in the hills.

A subterranean monster thought to surface occasionally was the *Ciuthach*, a cave-dwelling giant of long forgotten antiquity. In the *Celtic Review* (vol. IX) we find that the legends of the Ciuthach may have an *ultimate historical basis*.[77] This Ciuthach was evidently more primitive than the Gruagach which is described as a *supernatural wizard, often a giant*. The Gruagach means *the hairy one*.[78] Like the spell-casting Tuatha de Danaan these giants were regarded as wizards.

The common denominator between the names of all these giants is the -ach suffix which evidently is indicative of *larger than normal size*. Ath[ach], Dire[ach], Ciuth[ach] and Gruag[ach] all describe male beasts, however there existed other creatures that were noticeably female. In fact, the earliest appearance of a female giantess is the Tuatha de Danaan queen named Fuam[ach] in *Gods and Fighting Men* by Lady Gregory.[79]

The *Caille[ach] bheur* of the highlands was blue-faced, a hag who seems to be one of the clearest cases of a *supernatural creature who was once a primitive goddess, possibly among the ancient Britons and Celts*.[80] She is related to the Caille[ach] bera, which is a class of *gigantic hags* in the mountain wilderness of Ireland. Later she became reckoned as an evil spirit or fairy like the Danaanites.

To further link these monstrous hags to the giants of the Tuatha de Danaan and Firbolgs are the tales of the *Black Annis*. This female giantess was reclusive, a nocturnal hag *ever so tall* with long stringy hair, large teeth and feared by mothers with newborn children. The Black Annis was a witch giantess that *ate people*, with an appetite for infants. The name of this dark fairy, Annis, derives from the Celtic mother goddess Anu, which is a form of Danu of the Tuatha de Danaan, *Danaan* being a composite of Dagon-Anu (Ana-feminine form).[81]

Said to be a descendant of an ancient bloodthirsty goddess, Black Annis was one-eyed, livid-faced and long clawed.[82]

It appears that this Annis hag was similar to the Direach, a giant descendant of the Fomorian cyclopses. Long after the yore and legends of giants passed on to the realm of mere fable, the British and Irish of the Dark Age and Middle Age eras still told of gaunt wandering hags with bluish skin and unusual height. Like the female Grendel in *Beowulf* called an *accursed outcast* (line 1267), the Annis and Cailleach lived among ruins, caves and secluded woods, rarely daring to encroach upon human territories.

Another forlorn demonic like Grendel is an archaic being from the underworld named Aillen, *a restless remnant of an elder race, long ago forced by mortals into the other world beneath the Irish hills.*[83] Aillen was a musician of the Tuatha de Danaan of former times. Until Corineus destroyed his race. He was reduced to a hideous form that stalked the surface world only during All-Hallow's Eve (Halloween). This evil fairy is also described in *The Enchanted World...Night Creatures* as a *full two heads taller than any human.*[84] This physical description is significant because of its Egyptian parallel cited earlier in this book where the Philistines are depicted in Egyptian artistic reliefs as exactly two heads taller than their Egyptian adversaries. This *elder race* was none other than the Anakim-related Philistines from Canaan. In fact, Annis appears to relate directly to *Anak*, which finds its origin from the Sumerian Annuna, supernatural being that fathered the giants. *Smith's Bible Dictionary* also confirms this unique size difference, stating that the Anakim were a *race of tall people, who lived in Hebron...They appear on monuments of Egypt as tall and light colored, and are called the Tammahu, from the Hebrew Talmai.* Talmai was one of the great giants that the ten spies feared when they searched out Canaan, a son of Anak himself.

Another direct link the Tuatha de Danaan maintained with Canaan and their Philistine ancestors was their affinity for music and the playing of instruments. Like Aillen of the Danaan fairies *no people were more devoted to music than the inhabitants of Canaan...an inexhaustible treasure house of musicians.*[85]

The fairies became increasingly popular as the fears of giants subsided and became distorted with time and inconsistent oral tradition. The more renowned fairy folk were elves and goblins, both enchanting and sometimes ghastly remnants of the *legendary* Tuatha de Danaan that lived below Ireland. Mermaids and mermen were feared greatly as harbingers of destruction to the British and Irish who had no bridges to Europe or North America save by sea.

But be they land or sea, the common link between the physical traits of the various kinds of fairies on the British Isles and continental Europeans are the random deformities discovered when fairies are more closely examined. These include cleverly hidden mutations, aberrations, webbed fingers or toes, cloven hooves for feet concealed with long dresses and even cloven hands, bone deformations, missing limbs, etc. People associated these defects with evil, the fairies being demonic servants of the devil. It is quite probably that these mutations were caused by normal people engaging in incestuous affairs, genetic mutations caused by inbreeding. This was a very common practice among the biblical giants, forbidden by God, but passed down into human society. These unfortunate children were regarded by the ignorant commonfolk as children of the devil, and fairies. But it is true that not all of these cases were natural. The historic defects in fairies can be found more extensively in *An Encyclopedia of Fairies* by Katharine Briggs.[86]

These same deformities are what gave the son of the Philistine Anakim giant Goliath twelve fingers and toes. Inbreeding among the Nephilim nations and its mutating

322

effects became so pervasive in ancient Canaan that giant-kin peoples were raised to expand the gene-pool, nations such as the Avims, Horims, Sabeans and the Philistines. Because of genetic disfunctions unforseen by the Nephilim these giants forced lesser and weaker pure human nations to pay homage to them by sacrificing their daughters over as concubines for the giants.

The Canaanite nations were expelled from the Promise Land because they feared the Rephaim and Anakim that ruled over them. They were guilty of *giving over their daughters to false gods*. The Almighty told Abraham that in four hundred years his descendants would become a great nation, as the *stars of heaven*. This could not occur immediately because as God stated, *the sins of the Amorites was not yet full.*[87]

This is the story as presented in the Bible, a heavily redacted series of texts with whole inserts incorporated by Jewish priests seeking to place their own people into the center of ancient events. What can be gained here is the knowledge that giants were a very real presence and problem in antiquity whether men be allied to God or not.

26. The Zodiac...An Ancient Cataclysmic Impact Recorder

The 12 signs of the Zodiac were so important that the major civilizations after the Flood not only created entire pantheons of deities numbering 12 in commemoration of these stellar mysteries, but their priesthoods even created entire mythos to mask the fact that their gods were merely empty facades derived from the 12 signs of the Zodiac.

In the center of the Market place at Athens, Greece long ago stood a famous pillar with the inscription "The Twelve Gods." (1) As the center of Greek society all distances were measured from this pillar. Having been dedicated to the Zodiacal divinities [borrowed from Babylon] they were stellar guides used for terrestrial measurements of distance. This may have been the Altar of the Twelve Gods mentioned by Herodotus. (2)

The original preflood Zodiac was a book among the stars and its teachings were openly disseminated by the eight survivors to their offspring. After a few centuries when humanity began exploding populously at an exponential rate the newly arisen cults and priesthoods realized that only by concealing knowledge could they maintain control over the growing masses while also becoming the center of this renewing civilization. This corruption was absolute and continues today, for the Zodiac is still believed to be a hand-in-hand symbolism of a solar mythos. Nothing could be further from the truth.

There is a profound power the stars have over the human imagination. We gaze at the heavens on a starry night, transfixed as if we are supposed to be receiving something that lies at the edges of our memory. As imperfect beings staring into the vast depths of unimaginable distances, the appearance of the night sky and the inspirational currents that pass through our bodies resonate within our being an acute awareness that we are being watched, and called for. That knowledge was dispersed among the stars is a particularly old idea. Over 125 years ago the mystic Thomas Burgoyne wrote that the revelations of God are

". . . not lost to us today. The same book lies open before us that faced our ancient forefathers. It is standing out clear and distinct, waiting to be read by the sons of men." (3)

The Kabbalists believe that the future and God's divine plan for mankind was written in the stars long before the world was made (4), and this may be due to the Psalmist's passage that ". . . the heavens declare the glory of God; the firmament showeth His handiwork . . . night unto night showeth knowledge." (5) In the Book of Enoch we read, "O Enoch, look on the book which heaven has distilled: and reading that which is written upon it, understand every part of it. Then I looked on all which was written and understood all, reading the book and everything written in it, all the works of men." (6) Also in the Enochian records we learn that concerning the final Judgement ". . . there shall be writings and impressions above in heaven, and the angels may read them, and know what shall happen both to sinners and to the spirits of the humble." (7)

Not only the fixed stars were a part of this stellar alphabet and codified astronomy but also the planets, called by Stobaeus in Physica "Watchful Guardians." (8) The early concepts involved the planets as Watchers, an idea also mirrored in the Book of Enoch where we find that the planets ". . . behold the earth, and understand what is transacted, from the beginning to the end of it." (9) In Sumer the planets were called lu-bat, or Wandering Sheep or Revealers. There were even seven MASHU [shepherds], fixed stars on either side of the ecliptic to ensure that the planets did not deviate from their paths. (10)

The Zodiac was originally intended as an apocalypse recorder and its mysteries were taught by the Tetramorph, the Four Living Ones called Watchers that have dominion over the four quadrants of heaven. These four were marked by the Four Royal Stars of Aldebaran in Taurus, Regulus in Leo, Antares in Scorpio and Fomalhaut in Aquarius. In the book of Ezekiel and the Revelation these are the faces of the Watchers that hold up the Throne of God in heaven. Thus, the Bull, Lion, Eagle [Scorpio] and Man are the zo-on, or Living Beings. (11) The Zodiac refers to these four living beings but the priesthoods early on corrupted this by changing the symbolism and meaning of the 12 signs to confuse the 12 signs with the imagery of the Tetramorph, inventing animal forms and hybrids to conceal the true mysteries beneath. The mythographers made sure that their kings would assume the role of the Sun, and that the new stellar system would serve to convey that the threats of heaven that abide over mankind were done away with by the sun/hero king. Now, as one late philosopher would say, the Zodiac, ". . . like every skin, betrays something but conceals even more." (12)

Our discourse has barely scratched the surface of the secrets of the Zodiac, to unveil what the mythographers tried to conceal, excavating knowledge buried beneath layers of textual and mythological disinformation. The Zodiac today is consisted of 12 star patterns that in NO way conform to the mythological patterns assigned to them. How is this possible? Ancient people would developed images to assign to patterns of the stars they could identify with those images, but in EVERY case the houses of the Zodiac have imagery that does not match the constellation patterns.

The answer is simple. The Zodiac of Old does indeed match twelve star patterns but NOT the houses of the Zodiac known today. The Earth has MOVED, the pole star fell at least 30 degrees. The path of the sun and moon across the sky we see today is NOT the path the sun and moon took in antiquity.

Something terrible happened.

Pole Shift and Obliquity

The earth is tilted at 23° toward the plane of the ecliptic today, the axis it spins upon slightly wobbling as the planet orbits the sun while pointing at the pole star Polaris in the Little Bear. But this has not always been the case and many scientists postulate that this tragic inclination was the result of a cataclysmic impact of a gigantic asteroid some time in earth's remote past. (1) We are not without abundant geologic evidence of such massive impacts. The largest known crater in the world is the Vredefort Ring in South Africa which measures 186.4 miles in diameter and not far behind this one is the Sudbury Crater in Ontario, Canada at 155.3 miles in diameter. Also there is a 105.6 mile crater called the Chicxulub Crater near Yucatan, Mexico in the Gulf of Mexico. The scientists today are right, though they postulate such collisions are random events spread throughout vast epochs of time. But this is far from the truth.

 The scientists of today are little different than those of yesteryear. They are a virtual priesthood of knowledge, and from those priests and naturalists long ago we have many scientific observances preserved for us even from three and four millennia past. In the Babylonian tablet records there is found accounts of a demon lord called Kingu who was allied to the Chaos Dragon but was abruptly cut off by a "weapon not of war," a star spear. (2) The language employed in these texts seems to be the reverse of what we find in the biblical Revelation account where we read that Abaddon [cut off from others] is released from the Deep, or Place of the Lost, by a burning mountain that crashes into earth. By asteroid impact was the reign of the Anunnaki ended and the Eighth King imprisoned within the Abyss and by asteroid collision [Second Trumpet judgement] is the Eighth King [who is of the Seven] returned to kingship to fulfill the Sumerian King-List.

The crashing of an asteroid of immense size into the earth long ago is supported in the writings of the Sumerians who recorded that the Flood was preceded by a great thunder and large black clouds on the horizon. (3) The Rabbinical traditions hold that the firmament above [marine atmospheric canopy] flooded the earth by the falling of two stars. (4) The Revelation account maintains a similar motif with the descent of the asteroid of the Second Trumpet followed by the impact of the burning mountain called Wormwood in the Third Trumpet of the Apocalypse. The Enochian histories provide us a very scientific clue as to the approach of a planetoid with a strong magnetosphere that preceded the Great Flood causing a poleshift. In the Book of Enoch we read, "In those days Noah saw the earth became inclined, and that destruction approached . . . the earth labored, and [was] violently shaken." Readers of my published works will know this was planet Phoenix.

The early Hebrew stories tell that God threw down a pair of stars from the Pleiades star system to cause the Flood, and Mexican lore across the planet reveals that it was the passing of six stars called the Tzontemocque close to earth that initiated the Deluge according to an old colonial manuscript in the Spanish National Archives at

Madrid. Perhaps this is related to the Pleiades, which has six visible stars, and the Aztecs probably referred to this in their festival that commemorated the change of constellations after the Flood. Further, a 3000 year old Egyptian Twelfth Dynasty papyrus describes the Flood and its survivors. Accordingly, a star fell from the sky and burned everything before the Flood. In China a Jesuit missioner named Martinius was told that at the start of the second heaven and earth the world was shaken to its foundation and the sky sank lower to the north, the sun, moon and the stars all changing their positions, even the planets altering their courses. (5)

Grecian historical fragments masked in mythical garb tell us memories of poleshifts and their attendant destruction. Older traditions claim that ". . . Zeus, aided by Eris [Eye: metaphor for pole star], reversed the laws of nature, which hitherto had been immutable. Helios [sun], in mid-career [noon], wrested his chariot about and turned his horses toward the dawn. The Seven Pleiades and all the other stars, retraced their steps in Sympathy; and that evening, for the first and the last time, the sun set in the east." (6) The Greek legend of Phaethon is a preservation of a massive poleshift, the myth itself invented to explain the unprecedented phenomenon. Phaethon was the son of the Sun [Helios] who one day took charge of his father's sun-chariot but was immediately told that he was too young to handle the chariot horses that pulled the sun across the sky. But Phaethon disregarded the warning, the sun began its journey and reached the height of the sky when suddenly the chariot swung wide and even increased its speed. Phaethon struggled but he could not keep the sun from leaving its course as part of the sky grew dark and showed the sun descending upon Scorpio, then over to Cancer [a third of the Zodiac away]. Then the sun went back upward right before plunging down again and setting the world on fire. Valleys and mountains burned, streams turned to steam rivers and shrank as forests were consumed with flames. Then the sun was wrapped in thick smoke and disappeared over the sea quickly. (7)

Grecian historians, playwrights and philosophers also left behind fragments concerning a belief in this mysterious changing of the earth's pole. Euripides in his Electra (485-406 BCE) states that the stars long ago moved backwards and also recalled a change in the sun's movement, which he mentioned in Orestes. (8) Herodotus claims that the sun has twice risen where it was supposed to set (9) and in Book II of his Histories he wrote that the Egyptians recorded there to have been four changes in the sun's direction. (10) That the sun and stars would cease moving in the heavenly vault was a fear of the natural scientists in Aristotle's day according to his Book IX of Metaphysics. (11) Similar stories and facts are recorded by the Roman writer Solinus. (12).

Because of the relevance the subject of poleshift has to our thesis we must endure this tangent only long enough to understand that even in the ancient Americas these scientific phenomena were remembered and passed down all the way to modern times. Truly these memories are universal. It was a common belief among the various cultures of America long ago that the sun was much closer to the earth than it appears today (13), which is what one would expect when a thick marine atmosphere was in place that magnified the heavens, making the moon first and then the sun appear much larger than they actually were. Other traditions hold that the sun was once bound to a huge chain that let it swing from side to side long ago to the amazement of those on earth. The native Americans of California tell a story from of old that the sun fell by accident from the sky just around sunrise. Early American accounts say that the pillars of heaven broke and the heavens sunk northward and the sun darkened as the planets altered their courses. (14) Any deviations in the movement of the sun are poleshifts, but with the great migrations after successive catastrophic centuries, after the Flood knowledge was fragmented and lost, diluted into oral traditions with moral attachments. The occurrence of poleshifts were no longer understood and were merely recorded as changes in the sun's course over the sky. But this is not always the case. There are instances where the native American accounts do appear more scientific.

The natives of Greenland fear a group of evil spirits called the Inguersoit, a species of ghosts of those who died when the world was turned upside down in a flood. (15) The Hopi tell of a time called the Dark Midnight. Men learned trade and commerce and all sorts of information which caused the end of the world by greed. The earth tilted and all geography changed again and the world was flooded but the Hopi knew it was coming and had prepared a special cylindrical boat and survived. As did Noah of the bible, so too did the Hopi send out birds to see if any lands had surfaced. (16) Most poleshift memories are affixed to flood myths. The Mayan Book of the Popul Vuh of the Quiches of Guatemala we find that the god Huracan became angry and flooded the earth, killing mankind. This destruction of the earth by water was at the same time as a great conflagration that appeared to burn the heavens. (17)

28. Anunnaki Historical Epochs & Gamma Ray Bursts of Nibiru

The deeper we penetrate the architecture of reality the more we come in contact with coincidences that defy rational conclusions. Sentience ensnared in webs of deceit. We traverse through life through a fixed medium of probability molds that take on predictive values the more we recognize their presence. The Old World's time-keeping system involving Great Years is a case in point. A 600 year period.

The birth of the biblical Noah is in the 1056th year of the preflood calendar. Factoring the Phoenix Calendar we find that Year One was 3895 BCE, making Noah's birth year to be 2839 BCE, or year 1056. We can employ biblical chronologist Stephen Jones' chronology published in The Secrets of Time and find that in using the Bible, the Book of Jasher, works of Enoch, Jubilees and the Assyrian Eponyms, according to him Noah was born at precisely 2839 BCE. Two different sources, with Stephen Jones knowing nothing about the Phoenix or its orbital chronology. A third method is found in the birth of Abraham. The biblical material reveals that he was born 292 years after the Deluge in 2239 BCE, even Josephus writing that Abram was born in the 292nd year after the Flood. This would be 1947 BCE however, it is also 1948 Annus Mundi, or 1948 years from Year One in 3895 BCE. Thus Abraham's birth seems to be a conjunct between two calendrical systems, one counting forward in time and the other backward. This is possible because the two separate time-keeping systems counted as their first months totally different portions of the year, thus the overlap between 1948 AM and 1947 BCE could mark the exact same date if one system counts March 21st [vernal equinox] as New Year's Day and the other January 1st. At any rate, Abram was born 892 years after Noah in the Genesis/Jasher genealogy so Noah was born in 2839 BCE.

Why is this relative to Anunnaki studies? Well, 2839 BCE was exactly 600 years after the Anunnaki/Watchers appeared with ENKI in 3439 BCE and built Erudi (biblical Irad). It was 1200 years (600+600) after the appearance of the Moon in 4039 BCE (hollowed for observatory installations). Further, Noah's birth in 2839 BCE marks the final 600 years until the Great Flood in 2239 BCE, the month of May. Abraham's birth marked the intersect between two calendars just as Noah's birth marked the conjunct between two Great Years of 600 year epochs before the Flood. And we cannot omit this reference from the Genesis text- "...in the six hundredth year of Noah's life, in the second month, on the seventeenth day..." the floodwaters were upon the earth.

Here is something you just can't make up. In 1895 the historian J.D. Parsons wrote that Noah's birth was *"...at the meeting point of two of those famous cycles of six hundred years so often referred to by ancient writers."* (1) The import of this statement lies in the fact that Parsons did not have a chronology to back up the claim. His information was from an alternative source other than chronology.

The Anunnaki Chronology began in 5239 BCE, counting 600 years to 4639 BCE, then to 4039 BCE when the Moon appeared, then 600 more years to the arrival of the Anunnaki under ENKI in 3439 BCE. These 600 year epochs are mentioned by Josephus and also revered by the Sumerians as a duration specifically related to the Anunnaki, called a NER. These facts are detailed in my work, *Return of the Fallen Ones*. Robert Temple discovered that the later Babylonians preserved a tradition of the 600 year period, calling it the neros, a fact he obtained from "...an extremily obscure old book from early in the nineteenth century," titled The Celtic Druids (1827) by Geoffrey Higgins concerning Stonehenge and other British stone circles. (2) Interestingly, Zechariah Sitchin notes that the Sumerian cycle of 1800 years [600X3] was important to the Anunnaki for astronomical reason. (3) 3439 BCE was exactly the 1800th year of the Anunnaki NER Chronology of 600 year epochs that began 5239 BCE.

Concerning the 600 year calendrical nexus points when historical and traditional records claim great personages were born, died, important events unfolded, Edward Carpenter writing in 1920 seems keen to this phenomenon. He uncovered evidence in his researches prompting him to write- "Have there been in the course of human evolution certain, so to speak, nodal points, or periods in which the psychologic currents ran together and condensed themselves for a new start; and has such each node or point of condensation been marked by the appearance of an actual and heroic man who supplied a necessary impetus for the new departure, and gave his name to the resulting movement? Or, is it sufficient to suppose the automatic formation of such nodes or starting points without the intervention of any special hero or genius, and to imagine that in each case the mythmaking tendency of mankind CREATED a legendary and inspiring figure and worshipped the same..." (4) This is a profound statement made a century ago- that the collective psyche of humanity responds to the linear projections of a framework of nodal apertures in the fabric of space -time inducing us to either become aware of important persons appearing on those nodal dates, or that we invented them later and retrospectively assigned them to those nodal dates. No matter which is true the case set forth by Edward Carpenter is true and demonstrable.

Enoch appears (ENKI) as a great benefactor to humanity in 3439 BCE. 600 years later Noah appears in 2839 BCE who will be the savior of humanity through the global cataclysm. 600 years later this same Noah survives the Deluge in 2239 BCE preserving the seed of humanity. Whether any of this is true does not affect Carpenter's observations, for on those nodal dates we have by many different chronological methods ascertained these years to all be 600 years apart whether the stories are true or not. The Chinese maintained a tradition that the Great Flood actually marked a major division in time. (5) Additionally, 600 years after the Flood was 1639 BCE, the exact date Jacob (Israel) died and the promises of the covenant of Abraham passed to his sons, the patriarchs of many tribes that later become whole nations. We can't stop there because 600 years later we have 1039 BCE when David emerges as the savior hero of Israel in the slaying of Goliath the Philistine oppressor. This phenomenon was addressed by Acharya S. in *The Christ Conspiracy* when she wrote that it was taught long ago that every 600 years "a great man" arises or is born. (6)

No one can accuse me of inventing this 600 year timeline, it is ancient and well-documented. Nor did I date any of these events, which were already dated at 3439, 2239, 1639, 1039 BCE by other published sources as shown in my books *When the Sun Darkens, Anunnaki Homeworld* and *Nostradamus and the Planets of Apocalypse.* As many of my readers know, it is my belief that our reality matrix maintains characteristics of a hologram. It is my theory that this reality construct has dimensional architecture that maintains its structure over long periods of time, programmed routine. The 600 year NER, or Great Year, the Phoenix Cycle of 552 year epochs, the 414 year Cursed Earth chronology, the 138 year orbit of the Phoenix, 792 year orbit of NIBIRU, 394.5 year orbit of the Dark Satellite. Each one of these are well demonstrated through history in my research and they all lend proof of a vast invisible infrastructure built around and totally confining, mankind.

Anunnaki Orbital Chronology

Zechariah Sitchin, author of the popular Earth Chronicles series, never provided a chronology for the orbit of NIBIRU, but merely speculated that its orbit was 3600 years long. As seen in other posts this 3600 "years" was a glaring mistake on Mr. Sitchin's part involving the interpretation of the length of the Sumerian shar. We will not revisit that embarrassment here. Instead, I offer you the real and demonstrable orbit of the object called NIBIRU by Sitchin but probably known by other names to the ancients. My published works on the subject contain the source materials, so will upcoming posts.

3439 BCE...Primitive population of Neolithic humans reduced by a third in massive flooding. The year the Anunnaki/Anunna/Watchers/Enki/Enoch appeared and began building technolithic structures in what later would be called Egypt, 1200 years (432,000 days on 360-day year calendar) before the Great Flood of 2239 BCE. NIBIRU exited the inner solar system orbiting Sol.

2707 BCE...NIBIRU entered the inner system beginning its 60 year perihelion period. The 60 year window of opportunity for the Anunnaki to visit Earth is documented in Near Eastern texts;

2647 BCE...792 year orbit complete. A Chinese tradition concerning the 60 year period dates its origin to "2637 BCE." Knowing nothing about this NIBIRU orbital chronology, Robert Temple's independent research uncovered that ancient Egypts associated the 60 year period with the crocodile, a calendar sysmbol, Temple theorizing that the crocodile represented to them the amphibian aliens. 2647 BCE marked the Exodus of the Anunna from Earth, beginning the Abandonment & Shock Period of preflood humanity. Social unrest, wars, racial conflicts, rapid loss of technolithic knowledge initiating the Post-Technolithic Period. 2647 BCE was 408 years to the Great Flood in 2239 BCE, this 408 years remembered precisely by the ancient American cultures who claimed that the Fourth Age was the Water Sun epoch lasting 408 years, which began their calendar. To recall the exact amount of years, 408, is beyond coincidence. In ancient South America the people practiced ritaul magic in the designing of the gigantic geoglyphs of Nazca in an effort to induce the sky gods to return. All around the world cultures began erecting pyramids believing that by emulating the work of the gods (Anunnaki visitors), these gods would return.

[732 years pass with NIBIRU outside the Sol system on its orbit around Nemesis, the Dark Star, Sol's collapsed binary companion star being a dark brown dwarf. 60+732 years gives NIBIRU a total orbital period of 792 Earth years]

1915 BCE...NIBIRU entered the inner system beginning its 60 year perihelion period. Ancient Near East texts describe a terrible sky dragon and celestial war that shook the earth. Writings from India describe a great darkness during the day time and a rain of stones with flames from the sky.

1855 BCE...No records. NIBIRU exits Sol system. 792 year orbit complete.

[732 years pass with NIBIRU outside the Sol system on its orbit around Nemesis, the Dark Star, Sol's collapsed binary companion star being a dark brown dwarf. 60+732 years gives NIBIRU a total orbital period of 792 Earth years]

1123 BCE... NIBIRU entered the inner system beginning its 60 year perihelion period. A sky dragon appeared and changed the Mandate of Heaven in China; Shang Dynasty collapses

1063 BCE...No records. NIBIRU exits Sol system. 792 year orbit complete.

[732 years pass with NIBIRU outside the Sol system on its orbit around Nemesis, the Dark Star, Sol's collapsed binary companion star being a dark brown dwarf. 60+732 years gives NIBIRU a total orbital period of 792 Earth years]

331 BCE... NIBIRU entered the inner system beginning its 60 year perihelion period. The Macedonians under Alexander and the Persians under Darius III witnessed a partial eclipse. The Moon dimmed and the sky turned blood red. Modern eclipse computation programs calculate no eclipses for this period seen over the Near East. Weeks later Alexander's forces were terrified to see flames coming out of the sky.

271 BCE...Something totally eclipsed planet Venus . For this to occur, with Venus so close to Earth, an object of

great size had to have transited between them. 792 year orbit complete.

[732 years pass with NIBIRU outside the Sol system on its orbit around Nemesis, the Dark Star, Sol's collapsed binary companion star being a dark brown dwarf. 60+732 years gives NIBIRU a total orbital period of 792 Earth years]

462 CE... NIBIRU entered the inner system beginning its 60 year perihelion period. No records.

522 CE...792 year orbit complete. Earthquakes devastated Olympia in Greece. Sky dragons were seen over Britain, a celestial war of monsters, raining great droops of blood followed by a dearth. This could be Phoenix, as 522 CE in the only year in all recorded world history that NIBIRU and Phoenix were passing through inner solar system at same time. A strange star appeared over Britain, attached to a ray that ended in a dragon. 522 CE was the beginning of the Dark Age when written records became scarce.

[732 years pass with NIBIRU outside the Sol system on its orbit around Nemesis, the Dark Star, Sol's collapsed binary companion star being a dark brown dwarf. 60+732 years gives NIBIRU a total orbital period of 792 Earth years]

1254 CE... NIBIRU entered the inner system beginning its 60 year perihelion period. No records.

1314 CE...792 year orbit complete. Plague fogs, quakes and disasters in China but over Europe is seen a great Black Darkness that blots out the stars. This ends the period known as the Seven Comets Over Europe. The Great Famine of Europe from 1314-1317 CE began a 40 year period of disasters, plagues and famines worldwide that killed a third of the global population.

[732 years pass with NIBIRU outside the Sol system on its orbit around Nemesis, the Dark Star, Sol's collapsed binary companion star being a dark brown dwarf. 60+732 years gives NIBIRU a total orbital period of 792 Earth years]

2046 CE... NIBIRU entered the inner system beginning its 60 year perihelion period. Called Wormwood in the Apocalypse text, a third of humanity again killed just as in 3439 BCE. Anunnaki invasion of Earth (described bodily in Revelation prophecies). David Davidson's 80-year old research on geometry of Great Pyramid reveals that he was convinced that the monument conveyed an orbital chronology that ENDS in 2045 CE. It is the 2046 CE proximity of NIBIRU to Earth that reduces the day, night, sun, moon, and stars by a third because our planet will be MOVED and begin spinning faster causing destruction that will kill off a third of mankind.

2106 CE...792 year orbit complete. NIBIRU exits the Sol system after the Anunnaki on planet for 60 years. 2106 CE is the 6000th year from 3895 BCE that serves as the Ancient World's Year One, marking the year of a major poleshift that reset civilization back to a 0 point. This 3895 BCE global lithospheric displacement rearranging the coasts and continents, slipping entire landmasses beneath the seas, is the reason why in 3439 BCE when the Anunnaki arrived they found a human race living no different than animals (according to the Sumerian records and the archeological evidence). When the Anunnaki arrived it had been 456 years since the 3895 BCE poleshift had ended every civilization on the planet.

This orbital chronology is the subject matter of my book Anunnaki Homeworld and its data-packed sequel, Nostradamus and the Planets of Apocalypse. I have here provided the orbital history of NIBIRU but we have much ground to cover before we conclude that all the evidence has been amassed. My own books are packed with extensive bibliographies because I believe that all source materials need be honored, and that all who read my conclusions see for themselves that I invent no dates to support a theory, that the dates were already published in works preceding my own.

Out of the Deep...Anunnaki Overlords

The accounts of Anunna origin seem confusing- out of the sea or out of the sky. But the most popularized account is not original, but an anachronistic misunderstanding of older records. Originally, the oldest writings, Sumerian, depicted the Anunnaki as having dropped from heaven. They were not amphibian. Nephilim is Hebrew for the fallen ones, or those who dropped down .(1)   That this refers to fallen angels is purely religious invention.

After the Great Deluge the Sumerians texts were translated into Akkadian and Babylonian. These translators found multitudes of references to Anunnaki having appear on earth from "...out of the Deep." This Deep [ABZU] was originally an astronomical designation for the largely unknown abyss of southern hemispheric space...the region of space below our solar system that can not be viewed from the northern hemisphere. In Babylon artists showed gods emerging from the sea, a terrestrial abyss and soon after reliefs gave such marine deities amphibious characteristics. Later scribes compounded the association until the gods almost a thousand years after the Great Flood in 2239 BCE were represented as part fish. Even later in time they would be represented with wings to symbolize their origin from the sky and ability to fly. And the concept of angels was born.

Excavated tablets from the Sumerian city of Nippur tell of the arrival of the Anunna to a mountainous region. They set up a camp in a fertile valley and called their settlement EDIN. (2) These are the Kharsag Tablets, and EDIN is a name implying a walled enclosure. (3) An Anunna female called the Serpent Lady was among them, known as NINKHARSAG. In Egyptian, the hieroglyph and word for goddess also means serpent. (4) The explanation we get in Genesis that Eve means The Mother of All Living is a borrowing from the older goddess religion of antediluvian antiquity. The Mother Goddess was the center of all preflood religious observances.

From this anciently popular Sumerian account the Jews borrowing heavily from the Babylonian libraries invented the Adam, Eve, garden of Eden and serpent themes that found their way into the composition of Genesis. From EDIN groups of Anunna spread out to become the ruling elite over the indigenous humans who were living as beasts without culture, written language or an infrastructure. These Anunnaki founded the dragon and serpent dynasties so popular in traditions about the preflood world.

That the ancients provide no clear data on NIBIRU suggests that the knowledge of this object was already obscure by the advent of writing systems. The oldest known writings in the world do not antedate 2200 BCE. We have traditions claiming things were written down prior to this time and there are references in the oldest texts that they were copies of yet more ancient documents, but we simply have no examples. Even the most sophisticated technolithic architecture found in ancient Egypt is absolutely bereft of any hieroglyphs, pictographic texts or writing of any kind.

3439 BCE begins the 792 years of Anunnaki residence among humans on earth before the Flood, to the year 2647 BCE when NIBIRU passed through the inner solar system one last time prior to the Great Flood. Robert Temple had no date for this time but we'll borrow his terminology, this being the Anunnaki Contact Period. William Brambley called them the Custodial Society in his monumental work *The Gods of Eden*. NIBIRU is the Planet of the Crossing according to Zechariah Sitchin. NIBIRU is one of the 50 divine names in the Enuma Elish; the 49th name. (5) The Babylonian Enuma Elish reads- "Nibiru shall hold the crossing of heaven and earth...let 'crossing' be his name." (6) Robert Temple remarks that in the Enuma Elish text NIBIRU is described not as a planet but as a star. (7) Sitchin wrote that NIBIRU orbited its own star, not Sol, located in the Deep. It appeared in the Sol system seeking a new destiny [orbit]. When it appeared in the Sol system it had the longest circuit [orbit] of all of Sol's planets. (8) NIBIRU approached planet Tiamat and destroyed her, capturing some of her eleven moons, KINGU (Luna) among them. NIBIRU continued on, finding a destiny and returned to the Deep. (9) NIBIRU returned later to plunge through the debris of Tiamat and over time her remnants filled her former orbit as the Asteroid Belt. Sitchin noticed that the Sumerian records refer to NIBIRU as the Planet of the Crossing, that the other known planets were told not to cross above nor below (10), referring to the ecliptic plane on which all the other known planets orbit.

According to the author of Ancient Alien Question, NIBIRU's existence as a planet is questionable- no Sumerian texts call NIBIRU a planet. (11)   But NIBIRU is mentioned in post-Sumerian cuneiform texts but not as a mysterious planet, but as a description of known planets like Jupiter and Saturn as published in 1900 in *The Reports of the Magicians and Astrologers of Nineveh and Babylon in the British Museum* by Reginald Campbell. In fact, *before* Zechariah Sitchin was even born scholars were already confused about the identity of NIBIRU and in Campbell's work it is revealed that these men in the 1890s and 1900 arbitrarily began inserting *Jupiter* in the cuneiform translations where the word NIBIRU occurred. NIBIRU of the Anunnaki is more probably a dark red dwarf binary companion to Sol with an Anunna-populated world, moon or superconstruction that uses it as a ferry. It must also be noted that even a supergiant planet the size of Jupiter if near Pluto would be invisible to earth. Too far away. Neptune is huge and Uranus much closer to Earth and both gigantic worlds are invisible without telescopes.. NIBIRU will not be visible from earth until 2043 to 2045 before its arrival in November 2046. But by this time it won't matter. The Phoenix will have already transited and totally changed the contours of our world, coastlines, mountain ranges, drying ocean beds replacing many regions that were thickly populated just hours prior to its May 16th 2040 passage.

Evidence for the existence of the NIBIRU brown dwarf dark star derives from an unexpected source. Scientist Paul A. LaViolette, Ph.D. shows that the historic spacing of cosmic ray peaks in the geologic record shows that it occurred 14 times in the last 6000 years, gamma ray bursts bathed earth. The first saturation is approximately dated

3300 BCE. (12) The radio telescope findings are close to NIBIRU's 3439 BCE passage date. As an approximate they are exact. As the small brown dwarf star is within its perihelion period to Sol it would occasionally release energy in the form of flares spewing cosmic radioactive particles. Though LaViolette does not mention NIBIRU, the dating of the gamma ray bursts are too coincidental to ignore. These findings show that something saturates earth with a cloud of ionized gas. I venture that this object bursts with gamma ray activity upon close approach to perihelion, LaViolette documenting a period coinciding with the NIBIRU visitation from 1123-1063 BCE, again in 522 CE and 1314 CE. Because the perihelion period is 60 earth-years long before NIBIRU exits the inner system till its return 732 years later, seven of the cosmic ray peaks can be attributed to NIBIRU (50%), this including the first [3439 BCE] and the last time it was in the inner system in 1314 CE. About 40% of the gamma ray bursts occurred within 500 years of one another, 650-1050 CE (six bursts) and five of the six occurred as NIBIRU was returning toward the inner Sol system. These were not proximity saturations but immense wave fronts from detonations, or x-flare activity from NIBIRU or our own sun. LaViolettes research accounts for 13 of the 14 radiation pulses.

In late 1960s Dr. Anthony Hewish, 1974 Nobel Prize recipient in Physics, working at Mulard Radio Astronomy Observatory discovered in the southern sky radio emissions from an extinct star that had blown up or collapsed circa 4000 BC. Totally independently, at the same time, George Michanowsky, deciphered an ancient Sumerian star catalogue text concerning the same southern region of the heavens that told of a star explosion. (13) In my published works and other posts it is my position that this nova or binary companion collapse is what so heavily damaged the planets and moons of our solar system, the origin of Phoenix, the Dark Satellite and NIBIRU, the Astroid Belt and comets. The existence of a dark brown dwarf binary companion still near to the Sol system is the subject of Andy Lloyd's interesting work published as *The Dark Star*.

29. 600 Year Epochs of Anunnaki Chronology to 1962 CE

Charles Fort had a theory almost a century ago that Earth was being watched, observed by intelligent overseers, that mankind was considered as property. My research as published in several books seems to bear this out, none more than Descent of the Seven Kings where I detail and analyze the 600 year epochs of world history from 5239 BCE to 1962 CE that make up the Anunnaki NER Great Year Chronology.

In prior posts we have examined the 3439 BCE descent of the Watchers/Anunnaki and the person of ENKI/Enoch that occurred 600 years after the appearance of the Moon to orbit the Earth, or Capture of Luna. 3439 BCE appearance of the Anunna was also 600 years before the birth of Noah and the 1st regnal year of a dynasty of Nephilim Kings over Egypt. Noah's own birth was in the biblical narrative 600 years before the Great Flood of 2239 BCE, a Phoenix-caused cataclysm. This disaster that largely depopulated the planet was 600 years before the death of Jacob in 1639 BCE and introduction of the Egyptian-Josephite peoples into the family of Israel (Hyksos Amorites). Jacob (Israel) died 600 years before the 1039 BCE birth of David, the Nephilim-slayer, killer of

Goliath and other Anakim-Philistine giants who became King of Israel.

That some of these events NEVER happened does not matter, that David was borrowed from a Canaanite epic about a giant-slayer does not make a difference. That Noah was born at the beginning of a 600 year period and was still alive 600 years later when the Great Flood occurred, whether true or not, does not matter. The veracity of these accounts has little to do with what is occurring. The individual stories come from source materials from widely separated texts. When studied and put into their chronologies they all fit perfectly within the 600-year framework. How? The dates were derived from different authors and chronological studies, the biblical narratives, Book of Jasher, Enochian texts...how can real and fictive events thousands of years after they are said to have occurred, be put together in a perfectly sequencial timeline of 600-year intervals?

Everything we perceive in our reality is the echo of something actually thought of or implemented at a higher dimension. Charles Fort was not wrong- we are owned. Deceived. Even our histories are manufactured because these designs are control mechanisms and that allow offworld manipulators to guide the flow of modern events. The 600 year Anunnaki epochs are nodal points where religious programming is patterned, where actual governments are toppled and set backs designed so progress and development is impeded, and where humanity experiences tragic exterminations, whole populations decimated that are at peace and show signs of impending progress. Remember, our own modern technological, information-based civilization is less than

150 years old. If our owners only have a 600-year window of opportunity to base their projections on our progress to keep us at Ground Zero Development then they must have a continuous stream of data from observation posts (many lunar craters are such devices) as well as Earth-based agents.

The manipulation is ancient and quite revealing, demonstrating that (A) something wants to keep humans miseducated, ignorant and primitive, often introducing accusations against Group B; (B) something seeks to be mankind's benefactor but has been severely demonized throughout history. The Great Deluge story became the most prolific piece of propaganda ever. All variations of the idea attribute the blame for the Great Flood on earth to MAN for his rebellions against God and because of the wicked children of the angels who taught humans forbidden secrets- all lies being the opposite of the truth. The friendly Anunna who taught humans how to live were demonized by those Anunna seeking to keep mankind enslaved. After the Deluge in 2239 BCE the slavery continued in the form of religious programming. The priesthoods took the reins of public education and soon had all people believing they were born in sin. History repeated itself when the spiritually free movements of Gnosticism were stamped out by the official Roman Church that continued to perpetuate a religious institution inducing men to blame themselves for their physical and spiritual plight.

The 600 year intervals are curious because of the events that transpired and how those events shaped the histories that followed. Remember, our reality construct maintains the architecture of a hologram, events are not random but serve as reflections of prior events just as new events that unfold are actually ghosted reflections from a future already set in stone in the collective though we as individuals have great freedom to decide what, where we want to be. This is better covered in my work, Nostradamus and the Planets of Apocalypse. The underlying theme of the 600 year Anunnaki NER date-events is that of religious programming, not any particular religion for they all have their use in population control. The second theme evident is change of government. The third is widespread depopulations.

Continuing into more relative history, 600 years after the 1039 BCE birth of David was 439 BCE when the Parthenon Temple atop the Acropolis at Athens completed, exactly 3000 years after the Anunnaki/Watchers descended in 3439 BCE. 1800 years after the Deluge in 2239 BCE and 1200 years after the death of Jacob in 1639 BCE, 600 years after the birth of David. The Parthenon was adorned in fantastic reliefs of the War of the Titans and Giants with a depiction of Nereus, the ancient Achaean Noah who survived the Flood and whose Greek name preserved the Sumerian NER (=600) in NER-eus. This temple was the center of the Greek world and was built to commemorate a goddess, Athena, who epitomized the Virgin [parthenonos is Virgin Chamber]. This concept was born in the Near East when virgins were placed in opulent temple bedrooms to entice gods to descend.

Moving another 600 years we arrive at 162 CE when a pandemic disease afflicted China for eleven years and spread throughout the east to the west infecting the Roman Empire for 16 years. Entire provinces belonging to Rome were depopulated. Amidst the massive loss of life the Han Dynasty fell initiating an Asian Dark Age that lasted over four centuries until the emergence of the Tang Dynasty. (1)

Readers of my published works will know that 1902 was the end of the Cursed Earth system known in antiquity, a Phoenix calendar. 1902 CE began the Giza Course Countdown of pyramid levels to the final year when the Chief Cornerstone descends to finalize the monument, whatever or whomever this chief cornerstone is. In 1902 a farmer plowing a field near La Majorra in the mountains of Veracruz State discovered the Tuxtla Statuette, later acquired by the Smithsonian Institute. It was a squat, bullet-shaped headed human with a duck bill and wings covered in 75 Epi-Olmec glyphs. Its own inscribed Long-Calendar date is March 162 CE which in 1902 made it the oldest Long-Count calendar found. (2) Curious how this date of 162 CE marks a further end to an old culture that met a cataclysmic end toppling their civilization in 31 BCE at transit of Phoenix, now found in 1902 CE when Phoenix again transited bathing the planet in hundreds of millions of tons of red dust. This is exactly what you would expect in a holofield. Separate calendrical systems often intersect at key nodal points.

We move forward through history another 600 years. The Observers find humanity rising in population levels but most of the world suffers in a widespread Dark Age. Literacy is virtually nonexistent save for the quills of the priesthoods. The year is 762 CE. The Jewish Exilarch Solomon died, leader over foreign Jewish activities in Persia and throughout the Islamic world. His hereditary successor, his nephew Anan ben David Hassini, was rejected by the elders who opted instead to install his younger brother Chanaya as Exilarch. Anan fled to

Palestine founding his own synagogue, calling upon Jews everywhere to abandon the corrupt Talmud and obey only the inspired Word of God in the Pentateuch (Genesis to Deuteronomy). His sect became influential, known as the Karaites, or Followers of the Text, and Anan's view and teachings about Jesus was much more positive than the Talmudic one. He urged Jews to resist the Rabbinate, for he thoroughly believed that the rabbis were modern Pharisees bents on propagating the traditions of men rather than the will of heaven. (3)   This Kairite movement still exists today. This event of 762 CE caused a major rift in Judaism still extant today. The value of such division between groups of the same faith is that it perpetuates the belief system by both groups supporting it but differing only in minor issues. A control mechanism.

This year of 762 CE marked the first year of the Abbasid Dynasty in Baghdad. The region of ancient Babylon, Baghdad is thoroughly planned out and would remain a Muslim center even today.

On the other side of the planet 762 CE marked an important event.   The Mayan conclave met at Copan to correct the calendar. The skywatchers served as the culture's chronologists. Altar Q at Copan depicts these 16 skywatchers. The following year in 763 CE the decision of the Copan skywatchers was published on monuments throughout the realm of the Maya.(4) Interestingly, 762 CE is the 6000th year of the Anunnaki NER chronology of 600 year epochs from its start in 5239 BCE.

Continuing along the 600 year periods we get to 1362 CE.   England, long under French influence, in this year began opening Parliament in English rather than in French and English began in the language of the law courts as well.

(5)   This marks a major awakening among the English and French peoples as other nations in Europe begin to stir. Global depopulations occurred from 1314 CE passage of NIBIRU on through 1348 CE when the Great Black Death plague run its course. 1362 CE marks the beginning of exploration and awareness, the foundation of Western Civilization of post-Dark Age antiquity. In fact, in 1362 the Norse-Goth expedition of King Magnus of Norway surveyed North America and left behind the Kensington Stone inscription discovered in 1898 as proof of their presence across the interior. (6)   This region later to become Canada and the United States of America.

The final 600 year epoch ends in 1962 CE but the events of that year require an entire post unto themselves. If the Anunnaki NER Chronology of 600 year periods interest you, see even more data and chronological charts in *Return of the Fallen Ones*.

30. 1962 CE...The Final Year of Anunnaki NER Chronology

The 600 year Anunnaki NER Chronology throughout history has consistently visited upon us at those key nodal dates the themes of the Moon, of visitors from the Deep of space, of calendar systems and of religious programming. What exactly occurred in 5239 and 4639 BCE is purely conjectural, but the dates from 4039 BCE to 1962 CE, or 6000 years evenly, are not unknown. 1962 CE marks the end of the 600 year NER calendar of the Anunnaki so we should find that many events that transpired in this year directly reflect these same themes carried on through these epochs of human history.

1962 CE was the final year the astonishing underground cities of Turkey remained unknown and hidden. In 1963 the entrance to a vast subterranean metropolis called Derinkuyu was accidentally discovered, covering an estimated 2.5 square miles. It has between 18-20 underground levels though only 8 of them are open to the public. Advanced drainage, ventilation shafts have evidence of drilling- thousands of chambers to support a population between 100,000 and 200,000. Amazingly, underground tunnel systems connect Derinkuyu to other subterranean cities and a total of 36 such underworld cities have already been found by 2004. Derinkuyu is pre-Hittite, probably antediluvian or even PreAdamite (pre-4039 BCE) . Great planning was required and Andrew Collins theory is most plausible- these cities were designed by a population seeking protection from a coming force of nature, to avoid dying out in some foreseen cataclysmic episode. (1) In 1962 CE Arizona Cavalcade was published, written by Joseph Miller, which cites a 1909 Phoenix Gazette news article about the amazing discovery of a mysterious underground city complex in the Grand Canyon. (2) Underground facilities were built extensively at Giza in Egypt below the Great Pyramid but are closed off from pulic inspection today.

Such underground projects are not only on Earth. In 1962 CE meticulous observations of an anomalous bulge at the Martian equator by nine respected astronomers resulted with astrophysicist, Dr. E. J. Opik, concluding that such a bulge may be hollow, an artificial construction, like a shelter. (3) Vladimir Terziski, a Bulgarian-born engineer and physicist, claims there to be a joint U.S.-Russian base on Mars since 1962. Dr. Richard Boylan holds that we have had military bases on the Moon and Mars since 1962. (4) In

1962 CEs scientific examination of the Moon found that its interior was less dense than its interior; NASA scientist Gordon MacDonald concluded that "...it would seem that the Moon is more like a hollow than a homogenous sphere." (5) Jim Marrs quotes MIT's Sean C. Solomon concerning new findings by the lunar orbiter, "...indicating the frightening possibility that the Moon might be hollow." (Our Occult History p. 19) The hollow moon position was supported by Russian scientists Vasin and Shcherbakov, who claim that the Moon is not an artificial satillite but a hollowed-out planetoid fashioned by some advanced civilization. (6) In 1962 CE the U.S. landed Ranger 3 on the moon and John Glenn became first American to orbit the earth, doing it three times in a Mercury capsule called Friendship 7.

Radio telescopes in 1962 began detecting strong xrays coming from the Cygnus region of space, the Cygnus Rift, a great black tear in space. Scientists first detected solar wind in 1962 and on July 8th scientists detonated a megaton atomic weapon 248 miles above the earth. In 1962 the ultra secret Cheyenne Mountain Complex is completed near Colorado Springs, a massive underground facility with tunnel systems leading to other underground bases and underworld cities. Here, underneath the United States, the most intelligent people on the planet manufacture technologies unknown to the private sector. This is also the NORAD Command Center, the Air Force Space Command, the Space Defense Operations Center and the Air Defense Command. This complex provides a day to day picture of precisely what is in space and where it is located. (7) Many researchers are convinced that the Cheyenne Mountain underworld contains a whole joint human-extraterrestrial joint operations center. 1962 CE was first year of operations for Wright-Patterson Air Force Base's Foreign Technology Division. (8) Since 1947 as the T-2 Intelligence of Air Material Command, it was at Wright-Patterson Field that U.S. scientists attempted to reverse-engineer the debris from the Roswell UFO crash. The Naval Ordnance Lab manufactured Nitinol from the "memory metal" in 1962, a titanium-nickel alloy. Titanium was not a human discovery, but developed from the 1947 Roswell debris. Researchers note that prior to 1947 CE there exist no government references to titanium. (9)

1962 CE began the Close Encounters of the Fourth Kind-abductions of unwilling humans for genetic experimentations, fetal extractions and implantation of tracking devices. In 1962 scientists discovered that Venus is hot and rotates in a retrogade motion, both facts predicted by Immanuel Velikovsky. (10) In 1962 Dr. Carl Sagan urged the scientific community at the American Rocket Society in November to reexamine ancient myths and traditions for evidence and clues that Earth has been visited by extraterrestrial species in antiquity. (11) In 1962 CE Dr. James D. Watson and Francis Crick awarded the Nobel Prize for Physiology or Medicine for their discovery of the double-helix DNA construction. Crick holds that DNA is too complex and so perfect that it is not the result of evolution, that its origin lies elsewhere. DNA is alien. (12)

Many believe 1962 began a spiritual darkening over America, a curse on the nation. All those material blessings that made America supreme in the past began to wane-crude oil production, coal mining, steel manufacturing, pig iron production, nickel mining, aluminum and zinc, rubber, copper, lead, tin, bauxite, chromite, gold, electricity production. Merchant fleet tonnage diminished as did automobile production, as other nations began out-producing the United States. By 1966 the statistics were alarming, showing a rapid decline in all of these national resources productions. (13) In 1962 CE U.S. Supreme court on a 6-1 decision ruled it unconstitutional to pray in public schools. (14) The Southern Baptists went the opposite extreme, overwhelmingly passing a resolution concerning absolute faith in the biblical records as the infallible Word of God. (15) Few biblical scholars are Southern Baptists. That much of the biblical material is of proven Babylonian,

Elamite, Egyptian, Ionian and Gnostic origin is ignored. Even the Vatican was feeling it in 1962. Rome held a council of 3000 men under Pope John XXIII to consider ways it can relate to the 20th century world. (16) By 1962 the Vatican was losing the battle against Protestantism concerning the making available of the Holy Writ to the public which Rome refused to do for centuries. In 1962 the Christian Gideon's Association celebrated its 50,000,000th freely distributed King James Bible in hotels and other public places. (17)

The year 1962 CE is the 6000th year since the Capture of Luna, or Moon, once an inhabited world, which was 144 years before 3895 BCE when the lithospheric displacement virtually created a new heavens and new earth as ocean beds dried becoming new landmasses after populated continents became oceans beds. The year 1962 CE is also 144 years before 2106 CE, which is the 6000th year from the poleshift of 3895 BCE which began Year One of the 1656 years before the Great Flood in 2239 BCE. The Revelation prophecy of the coming of a new heavens and new earth is precise, but NOT as the religionists believe. It will occur in 2106 CE...a population-eradicating poleshift.

31. How to Predict the Future: Intro to Calendrical Isometrics

The horror comes in reality from the mathematical aspect of the event...no code of ethics are justifiable a priori in the face of the cruel mathematics that command our condition.

Albert Camus (1)

In 1973 the World Trade Center towers were completed in New York City. At that time, standing 110 stories each, these were the tallest buildings in the world. On February 21st of the same year an Israeli jet shot down a Libyan passenger airliner killing 103 people. These two events would appear to be unconnected, occurring in opposite hemispheres, to be separated in both time and space. But were they?

The destruction of the World Trade Center towers in 2001 popularly remembered as 911 is a day not easily erased from the minds of Americans. It is the one day in our collective pasts that we all recall perfectly what it was we were doing on that day. In the complex geometrical matrix of our lives we know precisely the TIME and LOCATION of our experiences as 911 unfolded.

But was this a predictable event? Is there a correlation between the World Trade Center destruction and the destruction of the Libyan passenger jet 28 years earlier? Is there a definite method by which anyone could predict a future event? Could it be possible that the future of any thing is hewn from its history?

The answer to all of these questions is yes.

The information detailed in this article will alter your perception of reality, for once the human mind is stretched by a new idea it can never go back to its original dimensions. (2) In order to fully comprehend how easy it is for one to perceive the future we must first understand the findings of some of the greatest minds who have ever pondered the subject.

Albert Einstein believed that time itself was a geometrical concept. (3) The world-famous physicist said that, "The future...is every whit as necessary and *determined* as the past," (4) and that, "People like us, who believe in physics, know that the distinctions between the past, present and future is only a stubbornly persistent illusion." (5) Einstein's opinion was not dissimilar from other great scientific minds.

The Russian physicist P.D. Ouspensky in the early 20th century in his epic work *Tertium Organum* wrote, "Future events are wholly contained in preceding ones, and if one could know the force and direction of all events which have happened up to the present, i.e. if we knew all the past, by this we could *know all the future*." (6) He too believed that time was a geometrical construction embedded within the human psyche. He further wrote, "The past and future are existing simultaneously on the lines perpendicular to our plane, and the past is identical with the future because phenomena come from both sides and go in *both directions*." (7)

If this is true then this concept must be demonstrated. If demonstration can be replicated many times then a fundamental aspect of our existence has been discovered. If the phenomena of an event is moving in two directions in time and space at the same time then we can perceive our space-time structure as acting similar to the ripples on the surface of a pool of water. An event happening right now in the present would correspond to the epicenter of a concentric pattern of wave-rings rippling up the surface of the pool after a drop of water fell upon the smooth surface. The ripples travelling to the left would symbolize *past events* while those moving toward the right were *future occurrences*. No matter how far the ripples travel they will always be equidistant from the epicenter of the ring formation. Each wave ring is the SAME distance from the center as the corresponding wave ring on the other side of the pool.

If this thesis is to be demonstrated and explained then we need to apply fixed terms to the particulars of this phenomenon. For our purposes here the drop [event] that creates the space-time structure [wave-rings] that issue out in both directions [past and future] is the center of the entire pattern. Thus, this is the *Isometric Epicenter*. This word, isometric, denotes something that goes in two directions at the same time, and in this case, we are referring to timelines [wave rings]. The epicenter is any event in history that one would want to know the future of.

The future of an event is represented by the wave-rings that travel to the right. but as these are merely the geometrical reflections of the same events that travelled to the left [past], then to understand the future events we must compare them with those that are equidistant from the Isometric Epicenter. For example, the third wave-ring to the right [future] is a *reflection* of the third wave-ring to the left [past]; around the perimeter of the rings all the way around the pool the rings are ONE AND THE SAME...only from the epicenter are they of any distance from one another. This is an *Isometric Projection,* the comparative analysis of an observer (historian or prophet) of two events, one in the past and one in the future both connected to a central event geometrically. This is Calendrical Isometrics. No further terms will be introduced in the exposition of this thesis.

We take for our Isometric Epicenter the year 1973 when the World Trade Center was completed in New York City as the tallest buildings in the world (in that year), the year Israelis shot down a passenger jet. In retrospect we see easily that 911 was 28 years after 1973, passenger jets destroying the WTC towers in 2001, skyscrapers wherein worked many thousands of people, a rather high centration of them being Jewish and Israeli. Studying the end of the WTC we are reminded of their beginning, in 1973, the isometric epicentral year. When looking backward to the geometrical space-time reflection of 2001 from 1973 we are taken back that same 28 years to the year 1945 and to a most remarkable and little-remembered event in American history that was NEVER mentioned by the media when the events of 911 were unfolding in 2001.

In 1945 a US B-25 bomber piloted by Lt. Col. William Smith crashed right through the 78-79th floors of the *tallest building in the world,* the Empire State Building, in New York City. The pilot was flying through low fog clouds and lost his bearings. The space-time reflection is hauntingly precise. It was United Airlines Flight 175 that slammed into the South Tower's 79-80th floors, a wing even striking the 78th floor according to David Icke in *Alice in Wonderland and the World Trade Center Disaster.*

Had an observer taken in to consideration this 1945 bomber accident involving the tallest building on earth in the city of New York when New York erected taller buildings, the WTC in 1973 which were the tallest structures in that year (a taller building was erected in 1974) he would have been able to predict that a plane or planes would strike the WTC in 2001. Another example can be made of the assassination of archduke Ferdinand that catapulted Europe into World War I. This assassination was carried out exactly 49 years after another high-level assassination in 1865, that of Abraham Lincoln. A researcher seeing the parallels between Lincoln and Ferdinand would quickly see that the two shared things in common. They both opposed the Banking cartel of the Rothschilds and were enemies of the internationalist Cryptocracy that now runs the entire world. The truth of both of their assassinations has been officially declared, but the truth is that they were carried out by the agents of the world banks. This researcher would then count 49 years into the future from the second assassination and find the third murder, this being the November assassination of President John F. Kennedy. Whole books, documentaries and articles have been written showing the uncanny parallels between Lincoln and Kennedy but what is largely unknown is that Kennedy was about to issue an Executive Order that would critically damage Rothschild control over American banks.

Every event of every second in space and time is geometrically connected isometrically to both past and future times and events. By analogy, our space-time structure is like this same pool of water, but instead of a single drop disturbing the smooth surface in to a pattern of ever-growing rings, every fraction of our own existence is permeated with wave-ripples from countless events from innumerous times that create interference patterns that slightly alter the future wave-rings [events] so that they never quite mirror exactly their past counterparts.

This is why there are slight deviations and that no future event can totally replicate a similar event in the past. But the phenomenon is real. It is demonstrable and the concept was understood by the ancients. To continue with our analogy, the fabric of reality is this pool of water as it would appear as thousands of raindrops slammed into its already rippling surface forming patterns within patterns. The ripples [events] do not hinder one another as they transect. They flow through one another. The space-time interface of multitudes of timelines all operating simultaneously is the cause for the effect we erroneously call *coincidence*.

Our predecessors believed that the knowledge of the future was accessible by the study of the past. A golden inscription discovered in the famous tomb of King Tutankhamen of Egypt reads, "I have seen the past; I know the future." (8) King Esarhaddon of Assyria in the 7th century BCE left behind a tablet inscription saying, "The future shall be like the past." (9) King Jedidyiah, better known as Solomon, author of Ecclesiastes, wrote, "That which hath been is now; and that which is to be hath already been; and God requireth that *which is past."*

Because the phenomenon of the passage of events through the space-time structure has the quality of being isometric, travelling both into the past and future at the same time, scholars five centuries ago like Firmicus Maternus were able to understand that "...the beginning of anything was to be found out by the unfolding of *historical events."* (10) More contemporary philosophers and historians have not deviated from this tenet. In his *Discourses,* Niccolo Machiavelli made two statements that capture our attention:

"If one examines with diligence the past, it is easy to foresee the future." Then he goes on to remark- "He who would foresee what has to be, should reflect on what has been, for everything that happens in the world at any time has a genuine resemblance to what happened in ancient times. (11)

There are few men alive who can boast of having researched more on our world's ancient beliefs and histories than Gerald Massey, author of the huge volumes titled *Ancient Egypt Light of the World* and *The Natural Genesis*. These immense tomes are packed with historical, anthropological and mythological data. Massey's *Lectures* book from the 1880s contains these statements he made- "The past is a region to explore...it is impossible to understand the present without the profoundest knowledge of the past." And, "Our past deeds must and *will* make our future fate." (12)

A contemporary of Massey was the occultist Franz Hartmann, who, in 1888 published a work on magic. Hartmann perceived that the entire universe is made up of matter that vibrates at different frequencies which gives different physical materials the densities they have. This is now a know fact about all physical objects, this illusory world that still mystifies even the quantum physicist. The number of vibrations at a given interval is what identified something from something else. What interests us here is that Hartmann wrote- "If everything has a certian number of vibrations, and if these vibrations increase or diminish at a certain ratio and in regular periods, a *knowledge of these numbers* will enable us to PREDICT A FUTURE EVENT." (13)

Calendrical Isometrics is the science of the future. Instead of counting vibrations the historian or prophet counts days or years as his numbers which are represented by the wave-rings upon the surface of the pool. A very relevant statement was uttered in 1902 by Judge Thomas Troward when he said, "The more deeply we investigate the world we live in, the more clear it must become to us that all our science is the translation into words or numerical symbols of that order which already exists." (14) Oswald Spengler agreed, writing in *The Decline of the West*, "...the most valuable thing in the classical mathematic is its proposition that *number* is the essence of all things *perceptible to the senses*." (15) Numbers serve as the alphabet in this system of analyzing history and the future, but it is the forward and backward isometric timelines that construct *sentences* out of these numerical letters we employ. And multiple isometric projections all linked to the same year form for us entire paragraphs, pages and even a whole book of knowledge about a future event.

Our present blindness to this phenomenon is partly because we have been duped by historians and chronologists over and again in to accepting that any particular calendar is of any importance, that the artificial strictures of mechanical time governs our existence. Nothing could be further from the truth. The historian Lewis Mumford summed it up perfectly in his monumental work titled *Technics and Civilization* when he wrote- *"Time is measured not by the calendar but by the events that occupy it."* (16)

That 1973 was our epicentral year in our study of the World Trade Center does not in any way restrict 1973 from being a part of other isometric projections. Many events occurred in 1973 and for every single individual event there are isometric projections connecting those events with both past and future events and times. This forward and backward pulse of the space-time continuum forms our every day reality. At 20 miles per second our planet moves around the sun immersed in an incomprehensible vast space-time structure virtually saturated with unseen events in motion. Current events are the space-time reflections of future phenomena not yet passed through.

In the year 1054 CE the entire world witnessed a stunning supernova in the Crab Nebula. Many Europeans and others named their children after the bright star explosion. Also in 1054 Pope Leo IX excommunicated the Patriarch of Constantinople which resulted in the great rift between the Eastern and Western Christian Church. This division was a loss of power for Italy, headed by the Papacy. Christianity emerged out of the roots of Judaism and Greek belief (Constantinople headed the Greek Church) and the two elements that stand out in 1054 are religious division and the appearance of a bright star. At this time in Europe the Jews were spread throughout the nations because the Romans had completely obliterated their nation and Jerusalem in the year 135 CE. All of the European powers at this time distrusted the Jewish people because of their conspiracies in the Muslim invasions of southern Europe when Jews opened the gates of several cities to allow the Moors and Saracens to invade. Christian peoples of Europe were offended because it was they who had taken the Jewish exiles in after their flight from Rome.

If we compare 135 CE to the year 1054 we find that they are 919 years apart. In 1054 the Roman power was weakened from a religious-political conflict, but in 135 CE the Romans were empowered and crushed the Jewish nation in the Bar Kochba Rebellion, which in Hebrew means *son of a star.*

Now when we search isometrically beyond 1054 in to the future this same 919 years we arrive at 1973 when Israel was attacked by an alliance of Islamic nations in the Yom

Kippur War. This religious-political war found Israel surrounded but totally victorious as they saved Jerusalem, the circumstances the same but only the outcome differing.

That every future is an echo of its past is demonstrated by this peculiar forward and backward trait embedded within the geometrical framework of history. Could it be possible that some men are influenced by a future that exists in space but has not yet transpired in time? Every second we spend in the present we are held together by an infinite amount of *pasts* as well as *futures,* we as sentient beings literally trapped at the intersect between two infinities. If the future did not yet exist somewhere *we could not exist either.* The space-time sequence of events is moored to something, be it a property of our collective psyche or an Eternal Mind (if there is a difference), somewhere, the future exists in space though unrealized in time. This was the belief 15 centuries ago by Augustine of Hippo-

Where did those who sang prophecies see these events if they do not yet exist? To see what has no existence is impossible. And those who narrate past history would surely not be telling the truth if they did not discern events by their soul's insight. If the past were nonexistent, it could not be discerned at all. Therefore, both future and path exist. (17)

And because it exists, interwoven into the matrix of the present and past, it is accessible. Our minds are open to every impression that touches us as we flow through our environments. We traverse our lives through a medium of innumerable contacts, immersed in an unfathomable multitude of places that remain nonlocal because physically we can only experience one *time* at a time. For this reason we are sometimes overcome with the sensation that we already know something that we also understand that we had never come in contact with, that we have seen or experienced something before though we have no memory of it. Or the feeling that we are being watched takes over us, that we have performed certain acts exactly in the same way we had done in the unremembered past. The sensations of deja vu, occurrences of retrocognition, synchronicity and coincidence are reminders that the world around us that we perceive through the agency of our limited senses is far greater than we are able to grasp.

Because the past can be attained by the agency of memory then this necessarily implies that the future can also be experienced, through *imagination.* Poetically, with the past as memory and the future perceived through imagination, then our present reality is the ever-fleeting passage of what's imagined in to what is remembered.

That prophets have foretold many recorded events long prior to their unfolding in the human drama is well attested in the literature of nations around the world spanning back millennia. What is not known is how they do it. We are given the answer that these men were touched by the Divine, and this could be so. We are created beings, the question being only the *identity* of our makers. Encoded within the structure of our own biological programs are precise geometrical informations. There appears to be a direct connection between our external space-time structural existence in material reality and our internal geometrical DNA makeup. The forward and backward property expounded upon in this work concerning historical timelines is scientifically referred to as a palindrome. This is a sequence of numbers that count both forward and backward from an epicentral point.

Intriguingly, it has been discovered that much of our DNA is structured in the form of palindromes, as yet "undeciphered sentences" that read both forward and backward mystifying the geneticists. In fact, perhaps as much as 95% of our DNA remains undeciphered according to Sol Luckman in *Conscious Healing.* (18) If this is the foundation of our body in the microscopic realm in which our psyche seems to be moored then naturally this is also a property of the universe we are suspended within. The macrocosm merely reflects the microcosm.

Isometric projections are real and measurable in the outer world of experiences because they reflect the inner world of man.

The famous critical thinker Rene Descartes wrote, "It were far better to never think of investigating truth at all, than to do so without a method." (19) Our method is to study what occurred during certain years, then to examine the past for events that were very similar in nature. The distance in time between these two events allows us to perceive when a similar event will occur in the future. When isometric patterns are detected we are afforded a window into the past to events preceding that molded the conditions in time and space to events that follow.

Through the study of calendrical isometrics we see more clearly who we are and where we came from...two requirements necessary when considering *where* we are going.

32. The Greatest Secret of Them All

My work, *Awaken the Immortal Within*, is for those who have searched for the truth all their life and know they have not found it. The rest of you are warned away.

Reality is an evasive witch, sweeping away paradigms with the dust of discovery. When a mortal approaches the hallowed realm of Verity, her substance becomes shadow, an immortal jest- the process of discovery exceeding our ability to fully process what it discovered.

Things are rarely as they appear. Because we think, we believe that we are alive, though some distant inner voice whispers secrets- it is the dead who gather to mourn the living...a funeral attracts a congregation of the lost. Or an ancient doctrine-when angels die they become mortal souls. The meaning of life evades the living because nothing is made alive until it dies. A terrible misunderstanding, misconception manufactured to deceive. We are carcasses of creativity ever compelled to call upon One that does not answer. Not yet.

Men fear the unknown, the decay of their prisons, unmindful that he is a spirit bound in bodily bondage. Cocooned immortality. The individual human is deity dismembered and deceived; billions of ethereal sparks in a ghostly fire. Such is the essence of material reality-all is a reflection of something else, like the future to the past. We sparks are the Undead, condemned to serve a sentence in a hell we call home, flowing through immateriality in a struggle like so many spermatozoon racing to fertilize the bondage of another immortal soul. A definition of tragedy: to be born into a realm of death and to grow into the blame.

Religionist beware, you will find no ally here. In death I walked that path till almost lost in darkness. The Deep has no greater voice than those who claim to come from God. It was from this Abyss I came, starving, that I finally found a truth.

Raised a staunch religionist, washed in blood that never flowed from a God who never walked, I was reborn, a spirit-filled unbeliever, crucified in criticism to observe clearly the stage and all that's hidden behind it. Woe unto the scribes! Line upon line, inventiveness masked as inspiration, words dropped by the whims of copyists as others were added, the far east robbed of its parables as the west lost its stage plays.

The Christian story a cosmopolitan drama, sculpture of Greek Platonism, Stoic austerity, Alexandrian learning, Ionian Mysteries and Egyptian wisdom, old Israelite eschatology altered into Jewish forgeries- a statuesque gnosis is this pillared story of the Gospel. A soup made of all the best ingredients.

In my search for the Savior I mistook my feelings for His fidelity. Seeking a cause I found a curse. In stepping off the carefully prepared path I saw its destination clearly-to pierce the Veil and fall into a pit. My religion a lie of Maya, I despaired and found no comfort. In wrath I wandered, separated from the world but with sight far and true. A prison world- the abyssal layers of dungeon realms perfected to confuse and confine a host of eternal spirits.

Us.

Intrepid sojourner, with rule and plumb line I searched the depth and marveled at my catch...lying leviathans of Judaism, deceitful monkeys of Hinduism, a hydra of a hundred denominations each guarding a portal to paradise. But the gates of hell are seminaries. The flocks are fleeced with offering plates while fed the grass of guilt. Teaching of a light they spread darkness, with healing on their tongues they spread plague with their handshakes, praising a Holy Spirit they mask the doubt within their own. Pastors and preachers, reverends and priests- a new species of devil, illusionists turning horns into halos, myths into money, hell into heaven...thundering the Word of God as if the voice of men could speak it.

Jesus is the drama of a paramount ideal, deification ex post facto, the sum total of many ancient parts. He is what we want not what we have. What we possess is actually so much more powerful. But for now, woe unto the scribes! In rewriting a stage play they invented redemption.

A definition of religion: spiritual population control propaganda by nonhuman overseers.

The slow developmental transition of eastern cosmology into the historic religions they became that eventually morphed into the mysticism of today is a steady record of mankind's attempts to make some sense of the recognizable unreality of his existence. The revolt against Maya, or man's horrific revelation that he is trapped in a multifaceted web of layered illusions designed to blind him from the interconnectedness of all things, resulted in complex philosophical systems that endeavored to justify why terrible things happened to good people. Or how it could be that the immoral and wicked not only remained unpunished, but prosper as well. A secret: there are no ethical considerations of the wolf when rending the rabbit.

Thus the knowledge of Maya, our prison holosphere, was corrupted by a false conception designed to rationalize these problems: the Karmaic Doctrine. The idea that what goes around comes around satisfied many who saw evidence of its operation in the manifestations of events in the lives of good and bad men. But some were not convinced. The believer in Karma saw only what Maya reflected, their own projections while the critic invented yet another doctrine to explain why he often saw no evidence of Karma at work. The new belief explained why there was so little perceived evidence of Karma, that Karmaic debt builds in one life to be discharged in another- or reincarnation.

The transmigration of souls is yet another desperate attempt of humanity to cope with the unfairness of reality, the bitter pain of loss, the unbending phenomenon of Murphy's Law, with death. Attempting to make sense of his twisted existence, man invented religion, sin-debt and Maya thus provided mankind with priests to help him interpret realities that burdened humanity with a need for redemption. The victims now blame themselves for their own spiritual enslavement and physical travails, woes compounded on the religious believer who suffers only because he believes he is meant to suffer.

I commend you for reading this far. In stripping away untruths to see what remains intact it is first necessary to cull the herd. What is REAL is always kept SECRET. Imagine the difficulty of a single spark within a fire realizing that it is the flame, so small a world, that confines it. Because it is the masses that make the holospheric matrix we find that the truth is for the individual and not the masses. A few individuals can share the truth, but not the many. If you are one of these people, this knowledge is for you. In absorbing what I share, you can become one with what I know.

You will become a rogue spirit adrift in a sea of humanity with coordinates to islands others cannot see, a vagabond of another vintage. You shall cope with the truth though you may not believe it. Not at first. By the act of looking you shall perceive invisible cords that pull and oppress others- forces that now shun you, that regard you as an aberrant malfunction in a system of controlled chaos. Infected with curiosity they will treat you as diseased, the bonds that earlier bound you will be severed to contain this contagion. Holospheric self-preservation. It passes poisons off as remedies, the healthy few in number. You shall become a medicine man with antidotes in the dark, carrying a torch bearing sacred fire lit by another. In the shadows of this flickering light are enemies encircled; they rage against revelations. Conspirators striving to darken the illumined. In searching, your gaze will reflect back upon yourself and a truth will be unveiled. A new scion to what lies hidden in the human race. The living emerge only after the egg is cracked...the womb torn. You will remember the future as you see clearly the past. Unto you, the reader, are secrets rendered, obscurities unobstructed. There is truth in what is written- "To him who hath, more will be given..." From opposing vantage points lucidity and lunacy are one: the visionary knowing the holosphere for what it is while the vision-afflicted knows things are wrong but knows not why.

The inheritance of knowledge is danger. Let the timid flee. Even immortals fear what a man can know.

Exhaustive research in comparative religions old and new, in occult and magical systems, in philosophical systems oriental and occident and in stringent analysis of multidisciplinary scientific experimentation of all things perceivable has forced upon us the demonstrable fact that reality is not real at all, that the physical is but a figment of the collective imagination, all things phenomenal are but phantasms of hive psyche. It has for over a century been known to science that the magnification of any solid material object reveals great distances of nothingness between objects like electrons and nuclei, and that electrons orbit far away from their nucleic host, change from wave forms to solid phenomena when observed. A physical object is distinguished from another only by the number of orbiting electrons. These atomic distances microscopically mirror their macroscopic counterparts- earth as an electron is 93 million miles away from its nucleic Sol and in the space between is nothing. Our sun is 4.2 light years from the closest stellar system, Alpha Centauri/Proxima. The distances between tiny nuclei are comparable to stars but when a nucleus is magnified enough we finally reach the foundation of physicality...an oscillating field. Pure energy with no physical property. Inside all material objects is more empty space than solid and the core solid nuclei are in essence miniscule entanglements of suspended energy. The world of existence is a property of perception. To believe we are physical beings in a material medium is tantamount to describing a breeze passing through fog.

From of old there are whispers. Hidden teachings borne from east to west, a secret ever known to but a few. The world is a complex construct, a prison of physicality designed to confine souls in an aura of sense-perception so perfectly fashioned as to deceive the imprisoned spirit. A dungeon realm of the Demiurge is this holosphere. Immortal beings in quarantine by an enemy in a prison of unknown origin designed to make its captives believe that they are a part of the Creation when they have actually been cut off. Held in place by a powerful, diabolical mind. Its victims immortal, they cannot be killed. So this Demiurge, the god of this world of sense-perception of his own design, invented a way to deceive eternal beings that they were mortal, that in living they now had to fear death.

This entity is not omnipotent, it is not a creator, but a manipulator. A human soul awakens, perceives the holospheric illusions for what they are, and then creates his own interference patterns, freed from the confines of ignorance. Thus the man is no longer a marionette. This sinister mind, the enemy, has no more power over the freed individual, who then writes their own destiny. Immersed in this thought medium the living souls are asleep. But one who awakens knows the holosphere for what it is- a mirror. This spirit projects his will, modifies the medium to conform to his wants, changes reality. He is a creator whom the destroyer no longer deceives.

We think in terms of gender and genera, polarizing everything passing through our sense-range. The acute mind knows that discoveries are not made by seeking similarities. We are prone to draw conclusions from the recognition of correlates. In this way we search the surface of phenomena without seeing its depth. To truly learn about a thing is to identify its distinctions, isolate disparities and see why it is dissimilar. Unfortunately, both methods of analysis merely reinforce the holospheric matrix that deceives us into believing in distinctions between things and concepts that really don't exist.

Anything we accept as true in essence becomes a trap, a model of confinement. One who looks at the world from inside his model can only interpret data through this sphere of belief-objectivity is impossible from within a believed worldview. The observer is trapped in subjective analysis though he believes he is objective. A man inside a bubble thinks his vision is clear though he must view things through this film, a watery lens that reflects back some light but distorts reflections due to its spheric curvature.

The man is oblivious of his prison. The outside world only partially influences him because the bubble reflects away data and phenomena he would have ordinarily perceived from a different vantage point.

The reality matrix is sufficiently complex enough to induce us to believe in it. The demon chaser finds demons, the dowser discovers water, the religionist sees reasons everywhere that give proof to his faith as the witch who knows she miscast her spell then suffers for it. The astronomer ever discovers more distance galaxies to replace prior universal boundaries first known only in theory, and the UFO researcher finds proof of extraterrestrials in testimonies, in video, on film, in ancient art, texts and even in biblical imagery. Wherever there are people to believe in something, the holosphere will provide evidence of its existence. Seek and ye shall find is a trap. Philosophies, faiths, conclusions of science all supported by evidence, proofs and conviction but all in opposition to one another. Reality is then a misnomer, disguised as duality, existence is a confluence of realities in myriads of superimposed minds-a multiplicity of surveyors observing architecture of their own collective construction. Only in a hologram can contrary realities coexist without contact.

Oliver Wendell Holmes said that when the human mind is stretched by a new idea it can never go back to its original dimensions. This is the value of learning, of absorbing new information from diverse sources. Public education saps the initiative, waters down what needs to be highlighted, levels the plateau of intellectual development striving to make equals of everyone...a control mechanism no different than organized religion. Both serve the same purpose. Our secular selves are taught that all mysteries are solved and that we are in control; our spiritual selves are quarantined with antiquated systems of thought made acceptable because the dictates were the words of a god. Both conceal the truth- we are NOT in control in the collective and our predicament is not the work of any deity. If the God of Judeo-Christianity truly wrote the Bible and made the world what it is today then any rational individual having reviewed the evidence will rightly determine that God is an enemy of mankind. And this, written by myself, comes from a man who spent the first 40 years of his life a stringent, washed-in-the-blood southern Baptist. Born again, twice-baptized, I have read the entire Bible through over fifty times in my life and have the notes to prove it.

Learning forces us to undergo an intellectual transformation and this is what makes the student open to all types of knowledge quite dangerous to the Establishment- our thoughts lay the foundations to future conditions, knowledge acquired changes us in subtle ways. We are told, warned actually, by great mentalists long ago, that a little learning is a dangerous thing. The more I distance myself from the core programming that had ensnared me most of my life the more I appreciate this statement. Now, with long experimentation, imagination, discovery and implementation of various systems of thought I can now clearly see by virtue of retrospect that all my life I experienced only those major events that I set in motion.

My life has not been measured from destination to destination, by periods of peace or discord, stability or chaos, stagnation or accomplishment. No, these are merely aspects of my space-time passage. My life has been measured by conscious decisions, the milestones of my existence being the exercise of discretion to either believe or disbelieve. Over the years I have maintained meticulous records detailing the events of my life which enabled me to see a definitive pattern between my attitude and my experiences. It is axiomatic that one's attitude is but a personality's outward manifestation of the condition of the mind. This being so, and demonstrated many times in my life, then I must conclude that I have never suffered anything other than what I expected to endure, my expectations a projection mentally reflected back to me as circumstances.

I have never really been surprised by anything that I have experienced be it positive or negative. With the conditions of my life derived from my own psyche, I am left with no one to blame but myself.

As a deist, a student of the Gnosis, I hold that God is a part of our reality. But as an anti-religionist I accept that he is still unknown to us. The creature and Creator are One and the interface between them is mental. We pray and never receive because the architecture of our 4th dimensional existence mandates that men do not receive what they want, but what they are. Edgar Cayce said that what a man thinks continually, he becomes. A lot about Cayce I dislike, but we agree on that one. But here's some quotes from men I have great affinity toward:

JAMES ALLEN WROTE, "LET A MAN RADICALLY ALTER HIS THOUGHTS, AND HE WILL BE

ASTONISHED AT THE RAPID TRANSFORMATION IT WILL EFFECT IN THE MATERIAL CONDITIONS OF HIS LIFE. MEN IMAGINE THAT THOUGHT CAN BE KEPT SECRET, BUT IT CANNOT, IT RAPIDLY CRYSTALLIZES INTO HABIT, AND HABIT SOLIDIFIES INTO "

RENE DESCARTES WROTE, "I AM MORE THAN I SUPPOSE MYSELF TO BE, AND PERHAPS ALL THOSE PERFECTIONS WHICH I ATTRIBUTE TO GOD ARE IN SOME WAY POTENTIALLY IN ME."

THOMAS TROWARD IN 1909 WROTE, "DO NOT EXPECT GOD TO DO FOR US WHAT HE CAN ONLY DO THROUGH US."

ERNEST HOLMES IN 1919 WROTE, "EXPECTATION IS A FORCE, EXPECT THE BEST TO HAPPEN...ONE WHO HAS LEARNED TO TRUST WILL NOT BE SURPRISED EVEN WHEN HE FINDS THINGS COMING FROM THE MOST UNEXPECTED SOURCES."

When one dissolves Christianity of its dressings this teaching, this ideology of faith is clearly found...that our physical reality is a mere reflection of inner ideas and convictions. Even Jesus in the Gospel narratives never healed anyone. Heed what Jesus said when others were healed who had come to him-

"ACCORDING TO YOUR FAITH BE IT UNTO YOU."

"THY FAITH HATH MADE THEE WHOLE."

"RECEIVE THY SIGHT, THY FAITH HATH SAVED THEE."

"BE NOT AFRAID, ONLY BELIEVE."

I know who I am and understand my place as I journey through this little corner of existence. As author of nephilimarchives.com it is important to me that you know I am no holier-than-thou type, no pompous moron stuck up with learning. I'm a good ol' boy who just happens to have a strange gift for memorizing things that interest me. At 40 years old I was awakened. The veil torn away I was made to see with clarity that everything I had studied for years had a focus, a direction. That the religious programming that had had me stuck over and over was a spiritual poison camouflaged as freedom. Absolute genius! To mask a dungeon with illusory trappings and then blame its inmates for its existence.

I am comfortable with who I am, an admixture of good and evil, a divided soul ever analyzing its other half, suspended between the holy and profane. A moralist, yes, but I still retain a capacity for wickedness. It is this ever-influencing of opposite attractions that builds character, our personas molded by our constant decisions.

If you want to fully understand the nature of reality and how we create circumstances governing our lives, if you want to know the precise mental formula you need to change the conditions of your life, then you are no different than I was not long ago. Your search ends here. Read *Awaken the Immortal Within,* available through Amazon.

* * * * *

Breshears is the host of www.archaix.com where can be found his 510-page epic work titled *Chronicon: Timelines of the Ancient Future*, a chronology of the

world cover 7000 years year-by-year from 5239 BCE to 2012 CE. Also on the site is *King of the Giants*, the life and histories of a Nephilim ruler named Amaruda-ak popularly known as Nimrod, and the compelling research titled *Chronotecture: Lost Science of Prophetic Engineering* that includes over 70 charts and illustrations demonstrating that the Great Pyramid is a calendar in stone. His day job as a graphic artist and website developer is found at www.ophisystems.com.

Jason M. Breshears is a researcher of the occult, chronology and antiquities. Eight of his published works are nonfiction with extensive bibliographies concerning fascinating information on ancient civilizations, cataclysms and the modern establishment's attempts to suppress these discoveries from the public today. Five of these works are published by Book Tree in San Diego.

The Lost Scriptures of Giza (2006, 2017 updated version) Kindle & paperback
When the Sun Darkens (2009) paperback
Anunnaki Homeworld (2011) paperback
Nostradamus and the Planets of Apocalypse (2013 Kindle & paperback
Return of the Fallen Ones (2017)

Other books by Breshears
Giants on Ancient Earth (2017) Kindle & paperback
Awaken the Immortal Within (2017) Kindle & paperback
Shocking Secrets of Antiquity (2017) Kindle & paperback

Fiction (The Oraclon Chronicles)

Dark Tales of Dagothar (2017) Kindle & paperback
Uprising: Darkfall of the Faeries (2017) Part 1 of The Oraclon Chronicles (Kindle & paperback)

Greric and the Witch of Dimwood (2017) Kindle &
paperback
The Cragly of Cindereach (2017) Kindle & paperback

Breshears has authored 17 books and several articles, 10
works available on Amazon. His research bibliography is
currently at 1207 nonfiction books read and data mined
during a 19 year period, approximately 250,000 pages from
many rare works as old as four hundred years, including
translations of texts dating as far back as four thousand
years. His core conclusions, discoveries and observations
are being released on www.archaix.com in 2018. As a pen
& ink illustrator and graphic artist, most of his book covers
and artwork are done by himself.

Breshears is one of the only researchers in the world who
specializes in ancient chronological systems, focusing on
global antiquities from 4309 BCE to 522 CE, many of his
historical discoveries can not be found in any other works.
For this reason he was awarded with multiple publishing
contracts with Book Tree in San Diego.

Personal Note from Jason- I'm witty with a dark sense of
humor, my pendulum swinging between gladiator and
goofball. I value smartasses. A free spirit, humor my ally,
I embrace my deviance often finding solace among the
shadows. I recognize that I see the world around me
through filters different than my peers. A pirate
philosopher playing both sinister and sacred, I honor no
God- my spirituality is measured in my actions toward
others. Implacable in my beliefs until overwhelmed with
new information, I love meatballs but dislike spaghetti,
scrape the good stuff out of tacos and subway sandwiches
and the toppings off of pizza. Life's too short for shells and
crusts. I sing in the shower, drink my coffee black, love

short-haired dogs and I'm hoping heaven has grilled-cheese sandwiches. I'm all-American, a patriot who has studied and admired the history of this great nation and I'm upset with the morons who are ruining it. My friends are few, but genuine. In a world that thrives on artificiality I take care to identify friends from fictions. In summary, I've never been accused of being normal.

My Philosophy- Though all men are created equal, they do not remain that way. In this age males are many but men are few. But there are some of us that rise above the rest and have the right to represent our gender as a whole...men of peace with capacity for war, we who speak what others are afraid to say, the apex of both the sacred and the profane. I am one of these men, just as evil as I am holy, separated by sin but bound to God, a student and teacher from the occult to Christianity. Poets and philosophers, visionaries and vikings, we few have a divine right to claim that we are men...all others are merely males. The following are my beliefs, the architecture of my personality:

* The man of principle never forgets what he is, because of what others are. -Baltasar Gracian

* The real voyage of discovery consists not in seeking new lands, but in seeing with new eyes. -Marcel Proust

* I am something more than I suppose myself to be, and perhaps all those perfections which I attribute to God are in some way potentially in me. -Rene Descartes

* A man's worth is not measured by his accomplishments, but in what he strives to accomplish. -Cicero, 1st cent. BCE

* LIVING is the purpose of life

* A person who sees what he wants to see, regardless of what appears, will some day experience in the outer what he so faithfully sees within. -Ernest Holmes, 1919

* Though we all live in the same world there are some of us who exist within an entirely different Universe- Me

Complete Bibliography of Cited Works

Stellar Theology and Masonic Astronomy: Robert Hewitt Brown, 1882 (D. Appleton & Co./reprint Book Tree)

The Book of the Damned: Charles Fort, 1919 (Bonnie & Liveright, NY/ reprint Book Tree)

The Watchers: Raymond E. Fowler (Bantam)

The Gods of Eden: William Brambley (Avon)

Gods of Eden: Egypt's Lost Legacy and the Genesis of Civilization: Andrew Collins (Bear & Co)

The Genesis race: Will Hart (Bear & Co)

The Chronology of Genesis: A Complete History of the Nephilim: Neil Zimmerer (Adventures Unlimited)

Elder Gods in Antiquity: M. Don Schorn (Ozark Mountain)

Our Haunted Planet: John Keel, 1971 (Glade Press/ reprint Book Tree)

Humanity's Extraterrestrial Origins: ET Influences on Humankind's Biological and Cultural Evolution: Dr. Arthur David Horn with Lynette Anne Mallory-Horn, 1994 (Silberschnur)

Mankind: Child of the Stars: Max Flindt & Otto O. Binder, 1974 (Ozark Mountain)

Flying Serpents and Dragons: Rene Andrew Bouley, 1990 (Book Tree)

Universal Laws Never Before Revealed: Keely's Secrets: Dale Pond, John Keely, Nikola Tesla, Edgar Cayce (The Message Group, 2007)

Stalking the Wild Pendulum: Itzhak Bentov (Destiny)

Tertium Organum: P.D. Ouspensky, 1919 (reprint Book Tree)

Antigravity and the World Grid: David Hatcher Childress (Adventures Unlimited)

Hesiod: Theognis: translated Dorothea Wender (Penguin)

Natural History: Pliny the Elder, trans. John F. Healy (Penguin)

Lucretius: On the Nature of the Universe: trans. Ronald Melville (Oxford World Classics)

Enuma Elish: Seven Tablets of Creation, Vol. I: L.W. King, 1902 (reprint Book Tree)

Epic of Gilgamesh: trans. Maureen Gallery Kovacs (Stanford University Press)

Epic of Gilgamesh: trans. N. K. Sandars (Penguin)

The Vedas: trans. Ralph T.B. Griffith, 1892 (reprint Book Tree)

Egyptian Book of the Dead: translated E.A. Wallis Budge (Grammercy Books)

Beowulf: trans. Burton Raffel (Mentor Books)

The Odyssey: Homer, trans. Robert Fitzgerald (Doubleday Anchor)

The Iliad: Homer, trans. Ennis Rees (Barnes & Noble)

The Aeneid: Virgil (Penguin)

Tales From Ovid: trans. Ted Hughes, from Metamorphosis (Farrar Straus Giroux)

The Great Pyramid: Its Secrets and Mysteries Revealed: Piazzi Smyth, 1880 (Bell Pub. NY, 1990 reprint from 1978 Outlet Book Co., orig. pub. by W. Isbister, London under title Our Inheritance in the Great Pyramid, 1880)

The Great Pyramid: Its Divine Message: D. Davidson & H. Aldersmith, 12th Ed. 1924 (reprint Book Tree)

The Origin and Significance of the Great Pyramid: C. Staniland Wake, 1882 (Reeves & Turner, reprinted by Book Tree)

Pyramid Quest: Robert Schoch & Robert McNally (Tarcher Penguin)

The Great Pyramids: Jean-Pierce Corteggiani (Discoveries, Abrams, NY)

Canaanite Myth & Hebrew Epic: Essays in the History of the Religion of Israel: Frank Moore Cross: 1973 (Harvard Univ. Press 1977)

Mysteries of Ancient South America: Harold T. Wilkins: 1947 (2000 Adventures Unlimited)

The History of Atlantis: Lewis Spence, 1926 (Rider & Co. London reprint 1996, Adventures Unlimited)

The Mystery of the Olmecs: David Hatcher Childress, 2007 (Adventures Unlimited)

The Doctrine of Sin in the Babylonian Religion: Julian Morganstern, 1905 (reprint 2002 The Book Tree)

Secrets of the Stones: John Mitchell, 1989 (Inner Traditions)

Space Travelers and the Genesis of the Human Form: Joan d'Arc, 2000 (Book Tree)

LIBER KAOS: Peter J. Carroll, 1992 (Samuel Weiser)

Discovering Ancient Giants: William A. Hinson, 2012 (Seaburn)

Taliesin: The Last Celtic Shaman: John Matthews, 1991, 2002 (Inner Traditions)

Secret Cities of Old South America: Harold T. Wilkins, 1952 (2003 Adventures Unlimited)

The Tigris Expedition: In Search of Our Beginnings: Thor Heyerdahl, 1981 (Doubleday & Co)

In the Hands of the Great Spirit: The 20,000 Year History of American Indians: Jake Page, 2003 (Free Press)

Breaking the Godspell: The Politics of Our Evolution: Neil Freer, 2000 (The Book Tree)

The Secret History of Extraterrestrials: Len Kasten, 2010 (Bear & Co.)

Mysteries of the Ancient World: 1979 (National Geographic Society)

Lost Civilizations: Leonard Cottrell, 1974 (Collins-Publishers Franklin Watts)

A Global History of Man: 1970, Leften S. Stavrianos, L.K. Andrews, J. R. McLane, F. Safford, J.E. Sheridan (Allyn & Bacon, INC)

Earth Under Fire: Humanity's Survival of the Ice Age: Paul A. LaViolette, Ph.D 1997 (2005 Book Tree)

From the Ashes of Angels: The Forbidden Legacy of a Fallen Race: Andrew Collins, 1996, 2001 (Bear & Co.)

The Lost Worlds of Ancient America: edited Frank Joseph 2012 (New Page Books)

The Origin of Biblical Traditions: Albert T. Clay, 1923 (Oxford Univ. Press, 1999 reprint Book Tree)

Our Occulted History: Do the Global Elite Conceal Ancient Aliens? Jim Marrs 2013 (William Morrow)

How the Sun-God Reached America: Dr. Reinoud M. de Jonge & Jay Stuart Wakefield, 2002 [ISBN 0-917054-19-9]

Atlantis in America: Navigators of the Ancient World: Ivar Zapp & George Erikson 1998 (Adventures Unlimited)

The Sirius Mystery: New Scientific Evidence of Alien Contact 5000 Years Ago: Robert Temple, 1998 (Destiny)

Ponder on This: Alice A. Bailey & Djwhal Khul, 1971 (Lucis Pub. Co. NY)

And the Truth Shall Set You Free: David Icke, 1995, 2004 [David Icke]

Atlantis: The Antediluvian World: Ignatius Donnelly, revisions by Egerton Sykes (Book Tree reprint)

The History of Atlantis: Lewis Spence, 1926 (1996 reprint Adventures Unlimited)

Our Sun-God: Christianity Before Christ: John Denham Parsons, 1895 (reprint Book Tree 2007)

Pagan and Christian Creeds: Edward Carpenter, 1920 (Harcourt Brace & Howe, reprint 1999 Book Tree)

Babylonian Influence on the Bible and Popular Beliefs: A Smythe Palmer, 1897 (2000 Book Tree)

Atlantis in America: Lewis Spence, 1925 (London, reprint Book Tree)

The Problem of Atlantis: Lewis Spence, 1924 (Rider & Son, reprint 2002 Book Tree)

The Message of the Sphinx: Graham Hancock & Robert Bauval 1996 (Three Rivers Press)

The United States and Britain in Prophecy: Herbert Armstrong

The Encyclopedia of World Facts and Dates: Gordon Carruth, 1993 (HarperCollinsPublishers)

Genes, Giants, Monsters and Men: Joseph P. Farrell, 2011 (Feral House)

Uriel's Machine: Christopher Knight & Robert Lomas, 2004 (Barnes & Noble Books)

The Trojan War: A New History: Barry Strauss, 2006 (Simon & Schuster)

Mysteries of Time and Space: Brad Steigler (Prentice Hall)

Worlds in Collision: Immanuel Velikovsky, 1950 (Victor Gollancz)

The Annals of the World: Deduced From the Origin of Time: James Ussher, Archbishop of Armaugh (London, 1658)

Atlantis Destroyed: Rodney Casteldon, 1998 (Routledge, London)

Underworld: The Mysterious Origins of Civilizations: Graham Hancock, 2002 (Three Rivers Press)

The Giza Prophecy: The Orion Code and the Secret Teachings of the Pyramids: Scott Creighton and Gary Osborn, 2012 (Bear & Co)

Atlantis Beneath the Ice: The Fate of the Lost Continent: Rand and Rose Flem-ath, 2012, revised from 1995 When the Sky Fell.

The Rise and Fall of Atlantis: J.S. Gordon, 2008 (Watkins Pub. London)

The Complete Books of Charles Fort: The Book of the Damned, Lo!, Wild Talents, New Lands (reprint Dover, NY 1974)

The Christ Conspiracy: The Greatest Story Ever Sold: Acharya S. 1999 (Adventures Unlimited)

History in Quotations: Reflecting 5000 Years in World History: M. J. Cohen and Dr. Major (Cassel)

Dark Moon: Apollo and the Whistleblowers: Mary Bennett and Mary S. Percy, 2003 (Adventures Unlimited)

Celtic Myths and Legends: T.W. Rollenston, 1917, 1990 (Dover)

How the Sun-God Reached America: c. 2500 BC: A Guide to Megalithic Sites: Dr. Reinoud M. de Jonge & Jay Stuart Wakefield (2002 MCS Inc.)

Alice in Wonderland and the World Trade Center Disaster: David Icke, 2002 (Bridge of Love)

Breaking the Godspell: The Politics of Our Evolution: Neil Freer, 2000 (Book Tree)

Fingerprints of the Gods: Graham Handcock, 1995 (Mandarin)

The Decline of the West: Oswald Spengler: abridged edition by Helmut Werner, 1991

City of God: Augustine: trans. Marcus Dods, 2009 (Hendrickson Pub.)

Ancient Mysteries: Peter James and Nick Thorpe (Ballantine)

The Destruction of Atlantis: Frank Joseph (Bear & Co.)

From Atlantis to the Sphinx: Colin Wilson (Fromm International)

Atlantis: Mother of Empires: Robert B. Stacey-Judd (Adventures Unlimited)

The Shadow of Atlantis: Alexander Braghine, 1940 (Adventures Unlimited)

Atlantis: The Antediluvian World: Ignatius Donnelly and Egerton Sykes (Kessenger, reprint Book Tree)

Atlantis in America: Navigators of the Ancient World: Ivar Zapp & George Erikson (Adventures Unlimited)

Secret Cities of Old South America: Harold T. Wilkins, 1952 (Adventures Unlimited)

Annals of Imperial Rome: Tacitus, trans. Michael Grant (Penguin)

Ages in chaos: From the Exodus to King Akhentaon: Immanuel Velikovsky, 1952 (reprint 2009 Paradigma)

Children of the Sun: A Study of the Egyptian Settlement of the Pacific: W.J. Perry, 1923 (Reprint Book Tree 2004)

The Problem of Atlantis: Lewis Spence, 1924 (reprint Book Tree)

Atlantis in America: Lewis Spence, 1925 (reprint Book Tree)

Egypt, Greece and Rome: Charles Freeman (Oxford University Press)

From the Ashes of Angels: Forbidden Legacy of a Fallen Race: Andrew Collins (Bear & Co.)

The Histories: Herodotus: trans. Aubrey de Selincourt/ revised John Marincola (Penguin)

The Two Babylons: Alexander Hislop (Loixeaux Brothers)

Archaeology: edited Paul G. Baun (Cambridge University Press)

Tracing Our Ancestors: Frederick Haberman (Covenant)

The Bible as History: Werner Keller (Bantam)

The Bible As It Was: James L. Kugel (Belnap Press, Harvard University)

The Doctrine of Sin in the Babylonian Religion: Julian Morganstern (Book Tree)

The Origin of Biblical Traditions: Hebrew Legends in Babylonia and Israel: Albert T. Clay 1923 (reprint Book Tree)

Babylonian Influence on the Bible and Popular Beliefs: A. Smyth Palmer, 1897 (reprint Book Tree)

Antiquities of the Jews: Flavius Joseph, trans. 1736 William Whiston (Hendrickson Publishers)

Cicero: On Goverment: Marcus Tullius Cicero: trans. Michael Grant (Penguin)

After the Flood: Bill Cooper, 1995 (New Wine Press)

Secrets of Time: Stephen Jones (God's Kingdom Ministries)

Earth Under Fire: Paul A. LaViolette Ph.D (Bear & Co.)

A Short History of the World: H.G. Wells (reprint Book Tree)

History of the Christian Religion to the Year Two Hundred: Charles B. Waite (C.V. Waite & Co.) 1900, 5th Edition, 6th Printing, 1992

Early Man and the Cosmos: Evan Hadingham (Walker & Co.)

The Enchanted World- Night Creatures: (Time-Life Books)

Bulfinch's Mythology: Edmund Fuller (Dell)

Encyclopedia of Fairies: Hobgoblins, Brownies, Bogies, and Other Supernatural Creatures: Katherine Briggs (Pantheon Books)

The Illustrated Book of Myths: Neil Philip (Dorling Kindersley)

Celtic Myth and Legend: Charles Squire (New Page Books)

Northern Tales: Howard Norman (Pantheon)

Book of the Hopi: Frank Waters (Penguin)

God is Red: Vine Deloria, Jr. (Delta Books)

The Natural Genesis, 1883 Gerald Massey (reprint Black Classic Press)

Ancient Egypt Light of the World: Gerald Massey, 1907 (reprint Black Classic Press)

Mythology: Edith Hamilton (Little, Brown and Co.)

Sun Lore of All Ages: (reprint Book Tree)

The Greek Myths: Robert Graves (Penguin)

Celtic Myth & Legend: An A-Z of People and Places: Mike Dixon-Kennedy (Blandford)

Our Sun-God: Christianity Before Christ: John Denham Parsons, 1895 (2007 reprint Book tree)

Secret Teachings of All Ages: Manly P. Hall (Philosophical Research Society)

Lost Cities of North and Central America: David Hatcher Childress (Adventures Unlimited)

Lost Cities of Atlantis, Ancient Europe and the Mediterrean: David Hatcher Childress (Adventures Unlimited)

Lost Cities of Ancient Lemuria and the Pacific: David Hatcher Childress (Adventures Unlimited)

Lost Cities of China, Central Asia and India: David Hatcher Childress (Adventures Unlimited)

Lost Cities and Ancient Mysteries of Africa and Arabia: David Hatcher Childress (Adventures Unlimited)

When the Sun Darkens: Jason Breshears, 2009 (Book Tree)

Anunnaki Homeworld: Jason Breshears, 2011 (Book Tree)

Lost Scriptures of Giza, Jason Breshears, 2006, 2017 (Book Tree)

Nostradamus and the Planets of Apocalypse: Jason Breshears, 2013 (Book Tree)

Secret to Changing Your Life: Jason Breshears, 2017 (Archaix)

Giants on Ancient Earth: An In-Depth Study on the Nephilim: Jason Breshears, 2017 (Archaix)

The End of Days: Armageddon and Prophecies of the Return: Zechariah Sitchin, 2006 (William Morrow)

Divine Encounters: Zechariah Sitchin (Avon)

The 12th Planet: Zechariah Sitchin (Avon)

Genesis Revisited: Zechariah Sitchin (Avon)

Stairway to Heaven: Zechariah Sitchin (Avon)

The Lost Book of Enki: Zechariah Sitchin (Bear & Co.)

The Wars of Gods and Men: Zechariah Sitchin (Avon)

When Time Began: Zechariah Sitchin (Avon)

The Lost Realms: Zechariah Sitchin (Avon)

Symbols, Sex and the Stars: Ernest Busenbark (Book Tree)

Book of Jasher: Albinus Alcuin 800 AD (reprint Book Tree)

Buber's Tanhuma Devarum 7 in Judaism, edited by Arthur Hertzberg, George Brazillar, NY 1962

Ancient Man: Handbook of Puzzling Artifacts: William Corliss (Sourcebook Project)

A New Look at God's True Calendar: Dankenbring (Triumph Prophetic Ministries)

The History of the Devil and the Idea of Evil: Paul Carus (Grammercy)

Giants, Dwarfs and Other Oddities: C.J.S. Thompson M.B.E. (Citadel Press)

The Divine Pymander: trans. John D. Chambers (reprint Book Tree)

The Practical Bible Dictionary and Concordance (Barbour)

The Student Bible Dictionary: Karen Dockrey, Johnny Godwin, Phyllis Godwin (Barbour)

Smith's Bible Dictionary (Barbour)

Plato: Five Great Dialogues: edited Louise Ropes Loomis (Grammercy)

The Philosophy of Aristotle: Renford Bambrough, 1963 (Mentor)

The Discourses: Nicolo Machievelli (Penguin)

The Myth of Sisyphus: Albert Camus 1942, trans. from French Justin O'Brien (Vintage)

Beyond Good and Evil: Frederick Nietzsche, 1886 (Walter Kaufmann trans. (Vintage)

The World As I See It: Albert Einstein, 1935 (reprint 2007 Book Tree)

The Story of Philosophy: Will Durant, 1926 (2006 Pocket Books)

Triumph of the Human Spirit: Paul Tice (Book Tree)

Shadow of Darkness, Dawning of Light: Paul Tice (Book Tree)

Simple Kabbala: Kim Zetter (Conari Press)

When Men Are Gods: G. Cope Schellhorn (Horus House Press)

The Book of Enoch: trans. Richard Lawrence (Artisan)

The Book of Enoch: trans. R. H. Charles 1912 (reprint Book Tree)

The Book of Jubilees: trans. Rev.George H. Schodde (Artisan)

The Archko Volume: trans. Drs. McIntosh & Twyman (reprint Book Tree)

The Dead Sea Scrolls: Michael Wise, Martin Abegg & Edward Cook (Harper SanFrancisco)

Lost Language of Symbolism: Harold 1912 (reprint Book Tree)

A Brief Tour Through Higher Consciousness: Itzhak Bentov, 2000 (Destiny)

The Art of Seduction: Robert Greene, 2001 (Penguin)

The Art of Worldly Wisdom: Collection of Baltasar Gracian, trans. Martin Fischer (Barnes & Noble)

The Secret Symbols of the Dollar Bill: David Ovason (Perennial Currents)

Darwin's Mistake: Hans Zillmer (Adventures Unlimited)

Evolution Cruncher: Vance Ferrell (Evolution FACTS)

Encyclopedia Americana (Grolier)

Crop Circles, Gods and Their Secrets: Robert Boerman (Frontier/Adventures Unlimited)

Strange Stories and Amazing Facts: 1977 (Readers Digest Association)

A Study of Numbers: R.A, Schwaller de Lubicz, 1950 (Inner Traditions)

The Dimensions of Paradise: John Mitchell (Adventures Unlimited)

The New View Over Atlantis: John Mitchell, 1969, 1973, 1983 (Harper & Row)

Survivors of Atlantis: Frank Joseph, 2004 (Bear & Co)

Round Towers of Atlantis: Henry O'Brien, 1834 (Adventures Unlimited)

Cosmos of the Ancients: Stefan Stenudd, 2007 (BookSurge)

The Land of Osiris: Stephen S. Mehler (Adventures Unlimited)

Cradle of Civilization: Samuel Noah Kramer, 1967 (Time-Life Books)

Maps of the Ancient Sea Kings: Advanced Civilizations in the Ice Age: Charles H. Hapgood (Turnstone)

Lost Worlds of Ancient America: edited Frank Joseph, 2012 (New Page Books)

Path to the Pole: Charles Hapgood (Adventures Unlimited)

Chariots of the Gods: Erich Von Daniken (Berkley Books)

Our Cosmic Ancestors: Maurice Chatelain (Temple of Golden Publications)

The Ancient Alien Question: Philip Coppens, 2012 (New Page Books)

Inside the Real Area 51: The Secret History of Wright Patterson: Thomas J. Carey & Donald R. Schmitt, 2013 (New Page Books)

The New World Order:A. Ralph Epperson, 2008 (Publius Press)

Into the Bermuda Triangle: Gian J. Quasar, 2004 (International Marine/McGraw Hill)

Proof of the Illuminati: Seth Payson, A.M. 1802 (Invisible College Press)

Phenomenal World: Joan d.Arc, 2000 (Book Tree)

And the Truth Shall Set You Free: David Icke, 1995, 2004 (David Icke)

Hyperspace: Michio Kaku, 1994 (Anchor Books, Oxford University Press)

Twilight of the Idols: Frederich Nietzsche (Penguin)

The Golden Bough: Sir James Frazer (Grammercy)

Three Books of Occult Philosophy:Henry Cornelius Agrippa, 16th cent. annotated Donald Tyson (Llewellyn)

Lectures: Gerald Massey, 1900 (reprint Book Tree)

Magic: White and Black: Franz Hartmann, M.D. 1888 (Book Tree)

The Hidden Power: And Other Papers on Mental Science: Thomas Troward, 1921 (reprint Book Tree)

Edgar Cayce's Story of the Origin and Destiny of Man: Lytle Robinson (Coward, McCann & Geoghegan, INC)

Wycliffe Bible Encyclopedia: Vol. I (Moody Press)

Dictionary of First Names: Patrick Hanks & Flavia Hodges (Oxford)

Herder Dictionary of Symbols: English trans. Boris Matthews (Chiron)

Dictionary of Deities and Demons of the Bible: edited Karel van der Toorn. Bob Becking & Peter Vander Horst (Brill: William B. Eerdman's)

The Popul Vuh: Lewis Spence, 1908, 1912 (reprint Book Tree 2003)

Simon Magus: His Philosophy and Teachings: G.R.S. Mead 1892 (Book Tree 2003)

Tales of the Prophets:Great Books of the Islamic World: Muhammed ibn abd Allah al-Kisai, trans. W.M. Thackston, Jr. (Great Books of the Islamic World)

The Mystery of the Oracles:Phillip Vandenberg, 1982 (Macmillan)

The History of the Christian Religion and Church During the First Three Centuries

Technics and Civilization: Lewis Mumford (Harcourt Brace & World INC)

Ancient Pagan and Modern Christian Symbolism: Thomas Inman, 1869 (Peter Eckler/ reprint Book Tree)

The Mystery of Numbers: Annemaries Schimmel (Oxford)

Nemesis: The Death Star: The Story of a Scientific Revolution: Dr. Richard Muller: 1988 (Weidenfeld & Nicolson)

The National Experience: Part I: A History of the United States to 1877: 5th Ed. (Harcourt Brace Jovanovich)

Poleshift: John White (ARE Press)

Genesis Commentary: Peter Ruckman

Epistle of Barnabas

Book of the Secrets of Enoch

Apology for Printers: Benjamin Franklin

Theogany: Hesiod

Doomsday: A View Through Time: Russell Chandler

247 referenced texts (not including biblical records)

Chapter-by-Chapter Citations

Petrified Jellyfish and Fossilized Humans Evidence of a Flash Frozen World

1. Book of the Damned p. 93; 2. ibid p. 103; 3. Atlantis in America p. 97-98; 4. Our Haunted Planet p. 7; 5. Livy I.55-56; 6. Evolution Cruncher 557-558; 7. Strange Stories and Amazing Facts p. 247-249; Readers Digest Ass. Montreal 1977; Evolution Cruncher 54; 8. Lost Cities of North and Central America p. 475; 9. Secret Cities of Old South America p. 285; 10. Evolution Cruncher p. 575-576; 11. Lost Cities of Atlantis, Ancient Europe...176; 12. Evolution Cruncher p. 576; 13. North American Indians p. 8; 14. Lost Cities of Atlantis, Ancient Europe...207; 15. Into the Bermuda Triangle p. 154; 16. Darwin's Mistake p. 35; 17. ibid p. 36; 18. Secret Cities of Old South America p. 288; 19. Evolution Cruncher p. 128

A Fossilized World vs. Scientific Fantasy

1. On Government, Cicero: The Brutus 277; 2. Atlantis in America p. 66, words of Spence; 3. Universal Laws Never Before Revealed p. 185; 4. Philosophy p. 58; Metaphysics book 4:4; 5. Twilight of the Idols p. 61; 6. Twilight of the Idols p. 101; 7. Proof of the Illuminati p. 144; 8. Annals III 18 p. 128; 9. Book of the Damned p. 115; 10. A Study of Numbers p. 9; 11. Evolution Cruncher p. 45; 12. Evolution Cruncher p. 59; 13. Evolution Cruncher p. 54; 14. Nemesis p. 137; 15. Maps of the Ancient Sea Kings p. 21; 16. Twilight of the Idols p. 61; 17. On the Nature of the Universe bk. 4 812-817; 18. A Brief Tour of Higher Consciousness xxiv; Stalking the Wild Pendulum p. 1; 19. Lost Cities of Ancient Lemuria and the Pacific p. 6; 20. Triumph of the Human Spirit p. 265; 21. Apology for

Printers; The National Experience p. 73; 22. Phenomenal World p. 33; 23. Book of the Damned p. 182; 24. Tacitus, Annals 4 57-58 p. 187; 25. Elegies 769-772; 26. Path to the Pole p. 62; 27. Path to the Pole p. 63; 28. Path to the Pole p. 65; 29. Darwin's Mistake p. 73; 30. Evolution Cruncher p. 192, 486; 31. Evolution Cruncher p. 203; 32. Darwin's Mistake p. 40; 33. Encyclopedia Americana Vol. 7 p. 579; 34. Evolution Cruncher p. 149; 35. Evolution Cruncher p. 478; Path to the Pole p. 303); 36. The Art of Worldly Wisdom p. 45; 37. Book of the Damned p. 11

Mysterious Origin and Fate of the Cro-Magnon People

1) Mankind: Child of the Stars p. 78; 2. Mankind: Child of the Stars p. 78; 3. Mankind: Child of the Stars p. 94; 4. Mankind: Child of the Stars p. 96; 5. Mankind: Child of the Stars p. 165; 6. And the Truth Shall Set You Free p. 12; 7. Mankind: Child of the Stars p. 80; 8. Our Occulted History p. 48; 9. ibid p. 48; 10. Mankind: Child of the Stars p. 50; 11. p. 97; 12. Mankind: Child of the Stars p. 77; 13. The History of Atlantis: Spence p. 80; 14. ibid p. 80; 15. Atlantis in America p. 37; 16. Elder Gods in Antiquity p. 91; 17. Mysteries of the Ancient World p. 18; 18. ibid p. 18; 19. Atlantis in America: Spence p. 36; 20. The History of Atlantis: Spence p. 81; 21. Atlantis in America: Spence p. 36; 22. Mysteries of the Ancient World p. 24-25; 23. Lost Cities of North and Central America p. 452-453; 24. ibid p. 452-453; 25. The Lost Worlds of Ancient America p. 236; 26. Elder Gods in Antiquity p. 89; 27. Flying Serpents and Dragons p. 161; 28. Our Occulted History p. 189; 29. The History of Atlantis p. 82; 30. ibid p. 82; 31. ibid p. 81; 32. ibid p. 84-85; 33. Atlantis in America p. 16; 34. ibid p. 34; 35. Divine Encounters p. 34; 36. The History of Atlantis p.

83; 37. ibid p. 83; 38. ibid p. 82; 39. ibid p. 82; 40. ibid p. 84; 41. Atlantis in America p. 96; 42. The History of Atlantis p. 85; 43. Atlantis in America p. 34; 44. Elder Gods in Antiquity p. 165

The Anunnaki Homeworld Nibiru and Once-Inhabited Planet...the Moon

(1) Genesis Revisited p. 114-115; (2) Our Occulted History p. 19; (3) ibid p. 19; (4) ibid p. 19; (5) Atlantis in America: Spence p. 232; (6) Our Occulted History p. 16-17; (7) ibid p. 18; (8) ibid p. 23; (9) Space Travelers and the Genesis of the Human Form, citing Velivoksky, Ovid); (10) Worlds in Collision: Velikovsky); (11) Atlantis: The Antediluvian World p. 38; (12) The Origin of Biblical Traditions p. 69; (13) The 12th Planet p. 233; (14) Ponder on This p. 272; (15) ibid p. 273; (16) The Giza Prophecy p. 127-1238, 235; (17) Earth Under Fire p. 81

PreFlood Memories of a Prior Creation

1. Enuma Elish: Seven Tablets of Creation Tablet 1 lines 23-24; 2. Babylonian Influence on the Bible and Popular Beliefs 5; 3. Babylonian Influence on the Bible and Popular Beliefs 80; 4. Philosophy of Aristotle 46; 5. Plato's Symposium, Dialogues of Plato 174; Theogany 27; 6. Symbols, Sex and the Stars 312; 7. The Vedas 105; 8. The Natural Genesis Vol. II 98; 9. Mythology 87; 10. Greek Myths 34; 11. Epistle of Barnabas 5:14

PreFlood Races Shocked at First Appearance of Caucasians

1. The Watchers; Raymond E. Fowler, pg. 224; 2. The Watchers; Raymond E. Fowler, pg. 229; 3. From Atlantis to the Sphinx; Colin Wilson, pg. 82; 4. Chariots of the Gods; Erich Von Daniken, pg. 27; 5. The Two Babylons; Alexander Hislop, pgs. 85-86; 6. From the Ashes of Angels p. 198; 7. From the Ashes of Angels p. 198-199; 8. From the Ashes of Angels p. 110-112; 9. From the Ashes of Angels p. 112; 10. Stairway to Heaven p. 147; 11. Stairway to Heaven, citing Enoch p. 147; 12. From the Ashes of Angels p. 35; 13. The Lost Book of Enki p. 204; 14. The 12th Planet p. 106; 15. Cradle of Civilization: Kramer p. 41; 16. The Lost Book of Enki p. 169; 17. Stairway to Heaven p. 198; 18. The Sirius Mystery p. 293; 19. From Atlantis to the Sphinx; Colin Wilson, pgs. 20-21; 20. From Atlantis to the Sphinx; Colin Wilson, pg. 135; 21. From Atlantis to the Sphinx; Colin Wilson, pg. 147; 22. From Atlantis to the Sphinx; Colin Wilson, pg. 147; 23. Mysteries of Ancient South America p. 109; 24. The Tigris Expedition p. 330; 25. Chariots of the Gods; Erich Von Daniken, pg. 93; 26. Gods of Eden: Brambley p. 34, 37; 27. Atlantis: The Antediluvian World p. 215; 28. Atlantis: The Antediluvian World p. 215; 29. The Wars of Gods and Men p. 64; 30. ibid p. 65; 31. The Lost Book of Enki p. 219; 32. ibid p. 229, 271

ADAMU...PreCaucasian Humans & Anunnaki Designer DNA Campaign Before the Flood

1. Atlantis: The Antediluvian World p. 179; 2. ibid p. 179; 3. Elder Gods of Antiquity p. 92; 4. The Genesis Race p. 27; 5. ibid p. 27; 6. Genes, Giants, Monsters and Men p. 225, 237; 7. Genes, Giants, Monsters and

Men p. 223; 8. In the Hands of the Great Spirit p. 12; 9. In the Hands of the Great Spirit p. 13; 10. In the Hands of the Great Spirit p. 14; 11. The Lost Worlds of Ancient America p. 258; 12. Atlantis: The Antediluvian World p. 249; 13. Atlantis: The Antediluvian World p. 249; 14. Atlantis: The Antediluvian World p. 249; 15. p. 250; 16. p. 250; 17. A Global History of Man p. 42; 18. Lost Cities of China, Central Asia and India p. 350-351; 19. p. 361; 20. Atlantis: The Antediluvian World p. 212-213; 21. Atlantis: The Antediluvian World p. 58

A Flood Before Noah's...Enoch and the Gihon Flood 3439 BCE

(1) The 12th Planet p. 291; (2) ibid p. 291; (3) Book of Jasher 2:3-7; (4) Flying Serpents and Dragons p. 132; (5) Ancient Egypt Light of the World Vol. II p. 567; (6) The Lost Book of Enki p. 8; (7) The Great Pyramid: Smythe p. 370

The Fallen Ones Came From Somewhere Else

(1) Fragments of a Forgotten Faith p. 26-27; (2) From the Ashes of Angels p. 360; (3) Our Occulted History p. 171; (4) The Genesis Race p. 168; (5) ibid p. 3; (6) ibid p. 4; (7) ibid p. 56; (8) ibid p. 75; (9) The History of Atlantis: Spence p. 104; (10) Atlantis: The Antediluvian World p. 108; (11) ibid p. 109; (12) ibid p. 184; (13) ibid p. 185; (14) ibid p. 189; (15) ibid p. 189; (16) ibid p. 189; (17) ibid p. 189

The 432,000 Years Was 432,000 Days [1200 years] From 3439 BCE Descent of the Watchers to the Great Flood 2239 BCE

(1) Discovering Ancient Giants p. 200-201; (2) Atlantis: The Antediluvian World p. 62; (3) The 12th Planet p. 247; (4) Secret Cities of Old South America p. 116; (5) The 12th Planet p. 248; (6) Atlantis: The Antediluvian World p. 168; (7) The 12th Planet p. 248); (8) Elder Gods in Antiquity p. 321; (9) The 12th Planet p. 247; (10) Underworld p. 239; (11) The Gods of Eden p. 44; (12) Atlantis: The Antediluvian World p. 174

PreFlood Calendars, the Goddess & the Seven Anunnaki Kings

1. The Natural Genesis VOl. II 147; 2. Babylonian Influence on the Bible and Popular Beliefs 58; 3. The Doctrine of Sin in the Babylonian Religion 92-93; 4. Secrets of Enoch 20:1; 5. Ancient Pagan and Modern Christian Symbolism 7 & The Mysteries of Numbers 150; 6. Jubilees 4:22-23; 7. The Doctrine of Sin in the Babylonian Religion 10-11; 8. Wars of Gods and Men 104; 9. Lost Language of Symbolism 12; 10. Lost Language of Symbolism 13-14; 11. Wycliffe Bible Dictionary 64; 12. Lost Language of Symbolism 13; 13. The Doctirne of Sin in the Babylonian Religion 87; 14. The Vedas 116; 15. The Doctrine of Sin in the Babylonian Religion 88; 16. Babylonian Influence on the Bible and Popular Beliefs 59; 17. Babylonian Influence on the Bible and Popular Beliefs 59; 18. The Natural Genesis Vol. II 149; 19. Book of the dead 509; 20. Book of Enoch, trans. Charles 18:6 notes; 21. Enoch 18:11-14, 21:1-3; 22. Revelation 17:3-11

Before the Flood...A Caucasian Civil War

1. And the Truth Shall Set You Free p. 5; 2. Humanity's Extraterrestrial Origins p. 98-99; (3) The Complete Works of Charles Fort p. 574

The Ten Kings of Atlantis, of the PreFlood World and Prophecy

(1) The Natural Genesis Vol. II p. 184; Atlantis: Antediluvian World p. 4, 7; (2) Atlantis: Mother of Empires p. ;212; Atlantis: Antediluvian World p. 4, 7; (3) John D. Morris, Back to Genesis, Institute for Creation Research; Secret Cities of Old Souther America p. 262; (4) The Doctrine of Sin in the Babylonian Religion p. 13; (5) The Doctrine of Sin in the Babylonian Religion p. 90-91; (6) The Natural Genesis VOl. I p. 322; (7) The Natural Genesis Vol. II p. 104; (8) Ancient Egypt Light of the World Vol. I p. 322; (9) The Doctrine of Sin in the Babylonian Religion p. 91: (10) The Doctrine of Sin in the Babylonian Religion p. 79; (11) The Natural Genesis VOl. II p. 84-85 & Ancient Egypt Light of the World Vol. I p. 323; (12) The Natural Genesis Vol. II p. 84-85

Annus Mundi Calendar, Abraham & the Secret Records of the Great Pyramid

1. The Great Pyramid: Its Divine Message 105, 76-77; 2. The Great Pyramid: Its Divine Message 555; 3. The Origin and Significance of the Great Pyramid 112-114; 4. The Origin and Significance of the Great Pyramid 112-114; 5. The Origin and Significance of the Great Pyramid 112-114; 6. The Land of Osiris 109

Abram and Giza in Egypt

1. Symbols, Sex and the Stars 310; 2. Dictionary of First Names 390; 3. Our Cosmic Ancestors 157; 4. Dimenions of Paradise 181; 5. Symbols, Sex and the Stars 168; 6. Symbols, Sex and the Stars 99; 7. The Mysteries of Numbers 150; 8. Herder Dictionary of Symbols 78; 9. Symbols, Sex and the Stars 355; 10. Student Bible Dictionary 39, see map; 11. Student Bible Dictionary 98; 12. Babylonian Influence on the Bible and Popular Belief 2; 13. Dictionary of Deities and Demons of the Bible 3; 14. The Bible as History 83

Great Pyramid Measured in Phoenix Orbits

1. Atlantis: The Antediluvian World p. 273; 2. The Message of the Sphinx p. 23; 3. The Ancient Alien Question p. 38; 4. ibid p. 95; 5. Lost Cities of Ancient Lemuria & the Pacific p. 170; 6. The Gods of Eden: Collins p. 55; 7. ibid p. 52; 8. The Message of the Sphinx p. 297

The Giza Deception & Sphinx Enigma...Architectural Misdirection

1. The Message of the Sphinx: Hancock & Bauval p. 10; 2. The Message of the Sphinx p. 13; 3. Dr. Klaus-Ulrich Groth, More Egyptian Underground Secrets Revealed: Legendary Times Vol. 9 No. 1 & 2 p. 10-11; 4. The Message of the Sphinx p. 162; 5. ibid p. 163; 6. Message

of the Sphinx p. 163; 7. The Rise and Fall of Atlantis: p. 325; 8. Our Occulted History p. 182; 9. Gods of Eden: Collins p. 170-171; 10. Gods of Eden: Collins p. 171; 11. The Sirius Mystery p. 12; 12. The Sirius Mystery p. 92; 13. The Genesis Race p. 178; 14. The Genesis Race p. 176; 15. The Popul Vuh p. 48; 16. Atlantis: The Antediluvian World p. 301; 17. The Stairway to Heaven p. 49; 18. The Message of the Sphinx p. 31

The Great Pyramid's 4900 Year Old Secret

1. Lost Civilizations p. 8; 2. ibid p. 14; 3. The Genesis Race p. 79; 4. Stairway to Heaven p. 376; 5. ibid p. 322; 6. Mysteries of the Ancient World p. 76; 7. Elder Gods in Antiquity p. 248; 8. Pyramids of the New World p. 13; 9. When Time Began p. 195; 10. Message of the Sphinx p. 200; 11. Lost Civilizations p. 40; 12. The Christ Conspiracy p. 379; 13. ibid p. 378; 14. The Message of the Sphinx p. 28; 15. Message of the Sphinx p. 31; 16. ibid p. 31; 17. The Gods of Eden: Collins p. 9-10; 18. The Great Pyramids: Corteggiani p. 47; 19. Lost Cities of Atlantis, Ancient Europe and the Mediterranean p. 29; 20. Lost Cities and Ancient Mysteries of Africa and Arabia p. 101; 21. The Gods of Eden: Collins p. 10; 22. ibid p. 119; 23. Our Occult History p. 85-86; 24. Lost Cities and Ancient Mysteries of Africa and Arabia p. 128; 25. The Gods of Eden: Collins p. 10; 26. Lost Cities and Ancient Mysteries of Africa and Arabia p. 128; 27. ibid p. 128; 28. The Wars of Gods and Men p. 205-206; 29. ibid p. 203; 30. ibid p. 215; 31. When Time Began p. 373; 32. ibid p. 105; 33. The 12th Planet p. 295; 34. ibid p. 295; 35. ibid p. 296; 36. The Wars of Gods and Men p. 140; 37. p. 140; 38. p. 140; 39. p. 140; 40. p. 140; 41. p. 140; 42. ibid p. 105; 43. The Wars of Gods and Men p. 143;

44. ibid p. 222; 45. The 12th Planet p. 296; 46. When Time Began p. 196; 47. ibid p. 156; 48. ibid p. 157; 49. ibid p. 165-166; 50. ibid p. 163; 51. The 12th Planet p. 91; 52. ibid p. 91; 53. ibid p. 91; 54. The Wars of Gods and Men p. 193

Great Pyramid Holographic Blueprint of World Destructions

1. Atlantis: The Antediluvian World p. 273); 2. The Message of the Sphinx p. 23; 3. The Ancient Alien Question p. 38; 4. ibid p. 95; 5.   Lost Cities of Ancient Lemuria & the Pacific p. 170; 6.   The Gods of Eden: Collins p. 55; 7. ibid p. 52; 8. Secret Symbols of the Dollar Bill p. 182; 9. Pyramid Quest p. 3; 10. The Secrets of the Stones: Michell p. 17; 11. The Secrets of the Stones: Michell p. 18; 12. The Message of the Sphinx p. 297;

2815 BCE Date of Great Pyramid Completion Imprinted in Holosphere

1. Edgar Cayce's Story of the Origin and Destiny of Man p. 60; 2. ibid p. 78; 3. Edgar Cayce's Story of the Origin and Destiny of Man p. 79; 4. The Giza Prophecy p. 145; 5. The New View Over Atlantis p. 155-156; 6. Elder Gods in Antiquity p. 321; 7. Worlds in Collision p. 46; 8. Simon Magus p. 51; 9. Gods of Eden p. 196: Collins; 10. Gods of Eden: Collins p. 196-197; 11. ibid p. 197-198; 12. Tales of the Prophets p. 14-15; 13. Dark Moon p. 432;

The Great Flood...Ancient & Modern Science on the Phoenix Cataclysm

(1) Book of Jasher 37:17-18; (2) Mysteries of Ancient South America p. 27; (3) ibid p. 27; (4) ibid p. 12-14; (5) ibid p. 32; (6) ibid p. 87; (7) ibid p. 12-13; (8) ibid p. 10

...Ancient & Modern Science

(1) The Genesis Race p. 211-212; (2) ibid p. 214; (3) ibid p. 212; (4) The Destruction of Atlantis p. 140; (5) The Book of Jasher 6:11, 13; (6) Earth Under Fire p. 235; (7) ibid p. 237-238; (8) Natural History: Universe and the World 97 p. 22; (9) On the Nature of the Universe, book 5 lines 324-330, book 6 lines 290-295; 585-590; (10) ibid book 5 lines 747-768; (11) The History of Atlantis: Spence p. 32; (12) When the Sun Darkens p. 85-86

Mysteries of Easter Island and the Flood of Ogyges 1687 BCE

(1) Mysteries of Ancient South America 25-26; (2) ibid p. 28; (3) ibid p. 27; (4) ibid p. 27; (5) Lost Cities of Ancient America and the Pacific p. 314; (6) Children of the Sun p. 154; (7) ibid p. 466

The Flood of Ogyges

(1) Atlantis: The Antediluvian World p. 81, 76; (2) Secret Cities of Old South America p. 417; (3) Worlds in Collision p. 162; (4) City of God, Augustine 21; (5) Survivors of Atlantis p. 62; (6) ibid p. 66; (7) ibid p. 46; (8) Egypt, Greece and Rome p. 15; (9) Mysteries of Old South America p. 21; (10) ibid p. 111; (11) Atlantis: The Antedilivian World p. 81; (12) Worlds in Collision p. 161;

(13) The History of Atlantis: Apence p. 31; (14) The Stairway to Heaven p. 233; (15) Atlantis: The Antediluvian World p. 51, 81; (16) ibid p. 81; (17) The Great Pyramid: Its Divine Message p. 5, 52

From Thales of Greece to the Olmecs of Ancient America...Phoenix Disasters

(1) Histories, Book I 74, Herodotus p. 30; (2) p. 122; (3) p. 45; (4) The Mystery of the Oracles p. 223; (5) The Mystery of the Oracles p. 224-225; (6) Atlantis Beneath the Ice p. 169; (7) The 12th Planet p. 63; (8) City of God, Augustine VIII ch. 2; (9) The Great Pyramid: Its Divine Message p. 103; (10) The Rise and Fall of Atlantis p. 4; (11) Natural History: The Universe and the World 53 p. 19-20, Pliny the Elder; (12) Cosmos of the Ancients p. 54-55

From Thales to the Dead Sea Scrolls

1. Josephus, antiquities 15.5.2; 2. Annals of the World: Ussher at 31 BC; 3. The Christ Conspiracy p. 312; 4. Canaanite Myth and Hebrew Epic p. 327; 5. Nostradamus and the Planets of Apocalypse p. 29; 6. ibid p. 29; 7. Annals of the World: Ussher at 30 BC; 8. The Lost Realms p. 104, Encyclopedia of World Facts and Dates p. 88; 9. Lost Worlds of Ancient America p. 138-139; 10. Breaking the Godspell p. 41

How Jesus Stole the Phoenix

(1) Gospel of Nicodemus 8:1 (2) Tacitus, Annals of Imperial Rome VI 25-28 notes pgs. 213-214 (3) Dr. McIntosh & Dr. Twyman, The Archko Volume (4)

Graham Hancock, Fingerprints of the Gods (5) Immanuel Velivoksky, Ages in Chaos, Vol. I p. 65 (6) Manly P. Hall, The Secret Teachings of All Ages, pgs. 245 (7) ibid (8) Robert Greene, The Art of Seduction p. 262 (9) Paul Tice, Shadow of Darkness, Dawning of Light p. 202 (10) Ernest Busenbark, Sex, Symbols and the Stars, foreward

Danaan Invaders Predict Darkening of the Sun...1135 BCE

(1) Atlantis: Mother of Empires p. 237; (2) Uriel's Machine p. 232; (3) p. 339; (4) The Lost Cities of Atlantis: Ancient Europe and the Mediterranean p. 438; (5) Atlantis: The Antediluvian World p. 252; (6) Secret Cities of Old South America p. 75; (7) Atlantis: The Antediluvian World p. 253; (8) ibid p. 258; (9) ibid p. 253; (10) ibid p. 253; (11) Atlantis: Mother of Empires p. 237; (12) Taleisin p. 250; (13) Round Towers of Atlantis: 386; (14) How the Sun-God Reached America p. 14-10; (15) see M. A. Rutot in L'Atlantide, Brussels, 1920 cited in Atlantis in America: Spence p. 202; (16) The Trojan War p. 187; (17) Atlantis Destroyed p. 168; (18) History in Quotations p. 40;

Giants on Ancient Earth & the Origin of Nephilim Theory

1. Archeaology: edited Paul G. Baun (Cambridge Univ. Press) p. 4-5); 2. Buber's Tanhuma Devarum 7 in Judaism, edited by Arthur Hertzberg p. 155, 156, George Brazillar, NY 1962); 3. Secret Cities of Old South America p. p. 46); 4. The Greek Myths p. 685-686; 5. The History of the Christian Religion and Church During the First Three Centuries p. 82; 6. Discovering Ancient Giants p. 15; 7. Lost Cities and Ancient Mysteries of South America p. 199; 8. Lost Cities of North and Central America p. 468; 9.

Discovering Ancient Giants p. 20; 10. Discovering Ancient Giants p. 20; 11. Discovering Ancient Giants p. 21; 12. Discovering Ancient Giants p. 48-49; 13. Lost Cities of Ancient Lemuria and the Pacific p. 194; 14. Discovering Ancient Giants p. 22, 67; 15. Lost Cities of Ancient Lemuria and the Pacific p. 193; 16. Lost Cities and Ancient Mysteries of South America p. 257; 17. Secret Cities of Old South America p. 42; 18. Elder Gods in Antiquity p. 288; 19. Space Travelers and the Genesis of the Human Form p. 93; 20. Our Occult History p. 38; 21. Ancient Man: Handbook of Puzzling Artifacts p. 685-686

Origin of Nephilim Theory...The Daughters of Men

1. The War Scroll, cited by Russell Chandler in Doomsday-A View Through Time; 2. The Book of Enoch, trans. Richard Lawrence, 1821 p. 87; 3. The Book of Enoch: trans. Richard Lawrence : introduction; 4. The Dead Sea Scrolls: Tales of the Patriarchs p. 76-77

Epics of the Giants

1. Beowulf; Burton Raffel, citation from Robert Creed in the Afterward, pg. 128; 2. Beowulf; Burton Raffel, introduction , ix; 3. Epic of Gilgamesh; N.K. Sandars, pgs. 46-47; 4. Beowulf; Bruton Raffel, lines 104-114; 5. Enoch 15:8; 6. Encyclopedia of Fairies; Katherine Briggs, pg. 298-299; 7. The History of the Devil and the Idea of Evil; Dr. Paul Carus, pg. 250; 8. Beowulf; Bruton Raffel, lines 419-421; 9. Beowulf; Bruton Raffel, lines 883-885; 10. After the Flood; William Cooper, pg. 229; 11. Beowulf; Bruton Raffel, lines 1264-1266; 12. The History of the Devil and the Idea of Evil; Dr. Paul Carus, pg. 250; 13. The Enchanted World...Night Creatures; Time Life Books, pg. 7, Perilous Paths Through the Dark; 14. Beowulf; Bruton

Raffel, lines 1545-1547; 15. Beowulf; Bruton Raffel,
lines 1557-1561; 16. Beowulf; Bruton Raffel, line
1666; 17.Beowulf; Bruton Raffel, lines 2135-2136;
18.Beowulf; Bruton Raffel, lines 1613-1616; 19.Enoch
66:14; 20. Beowulf; poem, line 732; 21. Beowulf;
poem, line 449; 22.Beowulf; poem, line 165;
23.Beowulf; poem, line 2090; 24.Beowulf; poem, line
2088; 25.Beowulf; poem, line 1267; 26.Beowulf; poem,
line 595; 27.Beowulf; poem, line 426; 28.Beowulf;
poem, lines 1345-1352; 29.Beowulf; poem, line 1647;
30.Beowulf; poem, line 1662; 31. Beowulf; poem, line
1677-1681; 32. Beowulf; lines 1694-1696, Burton
Raffel; 33. Tales From Ovid; Ted Hughes, pgs. 10-12;
34. Tales From Ovid; Ted Hughes, pgs. 13-14; 35.
Joshua 11:21-22; 36. Gods and Fighting Men; Lady
Gregory, cited in Katherine Briggs, Encyclopedia of
Fairies, pg. 87; 37. Beowulf; poem, line 1267; 38. Epic
of Gilgamesh; Maureen Kovacs; 39. Epic of Gilgamesh;
Maureen Kovacs; First tablet notes; 40. The Golden
Bough; James Frazer, pg. 50, footnote #4 on The
History of Egyptian Religion; 41. The History of the
Devil and the Idea of Evil; Dr. Paul Carus, pg. 3; 42.
Epic of Gilgamesh; N.K. Sandars; 43.Epic of
Gilgamesh; N.K. Sandars

Trojan Exiles of Albion...Isle of the Giants

1. Bulfinch's Mythology; Edmund Fuller, pg. 14
2. Bulfinch's Mythology; Edmund Fuller, pg. 282
3. pages 178-179
4. Encyclopedia of Fairies; Katherine Briggs, pg. 178
5. Apocalypse Chronicles; James Lloyd, Vol. 5 #1,
   The Queen of Heaven and the Fallen Stars, pg. 2
6. Encyclopedia of Fairies; Katherine Briggs, pg. 87

415

7. *Encyclopedia of Fairies*; Katherine Briggs, pg. 405 [Motif A1659.11]
8. *Epic of Gilgamesh*; N.K. Sandars, pg. 120

9. *Jasher* 12:52
10. *Epic of Gilgamesh*; N.K. Sandars, pg. 103
11. *Smith's Bible Dictionary* [Barbour], pg. 231
12. *The Bible as History*; Werner Keller, pg. 57
13. *Smith's Bible Dictionary* [Barbour], pg. 68
14. pages 76, 108
15. *Smith's Bible Dictionary* [Barbour], pg. 68
16. *Practical Bible Dictionary and Concordance* [Barbour], pg. 35 and *Smith's Bible Dictionary*, pg. 94
17. *Epic of Gilgamesh*; N.K. Sandars, pg. 16
18. *Tracing Our Ancestors*; Frederick Haberman, pg. 8
19. Number 21:33, Deut. 32:14, Isaiah 2:13, Zechariah 11:2
20. *Encyclopedia of Fairies*; Katherine Briggs, pg. 313
21. *Encyclopedia of Fairies*; Katherine Briggs, pg. 143
22. *Genesis Commentary*; Peter Ruckman, pg. 282
23. *Encyclopedia of Fairies*; Katherine Briggs, pg. 123
24. *Tracing Our Ancestors*; Frederick Haberman, pg. 79
25. *The Bible as History*; Werner Keller, pg. 151
26. *The Bible as History*; Werner Keller, pg. 177
27. *The Bible as History*; Werner Keller, pg. 86
28. *The Bible as History*; Werner Keller, pg. 209
29. *The Bible as History*; Werner Keller, pg. 209
30. *The Bible as History*; Werner Keller, pg. 212
31. page 179
32. *Encyclopedia of Fairies*; Katherine Briggs, pg. 479 [Motif S262]

33. *Encyclopedia of Fairies*; Katherine Briggs, pg. 179
34. *Encyclopedia of Fairies*; Katherine Briggs, pg. 8
35. *Encyclopedia of Fairies*; Katherine Briggs, pgs. 8, 123
36. *Encyclopedia of Fairies*; Katherine Briggs, pgs. 314-315
37. *Encyclopedia of Fairies*; Katherine Briggs, pg. 400
38. *Encyclopedia of Fairies*; Katherine Briggs, pg. 401
39. *Encyclopedia of Fairies*; Katherine Briggs, pg. 148
40. *Tracing Our Ancestors*; Frederick Haberman, pg. 118
41. *Encyclopedia of Fairies*; Katherine Briggs, pg. 87
42. *Encyclopedia of Fairies*; Katherine Briggs, pg. 253
43. *Encyclopedia of Fairies*; Katherine Briggs, pg. 393
44. Volume 1, Pg. 68
45. Cited by Katherine Briggs in an *Encyclopedia of Fairies*; pgs. 90-91
46. *After the Flood*; William Cooper, pgs. 222-223
47. page 3
48. *Tracing Our Ancestors*; Frederick Haberman, pg. 93
49. *Tracing Our Ancestors*; Frederick Haberman, pg. 94
50. *After the Flood*; William Cooper, pg. 202 [Dodanim]-203
51. *After the Flood*; William Cooper, pg. 199
52. *After the Flood*; William Cooper, pg204
53. page 204
54. *Bulfinch's Mythology*; Edmund Fuller, pg. 206
55. *Bulfinch's Mythology*; Edmund Fuller, pg. 284
56. page 95

57. *Tracing Our Ancestors*; Frederick Haberman, pg. 96
58. *After the Flood*; William Cooper, pg. 223
59. *Bulfinch's Mythology*; Edmund Fuller, pg. 283-284
60. *Tracing Our Ancestors*; Frederick Haberman, pg. 96

417

61. *Bulfinch's Mythology*; Edmund Fuller, pg. 188
62. *Odyssey*, Book Nine; (Homer) <u>New Coast and Poseidon's Son</u>. Robert Fitzgerald
63. *Bulfinch's Mythology*; Edmund Fuller, pg. 282
64. *Giants, Dwarfs and Other Oddities*; C.J.S. Thompson, M.B.E., pg. 18
65. *Giants, Dwarfs and Other Oddities*; C.J.S. Thompson, M.B.E., pgs. 18-19
66. *Encyclopedia of Fairies*; Katherine Briggs, pg. 479 [Motif 6100.1]
67. *Odyssey*, (Homer) Book Seven, <u>Gardens and Firelight</u>. Robert Fitzgerald
68. *Odyssey*, (Homer) Book Nine, <u>New Coasts and Poseidon's Son</u>. Robert Fitzgerald
69. *Bulfinch's Mythology*; Edmund Fuller, pg. 284
70. Cited by Frederick Haberman in *Tracing Our Ancestors*, pg. 78
71. *Jasher* 90:29
72. *Giants, Dwarfs and Other Oddities*; C.J.S. Thompson, M.B.E., pg. 138
73. *Tracing Our Ancestors*; Frederick Haberman, pg. 97
74. *Tracing Our Ancestors*; Frederick Haberman, pg. 97
75. *Bulfinch's Mythology*; Edmund Fuller, pg. 284
76. Cited by Katherine Briggs in an *Encyclopedia of Fairies*, pg. 102
77. *Encyclopedia of Fairies*; Katherine Briggs, pgs. 75-76
78. *Encyclopedia of Fairies*; Katherine Briggs, pgs. 206-207
79. *Encyclopedia of Fairies*; Katherine Briggs, pg. 123, citing Jane Wilde's *Ancient Legends of Ireland*
80. *Encyclopedia of Fairies*; Katherine Briggs, pg. 58
81. *Encyclopedia of Fairies*; Katherine Briggs, pg. 24

82. *The Enchanted World...Night Creatures*, pg. 21 [Time Life]

83. *The Enchanted World...Night Creatures* [Time Life]

84. page 35

85. *The Bible as History*; Werner Keller, pg. 191

86. Pages 92-93

87. Genesis 15:16

The Zodiac...An Ancient Cataclysmic Impact Recorder

1. Dimensions of Paradise 172; 2. Herodotus, The Histories Book II 7 p. 88; 3. The Light of Egypt Vol. I p. 65; 4. Simple Kabbalah 10; 5. Psalm 19:1-2; 6. Enoch 80:102; 7. Enoch 105:23; 8. The Divine Pymander 134; 9. Enoch 3:2; 10. Symbols, Sex and the Stars 280; 11. Stellar Theology and Masonic Astronomy 7; 12. Beyond Good and Evil 44

Pole Shift and Obliquity

1. The Shadow of Atlantis 112; 2. Enuma Elish: Seven Tablets of Creation VOl. II 209; 3. Chronology of Genesis: A Complete History of the Nephilim 1; 4. The Natural Genesis VOl. II 241; 5. Enoch 64:1-3; Destruction of Atlantis 120; Secret Cities of Old South America 48, 403; 6. Greek Myths 407; 7. Mythology 133; 8. Darwin's Mistake 95; 9. God's of Eden: Collins 21; 10. Darwin's Mistake 96; 11. Philosophy of Aristotle 116; 12. Darwin's Mistake 95; 13. Sun Lore of All Ages 6' 14. Sun Lore of All Ages 131; Antediluvian World 209; 15. The Natural Genesis Vol. II 220; 16. God is Red 155-156; 17. The Shadow of Atlantis 39

Anunnaki Historical Epochs & Gamma Ray Bursts of Nibiru

(1) Our Sun-God: Christianity Before Christ p. 33; (2) The Sirius Mystery p. 377; (3) Flying Serpents and Dragons p. 57; (4) Pagan and Christian Creeds p. 218; (5) The Great Pyramid: Its Divine Message p. 173; (6) The Christ Conspiracy p. 338

Out of the Deep...Anunnaki Overlords

(1) Flying Serpents and Dragons p. 86; (2) From the Ashes of Angels p. 205; (3) ibid p. 204; (4) The Sirius Mystery p. 267; (5) The Sirius Mystery p. 156; (6) ibid p. 157; (7) ibid p. 157; (8) The Lost Book of Enki p. 48-49; (9) ibid p. 52; (10) ibid p. 55; (11) The Ancient Alien Question p. 53; (12) Earth Under Fire p. 356-357; (13) The New World Order p. 94

600 Year Epochs of Anunnaki Chronology to 1962 CE

(1) A Short History of the World p. 128-129; (2) The Mystery of the Olmecs p. 199-200; (3) A New Look at God's True Calendar p. 55-56, Dankenbring (Triumph Prophetic Ministries); (4) The Lost Realms p. 79; (5) History in Quotations p. 211; (6) Ancient Mysteries p. 391

1962 CE...The Final Year of Anunnaki NER Chronology

(1) From the Ashes of Angels p. 283; (2) Lost Cities of North and Central America p. 316; (3) Elder Gods in Antiquity p. 67; (4) Secret History of Extraterrestrials p. 60; (5) Our Occulted History p. 19; (6) Space Travellers and the Genesis of the Human Form p. 28; (7) Alice in Wonderland and the World Trade Center Disaster p. 212-213; (8) Inside the Real Area 51 p. 63; (9) ibid p. 70-71;

(10) Our Haunted Planet p. 71-72; (11) ibid p. 39; (12) The Ancient Alien Question p. 227; (13) The United States and Britain in Prophecy p. 156-158; (14) Encyclopedia of World Dates and Facts p. 818-819; (15) ibid p. 818; (16) ibid p. 819; (17) ibid p. 819

How to Predict the Future: Intro to Calendrical Isometrics

1. Albert Camus, 1942, The Myth of Sisyphus; 2. Oliver Wendell Holmes; 3. Antigravity and the World Grid; 4. The World As I See It; 5. Hyperspace; 6. Tertium Organum; 7. ibid; 8. Crop Circles, Gods and Their Secrets; 9. The End of Days: Sitchin; 10. Three Books of Occult Philosophy; 11. The Discourses; 12. Lectures; 13. Magic: White and Black; 14. The Hidden Power: And Other Papers on Mental Science; 15. The Decline of the West; 16. Technics and Civilization; 17. City of God: Augustine; 18. Conscious Healing; 19. Key Philosophical Writings

Printed in Great Britain
by Amazon